# Frontiers in American Philosophy
## VOLUME I

# Frontiers in
# American Philosophy

## VOLUME I

Edited by Robert W. Burch
and Herman J. Saatkamp, Jr.

*Texas A&M University Press*
*College Station*

The paper used in this book meets the minimum requirements
of the American National Standard for Permanence
of Paper for Printed Library Materials, Z39.48-1984.
Binding materials have been chosen for durability.

*Library of Congress Cataloging-in-Publication Data*

Frontiers in American philosophy / edited by Robert W. Burch and
Herman J. Saatkamp, Jr. — 1st ed.
         p.      cm.
    ISBN 0-89096-495-5 (v. 1 : alk. paper)
    1. Philosophy—United States.    I. Burch, Robert W.    II. Saatkamp,
Herman J., Jr.
B893.F76     1992
191—dc20                                                    91-19447
                                                               CIP

# Contents

# Foreword

This is the first of two volumes based on papers presented at the Frontiers in American Philosophy Conference, Texas A&M University. Like the ancient Greek image of Janus, these articles look both forward and backward: forward through the major developments presently shaping future philosophical inquiry in the United States, and backward to the origins and plurality of the American intellectual heritage. The history, development, influence, and current edge of American philosophy are the subjects.

This volume is launched during the last decade of the twentieth century, a period when world citizenship and globalization are paramount. As a result, the articles in this work help to provide an understanding of the American intellectual legacies and prospects as we prepare for, and enter into, a new millennium. Not a parochial or narrow perspective, the focus on American philosophy is a concerted effort to sharpen the dialogue that clarifies and explicates American thought. Acknowledging the pluralism of American thought, there is no effort to define an American ethos. Instead, the volume is festive, celebrating the diversity of thought and influences in American philosophy.

This work is guided by the aurora of the twenty-first century and the seriousness of Santayana's oft-quoted remark: "Those who cannot remember the past are condemned to repeat it." With these as our cicerones, we offer these readings for your pleasure and knowledge.

Herman J. Saatkamp, Jr.

# Preface

ROBERT W. BURCH

This is the first of two volumes of proceedings of the international conference "Frontiers in American Philosophy," which was held in College Station, Texas, in early June of 1988. "Frontiers in American Philosophy" was conceived and then organized as a conference that would be dedicated to novel explorations of American philosophy. Hence the name "Frontiers." Participants were deliberately urged to strike out in new ways, new directions. The essays collected in this volume show, as the essays in volume 2 will also show, that participants' responses were faithful to the set task.

Although certain areas of possible novel exploration — such as the American philosophers' technical accomplishments in mathematical logic and philosophical analysis — are not heavily represented, other areas — such as metaphysics and social philosophy — are. And one cannot help but be struck by the extraordinary range of issues treated in these essays and by the American philosophers they concern.

It should not be surprising that a great many of the essays recur — either directly (as, for example, in the work of Putnam, Margolis, and Wallace) or else indirectly and by implication (as, for example, in the work of Thayer, Singer, and Oppenheim) — to that great axis of intellectual issues commonly known as the "realism/idealism" controversy. It seems fitting that so much of the discussion in this volume has reference to the possibility of some sort of middle position between what Putnam has called "external realism" and its antipode in some form of relativistic subjectivism. For such a middle position is, in the last analysis, the core meaning for the American philosophers of "pragmatism."

The conference "Frontiers in American Philosophy" was made possible by funds from Texas A&M University, funds which were disbursed through the College of Liberal Arts of the university. I would like to thank the university, the College of Liberal Arts, and especially Dean Daniel Fallon, who masterminded the obtaining of the funds and thus made possible the "Frontiers" conference, and with it the present volume and the subsequent one.

# Introduction

JOHN J. McDERMOTT

Let us take a walk with Walt Whitman,
A Kosmos of Manhattan the Son:

"You shall no longer take things at second or third hand nor look
through the eyes of the dead nor feed on spectres in books.
You shall not look through my eyes either, nor take things from me.
You shall listen to all sides and filter them from yourself."

## Roots/Edges

The past as Prologue to creative oblivion
And so — America
One of a kind, but special
Nonetheless —
Pockmarked, heroic, bewildered
Arrogant, sensitive, never
Plodding
Aboard the Arbella — Bible in hand
Rickets, scurvy and rats
Everywhere
We shall be a City on a Hill
The Lord's Plantation
And the eyes of all the
World
Shall be upon us.
No easy burden, that.
Redeemed
Only somewhat, they, we, say —

John Winthrop to his
Beloved Margaret
How fortunate — fortunate indeed
Are we.
Half of my siblings, half of our
children
One of my three wives, you
still alive.
God is good
From Sudbury to Marlborough
A stone taken from
Meeting House hill
A new start, the Alleghenies,
The Appalachians
On to the alleged
Northwest Territory
O'MacKinac
O'Saginaw
The great plains await
As white man and white woman
Bible in hand, once again
Forage and deforest
Oblivious
To the red that floods the land
Amerindian — Amerindian
Shoshone, Osage, Apache
Iroquois, Blackfeet
The Christian Chief Joseph
Betrayed by us
As the Nez Perce bite the dust
Victims of cultural genocide
Listen — Listen to the Jesuit
Father Hennepin
Why, Why, he plaintively asks?
How is it that our Indian
Brothers and Sisters, pagans all,
Be more Christian than we,
How. Yes How!
At that point, nothing, nothing
Said about the browning of
America
Yet, try the Camino Real

Try the Santa Fe Trail
Try the Rio Grande
To this day
By fatal boxcar
By car trunk
By wading among the snakes
Slicing through the anchor fence
America—and ye shall be free
Maybe—
Roots, Ah roots—
The deep irony of Haley's Roots
No! Not Haley's comet
Haley's Roots
The Dahomean—kidnapped
Look to it—Boy!
Come here—Girl!
Leroy! a slash for that clandestine
Reading
Trapped between the scissoring
From a magnificent
Non-literate gesture culture as
Embodied, and so liturgically,
Ritually thick
As in the world of Africa
Yet prevented, a euphemism for
Slavery
From getting it on with the book.
Rachel! Do not let me catch you
Ever, Ever
Reading
Across the Great Plains
Bush by brackish water
Trapped in the Humboldt Sink
The pregnant Sara Royce
The Donner party (now the
Recipients of ORV)
Ate each other.
From St. Jo to Sacramento
Arrows in the neck, Pony
Express—detritus
Horses presaging the telegraph
Pole

From Peck Slip to the Barbary Coast
O Columbia—Gem of the Ocean.
Stained with heroism and
Madness
The American Frontier
Frontier of Valor
Frontier of Sadness
Frontier of Violence
Frontier of Courage
Frontier of Trashing
Of Beginning again and again
Of novelty
Of loneliness
America, America, America
Named for a pickle dealer
In need of a Latin feminine case ending.
Cosmographicae Introductio of 1507
Europa, Asia, Africa and
America.
Oy Vey—and who are they?
Not a new place, not a new thing
Nay—A mundus novus
A new world—
America.

A truck-stop outside of Des Moines
The blitzed copper veins of
Anaconda and Butte
Montana
Whitesand, corn rows, endless
Wheat, breezing in the Iowa still.
Gunnison, San Joaquin
Even Hoosiers
Franconia notch, Pennsylvania Station
Hatteras and Everglades
A brace of panhandles
Chattanooga, parden me boy
Kimosabe
Hi Ho Silver—Away
The silver bullet of
The midnight special
Dens of crack

Crinolines and bouffant
For the day will live in
infamy
As will My Lai
From the LBJ lie, low to Haiphong
Who would have thought
He was such a nice boy
The McDonalds of San Ysidro
as Beirut
When black boys and black girls
Hold hands with white boys
and white girls
From the granite hills of
New Hampshire
To Stone Mountain of Georgia
To the curvaceous shores
of California
A King among pygmies
Gun him down
Ask not what your country
can do for you
But ask what you can do
for your country
Gun him down
We can do better
Gun him down
The 'Natural' as Ruthian
Greta and Marilyn
Clark and Gary
Here's looking at you
As time goes by with
A grapefruit in your face
You can of course, go uptown
Or downtown — by the
A train
Unless you come from Wharton
Or the B. school
Complete with Wall Street
Attache
Cocaine-lined, white collared
Subtle violence
Hey there, can you spare a dime

Over there, over there
Let us make the world
Safe for democracy
As we wallow in our
Augean stable.
Many mice make a Meese
Tammany and Teapot Dome
Karl Marx said it was a sell-out
The lefties call it co-optation
But my Mama lives on your
Social Security
Only in America—says
Harry Golden
As Niagara Falls into
The wedding gown
Flivvers and flappers
Bathtub gin
Shitkickers and yuppies, the latter
alas
Edison and Lincoln
The Jeffersonian City as a canker
Land, always land,
But only for the few
Burn baby burn
The arch—the sluices in the
High Missouri
Burn baby burn
After all, business is business
The business of America
is Business.
Bible in hand, preaching the
Carnegie Gospel of wealth
On the road and by the
Way
Can you spare a dime.
The word is German
Heimlosigkeit
The phenomenon is American
I ain't got no place to go
Homeless!
The world at large, the planet
Global culture

Chastises America
Get your act together
Confusion reigns, they say.
Not confusion, say I
Ambiguity
Say I
Despite the philosophers of the new
stripe
The big questions are irresolute
Should we emulate Famulus in
Goethe's Faust
Who, upon peering into the world of
Intellect
Announced and pronounced
How impressed he was with how
Wondrously far he has come
Or, should we emulate that
Stunning vignette of
Camus in L'Etranger
Until now I have not thought about it;
But now that I have thought about it, No!
I want to live only with that which I know.
Derby day, Dr. J.
Why is the American National pastime
A game that can be tied to infinity
Schenley, Shaker and Scarsdale
Hough and Watts
White and Black
Can you spare a dime
The braggart Swaggart
Does not know a red light from
Bible in hand.
Why not listen to Matisse
L'exactitude ne pas verité
America — ambiguity
Quo vadis. I have not the slightest
idea.
Why go — then?
Precisely.
As the parade goes by —
Hey Camerado —
I love you.

They do not answer —
Hey there — no matter.
When you come, as you will,
to look for me —
Find me under your boot soles.
I am — will be
the leaves of grass —

*Benedicite*

# DIVERSE THEMES IN AMERICAN PHILOSOPHY

# James's Theory of Perception:
# A Reading of the
# *Essays in Radical Empiricism*

HILARY PUTNAM

Although James is usually thought of as a "literary" philosopher, in the *Essays in Radical Empiricism* James wrote what even Bertrand Russell recognized to be serious technical philosophy.[1] And indeed, these essays have the mysterious sort of depth that the most puzzling passages of the great philosophers seem to have: say, the Transcendental Deduction, in the case of Kant, and the Private Language Argument in the case of Wittgenstein. These essays—especially the fourth, "How Two Minds Can Know One Thing"—are difficult writings, whose importance in understanding James's views cannot be overestimated.

James himself would have said, "These views presuppose pragmatism, but not vice versa." Bertrand Russell would have said that James was wrong about the presupposing of pragmatism; that pragmatism and radical empiricism (or at least what was correct about radical empiricism) were totally independent, and, indeed, Russell rejected James's pragmatism and accepted a significant aspect of his radical empiricism. And, in fact, what James actually says isn't quite that radical empiricism presupposes pragmatism; what he claims is that his pragmatism is a "propaedeutic" to radical empiricism. The idea must be that pragmatism is not strictly presupposed by radical empiricism, but nevertheless it is a good idea to have read— and, James would hope, to have accepted—pragmatism as what James called a "genetic theory of truth" before tackling these essays.

But the term "theory of truth" is one of the problems in understanding James's philosophy. In what sense is it a *theory* of truth? (The qualifier "genetic" indicates it isn't a straightforward theory of the "essence" of truth.) And how are the vague terms that James employs in connection with his theory of truth—terms like "function" and "satisfaction"—supposed to clarify the notion of truth?[2] But, in any case, James thinks that accepting the thing he calls a "theory of truth" is a propaedeutic towards understanding radical empiricism. On the other hand, it would be wrong to think of James as a philosopher whose primary interest is in theory of perception, or even in resolving the subject-object dichotomy. We cannot suppost that all of James's grand remarks about life, morality, and religious belief are a mere propaedeutic to a discussion of the really interesting question whether two different people see the same Memorial Hall. Obviously, it is the other way around. James does not think that radical empiricism is irrelevant to the rest of his philosophy. It may be that, if anything, the *Essays in Radical Empiricism* is best thought of as a propaedeutic to James's pragmatism.

If we regard the radical empiricism as being propaedeutic to James's pragmatism, rather than the other way around, we can see that the rather cold metaphysical picture James presents in these essays is meant to turn hot. In the present essay I shall not, however, attempt to read *Pragmatism* in the light of radical empiricism, although that is something I may do in future publications. For now, let me note that when I do teach James's *Pragmatism,* my custom is to go through the lectures almost line by line. I think that is valuable in the case of *Pragmatism,* because the first impression is that the lectures are easy, and because James seems to write so clearly and so well; but if one is receptive to James's message at all, one soon realizes that something is happening which is very nuanced, and the problem is getting the nuance. In the *Essays in Radical Empiricism,* by contrast, we are dealing with a mass of technical detail, and therefore I am going to adopt the opposite strategy of standing back from the technical detail, and trying to summarize the picture.

It is a very unconventional picture. I had an idea as to what it might be in the late seventies, when Dieter Henrich gave a seminar on Kant's Transcendental Deduction at Harvard. Henrich was lecturing on the unity of the self, and making the point that, in spite of all the phenomenal disunity of the self, which Kant was well aware of, Kant thought that in some transcendental sense the "I," the "I" in "I think," the "I" to which I am prepared to relate all my representations, is metaphysically a unity. And the world is metaphysically a unity. And Henrich described Kant's problem as establishing the connection between the unity of the world and the unity of the self. In some way these are transcendentally interdependent. And it occurred to me as he was saying all this that James's view might be summarized in the following way: the self isn't a unity and the world isn't a unity, and so Kant had the wrong problem. The problem shouldn't be to show that the unity of the world is correlative with the unity of the self, but to show that the disunity of the world is correlative with the disunity of the self.

## James and Darwin

In one of his lectures on *Pragmatism* — the lecture on The One and The Many — James says that there are ways of looking at the world in which it is a unity and ways of looking at it in which it is a disunity; but, he says, the pragmatist temperament favors, stresses, sees as of primary importance, the disunities, the pluralities. And this is not a mere "psychological" observation, for the whole message of the book, *Pragmatism,* is that temperament is all important, and pragmatism itself, after all, is an attempt to change your temperament, to make yourself into a different sort of person.

James is out of sympathy with what he calls the "rationalist" temperament, the temperament that sees unity as the most important thing. Of course, both temperaments have had their victories, the rationalist temperament most notably in mathematics; but a good example of the temperament James prefers would be Charles Darwin. (James was an enthusiastic supporter of Darwin at a time when there was hardly an experimental biologist who believed in natural selection.)

Many things make Darwin an appropriate representative of the pragmatist temperament. For one thing, Darwin was a writer who consciously used literary devices in presenting his scientific theories. (In the last few years there have been several articles in the *New York Times Book Review* about the influence of Darwin's use of narrative devices on the modern novel.) And I believe that this crossing of the lines between literature and science would have delighted James. (Certainly his *Principles of Psychology* crosses them.) But this is not what I have in mind at the moment. Let us recall Darwin's theory. As Ernst Mayr has repeatedly pointed out, it is a mistake to think that Darwin's theory had a single postulate, the postulate of natural selection.[3] Darwin's theory had many parts. First, evolution. At the end of the nineteenth century, almost everybody believed in evolution, but very few people believed in natural selection. (Think of Lamarck, not to speak of Hegel, or of Herbert Spencer.) Second, Darwin believed in common descent, for example, we and the other simians have a common descent. That suggestion of Darwin's was widely accepted by biologists, who did not regard it as a speculation outside the bounds of experimental biology. This Darwinian idea was accepted because it at once made sense of taxonomy. Although today's "creationist" debates sometimes convey the impression that scientists accepted evolution and common descent because they accepted natural selection, this is not the case. Natural selection was the controversial element in Darwin's story. And one of the most important aspects of Darwin's new way of thinking about the world, the way based on the idea of natural selection, is what Mayr calls Darwin's "anti-essentialism."

It is an interesting fact that the people who produced the theory of natural selection, Darwin and his co-discoverer Wallace, and the people who early became converts to it, were naturalists, not experimentalists; they were people who had been to odd places and seen a lot of flora and fauna. These people didn't perform experiments, but they did an enormous amount of observing and comparing, and what they were interested in was variation. The traditional view in biology, the view associated with Aristotle (and, perhaps more fairly, with Plato) is that the real reality, the essence, is the *type*. In this traditional view, there is such a thing as the essence of a cat, that is, of the type Cat, and there is such a thing as the essence of a dog, that is, of the type Dog, and this essence is what is of scientific importance and interest. (As Mayr has remarked, racism can be viewed as an expression of this kind of essentialistic thinking; the racist thinks of blacks and whites and Jews and Caucasians and Asiatics as types with essential characteristics, rather than as huge populations that exhibit immense variation and have enormous amounts of genetic overlap.) But for Darwin there was a flip: the reality is the variation. In a Darwinian view, no two humans are identical, not even identical twins. Even if the genotypes are identical, how they are expressed is not quite identical. No two human beings, no two rabbits, no two mice, no two cockroaches, no two amoebas are identical. Although there is a "central tendency," this "central tendency" is simply an average; Darwin would say that it is a mere abstraction. The very thing that is the true reality to the rationalist temperament becomes a mere mathematical abstraction to the Darwinian. "See, you can add up a lot of numbers and divide by N, the number of things in the population, and you think you have some kind of transcendental reality," a Darwinian might scoff. Even averages change, the Darwinian points out; the average height we have seen in country after country has changed as food habits have changed; there have been enormous jumps without any corresponding jumps in the gene pool.

Now, this Darwinian attitude, the attitude that says that the reality is the individual with all his uniqueness, his variation — opens the way for the idea that species slide into one another — exactly what "Aristotelians" thought was prohibited. If there is an eternal essence of Ape and and eternal essence of Human, how can one of those slide into the other? But once you say, "All there is is variation," all there is is individuals in their variety, you have totally changed the picture. We might say that, in this respect, Darwin was the most "pragmatic" of scientists.

I don't want to give the impression that we should (or that James thinks we should) *never* think in the "essentialist" or "rationalist" way. I have already mentioned the success of rationalistic ways of thinking in pure mathematics. And one could also cite aspects of contemporary physics as representing a limited but important success of "rationalism," in James's sense of the term. In fundamental physics, it is important that one electron is absolutely the same as every other electron. But James wants to remind us that even though the rationalistic type of thinking has its place — it is sometimes pragmatically effective — once it becomes one's only way of thinking, one is bound to lose the world for a beautiful model. I believe that this is a central part of the message of these essays.

### Reality and Unrealities: From Universe to Pluriverse

I state all this because, although in one way James is taking on a classical problem, the so-called "problem of perception," and speaking to classical issues — What about illusion, What about hallucination, and so on — James does not believe that he can convince us that direct realism can be right, and all the sophisticated philosophical objections to it that have become familiar since Descartes can be wrong, without providing a "metaphysics," in a certain sense. To redescribe perception, James has to redescribe reality — but "reality" is a funny term here. For there is a sense in which James is describing *more* than just reality.

Now, how can one provide a description of *more* than reality? You can describe more than reality if reality isn't all there is. There is also unreality. And part of the extreme pluralist view that lies behind James's metaphysics is just that: that reality isn't all there is, that there is also unreality, or rather that there are, "intentionally, at any rate," unreal entities.[4]

James is, of course, not the only philosopher to think something like this: the name of Meinong springs to mind. And there are even logically minded philosophers who have tried to show that quantification over "Meinongian objects" can be made consistent, by formalizing Meinong's ideas. And I have no doubt that one could formalize James as well. But part of the reason that James is not read all that much by analytic philosophers is that he doesn't consider issues of formalization — not because he is unwilling to argue, for in these essays he is arguing, and very technically, but because his stream in philosophy does not come from Frege and

Russell, doesn't come from an interest in mathematical logic. Peirce is much easier for an analytic philosopher to relate to, because Peirce was a logician. James was trained in psychology, or what he called psychology, which is also not exactly what we call psychology today — which adds to the difficulty.

Nevertheless, James is not really inconsistent. The qualifier, "intentionally, at any rate," which James places before his claim that mental knives and real knives have the same "natures," is a way of restoring consistency, as is the distinction between an attribute's being part of the "nature" of an "experience" *adjectively* and its being part of the nature of the "experience" intentionally. But I shall not ask us to be *too* charitable. James's thought is certainly vague in part, which is why different people who were sympathetic to (some of) James's ideas could take quite different morals from them. (Russell and Husserl are good examples.) James is starting something in these essays, but what he is starting can be continued in different ways. So I believe it would still be an interesting project to study James's radical empiricism and then to look at how Russell reads it, leaving out the Meinongian objects (say, in *The Analysis of Mind,* when you see James's *Essays in Radical Empiricism* as a forerunner of Russell's neutral monism), on the one hand, and, on the other hand, how Husserl reads it (when you see the same essays as a forerunner of phenomenology). Phenomenologists themselves have written about this last, but it would also be of interest for someone who is not in that movement to take a look at this question.

But anyway . . . What does it *mean* to say *there are* objects that aren't real? The very words explode from the page, from a logician's point of view. You ought to have subscripts on "are" and "real." You should write, "There are$_1$ objects that don't exist$_2$" or something like that. James tries to help us out with his term "pure experience," but that is somewhat of a trap, partly because James is ambivalent. Sometimes he does have a metaphysics of pure experience, and at other times he seems to draw back from this melting of pure experience into a substance, and so on. But also, quite apart from the issues about whether "pure experience" is some sort of metaphysical substance, it is hard for present-day Anglo-Saxon philosophers to understand the ways in which James and his contemporaries used the word "experience." James and his contemporaries were much more familiar with German philosophy than we are today. In the English-speaking, as opposed to the German-speaking, philosophical world, "experience" has tended to mean "sensation." So there is a tendency today to read "world of pure experience" as "world of pure sensation," which totally misses what James is talking about. So let me, at least to start with, try to present James's view using this word "experience" as little as possible.

One reason to avoid the word "experience," at least until one has gotten some way into James's philosophy, is that if we use that word too early we may fail to realize that one of the things James wants to do is change our idea of what "experience" *is*. Of course, James also tries to change our view of what experience is in the *Principles of Psychology*. Experience, we learn there, is "thought and sensation fused." But there are interpretative problems with the *Principles of Psychology* too. So what term shall I use? I have said that James's theory isn't a "theory of reality," because reality is only a part of what it is a theory of, and I don't want to use the term "pure experience" (at least not yet). I don't want to say it is a theory of the universe *tout court,* because we might think of the universe as a unity. So let me say that James's theory is a theory of the *pluriverse.* I think that is a term that does justice to James view. Out there is the pluriverse. (We recall that perhaps the most quoted remark of James, after "it's true if it works," is that reality is a "blooming buzzing confusion.") After all, the last book James wrote he called *A Pluralistic Universe.* And that title clearly suggests talking of a "pluriverse."

So there is the pluriverse that contains everything, but we have to ask, "What is everything?" because, as already indicated, there is going to be a lot more in the pluriverse ("intentionally, at any rate") than in any standard rationalist or empiricist universe. James might well have said to all other philosophers, "There are more things between heaven and earth than dreamed of in your philosophy, Horatio."

## The Pluriverse, Reality, and the Ongoing Community

For the moment the pluriverse is just a placeholder, about which all I have said is that there is going to be a lot there. Within the pluriverse there is a part — and, if I were to sketch it on a blackboard, I should draw it with fuzzy edges — which James will call "reality." That sounds as if Reality is properly contained in the pluriverse; and that is the way James sometimes writes, when he "lets himself go," for example in "Does 'Consciousness' Exist": "Mental knives may be sharp, but they won't cut real wood. . . . With 'real' objects on the contrary [note the shudder quotes!], consequences always accrue; and thus the real objects get sifted from the mental ones, the things from our thoughts of them, fanciful or true, and precipitated together as the stable part of the whole-experience-chaos, under the name of the physical world. Of this our perceptual experiences are the nucleus, they being the originally *strong* experiences. We add a lot of conceptual experiences to them, making these strong also in imagination, and building out the remoter parts of the physical world by their means; and around this core of reality the world of laxly connected fancies and mere rhapsodical objects floats like a bank of clouds."[5]

Taken according to the letter, this means that there are a lot of things in the pluriverse which aren't "real" but which are still in some sense *there*. As I have already explained, James does not worry about how one would say that *nicely* (i.e., how one would "formalize such an ontology").

Let us take an example that is close to but not quite the same as the one James uses. Suppose that someone hallucinates a fire. (James considers someone *imagining* a fire.) The fire, considered as a fire, is not part of what we call "reality." James speaks of unreal things such as this fire as not having "general validity."[6] The term "general validity" indicates that what we call reality is in some way *shared*. But "shared" does not mean shared by just one particular "culture." There is not one single line in James's writing that takes "general validity" to mean general validity *in a particular culture.*[7]

The problem of what constitutes "general validity" is not very often a real problem when we are talking about tables and chairs. It is when one gets to the areas that most interest James, the areas of ethics and religion, that the meaning of "general validity" becomes problematic. In "William James' Ideas," Ruth Anna Putnam and I argue that James should be thought of as having what we called an "imperfect procedural conception" of validity in such areas; but a discussion of this would take us beyond the bounds of the present paper.[8] What is important, if we are right, is that the effort to get general agreement, the effort to find "inclusive ideals" that can be shared, is an essential aspect of the procedure to be used in such areas. What has general validity is not always what satisfies standards that are already shared in a community; sometimes the problem is to *come to agreement on the standards* and not just to find what conforms to standards that we have already agreed upon; but the theme of sharing, of "general" validity, is still present in James thought, even here.


## The Hallucinatory Fire Again

Let us return to the example of the "unreal" fire, the fire that someone hallucinates. Well, is it really a fire? It isn't real, so can it be a fire? Does it have flames? Is it *hot?*

As noted above, James is not a logician, and here he has to struggle for a terminology. What he says is that such an entity is connected with the property of being hot (being a fire, having flames, etc.) "intentionally" but not "adjectively."[9] It possesses being hot — being hot is part of its "nature" — but not as an attribute. You cannot simply say — let me now use James's expression, "pure experience," with all its dangers, just to have some term for this funny object — you cannot simply say that this "pure experience" *has* the attribute "hot"; you cannot simply say it *has* flames. We can only say that "is hot" is an attribute of a "pure experience" if the statement that that "pure experience" is hot is a statement about a reality.

But even that is too simple. James is more nuanced than that. In James's view the *same* pure experience may be *in here* under one description and *out there* under another description. More precisely, since James thinks of "location" as an *external relation,* the same "pure experience" may have one "location" ("in my mind") when "taken with one system of associations" and a different location (in physical space) when taken as belonging with a different system of associations.[10] If I am the person having the hallucination, and I say that it is a real fire, I am making a mistake. Under the description "real fire" that "pure experience" belongs outside of reality, it doesn't have general validity. But if you describe what is in a sense the same "pure experience" as a psychiatrist would describe it, as John Smith's hallucination, then under that description the same pure experience is a piece of reality — albeit a member of the class "hallucinatory experience" and not a member of the class "fire." So basically the word "reality" is correlative to the word "truth." If the description is "true," then under that description the "pure experience" is a reality; if the description is false, then under that description it isn't a reality. And the same "pure experience" may possess both true descriptions and false ones.

Moreover, the "external relations" James speaks of are not merely arbitrary associations; they are *experienced* relations, leadings-to and terminatings-in and representings; and James is a realist about experienced relations.[11] An aspect of this realism which I plan to discuss in future publications is his realism about *intentional relations* (as when he writes that one "pure experience" may be *about* another, or *represent* another, or *refer* to another). In my opinion, failure to see that, whatever James's "theory of truth" may be, it is *not* an attempt to *reduce intentional to non-intentional notions* is one of the fundamental sources of the many misunderstandings that have arisen in connection with it.

It follows that, in James's system, every "pure experience" is a part of reality under *some* description. (I cannot go into the details here; but the example of the way the mental fire is a part of reality under the description "John's image of a fire" — or better, "the inner content" of John's imagining a fire — respectively, thinking of a fire, having the illusion of a fire, hallucinating a fire, as the case may be, may serve to give the idea.)[12] Consequently, James does not, at the end of the day, have as severe problems as the Meinongians do: everything in James's "ontology," everything James quantifies over, is a perfectly kosher object, a perfectly real thing, under an appropriate external relation. What looked initially like "Meinongian objects" turn out to be real (albeit "subjective") objects which possess properties "intentionally" that they do not possess adjectively.

## The Purpose of James's Ontology

If I haven't gotten James all wrong, the machinery he develops in the *Essays in Radical Empiricism* has to connect with James's wider moral-religious-ideological concerns. It cannot be that he is doing all this just for the sake of a theory of perception. But in this essay I am putting all that aside, and looking at James as a theorist of perception. In that narrow context, saying that there are bits of pure experience that are not part of "this core of reality"[13] — at least, not according to the description which is suggested by their 'natures' — is going to be important in providing an alternative account of what may be called the subject-object distinction, or in overcoming the subject-object dichotomy.

Remember, there are certain very simple arguments, arguments with which we have been familiar since Descartes' *Meditations,* which philosophers have believed to show that what we directly and immediately perceive is subjective. Now, that view is not always *wholly* wrong, in James's view. If John Smith hallucinates a fire in the wastebasket, then under the description "fire burning in the wastebasket" what John Smith perceives is subjective. Obviously one cannot say that we immediately perceive the external world and only the external world, and everything we think we immediately perceive is really "out there." Like Peter Strawson[14] James wants to separate the questions, "Do we immediately perceive external things?" and "Do we perceive external things incorrigibly?" If we stated the traditional argument in a nutshell, stated it in a very unsophisticated way, it might be: "If we immediately perceived the external world, we would perceive it incorrigibly. But we don't perceive it incorrigibly, therefore we don't perceive it immediately." But James wants to say that we can perceive external things immediately, and we don't perceive them incorrigibly. Immediacy is not the same as incorrigibility.

Now, there are post–World War II Anglo-Saxon philosophers who followed this line without being aware that in any respect they were following the path that James had blazed many decades before. For example, although there are obvious and major difference between Austin's *Sense and Sensibilia* and James's *Essays in Radical Empiricism,* in one respect

Austin follows James's line exactly: Austin too thinks the right strategy is to challenge the supposedly obvious link between "directness" and "incorrigibility."

## The Seventeenth-Century Picture Criticized

Let us recall Berkeley's notorious slogan *esse est percipi,* to be is to be perceived. Philosophers rejected Berkeley's claim that *everything there is* is perceived. But almost all philosophers agreed with him about what is immediately perceived. If there is something you immediately perceive, the view runs, it must have all and only the properties it seems to have. Later on, after the term "sense datum" was invented, they would argue, "A physical thing might have one property and seem to have another; but how could the sense data that are produced in me by that physical thing seem to have one property and really have another? The sense datum *is* the appearance." That makes it sound like a definition, right? Appearances are one set of objects and external things are another set of objects, and how can the appearances have properties other than the ones they *appear* to have? Appearances are a set of objects for which the principle *esse est percipi* is true.

A further feature of the traditional picture is that the physical thing does not have the property of color. As Strawson points out, in a common-sense view, physical objects are recognized by us through the colored surfaces that they present; we see colors distributed on (objective) surfaces in an objective space.[15] The things we say about these objects and their colors and movements are taken as *data* in scientific theory construction. So the view that science has shown that there aren't *really* any colors "out there" has the peculiar consequence that science has demolished its own data! In the traditional view the "subjective" table, the phenomenal table, has color properties, while the "objective" table has only dispositions to produce color sensations. One might say that the physical table is rather "ghostly" in the traditional view, and indeed, it was often claimed by epistemologists that the average person is a "naive realist" who has an incorrigible tendency to *identify* phenomenal tables with physical ones.

Note also that something analogous to hallucination happens even in veridical perception, in the traditional view. I immediately perceive something subjective — the sense data — even when I see a real fire; and I might perceive qualitatively identical subjective objects if I were to hallucinate a fire. This is why the traditional view is correctly described as a mind-body dualism. The sense data I have in the case of veridical perception as well as in the case of hallucination are mental, and the physical chair is material. So the traditional cut is not between real objects and unreal objects that have *some* kind of existence — what phenomenologists call "intentional inexistence" — the cut is between mind and matter.

In sharp contrast to all this, James's picture is that when I have a veridical perception of a fire I don't see a private sense datum of a fire and infer the fire. I just see the fire. When I have a hallucination, in James's picture what I see is a fire that isn't really there.

The traditional move — which was thought to preclude the very possibility of such a move as this (although some interpreters think Thomas Reid may have anticipated it, nonetheless) — was to ask the "stumper," "If you directly see a totally different thing when you see a fire and when you see a hallucination, then why do you (as it might be) think you see a fire when you see a hallucination?" This question was thought to have one (and only one) possible answer.[16] In fact, different theories of perception give it quite different answers. The sense datum theory says that the sense data of the person who hallucinates a fire are similar to the sense data the person would perceive if he saw a real fire. So the hallucinatory fire is not similar to a real fire (in the traditional picture there is at most a problematical "correspondence" between the real fire and any sense data at all), but it is similar to the sense data produced by the presence of a real fire. James proposes the stunningly simple — maybe it is preposterous, I don't care, but it is stunningly simple — alternative that the hallucinatory object is similar in a certain way to the real object. You mistake the hallucination for a real chair because it *looks* like a real chair.

Notice that James is blocking one of the standard arguments for sense data, the argument that goes like this: "You are going to have to admit that all we perceive are sense data in at least one case, the case of hallucinations. When I hallucinate a chair (that isn't there), you can't say I see an external object, because there is no external chair for me to be seeing. It could even be that I'm in a totally dark room, and there is nothing before my eyes except blackness. Yet if I hallucinate a chair, I am directly presented with something. [J. L. Austin would challenge even that statement.] What I'm presented with, then, by universal agreement, is not a real external thing. What is it? It is something mental. So let us call it a sense datum. So we've agreed that in at least one case, when someone thinks he is perceiving a physical object, what he is really perceiving is something mental (is a sense datum). So it is plausible to suppose that even when it is a veridical perception, what you are directly perceiving is a sense datum."

Boom. Suddenly the external world has been taken away from you, and you never perceive anything directly except your own sense data. And James is perhaps the first philosopher — certainly the first twentieth-century philosopher — to cry, "Stop!"

The whole point of sense datum theory in epistemology was to provide a foundation for knowledge. I contend that — whether it is the alternative we would accept today or not — James succeeded in showing that there is a consistent alternative to sense datum theory. And if James succeeded in even that much, then he performed something stunning, because then sense datum theory cannot be the basis or foundation of our knowledge; at best it is just one more theory. And in fact, James did succeed in worrying philosophers. Russell credits James with moving him from the sense datum theory to the the theory of the *Analysis of Mind,* [17] and (perhaps as a result of Russell's shift) Moore began worrying about many of the possibilities raised by James's theory (e.g., could one sense datum be perceived by two minds, could there be "ownerless" sense data, could a sense datum actually be *part of the surface* of a physical object? — worries that are quite unprecedented before this time). The possibilities raised by James's theory had a corrosive effect, because once Moore realized that it was just an assumption that sense data had this property, just an assumption that they had this other property, the whole thing began to unravel.

So James was saying, "Here is an alternative hypothesis: Sometimes we see real chairs and real fires, and I don't mean that we directly see something mental and do some inferring. Sometimes we see objects that are — under some description — private. And a private object can *resemble* a public object."

Now, this isn't quite right as an account of James's view. The following qualification has to be introduced. A hallucinatory fire isn't hot in quite the way that a real fire is hot — a real fire is hot because the real fire has the properties of being a fire and being hot *adjectively.* The hallucinatory fire is connected to the properties "is a fire" and "is hot," but not adjectively. Nevertheless, at a certain level of abstraction, there is a similarity between the real fire and the hallucinatory fire. Some of the same properties belong to the "nature" of the "pure experience" that constitutes the hallucination and to the "nature" of a real fire. That is why the person who is subject to the hallucination (or to the illusion, in the case of a more mundane sort of perceptual error) mistakes the private fire for a real fire. He thinks that "the fire" has the properties he is aware of adjectively. He thinks his "pure experience" has general validity.

In sum, James argues that all the traditional epistemologist has shown by appealing to hallucinations (and other illusions) is that we *sometimes* experience things that are, in the traditional terminology, "mental." He hasn't shown that we *never* directly perceive parts of reality as they are. The essay "How Two Minds Can See One Thing" plays an extremely important role in the presentation of this argument. On the traditional theory, if you and I stand, say, in front of Gund Hall on the Harvard campus

and look at Memorial Hall, then even if we stand side by side, and even
if the difference in parallax is too slight to make a difference to our visual
experiences, even if our perceptual apparatus is in the same condition, even
if we are identical twins, we don't directly perceive numerically the same
object. You perceive your sense data of Memorial Hall, and I perceive my
sense data of Memorial Hall. But James wants to say that it is possible
that you and I could both directly perceive the identical external Memorial
Hall, and the identical external aspect of Memorial Hall. As he himself
puts it, "our minds meet in a world of objects which would still be there
if one or several of the minds were destroyed."[18] So, James is saying, "naive
realism" is right in its most important claim, that immediate perception
of external things is possible.

## Two Objections to James's Theory

Let us stop for a moment and consider a couple of possible objections
to James's theory. First of all, there is the obvious objection that the skeptical epistemological problem has not been met. Even if we accept everything James says, a traditional epistemologist would say, there is still no
way to *know* when we are hallucinating and when we are not.

To this objection James would reply that the problem is worse for the
traditional theory. James begins his presentation of his own theory by explaining that the traditional theory puts each mind in a private world. Or,
as James himself puts it, "[for the Berkeleyan school] our lives are a con-
geries of solipsisms out of which in strict logic only a God could compose
a universe even of discourse. . . . If the body that you actuate is not the
very body that I see there, but some duplicate body of your own with which
that has nothing to do, we belong to different universes, you and I, and
for me to speak of you is folly."[19] In short, James does not see how several
minds, each acquainted *only* with its own private objects, could arrive by
any process of inference at knowledge or even thought of one another.

James is not, of course, going to give an "answer" to skepticism in the
sense of a rationalist answer. Indeed, James may have been the first to use
the metaphor of a "foundationless" philosophy — I am thinking of the letter to Francois Pillon in which James writes, "I fear you may find my philosophy too *bottomless* and romantic."[20] James is not going to give an
answer to skepticism that is deeper than the perspective of shared human
experience (to this extent, Rorty is right). But even the notion of *sharing*
experience makes no sense in the traditional theory, James is claiming.
Here am I, in my private world, having experiences that are qualitatively

like experiences you are having in your private world, but what is the connection? If you say "simultaneity" for example, what does *that* come to?

The advantage of pragmatism over foundationalist epistemology, in James's view, is that — as James argues in the *Lectures on Pragmatism* — the way in which pragmatist philosophers answer skeptical doubts is the way in which skeptical doubts are answered in practice, by appealing to tests that in fact work in our lives. If I think that what I see may be an illusion, I try looking at it from a different position, or I ask other people to take a look. If no one is with me, I take a photograph of it (if I have a camera with me). If that is not possible, I may examine the situation at a later time, and make inferences.

If we take seriously the idea that there are not *two* criteria or sets of criteria for "reality" — "common sense" criteria and philosophical criteria — but only one,[21] then we are led naturally to the view that what demarcates "reality" is something human, not something abstract called "being real." To use the analogy with Darwinism that I suggested earlier, there is not one abstract property of being real, there is only variation. When one understands Darwinism, one's first reaction may be, "If Darwin is right, we can't speak of species any more." And the answer is, "You can, but you have to think of species in a new way." You have to learn what Mayr calls 'population thinking.' One *can* group cats together, even though they don't possess a common 'essence.' One has to look for groups that it is *functional* to group together for certain purposes, for instance understanding the history of the various phenotypes and genotypes that we see around us. I stress the analogy to Darwinism because the adjective that qualifies "theory of truth" in James's *Pragmatism* is "genetic." I think that we would be right to say that what James is describing when he writes about truth is a historical process, just as Darwin is describing a historical process. When James writes about truth, he describes the process by which we come to call things true; and when James writes about "reality" he describes the process by which we come to call things "real."

Up to a point, this can sound like what a sense datum theorist (say, C. I. Lewis — the only philosopher to call himself a "pragmatist" who believed in sense data) would say. For James, Memorial Hall is the sum of its various aspects — its spatial extension, its color properties, its solidity, its massiveness, and so forth. And if enough of those aspects are shared, it is what we call a real building. Now, many phenomenalists would talk the same way. But there's a difference. For a phenomenalist, "shared" does not mean literally shared, because two people can't literally share a percept, they can only have similar percepts. And the phenomenalist has an obvious problem, since one person might be seeing a building like Memorial Hall in Cambridge, another might be seeing a building like Memorial Hall in China (if there were one), another might be seeing a building like Memorial Hall in Switzerland, and so on, and these sense data, although "similar," would not form the right kind of "bundle" to constitute a single building. So the sense datum theorist says, "If people go to the same place, then . . . (I used the word "place")." And, in fact, the critics of the sense datum theory pointed out that when phenomenalists stated the conditions under which people were supposed to have the sense data that constitute a given external thing, they invariably had to use not sense datum language but material object language. But James escapes *this* difficulty, at least, because he has not ruled out objective language, the language of two perceivers seeing the same thing, from the very beginning, as the phenomenalist has.[22]

In sum, James's account of "reality" fits with his pragmatism inasmuch as the natural history, the genesis, of the notion of reality, will turn out to be the same as the natural history of the notion of truth. And how could truth be shared if reality couldn't be shared?

A more serious objection is the following: Consider a case in which an individual experiences something he considers real (we suppose the individual is alone at the time), but later other people say he couldn't have seen any such thing. Is the individual simply "voted down"? (This is how a student once actually put this objection.) James has an easy answer to this objection: What is "shared" in James's sense is not just a matter of something like a "vote," but rather a matter of the whole course of future experience, of the "final opinion." But someone who is a realist about the past (as, I confess, I am) may still be troubled. How can the truth of a statement about the past be a function of *present and future* experience?

One answer—the answer C. I. Lewis would have given—would be that the individual might have been right even if the experiences people actually have later seem to "verify" that he was wrong: whether he was right depends not (merely) on what people in fact experience later, but on what they (counter-factually) *would* have experienced *if* they had looked, touched, and so forth. This is a sensible answer, but I am convinced that it would not have been James's answer. I believe that the overwhelming weight of the textual evidence is that James had what is sometimes called an "inference license" view of counterfactuals. A counterfactual can indeed be true in the sense that experience—*actual* experience—licences us to behave as if it were true; but James has no room for the idea that there are true statements about the past that we shall *never* know to be true.[23]

For better or for worse, I think James is committed to the view that statements about the past that do not square properly with present and future experience are simply not true. I confess that I find this kind of antirealism about the past a sure sign of a mistake, whenever, and wherever it occurs; it could be argued, however, that what commits James to this mistake is not his "ontology" but his way of understanding counterfactuals (his "actualism," as one might term it).

## Other Aspects of James's Radical Empiricism

I want to put one or two more pieces into this picture, and then I should invite you to reread the *Essays in Radical Empiricism,* for my purpose is not to offer a substitute for reading these essays, but to offer an introduction to them. What becomes of the mind in James's picture? Obviously, there is not going to be any such thing as the "essence" of the mind in James's picture. Indeed, James agrees with Hume that in a certain way the mind is a plurality, not a unity. There are, of course, long discussions of this issue in *The Principles of Psychology.* But we can bring out the disagreement with Hume — or one of the disagreements with Hume, for there are many[24] — by considering again James's example of viewing Memorial Hall. As we already saw, if I stand at a distance of two hundred feet from Memorial Hall, the "Memorial Hall" I see is, under one description, in my mind (and, if I believe in mind-brain identity, as Russell at times did, then the percept is in my brain). Under another description (another "external relation") the "Memorial Hall" is two hundred feet from my body. My mind "intersects" objects at a distance from me. In fact, as we shall see in a moment, one's mind can "intersect" as much of the pluriverse as one is able to conceive.

The point behind this last remark is what I have so far left out of my account: both reality and the part of the pluriverse we don't call reality contain things other than percepts. A respect in which James is unlike any empiricist before him (and much more like the phenomenologists who followed him) is in *putting conception on a plane with perception.* An object that is conceived (the "intentional object" of a thought, in the phenomenological sense) is also part of the pluriverse and may or may not be part of reality. Now this is a fantastic transformation of empiricism. James is certainly painting a metaphysical picture, there is no getting away from it. But the effect of this metaphysics is quite fascinating, because it results in a novel move away from positivism. Up to now, I have made James sound quite close to positivism, at least as far as thoughts about middle-sized dry goods are concerned. It sounds, from what I have said so far, as if a table, for example, consists of its perceptual aspects, its solidity, its spatiality, its color, although those perceptual aspects are (in the appropriate "context" or "external relation") not in my brain but standing in front of me. It must seem that talk about the atoms of which the table consists must be construed as highly derived talk about what percepts you would have if you were to make certain experiments. James's view does not have that consequence, because although it is true that I cannot see or feel the atoms of which the table consists, I can *conceive* of them. I can "build out" the table with my conceptions of theoretical entities of all kinds. This may, by the way, be an idea James gets from Kant. James doesn't admit he gets *anything* from Kant, ever, but in a certain reading of Kant all representations are on a par — even sensations are, in a way, minimum representations. But I shall not speculate about sources; suffice it to say that, as I read these essays, when I conceive of the table as having atoms scattered through it, those atoms are also part of the pluriverse.

This aspect of James's theory is also a reason for describing it as proto-phenomenology. If we "bracket" the question of the truth of radical empiricism as a metaphysical theory of the stuff of the pluriverse — and I have intentionally used the phenomenological term "bracket" — then we at once open the door to Husserl's grand project of trying to describe experience without either presupposing or imposing anything like the traditional sense datum theory, of describing it as it is actually *vorgegeben*. But I don't know enough about phenomenology to pursue this thought further.

## Conclusion

It will be seen that in the last two sections of this paper, I have distanced myself at certain points from James's views. A metaphysics in which reality consists of intentional objects which are in turn the "natures" of bits of "pure experience" is, I confess, too rich for my battered digestive system. But what I hope to have brought out in this account is the *depth* of the problems James was dealing with. Even today, when the idea of "incorrigibility" has been given up, belief in something like the sense datum theory is as strong as ever, if unacknowledged. (The theory is more powerful than ever precisely because it is unacknowledged.) Cognitive science is full of thinly disguised mixtures of sense datum theory and identity theory. But James struck, I believe, the opening blow in the unfinished war against the sense datum theory. Showing that at least one alternative exists — that the mere existence of illusions, errors, dreams, and the extreme phenomenon of hallucination does not, in and of itself, *force* one to accept anything like the traditional sense datum theory; that the sense datum theory is a *hypothesis* (and, I would add, a most peculiar one), and for that reason sense data cannot possibly be a *foundation* for empirical knowledge — was, I believe, an epochal achievement. Others have continued the fight in different ways, and put yet other alternatives before us — I am thinking of Austin's *Sense and Sensibilia* — but it is time we were aware that this is part of what James was doing as well.

Those who defend the sense datum theory of perception today (nowadays, sense data are usually renamed "perceptual states," or something like that, and are usually identified with brain-states and/or functional states), may reply that they are not trying to do "foundationalist epistemology." They are only trying to do "philosophical psychology," they will say. But the very assumption that there must be such things as "perceptual states" (where this doesn't merely mean that the brain is involved in perception, but that seeing a rose and hallucinating a rose have a "similarity" that is *explained* by the idea that the two subjects are in "the same perceptual state") packs in the idea that there are *states* that are, in some way, also *appearances* and those states are *inside* us; and this is just the picture from whose grip James was to trying to free us.[25] It is amazing how hard it is to get back to the idea that we do, after all, normally perceive what is out there, not something "in here."

I believe that James was on the right track, and that Austin was on the right track, even if neither of them quite finished the job. I know that James is normally seen as an *inspiring* philosopher — often in a pejorative sense of "inspiring." The purpose of this paper has been to suggest that he was also a deep thinker, who struggled with incredibly deep questions. His solutions may have been "crazy" — but as Wittgenstein remarked in a private note, "It is only by thinking even more crazily than philosophers do that you can solve their problems."[26]

## Notes

1. "The view that seems to me to reconcile the materialistic tendency of psychology with the anti-materialistic tendency of physics is the view of William James and the American new realists, according to which the 'stuff' of the world is neither mental nor material, but a 'neutral stuff,' out of which both are constructed. I have endeavored in this work to develop this view in some detail as regards the phenomena with which psychology is concerned" (Bertrand Russell, *The Analysis of Mind* [London: George Allen and Unwin; New York: Macmillan, 1921], p. 6). "Their views [those of the 'new realists'], which are chiefly held in America, are in large measure derived from William James, and before going further it will be well to consider the revolutionary doctrine which he advocated. I believe this doctrine contains important new truth, and what I shall have to say will be in a considerable measure inspired by it" (Russell, *The Analysis of Mind,* p. 22).

2. In Hilary Putnam and Ruth Anna Putnam, "William James' Ideas," *Raritan*

(Feb. 1989), Ruth Anna Putnam and I argue that what James is offering is, in fact, a complex "imperfect procedural conception" of truth.

3. Ernst Mayr, *Evolution and the Diversity of Life* (Cambridge, Mass.: Belknap Press of Harvard University Press, 1976).

4. William James, *Essays in Radical Empiricism,* ed. F. Burkhardt and F. Bowers, introd. John J. McDermott (Cambridge, Mass.: Harvard University Press, [1912] 1976), p. 17.

5. Ibid., pp. 17–18.

6. Ibid., p. 11.

7. I take it, rather, that the "we" in James's writing is supposed to include the great majority of all human beings. His famous images of cosmic struggle between good and evil, which will go on until "the last man," and which may well involve supernatural beings, if there are supernatural beings, or at any rate beings of other orders of reality (since belief in such higher orders of reality is regarded as something positive in many of James's writings, including "The Will to Believe" and the *Varieties of Religious Experience*), suggest that the relevant community is at least as inclusive as (and potentially more inclusive than) the entire human species.

8. Putnam and Putnam, "William James' Ideas."

9. James, *Radical Empiricism,* p. 17.

10. Ibid., p. 8.

11. Ibid., p. 10.

12. Ibid., p. 9.

13. Ibid., p. 18.

14. Peter Strawson, "Perception and Its Objects," in *Perception and Identity: Essays Presented to A. J. Ayer,* ed. G. F. Macdonald (Ithaca, N.Y.,: Cornell University Press, 1979).

15. Ibid.

16. The answer given by the sense datum theory is probably the answer that the average person accepts today, without being aware that this theory became the "obvious" one at a particular historical moment. Here Foucault is right; there is something fascinating in the phenomenon of a philosophy seeping down to lay people—those who think of themselves as *anti*philosophical—and in the way western culture is deeply imbued not with one philosophy but with these changing philosophies.

17. See note 1.

18. James, *Radical Empiricism,* p. 39.

19. Ibid., p. 37.

20. Quoted in McDermott's introduction to James, *Radical Empiricism,* p. xxvi.

21. An idea that also figures in Wittgenstein's later philosophy! See, for example, Ludwig Wittgenstein, *Philosophical Investigations,* trans. G.E.M. Anscombe (New York: Macmillan, 1953), §208ff.

22. Of course, James differs from the phenomenalist in another respect: James is not trying to *translate* material object language into a different language.

23. This is how I would read the following passage from Lecture VI of *Pragmatism:* "The stream of time can be remounted only verbally or verified indirectly, by present prolongations or effects of what the past harbored. Yet if they agree with those verbalities and affects, we can know that our ideas of the past are true" (William James, *Pragmatism,* ed. Ralph Barton Perry [New York: Meridian New American Library, (1907) 1955], p. 141).

24. James's belief in the reality of "experienced relations" and the doctrine that one "pure experience" can be (irreducibly) *about* another "pure experience" are important disagreements with Hume. If James and Hume both have "bundle theories" of the mind, James at least has more "glue" available in his philosophy to hold such bundles together.

25. The presupposition is made less, not more, tenable by identifying the "perceptual states" in question with brain states; for a moment's thought suffices to see that if "perceptual states" are supposed to correspond to *appearances,* then they *cannot* be identical with brain state *types* (two *type* brain states that are "adjacent" in a perceptual dimension will always have realizations that are much less than a threshold apart; in such a case, one will not be in the same [perceptual] brain state, but there will be no difference in the way things *appear* to one). Although it is more difficult to argue that "token-token identity" is also a hopelessly confused idea, I believe that in fact it is.

26. Ludwig Wittgenstein (posthumous), *Culture and Value,* trans. Peter Winch (Chicago: University of Chicago Press, 1977), p. 75.

# A Convergence of Pragmatisms

## JOSEPH MARGOLIS

### I

Almost without exception, the attractive philosophies of the late twentieth century reject the cognitive transparency of nature and reality. Their convergence, however, does not signify that they arrived at that common conviction by common strategies. Even formulating this finding as we have harbors a bias that, in its near invisibility, obscures essential differences among those we might wish to bring together. For instance, to "reject the transparency of nature" suggests that there is a structured but cognitively alien independent world that our inquiries cannot quite capture but that we must consider in correcting whatever we offer as the fruits of a realist science and inquiry. That leads to the development of what we may call "critique," the adjustment of our first-order findings about the world in terms of speculations internal to the same intransparencies that infect those findings. One may well wonder what the point and presumed rigor of such correction can possibly be if intransparency holds.

The answer, broadly speaking, is that there *are rational* reforms that are possible nonetheless — for example, in terms of predictive and explanatory power, the salient successes of invention and technological intervention, and the persistent interests and perceptions of the race. *Critique,* then, is or includes a second-order reflection on the cognitional powers of human beings typically viewed as intransparent as the first-order inquiries it means to direct, by which we make as rational a bet as we can about the descriptive and explanatory promise of all the strategies of science we can imagine. Ian Hacking, for instance, says that he has been a "scientific realist" ever since he was persuaded that there are electrons. "So far as I'm concerned, if you can spray them then they are real."[1] What he means is that certain ingenious improvements on J. A. Millikan's original 1908 experiment designed to measure the charge on the postulated fundamental unit of electric charge, the electron, involved a technical intervention described as "spray[ing] a niobium ball 107 times larger than the drop of oil [Millikan worked with] with positrons to increase the charge or with electrons to decrease the charge."[2] The improved experimental results favorably indicated the existence of electrically charged quarks. Nevertheless, Hacking avoids all formal arguments meant to be rigorous and decisive on such matters as that of settling the rational method or paradigm of science or of fixing the sense in which a prior answer to the question of rationality in science can serve as a foundation on which to decide the question of realism in science: "You will find that I dismiss most questions about rationality and am a realist on only the most pragmatic of grounds."[3] Similarly, Bas van Fraassen, speculating about what he takes to be a more economical and more rigorous conceptual strategy, pits empiricism against positivism with regard to scientific realism and maintains that "empiricism requires theories only to give a true account *of what is observable,* counting further postulated structure as a means to that end. . . . My own view is that empiricism is correct, but could not live in the linguistic form the positivists gave it."[4]

Hacking and van Fraassen disagree, of course. Van Fraassen deliberately sets out "to develop a constructive alternative to scientific realism";[5] and Hacking pretty well subscribes to the view (which he labels "scientific realism") that "says that the entities, states and processes described by correct theories really do exist."[6] Also, instead of speaking of scientific rationality directly, van Fraassen, who also reports the Millikan experiments, speaks of the "virtues" of scientific theories, including their alleged "pragmatic virtues." Van Fraassen means, in assessing these virtues, to weigh the effective role of "background theory" in the description of what, observationally, obtains. He insists that "what is observable [is] a theory-independent question"; but, in holding to that claim, he admits that observation is always formulated within a "conceptual framework" and may, to that extent, be benignly "theory-dependent." He does not actually offer criteria for a clean demarcation.[7] No one does. Nevertheless, contrary to the scientific realist's way of describing things[8] and by way of a parody of Clausewitz, van Fraassen maintains that "experimentation is the continuation of theory construction by other means."[9] Our concern, here, is not to resolve the dispute between the scientific realist and the antirealist[10] but to offer evidence of how that deep division may yet manifest a deeper convergence on the matter of rejecting the transparency of nature. Van Fraassen's thesis is difficult to maintain precisely because, unlike the classical empiricists and the early positivists, he has no self-evident protocol sentences in his back pocket. Nevertheless, there *is* an extremely important theoretical dispute that obtains between the realist and the anti-realist;

and about *that* we may say that: (1) it is or entails a second-order dispute, a dispute involving critique; and (2) its resolution bears jointly, even symbiotically, on the fate of realism and rationality. Van Fraassen links the two issues in the following way: the essential "virtue" of a scientific theory, he says, the only one involved in its rational acceptance, is what is implicated in "the belief that the theory is empirically adequate [to the observational facts]"; "more than belief is [always] involved," however, "a commitment to the further confrontation of new phenomena within the framework of that theory, a commitment to a research programme, and a wager that all relevant phenomena can be accounted for without giving up that theory." This further commitment implicates what Van Fraassen terms "pragmatic virtues," which are entirely distinct from the virtue of science as such. Both, however, signify the exercise of rationality: the one, in the explanatory work of science proper; the other, in the human context in which we risk ourselves in guessing at what will best instantiate the fixed virtue of science.[11] There are surprisingly straightforward lessons to be drawn from this little vignette. First of all, the first-order pursuit of truth in science, the pursuit of the facts about the real world, does not require cognitive transparency and does not entail agreement about the nature of science, truth, reality, or rationality. Second, under the condition of rejecting transparency, it is conceptually baffling or impossible to admit the first-order objective of science without also admitting the viability of second-order questions of critique or legitimation. Third, the resolution of the second-order question of how to characterize the realist objective of science and our best strategies for advancing or achieving it is, in part at least, a second-order answer to the question of what we should understand as human rationality. Fourth, since the notions of science, truth, reality, and rationality are conceptually interdependent and inseparable, there can, ultimately, be no second-order disjunction between *theoretical* concerns with truth and reality and *practical* concerns with rationality and virtue.

In a word, our best picture of the way the world is and of how we should conduct ourselves is one. It is perhaps fairly viewed as the deep consequence of denying transparency, of admitting that the real world we describe is only the world we posit as a world *we do not merely posit,* within the incompletely fathomable limits of the conceptual powers by which we do that. Indeed, conceding a certain abstractness, this formulation is a fair recovery of Charles Sanders Peirce's pragmaticism, which, it may be said, construes both truth and reality in terms of the infinitely continued practice of an infinite community — what has been characterized somewhat more narrowly and more misleadingly (by Hacking, for instance, speaking of Hilary Putnam as a modern-day Peircean Peirceanizing Kant) as merely "substitut[ing] method for truth."[12]

Arguably, Peirce did *not* substitute method for truth, actually, *could not* have formulated a fixed and finite method for an infinite community infinitely set in a reflexively critical way to review whatever provisional method of science and truth-value policy that community might be supposed to have hit upon in passing from provisional stage to provisional stage. To read Peirce this way is to deny that rationality can be captured by explicit universal principles or rules *and* at the same time (again against Hacking's reading, also contrary to Peirce's own fears about being misunderstood), it is to allow for James's and Dewey's more immediate preoccupation with what meets our present "practical" needs or is "warrantably assertible" here and now.[13] It is reasonably clear, though never satisfactorily so explained by James and Dewey, that *they* fully intended to reconcile their own views with Peirce's.[14] It is also embarrassingly clear that neither Peirce nor James nor Dewey ever quite managed to formulate in *one* account the conceptual relationship between the infinite process of pursuing truth and the finite provisional phases of that process within which truth-values could be justifiably assigned and altered. It is surely the case— one would hope that Peirce himself fully realized—that the famous "pragmatist" doctrine, the doctrine that "the opinion which is fated to be ultimately agreed to by all who investigate is what we mean by the truth and [that] the object represented in this opinion is the real," was itself a *mythic* rather than a *critical* account of the method of rational inquiry.[15] It could not have been more than an account of the holistic, infinite context within which determinate assignments of truth-values or truth-like values in the finite phases of inquiry were linked to a conception of truth and reality without actually invoking (or being able to invoke), distributively, criteria of truth and reality in an operational way *under that conception.* Anything more or less would have been utterly incoherent.[16] The pragmatist theory, however, *does* require *that* conception in order to adjust and legitimate the grounds or criteria *for* the assignment of truth-values.

## II

We have been drawn here, ineluctably but rather too easily, into several thickets of dispute—one, the realist/antirealist quarrel; another, the quarrel about the proper relationship among the principal American pragmatists and about the proper interpretation of their respective claims. What

we had begun with, however, was merely the late twentieth-century repudiation of transparency and whatever possible misunderstandings that seemingly straightforward commitment might engender. The repudiation of
transparency has also come to mean something fundamentally different
from what we have been laboring to gain control of along the lines of the
two sorts of quarrel already sampled. It means (to some at least) that, in
repudiating transparency, one should also repudiate critique or second-order
legitimation itself — either in the sense of falling back to the first-order concern with truth in science (without invoking or without the need to invoke
a philosophical theory of truth at all) or in the sense of eliminating all
talk of truth even at the level of first-order scientific discourse (on the
grounds that to introduce truth there *is* already to oblige ourselves to acknowledge the conceptual relevance, even ineliminability, of second-order
legitimative questions). The first of these two strategies is Richard Rorty's;
the second is Jean-Francois Lyotard's. The first is explicitly labeled a form
of pragmatism; the second demonstrates the dialectical entanglement of
that sort of pragmatism with French poststructuralism. Both, in fact, may
rightly be termed versions of philosophical postmodernism, and both are
incoherent. But the charge remains to be shown.

Rorty seems quite straightforward in his indictment: a pragmatist "theory [he says] says that truth is not the sort of thing one should expect to
have a philosophically interesting theory about. For pragmatists, 'truth'
is just the name of a property that all true statements share."[17] There is
a certain slyness in the remark, however, What Rorty obviously means by
"a philosophically interesting theory" of truth is one that offers epistemologically prior, legitimated criteria by which distributed claims could be
said to be true or to describe the real world under and (perhaps) only under
that theory; he also means that a philosophical account of the conception
of truth or of the relation between truth and reality that did not entail
such explicit criteria would not be appropriately "interesting"; *and* he means
that the distributed statements of science and of serious inquiry do contain a significant number that *are true* and may be marked as true in spite
of our lacking any philosophically interesting theory of truth at all. Several counterconsiderations suggest themselves. First of all, it is clear from
what has already been said that Peirce believed that his theory of truth
and reality was philosophically quite interesting, even indispensable, precisely because it did not (and could not) yield the privileged criteria Rorty
insinuated would alone — however fatally inaccessible — establish any particular theory as an interesting theory.[18] Peirce seems convinced that it is
just the blindness of our rational efforts *now* regarding whatever would
be discerned as true and real in the limit of the infinite process of inquiry
that makes a theory of truth "interesting" *all the while we pursue our finite*

*inquiries.* That is the point of reconciling James's and Dewey's sorts of theory with Peirce's, though not necessarily their own particular doctrines. In any case, Rorty surely misrepresents the pragmatist tradition he reports. Second, the question arises as to just what we (and Rorty) might mean by saying that a whole lot of "statements" do *have* a certain property in common in being "true statements." It is the property of actually being true? Is it the property of being assigned (for some reason that does not invoke the use of "interesting" theories) the predicate "true"? And what, if anything, is the difference between these two options?

Rorty warns us that "pragmatists are saying that the best hope for philosophy is not to practice Philosophy," that "true sentences are not true because they correspond to reality, and so there is no need to worry what sort of reality, if any, a given sentence corresponds to—no need to worry about what 'makes' it true."[19] Nevertheless, this leaves utterly unsettled the sense in which we even bother to say that certain statements *are* true and others are not.

Rorty believes he does address the question responsively: "The issue is one about whether philosophy should try to find natural starting points that are distinct from cultural traditions, or whether all philosophy should do is compare and contrast cultural traditions."[20] His preference is clearly for the second option. "Pragmatism," he says, "denies the possibility of getting beyond the Sellarsian notion of 'seeing how things hang together'— which, for the bookish intellectual of recent times, means seeing how all the various vocabularies of all the various epochs and cultures hang together."[21] A very neat formula, this; but it is neither Hegelian nor Sellarsian, as Rorty would have us believe, and it is inadequate in any case.

The simple truth is that *how* the various epochs "hang together" invokes questions of relevance for a given practice as well as reasonable norms by which that practice should be guided or governed. There's no meaningful perception of how "all" cultures hang together without some conceptual direction regarding the supposed purpose of science or of other inquiries; and that is just what Peirce obviously meant to supply in offering his "interesting" theory. The predicate "true" is hardly negligible or redundant, in the plain sense that its *use* implicates a policy about *how* rationally or rightly to determine truth-value assignments in the short run (*and* about *which* assignments to allow) in accord with a defensible conception of the relationship between truth and reality in the long run. That connection can hardly fail to be disputatious; but it is also not eliminable, particularly where intransparency is concerned.

In short, it is the *practical* prospect of committing our very limited resources in constructing a systematic account of the truth about nature that obliges us to pursue the legitimative question. *To fail to pursue it would be irrational.* Since Rorty is a firm believer in the viability and perceived worth of first-order science, he can have no objection to the sustained use of the predicate "true" in constative or assertoric discourse there. But since he also objects to any and every use of constative discourse in second-order legitimative inquiry, he clearly believes that first-order discourse need not violate our stand against transparency in spite of the fact that all philosophical second-order, critical or legitimative discourse must violate that same stand. Nowhere, however, in Rorty's extensive writings is there a single demonstration that legitimative discourse is necessarily committed to transparency because of its taking truth-values.

How thin Rorty's objection to the "Philosophers" actually is may be guessed from the following remark:

> The intuitive realist [the prime opponent of the pragmatist] thinks that there is such a thing as Philosophical truth [transparently given] because he thinks that, deep down beneath all the texts, there is something [intuitively, non-linguistically discernible] which is not just one more text but that to which various texts are trying to be "adequate" [a "bedrock"]. The pragmatist does not think that there is anything like that. He does not even think that there is anything isolable as "the purposes which we construct vocabularies and cultures to fulfill" against which to test vocabularies and cultures. But he *does* think that in the process of playing vocabularies and cultures off against one another, *we produce new and better ways of talking and acting — not better by reference to a previously known standard, but just better in the sense that they come to seem clearly better than their predecessors.*[22]

This gives Rorty's game entirely away. For, *if* the legitimation or critique of "vocabularies and cultures" *can* yield changes that "seem clearly better" in terms of the shifting experience of a society — where "seem" now means that transparency is abandoned and that would-be rational strategies are still needed and open to just the appraisals Rorty admits obtain *within* the limits of "all" remembered practices — then, contrary to his own intention, *Rorty has actually managed to disjoin legitimation and the fatal commitment to transparency.* Either he denies that he has done so (which is false), or else he denies that that entails the recovery of false "Philosophy" (which is either vacuously true or else patently absurd). The short truth is that first-order constative talk entails second-order legitimative talk, that the use of the predicate "true" implicates epistemological norms that can never be altogether detached from the internal, historicized, nonprivileged practices of the viable society that first generated them. But why need they be more? Rorty's complaint is an entirely dispensable nostalgia that has no theoretical force.

His argument is not important in itself, except for its modishness. It is in a way the pop version of Quine's earlier attempt to "naturalize" epistemology: to encourage us, as Hilary Putnam compellingly shows, to "abandon the notions of justification, good reason, warranted assertion, and so on"—"to 'rule out the normative.'"[23] If truth is a normative notion, then, as Putnam concludes, "the elimination of the normative is attempted mental suicide . . . and there is no eliminating the normative."[24] Of course, to accept that finding is, effectively, to recover transcendental, legitimative, critical, second-order discourse: First-order science without second-order philosophy is seen to be blind; second-order philosophy without first-order science remains empty; and the distinction between the two proves to be a second-order distinction.[25] Still, to draw this conclusion is not yet to supply an adequate account of legitimation.

# III

Elsewhere, Rorty explicitly links his rejection of critique or legitimation to his own conception of rationality. First of all, he openly adopts Lyotard's view of "the postmodern attitude," that is, the "distrust of metanarratives," the distrust of "stories which purport to justify loyalty to, or breaks with, certain contemporary communities, but which are neither historical narratives about what these or other communities have done in the past nor scenarios about what they might do in the future."[26] Second, he attempts to show how to recover and reinterpret "bourgeois liberal institutions" in a way to "suit the needs of us postmodernist bourgeois liberals," in a way that "might convince our society that loyalty to itself is morality enough, and that such loyalty no longer needs an ahistorical backup."[27] What he really means is that a generous and courageous policy of philosophical laissez-faire is both quite sufficient for the flourishing of first-order science *and all we could rationally support in any case.* But what if he is wrong—empirically? What if the scientific community, faced with an extremely large array of substantive and methodological options of its own invention, which it cannot possibly exhaust in real-time terms—say, contrary to Karl Popper's optimistic utopianism—finds that it must (for the gravest practical or existential reasons: impending world drought, for instance) speculate here and now on the best rational bet it can muster from the internal history of its own perceived successes and failures?

To see the point is to recover Peirce's thesis (on the reading we have just offered) and to condemn Rorty's recommendation as irresponsible and incoherent. There can be no first-order science that ignores or disallows the testing of truth-claims, and there cannot be any rational policy regarding how we should manage the assignment of truth-values in science that does not implicate second-order legitimative concerns. Not to put too fine a point on it, Rorty either cheats in his characterization of bourgeois values or else he is hopelessly wide of the mark. Legitimation need not presume cognitive privilege of any sort, and it is more rather than less essential to rational behavior where transparency is denied and where the human existential quandary is more baffling and more insistent *because* transparency is denied.

It is, therefore, not surprising that Rorty turns Quinean in explaining himself and in attempting to persuade the rest of us:

> On a Quinean view, rational behavior is just adaptive behavior of a sort which roughly parallels the behavior, in similar circumstances, of the other members of some relevant community. Irrationality, in both physics and ethics, is a matter of behavior that leads one to abandon, or be stripped of, membership in some such community. For some purposes this adaptive behavior is aptly described as "learning" or "computing" or "redistribution of electrical charges in neural tissue," and for others as "deliberation" or "choice." None of these vocabularies is privileged against another.[28]

This is nonsense, however. Rorty is attempting — impossibly — to recover the normative as purely decriptive or as nakedly rhetorical and to disallow in the bargain the critical or legitimative altogether.

It does not take much to see that Putnam's challenge to Quine is intended to apply to Rorty's thesis as well. In fact, Putnam explicitly draws the connection: "I count Richard Rorty as a cultural relativist," he says, "because his explicit formulations are relativist ones (he identifies truth with right assertibility by the standards of one's cultural peers, for example), and because his entire attack on traditional philosophy is mounted on the basis that the nature of reason and representation are nonproblems, because the only kind of truth it makes sense to seek is to convince one's cultural pers."[29]

We must be careful here. We can and must join Putnam in recovering the notion of an "interesting" theory of truth, the indissoluble linkage between theoretical and practical concerns, and the viability and ineliminability of transcendental or legitimative questions — all under the constraint of abandoning transparency and cognitive privilege. To do so is simply to recover the essential nerve of a Peircean pragmatism. But Putnam puts his own argument in terms of certain charges against relativism, and that may be shown to be a much larger and much more delicate matter than Putnam concedes — *or* than Peirce anticipates. The simple truth is that it does not follow, or it has not yet been shown to follow, that the recovery of second-order discourse entails the defeat of relativism (Putnam's thesis) any more than it follows that an adherence to such normative discourse entails an adherence to cognitive privilege (Rorty's thesis). There is an exceptionally large lacuna that stares us in the face in the pitched opposition between Rorty and Putnam. We shall return to it in a moment.

For his part, Lyotard is nimbler than Rorty. Because *he* realizes that once we admit science as knowledge, once we acknowledge science as a paradigm of the pursuit of what is true about the world, we cannot fail to admit the relevance of legitimative questions. The only way to defeat the tentacular enterprise of legitimation—Lyotard has Jürgen Habermas preeminently in mind, of course—is to construe *knowledge* (*savoir*) as nothing more than a form of play. The preposterousness of the proposal is a tribute to Lyotard's consistency—at the price, however, of a deeper incoherence. "A science, Lyotard says, that has not legitimated itself is not a true science; if the discourse that was meant to legitimate it seems to belong to a prescientific form of knowledge, like a "vulgar" narrative, it is demoted to the lowest rank, that of an ideology or instrument of power. And this always happens if the rules of the science game that discourse denounces as empirical are applied to science itself.[30] Lyotard treats knowledge essentially as "know-how" (*savoir-faire*), which he dubs "narrative knowledge" or "narration," an aptitude never reducible "to science or even to learning (*connaissance*)." The reason is straightforward: science requires legitimation, which Lyotard repudiates, and learning "is the set of statements that, to the exclusion of all other statements, denote or describe objects and may be declared true or false," which would require legitimation.[31] Lyotard's motivation is not uninteresting, it may be said: it is intended to wed a touch of Marx (*praxis*), a touch of Foucault (*epistemes*), and a touch of Wittgenstein (*Lebensformen*).[32] But it is driven by the absurdity of its own dialectical requirements to announce that *postmodern* science has as its "model of legitimation . . . nothing to do with maximized performance [that is, the improvement of research programs or the like], but has as its basis difference understood as paralogy."[33] If, in any sense, paralogy could be endorsed, it would be endorsed *in* the name of "maximized performance"—ironically in Peirce's sense, shorn of Peirce's own somewhat too simple optimism.

Part of Lyotard's effort is sheer bravado, the wish to break up at any price the steady *bürgerlich* sobreity of Habermas's consensual and emancipative notion of legitimation[34] (what Lyotard treats as a failed modernism);[35] part of it is informed by a genuine appreciation of the discontinuity of scientific gains that break out of prior paradigms (somewhat along the lines Kuhn and Feyerabend have always emphasized);[36] and part of it is just lost in an irrationality that refuses to pay attention to the fact *that the fact that* "the continuous differentiable function [of research] is losing its preeminence as a paradigm of knowledge and prediction" is itself consensually confirmed (if it is confirmed) within the practice of sci-

ence and against mere wild paralogy.[37] Hence, even when he proclaims
that the postmodern orientation signifies "another goal within the system"
of knowledge — consequently, a goal affecting the rules of science, namely,
that of "the quest for paralogy" — Lyotard really means (he cannot but mean)
to favor a certain openness to prospects of discovery (*difference*) regarding
the nature of the world that a mere *modernist* science would fail to notice.[38]
This, then, also explains what he means, in closing his essay, in joining
science and politics — "a politics that would respect both the desire for justice and the desire for the unknown," because knowledge or information
is "inexhaustible" and because at no point in any "language game" (the
game of science preeminently) would any position have "exhausted its
stakes."[39] The simple trouble is that Lyotard *cannot* (any more than could
Feyerabend before him — recommending Galileo, who defied the apparent
canons of his own day)[40] account for the tolerance of the open-ended nature of science and its often maverick discoveries. Both his vision of science and his vision of politics are ultimately incoherent (and recall, in this
respect, Michel Foucault's similar, self-acknowledged failing).[41]

# IV

We are at a crossroads here. We have been tracing the dispute about
the relationship between first- and second-order discourse in terms of the
avoidability of cognitive privilege and transparency. This has led us to see
how the dispute affects the realist/antirealist quarrel, the quarrel about the
relationship between Peircean long run and the Jamesian and Deweyan
short run, and the quarrel between modernists and postmodernists. It could
also have been pursued in terms of the quarrel about whether all science
and rational inquiry must subscribe to bipolar values, excluded middle,
or *tertium non datur;* for, if privilege is abandoned, then, even on antirealist grounds (of Michael Dummett's sort, for instance) though not exclusively
on such grounds, it may well be the case that, for particular sectors of
the world, only a relativistic model of truth-value assignments could be
convincingly legitimated — that is, a model that was relativistic in the moderate sense of allowing only for the empirical support of judgments that,
on a bipolar model but not now, would yield incompatible or contradictory truths.[42] Put another way, what we have been pursuing are the converging pragmatist themes of a large variety of competing views dialectically
paired to show how they approach one another from decidedly different
contexts of debate.

But there is a larger prize in the offing. We have recovered, we may claim, a sense of the need for second-order legitimation, a sense of the very legitimacy of legitimation. But we have not actually considered its most salient features under the constraint of abandoning transparency. The recovery of transcendental, second-order, critical, or what Habermas tends to call "pragmatic" questions is the principal theme of what Rorty and Lyotard inveigh against as the project of philosophical modernism.[43] Granted, now, that it cannot be avoided, what can we say about legitimation's most disputed properties?

In a very pretty way, the best clues may be had by reviewing the manner of recovery proposed by Habermas and Putnam — who may fairly be regarded as two quite different stalwarts of modernism. Our argument will find that *if* legitimation is to be recovered in either of their ways, then, not too surprisingly, the postmodernists would be right to challenge legitimation as a form of privilege; but it will also find that legitimation need not be thus recovered, that it must (instead) undergo a sea change as a result of acknowledging such constraints as: (a) the loss of privilege and transparency; (b) the preformation of our cognitional and active powers; (c) the historicity of human existence; (d) the occurrence of discontinuities and incommensurabilities affecting our cognitive schemes; (e) the incliminability of perspectivism in discourse and life; and (f) the hermeneutic or intentional complexity of human self-understanding. It would be too much to attempt to pursue all of these matters here, although we may claim in a blanket way that the import of (a)–(f) really signifies the strong convergence of a phenomenologized naturalism and a naturalized phenomenology — which is to say, a convergence of nearly all the principal currents of contemporary philosophy along pragmatist lines.[44] We shall have to economize, however, and risk slighting that larger finding by favoring a certain indirection.

Consider Habermas. He rejects Kantian transcendental arguments for several compelling reasons that, in effect, he shares with Rorty's postmodern critique. For one thing, Kantian transcendental arguments are foundationalist, privileged, committed to a higher epistemological resource than is available in first-order science, by which its own cognitive limits and capabilities are supposed to be defined. "This," says Habermas, "is tantamount to an act of ushering the sciences to their proper place."[45] Second, Kantian arguments segregate one from another what Max Weber calls the "value spheres of culture" and assume, therefore, "the role of the highest [in fact, a completely 'ahistorical' role as] arbiter for all matters, including culture as a whole."[46] Habermas concedes Rorty's effective critique here. But he adds at once: "I have trouble accepting [Rorty's] conclusion, which is that if philosophy foreswears these two roles, it must also surrender the function of being the guardian of rationality. If I understand Rorty, he is saying that the new modesty of philosophy involves the abandonment of any claim to reason—the very claim that has marked philosophical thought since its inception. Rorty not only argues for the demise of philosophy. He also unflinchingly accepts the end of the belief that ideas like truth or the unconditional with their transcending power are a necessary condition of humane forms of collective life."[47]

The essential virtue of Habermas's strategy lies in his holding fast to the indissoluble linkage between theoretical and practical concerns, to grasping the symbiosis of first- and second-order discourse as inexorably invoking that linkage, and to locating all our efforts to define the effectiveness of legitimative work entirely within the flux of history. Habermas is sanguine about the prospects of legitimative discourse. In fact he reviews six distinct positions—three Kantian and three Hegelian—which set in a dialectical way the problem of recovering anything of the original transcendental objective. He summarizes rather breezily the upshot of "analytic philosophy" (Strawson), "constructivism" (Lorenzen), "critical-rationalism" (Popper), "materialism" (Lukacs), "practicism" (Korsch and Freyer), and "negativism" (Adorno), and the work of their opposite numbers, and announces with some warmth that "they still say *something* about the indispensable conditions of claims to the validity of those opinions we hold to be justified, claims that transcend all restrictions of time and place." At this point, Habermas finds a stronger resource in pragmatism and hermeneutic philosophy, since *they* "oust the traditional notion of the solitary subject that confronts objects and becomes reflective only by turning itself into an object. In its place they put an idea of cognition that is mediated by language and linked to action."[48]

The outlines of Habermas's recovery of pragmatic universals are very well known.[49] But its conceptual engine may have been ignored. It is simply this: Emancipative reason, the capacity to discern "the indispensable [universal] conditions" of all thought and action "transcend[ing] all restrictions of time and place," *is never itself so constituted as a historicized artifact or phenomenon that its best critical conjectures are inherently incapable of the full discovery to be assigned.* Habermas never answers the objection here implied (that is, the objection that he never explains how to distinguish between the genuinely "indispensable" conditions and whatever conditions merely appear as consensually favored under historical circumstances)—which, it should be said, is *not* tantamount to disallowing transcendental or pragmatic legitimation or to disallowing our postulating reasonable candidates for universalist standing. Habermas cannot show—and has never shown, despite the most strenuous efforts—that actual discourse and action *are* grounded in the putatively "indispensable" formal conditions he affirms, what he calls "the universal and necessary conditions of communicative action,"[50] or that we *are normatively committed* to those universals even if they are not actually instantiated in every successful communication. These conditions include of course the elements of the famous tetrad: truth, rightness, truthfulness, and comprehensibility.[51] What Habermas has never quite grasped is that *if* philosophy is, as he says, to be "the guardian of rationality," then the universalism he seeks must yield universal *criteria,* criteria transcending "all restrictions of time or place," criteria demonstrably unavoidable in all communicative action.

The truth is that Habermas suffers from a Kantian nostalgia that he has effectively rendered himself incapable of relieving. He admits that actual communicative action succeeds without subscribing to his conditions; and he fails to show how his own would-be norms are nonvacuously entailed or presupposed in every would-be rational endeavor — for instance, in pursuing scientific inquiries. He simply cannot reconcile universalism (the belief that there are determinate transhistorical norms of rational thought and action adequate for the direction of human life) and historicism (the belief that the structures of human life including the norms of rationality are inherently formed within the tacit limits of the biology of the species by the contingencies of cultural history).[52] Habermas's own resolution simply affirms: "I think pragmatism and hermeneutics have joined forces to answer this question [in effect, the question of the reintegration of universalism and historicism], by attributing epistemic authority to *the community of all who cooperate and speak with one another.* Everyday communication makes possible a kind of understanding that is based on claims to validity, thus furnishing the only real alternative to exerting influence on one another, which is always more or less coercive. The validity claims that we raise in conversation — that is, when we say something with conviction — transcend this specific conversational context, pointing to something beyond the spatio-temporal ambit of the occasion."[53] But the least reflection shows that, here, Habermas has simply reintroduced the completely unresolved difficulty of reconciling James's and Dewey's short-run criteria for truth-value assignments with Peirce's long-run conception of truth *sans* criteria, that is, the difficulty of reconciling local or historicized communicative practices with the utopian vision of the self-understanding of the infinite community of humankind or of all possible forms of intelligence.

Putnam's alternative version of modernism — to use the term in the pejorative sense the postmodernists favor — is rather more difficult to fix. It is, however, committed to the same "transcendence" of reason that Habermas pursues by another means. "Philosophers who lose sight of the tran-

scendence of reason," Putnam says, "become cultural (or historical) relativists. . . . [And,] at bottom there is a deep irrationalism in cultural relativism, a denial of the possibility of thinking (as opposed to making noises
in counterpoint or in chorus)."[54] In short, Putnam means to oppose Quine
and Rorty for the same reason, namely, their failure to acknowledge the
need for transcendental or legitimative norms of inquiry and action (reason); and, in opposing them, he means to recover such norms (in what
he regards as a somewhat Kantian spirit) in ways that escape cultural relativism, that "transcend" history, that provide universal constraints. But he
fails and must fail in this: He shows neither that we can escape nor how
we can escape nor that not escaping entails incoherence. The collapse
of his proposal, together with that of Habermas, sends a very strong signal regarding the future prospects of the pragmatism we are gradually
defining.

The issue may be put this way. At the present time, there are those — call
them philosophical postmodernists (Rorty and Lyotard explicitly, Foucault
and Nietzsche by temperament) — who reject all transcendental, second-
order, legitimative, critical discourse *in* rejecting cognitive privilege and
transparency, within the flux of history. They are all relativists of some
sort (or "worse"). Richard Bernstein, for one, has caught the fever and
the sense of the infection (among the champions of "objectivism, foundationalism, ultimate grounding of knowledge, science, philosophy, and language" — champions he actually opposes) when he equates the pernicious
doctrines of "relativism, skepticism, historicism, and nihilism" with one
another, also incommensurabilism, as being more or less the same teaching.[55] On the other hand, there are those — call them philosophical modernists (Habermas and Putnam explicitly, Gadamer, Ricoeur, Charles Taylor by implication) — who insist that transcendental or legitimative discourse
must, in being ineliminable, also be universalistic. They are all opponents
of one or another sort of relativism of the varieties Bernstein collects and
condemns. We have already encountered a clear expression of this teaching in Habermas himself.

There is today almost no advocate of critical or legitimative discourse
of an affirmative, productive sort who combines a defense of its ineliminability and the coherence of advocating legitimation *in* a relativistic,
historicized, antiuniversalistic spirit.[56] But that is precisely where the argument leads. Against the postmodernists, we may affirm that first- and
second-order discourse is inextricably linked; against the modernists, we
may affirm that second-order discourse cannot remain universalistic in
avoiding, within history, the pretensions of cognitive privilege. *The validity of legitimative arguments does not require that they actually be defen-*

*sibly universalistic* — in spite of the fact that, within the boundaries of one's conceptual horizon, every would-be defense must seek to encompass all that is argumentatively relevant. We search for universal scope in legitimative contexts, just as we do in projecting the would-be laws of nature; but, in legitimation as in explanatory science, we cannot actually — within anything like the pragmatist idiom that would reconcile Peirce's long run and James's and Dewey's short run — unite historicism and universalism. Putnam is particularly instructive here because, in pursuing the modernist option, he inadvertently discloses the *tenability* of what he calls "cultural relativism," and he does so against his own thesis. But the matter is admittedly complicated.

Recall that Putnam opposes those who would "naturalize" epistemology (Quine, Rorty) as philosophically "suicidal"; and that he opposes "metaphysical realists" (say, Russell and Moore at least) as "incoherent."[57] Now, Putnam himself brings these two themes together in conceding that standards of "truth and rational acceptability" can be formulated only relative to the "interests and saliencies" of our cultural history, while at the same time he repudiates "cultural relativism" as "incoherent" and "irrational."[58]

Here is a fair clue to his objection: "What I am saying," he explains, "is that the 'standards' accepted in a culture or a sub-culture, either explicitly or implicitly, cannot *define* what reason is, even in context, because they *presuppose* reason (reasonableness) for their interpretation. On the one hand, there is no notion of reasonableness at all without cultures, practices, procedures; on the other hand, the cultures, practices, procedures we inherit are not an algorithm to be slavishly followed. . . . Reason is, in this sense, both immanent (not to be found outside of concrete language games and institutions) and transcendent (a regulative idea that we use to criticize the conduct of all activities and institutions)."[59] This, of course, is what Putnam intends by characterizing his own stance as a sort of Peirceanized Kantianism.[60] But he really means to reject: (1) any mere "natural" consensus as fully legitimative (in a very strong sense directed against Rorty, say) *and* (2) any pretension that there is a genuinely "universal ethic" or consensual "authority" that an ongoing Peircean-like inquiry could yield in the short run (explicitly against Habermas and Karl-Otto Apel).[61] Thus far, it would appear that Putnam means to endorse a form of relativism. But his intention is to expose cultural relativism as incoherent. How does he gain his objective?

Putnam correctly fixes the locus of the relativist dispute: on the one hand, discourse that invites ascriptions of truth, rationality, rightness, and the like makes "sense [only] against the background of an inherited tradition"; and, on the other, "traditions themselves can be criticized."[62] This is what any viable theory of inquiry, rational conduct, or science must accommodate if it eschews privilege and embeds human practices in historical contingencies. Putnam views these conditions as quite beyond the resources of cultural relativism; but others, Alasdair MacIntyre for instance, are persuaded that relativism is actually capable of meeting the challenge. The answer to Putnam's charge against relativism requires no more than a purely formal consideration, for there is no sustained discussion, in Putnam's account, of what a tradition or historical practice is; although once we see the formal question correctly, we can move at once to a more substantive defense of relativism itself.

Putnam insists that "there is no eliminating the normative" — by which he means that legitimative discourse is inherently normative and cannot be reduced to the "naturalistic" or first-order discourse of psychology or of any other science.[63] But he also means, as we have already remarked, that "consensus presupposes reason rather than defin[es] it."[64] Now this is at best unclear and at worst seriously mistaken. Relativism hangs in the balance because, as Putnam also says, "we don't have an Archimedean point; we always speak the language of a time and place; but the rightness and wrongness of what we say is not *just* for a time and a place."[65]

Consensus *presupposes* rationality, in the uncomplicated sense that first-order "naturalistic" discourse presupposes *its* being subject to second-order normative or legitimative discourse; but it does not presuppose rationality in the further sense that *there is* a discernible, transhistorical, "absolute," or "universal" norm *that is presupposed in* every effort at inquiry or consensus. Putnam says as much. But if that is true, then it is quite impossible to escape cultural relativism *if* by that we mean (as seems reasonable) no more than to accommodate (1) the embedding of inquiry in a historical cultural or tradition having normative force and (2) the critical recognition that such a tradition is itself always open to further normative criticism.

Habermas appears to escape relativism because *he* attenuates the *confirmation* of his pragmatic universals within the Peircean long run, although he finds that he can *state* those universals in the short run. Quite a trick. Putnam also mysteriously appears to escape relativism because he does not take sufficient care to explain what he means by the term "presuppose": he seems to mean that Habermas's strategy is illicit (which it surely is) but that the rational norms by which we criticize provisional (historicized) posits of the norms of rationality are themselves presupposed by something like Peirce's long run in spite of our being unable, or our not needing, to specify those norms *in the short run*. But *that* he cannot (on his own view) supply any long-run norms *in* the short run demonstrates at a stroke that Putnam cannot escape cultural relativism. Q.E.D.

## V

Here then is the master significance of Peirce's fallibilism, the sense in which all current theories tend irresistibly to converge in a pragmatist manner. Putnam's mistake is understandable, but not elementary. It surely does not follow, as Putnam correctly insists, that, because a truth-claim depends for its meaning, for its truth-value assignment, for its "rightness and wrongness," *on* a particular language *L* or a particular culture *C,* it is also merely true-in-*L* or right-in-*C*. That *is* a vicious mistake rightly discounted as an incoherent form of relativism. But cultural relativism does not affirm *that* (or does not do so, on a reasonable reading). *All* that is needed is the concession that the *rational* correction of the historically embedded norms by which what, in *L* or in *C,* is affirmed as true or right is itself embedded in *L'* or *C'* (rationally corrected from the other) and that, there (as before), what is, in *L'* or *C',* truly or rightly affirmed, is not merely true-in-*L'* or right-in-*C'*. Putnam is quite wrong to say, therefore, that "philosophy, as culture-bound reflection and argument about eternal questions, *is* both in time and in eternity."[66] *In* time, it only ventures to speculate about eternity. *That is* cultural relativism, at least on its formal side.

Perhaps a final remark is wanted, in order to round things out. Alasdair MacIntyre provides a successful sketch of a viable cultural relativism that meets all of Putnam's fair conditions and eschews "eternity." Roughly speaking his strategy, in moral and political discourse, is the analogue of what Thomas Kuhn offers (or should have offered if he had grasped the full complexity of his own position) in regard to the discourse of science. MacIntyre postulates that a failure of translatability (or translation) between two cultures or subcultures is no more than an incompatibility or conflict or incommensurability between them regarding some set of claims or recommended conduct. His account depends only on: (a) excluding "the possibility of appeal to some neutral or independent standard of rational justification [that is, independent of one's historical tradition] to justify the choice of one set of beliefs, one way of life, one linguistic community rather than the other";[67] (b) acknowledging that "relativism [can] be transcended," in the sense that "we are [not] condemned to or imprisoned within our own particular standpoint, [unable] to controvert that of others only by appealing to standards that already presuppose the standpoint of our own prejudices";[68] and (c) acknowledging, further, that, *in* transcending the relativism of a given phase of one's tradition and practice, one is *not* transcending tradition or practice altogether. Nothing could be simpler or more compelling.

MacIntyre explains the option very clearly:

> Rationality, understood within some particular tradition with its own spe-
> cific conceptual scheme and problematic, . . . nonetheless requires *qua* ra-
> tionality a recognition that the rational inadequacies of that tradition from
> its own point of view — and every tradition *must from the point of view of
> its own problematic* view itself as to some degree inadequate — may at any
> time prove to be such that perhaps only the resources provided by some quite
> alien tradition . . . will enable us to identify and understand the limitations
> of our own tradition; and this provision may require that we transfer our
> allegiance to that hitherto alien tradition.[69]

Soften or problematize MacIntyre's *own* sense of the determinacy of
one's "tradition," one's "problematic," one's "specific conceptual scheme"
and specific norms of rationality, and you will have a full-fledged cultural
relativism that is both viable and *inescapable*. The excessively sanguine
use to which MacIntyre puts his own conception, in *After Virtue,* may
well be challenged without at all calling into question the general relativistic strategy by which he arrives at his own particular conviction.[70]

In a word, relativism *is* an ineliminable ingredient of the convergent
pragmatisms we have been tracing through the most prominent varieties
of late twentieth-century philosophies. It is not a stupid relativism — Pro-
tagoreanism, say, according to the usual prejudice; although Protagoras's
own doctrine of man as the measure, possibly directed against Parmenides's
exclusive way of truth, may be plausibly interpreted as recommending that
we waive the law of excluded middle *and* even *tertium non datur* (in which
case it need not be self-contradictory). Nor is it stupid in the manner of
radical incommensurabilism. It need only countenance moderate incommensurabilities of actual translation and conceptual isomorphism, while
denying unintelligibility and incomparability. Once it does that, it provides
easily enough for "internalist" evidence of methodological impasse and
rational improvement — perceived withal only within horizonal limits. Finally, the relativism here envisioned can claim logical resources of a suitably robust sort, synchronic as well as diachronic, because, in waiving *tertium non datur* (where needed), it can bring to bear relevance constraints
on any array of truth-claims and would-be rational commitments such that
claims and commitments that, on a model of bivalent or bipolar truth-
values would yield contradictories and incompatibles, need not do so now
or be judged to do so now. It will yield, instead, a plural array of what
we may call "incongruent" claims and commitments, that is, claims that
preclude a strong convergence toward uniquely determined truths or
uniquely determined rational commitments. It will therefore preclude the
very viability of universalistic norms.[71]

The upshot is quite straightforward. The entire thrust of late twentieth-
century philosophies, sprawling across the divide of Anglo-American and

continental European currents, is now perceptibly and justifiably converging on: (1) the rejection of universalisms of every sort, but not mere "indicative" universals (like mortality) or "horizonal" (or second-order) universals (like provisional internalist canons of rational inquiry); (2) the recovery of legitimation, critique, transcendental argument within the limits of (1); hence, (3) the redefinition of the norms of rationality in relativistic terms constrained by (1) and (2). Adherence to the themes of (1) — (3) constitutes the dawning *pragmatism* of our age. In fact, it constitutes a new resolution of the deep puzzle joining and separating Peirce and James and Dewey; for, now, both the long run and the short run are relativistically infected and equally internalist in resource. Even the realism every anti-realism must aspire to is no more privileged, no less internal or horizonal, than the piecemeal, distributive, first-order practices of societies that continue to be viable here and now. The rejection of this third option entails a retreat to that impossible modernism theorists like Habermas and Apel heroically practice (the recovery of universalism) or the equally impossible but obscured modernism theorists like Gadamer and Charles Taylor and MacIntyre and Putnam practice (call it "traditionalism") by which they (magically) pretend to recover within the shifting traditions of the race what the franker advocates of cognitive privilege treat as timelessly evident. Or else it entails a retreat to the incoherence of that hopeless postmodernism theorists like Rorty and Lyotard pretend to rescue by disjoining first-order and second-order discourse — a retreat that, in effect, is ultimately indistinguishable from sheer irrationality.

There appear to be no other options.

# Notes

1. Ian Hacking, *Representing and Intervening: Introductory Topics in the Philosophy of Natural Science* (Cambridge: Cambridge University Press, 1983), p. 23.

2. Ibid., p. 23.

3. Ibid., p. 2, in the context of chap. 1.

4. Bas C. van Fraassen, *The Scientific Image* (Oxford: Clarendon Press, 1980), p. 3.

5. Ibid., p. vii.

6. Ibid., p. 21.

7. Ibid., pp. 57–58; cf. pp. 75–77.

8. In effect, contrary to Richard Boyd's "Realism, Underdetermination, and a Causal Theory of Evidence," *Nous* 7(1973), pp. 1–12.

9. Van Fraassen, *Scientific Image,* p. 77.

    10. See Joseph Margolis, *Pragmatism without Foundations: Reconciling Realism and Relativism* (Oxford: Basil Blackwell, 1986).
    11. Ibid., pp. 87–88.
    12. Hacking, *Representing and Intervening,* p. 60. See Charles Sanders Peirce, "Some Consequences of Four Incapacities," in *Values in a Universe of Chance: Selected Writings of Charles S. Peirce (1839–1914),* ed. Philip R. Weiner (Garden City, N.Y.: Doubleday Anchor Books, 1958), particularly p. 89 (the essay is cited by Hacking); see also Hilary Putnam, "Two Philosophical Perspectives," in *Reason, Truth and History* (Cambridge: Cambridge University Press, 1981) (also cited by Hacking).
    13. See William James, *Pragmatism* (New York: Longmans, Green, 1907); William James, "Humanism and Truth," in *The Meaning of Truth: A Sequel to "Pragmatism"* (New York: Longmans, Green, 1909); and John Dewey, *Logic: The Theory of Inquiry* (New York: Henry Holt, 1938), chaps. 6–7.
    14. See, for instance, Dewey, *Logic,* p. 345n.6.
    15. Peirce, "How to Make Our Ideas Clear," in *Values in a Universe of Chance,* p. 133.
    16. This is the weakness of Hacking's account (in *Representing and Intervening,* chap. 4) and also of Israel Scheffler's reading, in *Four Pragmatists: A Critical Introduction to Peirce, James, Mead, and Dewey* (London: Routledge and Kegan Paul, 1974), chap. 2.
    17. Richard Rorty, "Pragmatism and Philosophy," in *Consequences of Pragmatism: Essays, 1972–1980* (Minneapolis: University of Minnesota Press, 1982), p. xiii.
    18. See Richard Rorty, *Philosophy and the Mirror of Nature* (Princeton: Princeton University Press, 1979).
    19. Rorty, *Consequences of Pragmatism,* pp. xvi, xx.
    20. Ibid., p. xxxvii.
    21. Ibid., p. xxxviii; cf. p. xli.
    22. Ibid., p. xxxvii; italics added (except for "seem" in the final line).
    23. See W. V. Quine, "Epistemology Naturalized," in *Ontological Relativity and Other Essays* (New York: Columbia University Press, 1969); and Hilary Putnam, "Why Reason Can't Be Naturalized," *Synthese* 7 (1982), rpt. in *After Philosophy, End or Transformation?,* ed. Kenneth Baynes *et al.* (Cambridge: MIT Press, 1987), p. 239. Putnam reports that Quine has denied in conversation that he did mean to "rule out the normative."
    24. Putnam, "Why Reason Can't Be Naturalized," pp. 241–42.
    25. See, further, Margolis, *Pragmatism without Foundations.*
    26. Richard Rorty, "Postmodern Bourgeois Liberalism," *Journal of Philosophy* 80 (1983), p. 583, rpt. in *Hermeneutics and Praxis,* ed. Robert Hollinger (Notre Dame: University of Notre Dame Press, 1985), p. 216.
    27. Ibid.
    28. Ibid., p. 217.
    29. Putnam, "Why Reason Can't Be Naturalized," pp. 228–29.
    30. Jean-Francois Lyotard, *The Postmodern Condition: A Report on Knowledge,* trans. Geoff Bennington and Brian Massumi (Minneapolis: University of Minnesota Press, 1984), p. 38.
    31. Ibid., pp. 18, 19.
    32. Cf. ibid., pp. 40–41.
    33. Ibid., p. 60, in the context of pp. 60–67.

34. Cf. ibid., pp. 60, 65–66.

35. Ibid., p. xxiii.

36. Ibid., p. 60.

37. Ibid.

38. Ibid., pp. 65–66.

39. Ibid., p. 67.

40. See Paul Feyerabend, *Against Method* (London: NLB, 1975).

41. See "Questions of Method: An Interview with Michael Foucault," trans. Alan Bass, *Ideology and Consciousness* 8 (1981), rpt. in *After Philosophy,* ed. Kenneth Baynes *et al.,* pp. 111–12; "What historical knowledge is possible of a history that itself produces the true/false distinction on which such knowledge depends? . . . isn't the most general of political problems the problem of truth? How can one analyze the connection between ways of distinguishing true and false and ways of governing oneself and others? The search for a new foundation for each of these practices, in itself and relative to the other, the will to discover a different way of governing oneself through a different way of dividing up true and false—this is what I would call "political *spiritualité.*" Foucault introduces the comment, remarking, "The question that I won't succeed in answering here but have been asking myself from the beginning is roughly the following: What is history, given there is continually being produced within it a separation of true and false?" Cf. also Michel Foucault, "The Subject and Power," which appears as an afterword in Hubert L. Dreyfus and Paul Rabinow, *Michel Foucault: Beyond Structuralism and Hermeneutics* (Chicago: University of Chicago Press, 1982).

42. See Margolis, *Pragmatism without Foundations,* part 1; also, Margolis, *Science without Unity: Reconciling the Human and Natural Sciences* (Oxford: Basil Blackwell, 1987), chaps. 1–2; see also Michael Dummett, *Truth and Other Enigmas* (Cambridge, Mass.: Harvard University Press, 1978)

43. See Jürgen Habermas, "What Is Universal Pragmatics?" in *Communication and the Evolution of Society,* trans. Thomas McCarthy (Boston: Beacon Press, 1979).

44. For the details, see Joseph Margolis, *Texts without Referents; Reconciling Science and Narrative* (Oxford: Basil Blackwell, 1988), chap. 3; also Margolis, "Overcoming Philosophical Strabism and Philosophical Diplopia," to be presented at the Merleau-Ponty Circle, September 1988, Villanova University, Villanova, Pennsylvania.

45. Jürgen Habermas, "Philosophy as Stand-In and Interpreter," in *After Philosophy,* ed. Kenneth Baynes *et al.,* p. 297. Cf. Rorty, *Philosophy and the Mirror of Nature,* chap. 8.

46. Ibid.

47. Ibid., p. 298.

48. Ibid., p. 304.

49. See Jürgen Habermas, *Reason and the Rationalization of Society* (*vol. 1 of The Theory of Communicative Action*), trans. Thomas McCarthy (Boston: Beacon Press, 1984), chap. 1.

50. Ibid., p. 139.

51. See Habermas, "What Is Universal Pragmatics?"

52. See Margolis, *Pragmatism without Foundations,* part 1.

53. Habermas, "Philosophy as Stand-In and Interpreter," p. 315; italics added.

54. Putnam, "Why Reason Can't Be Naturalized," pp. 228–29.

55. Richard J. Bernstein, *Beyond Objectivism and Relativism* (Philadelphia: University of Pennsylvania Press, 1983), p. 2.

56. The most ramified attempt to date to construct such a theory appears in Margolis, *Pragmatism without Foundations*. A briefer argument which appears to share a similar strategy (though not entirely the same particular taste) may be found in Alasdair MacIntyre, "Relativism, Power, and Philosophy," in *Proceedings and Addresses of the American Philosophical Association* (Newark, Del.: American Philosophical Association, 1985), rpt. in *After Philosophy*, ed. Kenneth Baynes *et al.*

57. See Hilary Putnam, *Philosophical Papers*, vol. 3 (Cambridge: Cambridge University Press, 1983).

58. Putnam, "Why Reason Can't Be Naturalized," pp. 226–29.

59. Ibid., p. 228.

60. Putnam, *Reason, Truth and History*, p. x; cf. Putnam, "Two Philosophical Perspectives." See also Putnam, *The Many Faces of Realism* (LaSalle, Ill.: Open Court, 1987).

61. Putnam, *The Many Faces of Realism*, pp. 53–56. See Karl-Otto Apel, "The Problem of Philosophical Foundations in Light of a Transcendental Pragmatics of Language," rev. and trans. Karl Richard Pavlovic, modified by Karl-Otto Apel, in *After Philosophy*, ed. Kenneth Baynes *et al.*, pp. 53–56.

62. Putnam, "Why Reason Can't Be Naturalized," p. 227.

63. Ibid., p. 242.

64. Ibid., p. 235.

65. Ibid., p. 242.

66. Ibid.; italics added.

67. MacIntyre, "Relativism, Power, and Philosophy," p. 394.

68. Ibid., pp. 405, 406.

69. Ibid., p. 408; italics added.

70. See Alasdair MacIntyre, *After Virtue*, 2nd ed. (Notre Dame: University of Notre Dame Press, 1984). It is curious that MacIntyre actually formulates the thesis here developed only in the postscript to the second edition of *After Virtue*. The account implied is not clearly stated in the body of the book. Also, it is reasonably clear that MacIntyre's use of his own strategy is intended to service a form of traditionalism freed from any explicit essentialism or the like. See Margolis, *Pragmatism without Foundations*, chap. 2.

71. This is the principal thrust of *Pragmatism without Foundations* and of the introduction to *Science without Unity*.

# Vanishing Frontiers
# in American Philosophy:
# Two Dogmas of Idealism

RALPH W. SLEEPER

My title alludes to two famous papers. The first is John Dewey's essay, "The Vanishing Subject in the Psychology of James," first published in the *Journal of Philosophy* in 1940. The second is Willard Quine's "Two Dogmas of Empiricism," a paper read a decade later at the Eastern Division meeting of the American Philosophical Association and subsequently published in the *Philosophical Review* of January, 1951.

Two brief quotations, one from each, will show why I have borrowed from them not just the style of my title but the theme of what follows. From Dewey the text is this: "Philosophy will not be emancipated to perform its own task and function until psychology is purged, as a whole and in all its special topics, of the last remnants of dualism."[1] And this from Quine: "Carnap, Lewis, and others take a pragmatic stand on the question of choosing between language forms, scientific frameworks; but their pragmatism leaves off at the imagined boundary between the analytic and the synthetic. In repudiating such a boundary I espouse a more thorough pragmatism.[2]

There is more than one way to link these texts. The path that I take is, perhaps, a less familiar one. It leads across the map of "Classical American Philosophy" in its own way, exploring imagined boundaries and vanishing frontiers.

One result of this exploration is the discovery that two dogmas of idealism still haunt the territory. One is the belief that an impassable abyss divides the external "noumenal" world from the internal "phenomenal" world of experience. The other is a belief that some form of transcendental argument — or logic — is a viable bridge between them.

Though both dogmas have early roots in empiricism, I call them dogmas of idealism in recognition of their Kantian origins, and of the fact that it is from that tradition that they have come to influence American philosophy from Emerson to Peirce, Royce, and Lewis. It is by his repeated attacks on that tradition — and its dogmas — that John Dewey commenced its repudiation.

One consequence of that repudiation is the rejection of the "metaphysics of experience," as Kant called it, and its reconstruction as the metaphysics of existence. This antifoundational move against traditional "first philosophy" helps to close the gap between speculative metaphysics and natural science. Another effect is the healing of the schism between the epistemology of facts and the knowledge of values. Both are features of a reconstructed pragmatism, one that reassigns the tasks of both metaphysics and logic.

Relieved of its foundational role as "first philosophy," metaphysics is reconstituted as the background theory of criticism. Relieved of its normative role in relation to science, logic is reinstated as the empirical theory of inquiry. Both of these moves bespeak a more thoroughgoing pragmatism — and a more radical empiricism.

Kant's exclusion of the noumenal world of things-in-themselves from the phenomenal world of experience was, as I have said, anticipated by the empiricists. Hume's skepticism about our ability to experience anything like a metaphysically fixed and universally valid law of causality, when placed in relation to Berkeley's contrary reduction of the real to experience, is a signpost on the road to Kant's restriction of experience to the phenomenal world. Another is Leibniz's devotion to truths of reason that hold in all possible worlds, the stimulus for Locke's account of truths belonging to the essences of things, truths that are eternal and that can be found out only by examining our own ideas.

But it is the consequences of these dogmas and not their origins that concern me here. First among them is the restriction of experience implicit in the exclusion of the thing-in-itself from empirical access. Denied entry to this much of the external world, reason is turned inward upon itself and to the attenuated experience of the phenomenal world. Within these constraints the search for categories upon which to found the structures of knowledge becomes a quest for the *a priori* conditions of experience. It is a search that, deflected from the possibility of discovering the categories of being or of existence, throws reason back upon its own resources. Metaphysics, thus restricted to the content of experience and the *a priori* forms of its reception, becomes, as it were, a branch of logic; its categories are conceived as the *a priori* forms of experience and are reached as the logical products of transcendental deduction.

Kant's confidence in this deduction arises, no doubt, from the Aristotelian notion of essence. For it was upon that notion that the syllogistic logic of subject-predicate relations and deductive inference is founded. But while Aristotle's logic was clearly based on his metaphysics — his "first philosophy" — Kant's procedure was to base his metaphysics on his logic, the "perfected form of the syllogism," as Dewey sometimes called it. This startling reversal — in which Dewey discerned the foundation of all "ontological logics" and which he condemned from time to time as "the philosophers' fallacy" — is the dark side of what Kant himself called his "Copernican revolution" in metaphysics.

Enthusiasm for Kant's two dogmas among nineteenth-century continental metaphysicians and logicians was unrestrained, and a flourishing market was soon created for a variety of ways of understanding their consequences, or for rejecting them altogether by means of one reductionism or another. Absolute idealism was one alternative, and materialism another, the dialectical logic of the one suggesting the ontological structure of the other.

By the end of the century, of course, the market was dominated by this Hegelian turn in metaphysics. But in logic, transcending even Hegel, logical idealism was already at apogee in the "logicism" of Frege. For it was, after all, Frege who announced the final hegemony of transcendental logic. It is not just that logic gives us the laws of mathematics, or even the laws of nature, as some had supposed, but that "logic gives us the laws of the laws of nature."[3]

In tracing the path of this triumph of logical transcendentalism to the United States I pass over the British idealists, noting their contrary move in psychologizing logic after the manner of Mill, a move that issued in Shadworth Hodgson's fabulous four-volume *Metaphysics of Experience* by the end of the century, and that had a profound impact on William James.[4] I likewise pass over Emerson's transcendental turn, by acknowledging what John McDermott has poignantly — and accurately — called his "Spires of Influence" upon classical American philosophy, and move directly to the period following.[5]

It is the period of the birth of pragmatism and of the burgeoning influence of Charles S. Peirce. Recalling his early mathematical background it is easy to see why Peirce's philosophical development followed a path that suggests parallels with Frege's, avoiding by the narrowest of margins a final confluence. By the close of the century American mathematicians were already well conditioned by the work of Dedekind and others to accept that form of transcendental logic that issues in "logicism." But it was not until the work of Peirce that its wider implications were much debated here.

This doctrine, finally made famous by Frege and Russell, held that all mathematical forms can be derived from the forms of logic. Moreover, its corollary — that all the sciences rest ultimately upon these same foundations — was already at issue in the United States. Peirce's own father, Benjamin, had made it so by mid-century, even though he also held that it is more likely that logic can be derived from mathematics than the other way around.[6]

Charles himself was on the brink of accepting a version of the doctrine as early as his 1865 Harvard lectures, "On the Logic of Science." He was still on the edge in his 1869 paper "On the Grounds and Validity of the Laws of Logic." But it was this paper, as Max Fisch points out, that Peirce would later see had already "adumbrated" his nomination of logic to the position of "Critic," forecasting the transition from a view of logic as non-normative of science to the assignment of logic to its normative role.[7]

Even this move in the direction of logicism, however, did not suffice to take him over the edge. Nor was it enough to commit him to either of the dogmas to which I am attending. Although Peirce was clearly well down the road to doing so in mathematics, his conception of the relation of logic as "Critic" to mathematics, and hence to metaphysics, had not yet been worked out. Nor would it be until the development of the doctrine of "synechism" in the 1890s. In that doctrine Fregean logicism is transcended — or perhaps it should be said that it is contained in a higher synthesis — for it "carries along with it," as Peirce himself says, "first, a logical realism of the most profound type; second, objective idealism; third, tychism, with its consequent thoroughgoing evolutionism."[8] It was a stunning combination, not least for its striking discovery of an ingenious way of resolving the conflict between Darwinian and Lamarckian evolutionism.

This remarkable synthesis, as again Fisch points out, had already been implicit in Peirce's reaction to Darwinism from the beginning, "At least from the summer of 1859 onward, one of Peirce's main metaphysical concerns was to establish that, contrary to what some metaphysicians were saying, we can reason mathematically and logically about infinity and therefore about continuity. On that assumption, synechism became a regulative principle first of logic and then of metaphysics."[9]

It is not that Peirce rejects Darwinism and adopts the Lamarckian persuasion in revulsion from the Darwinian hypothesis of the descent of man from simian origins, but that he needs Lamarckism to account for the ascent of "Platonic forms."[10] He needs both theories. While Darwinism accords well with "fallibilism" and its expression in "tychist" cosmology, it is Lamarckism that allows for a superior account of the evolution of what he sometimes calls "Platonic forms" or "generals," and sometimes refers to as "Scotistic reals." The doctrine of synechism is designed to provide a transcendental argument that will continuously link them in the tandem processes of "evolutionary love."

It is not my purpose here to examine in detail the structure of that argument, but a sense of how it goes can be gleaned from Peirce's essay, "What Pragmatism Is."[11] There Peirce elaborates the point that synechism is intended to connect the real — which he defines as "being as it is regardless of what you or I may think about it" — with what is "destined" to be believed as a consequence of the continuity of inquiry. He wants to show that what is antecedently and independently real — thus noumenally real? — is a causally efficacious external constraint on the direction and process of inquiry.[12] Peirce, of course, would not want the evident processive dualism of his synechism to be laid to his tacit acceptance of the Kantian dogmas, or their ghostly remains. But why not? Why not explain the shift from pragmatism to "pragmaticism" that way, as well as by invoking Peirce's reluctance to follow either James or Dewey down the more radical paths of empiricism that they were exploring?

Royce, of course, shows none of Peirce's hesitancy. Rejecting James's metaphysics altogether, but clinging to Peirce's conception of continuity, Royce embraces not one but both of Kant's dogmas. In two recent and important articles Robert Burch has pointed out some of the remarkable consequences of this turn by Royce.[13] Among them is not merely Royce's realization of the link between his own form of transcendental argumentation and Kant's, exemplified in *The World and the Individual* and the *Lectures on Modern Idealism,* but the revival of his own interest in mathematical and logical studies that led to his fascination with Russell's turn to Frege in 1903, and to Russell's period of "Platonism" in mathematics and science that followed.

Moreover, Royce's capitulation to transcendental logic, complete by 1892, was, in many respects, recapitulated by Lewis. For, despite his rejection of both Peirce's latent and Royce's overt idealism — and his loyalty to James — Lewis's "conceptual pragmatism" owes more to Royce and to Peirce than we are in the habit of conceding. Despite the intention of the "Pragmatic *A Priori,*" moreover, there is little in *Mind and the World Order* to remind us of either James or Dewey. In the end, as Quine suggests, it was his commitment to a transcendental logic that stopped him short of the full commitment to empirical naturalism that James and Dewey had made.

In his superb study of James, Gerald Myers shows that it is not easy to say just when James gave up on the two dogmas of idealism — if, indeed, he ever did.[14] But surely Dewey got it right when he saw, both early and late, that what may have been a commitment to at least one persistent consequence of this dualism was already at the "vanishing" point in the

*Principles of Psychology* — even if James himself was not yet prepared to acknowledge the fact. But Dewey was observing the development of James's psychology from a vantage point denied to James himself.[15] He had already rejected Peirce's program in normative transcendental logic by the time that the *Principles* was published. Unlike James, Dewey loved logic. He enjoyed teaching it and did so for most of his life. It might not even be too much to say that, in the end, he did his best work in logic.

Dewey's interest in refuting the claims of Kantian transcendental logic began early and never ceased.[16] Even while he was still under the influence of George Sylvester Morris, whose 1886 book on Kant's first *Critique* adopts the line of psychologism in logic that Dewey briefly followed, it is clear that Dewey was less interested in defending psychologism than in rebutting the arguments of the transcendentalists.[17] In a series of articles published in *Mind* in the 1880s, Dewey repeatedly argued the thesis that, as he succinctly put it in 1886, "in truth we do not go from logic to nature at all. The movement is a reverse movement. . . . The logical movement considered by itself, is always balancing in unstable equilibrium between dualism and pantheism. . . . Logic cannot reach, however much it may point to, an actual individual."[18] In this thesis, drawn from Hegel and distinguishing between symbolic "pointing" and actual "reaching," Dewey anticipates the now familiar distinction between a variable and its value, and the ontological implications thereof.

Just a few months after this appeared in *Mind* under the title "Psychology as Scientific Method," Dewey again attacked the method of transcendentalist logic and its "metaphysics of experience" in direct response to Shadworth Hodgson's criticism.[19] It is abundantly clear from the tenor and tone of Dewey's response that his own rejection of the two dogmas of idealism that Hodgson's "metaphysics of experience" embraced was now complete. All that remained for Dewey was the reconstruction of psychology, and its method, as the "logic of experience" in the 1903 *Studies.*

Since I've tried to trace the process of that reconstruction elsewhere,[20] let me devote what remains of my paper to a few of its consequences. Among them are those already noted by reference to Quine's essay, "Two Dogmas of Empiricism." From the outset, Dewey's conception of logic as an empirical science erased the boundary between the analytic and synthetic. The alleged boundary between fact and value soon followed.

But are these the consequences of the system that Peirce was trying to work out? Was it, indeed, pragmatism at all? The evidence suggests that Dewey's earliest efforts at logical reconstruction had little or nothing to do with pragmatism, at least as conceived by Peirce in the *Scientific Monthly* articles of 1886–87, even after James made them famous by his 1898 California address. Dewey had been attacking Peirce's conception of logic — if indirectly — all along, and so it is not at all puzzling that he failed to embrace those maxims and the tag attached. Moreover, as his 1896 essay, "The Reflex Arc Concept in Psychology," shows, Dewey did not yet think of James's radical empiricism as sufficiently free of the Kantian dogmas either. Dewey was already introducing the transactional approach to inquiry and the "logic of experience" that were to occupy him for the rest of his life.

The fact is, I think, that Dewey was astonished to learn of James's enthusiasm for the 1903 *Studies in Logical Theory,* which does not so much as mention pragmatism or radical empiricism. Peirce's response to the *Studies* was, of course, very different and clearly came as no surprise to Dewey. Shocked at the naive impudence of Dewey's empirical approach to logic, Peirce showed — in a letter of 1905 — that he well understood the challenge to the doctrine of synechism implicit in the *Studies,* and warned Dewey against further incursions into the territory that he had marked out for himself in the researches that had absorbed him — as he puts it — "for the last eighteen years."[21] It is easy to see why Dewey could not have believed himself a pragmatist at all.

In the end, of course, Dewey's acceptance of the epithet — or soft impeachment — of "pragmatism" would depend on how its terms were to be construed. Many factors contributed to the studied phrases in which Dewey finally stated that construal in 1938, and to his acceptance of the tag that Peirce had invented so long ago. They appear in the *Introduction to Logic: The Theory of Inquiry:* "The word 'Pragmatism' does not, I think, occur in the text. Perhaps the word lends itself to misconception. At all events, so much misunderstanding and relatively futile controversy have gathered about the word that it seemed advisable to avoid its use. But in the proper interpretation of 'pragmatic,' namely the function of consequences as necessary tests of the validity of propositions, provided these consequences are operationally instituted and are such as to resolve the specific problem evoking the operations, the text that follows is thoroughly pragmatic."[22] Perhaps what has been misleading us all along is what appears just a few lines below. For there Dewey says, "I should state explicitly that, with the outstanding exception of Peirce, I have learned most from writers with whose positions I have in the end been compelled to disagree." But, surely, we should not have been misled at all. For what follows is a thoroughgoing and systematic reconstruction of Peirce's doctrine of continuity, that is, of synechism.

Its consequences are those that we must expect from the final rejection of idealism and its persistent dogmas: a pragmatism that embraces its own "pragmatic realism" with its piecemeal character, and all the limitations, uncertainties, and vagueness that go with it.[23]

Putnam, Goodman, and others take a pragmatic stand on the question of choosing between realism and idealism, but their realism sometimes leaves off at the imagined boundary between the "internal" and "external" worlds. Quine does not seem similarly afflicted, although his insistence upon the special treatment of abstract entities suggests that he is closer to Peirce than he would willingly concede, that a trace remains of the transcendental mathematicism of Peirce in at least this one segment of his ontology. Goodman would excise such traces by accepting Quine's abstract entities as parts of a world "version," one among many such versions in his vision of "irrealism." His pluralism in "worldmaking" is successor to James's.[24]

Donald Davidson takes a pragmatic stand in respect of both Kant's dogmas, at least in rejecting the dualism of scheme and content, of mental states and mental objects.[25] But the theory of "truth without reference" seems to imply that transcendental arguments may sometimes be necessary. And Putnam, at times, seems to say outright that they are necessary.[26] Davidson invokes something like a transcendental argument in his efforts aimed at rescuing propositional attitudes from cognitive limbo. We need them, he tells us, if we are ever to make sense of the world of our experience.[27] And Putnam, invoking a similar line to justify the objectivity of value judgments in his Carus Lectures, remarks on its connection to Peirce's line and that which moves both Apel and Husserl to versions of transcendentalism.[28]

But the unabashed acceptance of the Kantian dogmas by Husserl and Apel is hardly the style that leads to the more thorough pragmatism envisaged by either Dewey or Quine. Perhaps Putnam's troubles stem from the Kantian turn that he takes in *Reason, Truth and History,* for that suggests to Margolis — and I think that Margolis is right about this — the necessity that Putnam faces of working out a transcendental argument to resolve the dualism of internal versus external realism.[29]

In reconstructing Peirce's synechism to get rid of its dualist ontology, Dewey espouses a more coherent theory of experience and of inquiry, as well as the more coherent version of realism that goes with it. (More coherent because it is piecemeal, and not perfectly "holistic.") The reconstructed theory of the continuity of inquiry supports a more thorough pragmatism, one that recognizes, as Stan Thayer puts it, that "logic has an ontology and ontology a logic; thought and things are causally linked in a circuit of existential transactions."[30]

Putnam sometimes seems to appreciate this feature of Dewey's methods, perhaps when he is reminded of it by Nelson Goodman, or Ruth Anna Putnam.[31] Then again, he sometimes forgets it, perhaps when distracted by the lure of modal logics or the attraction of Kantian moral images. But it is just because our practices are causally linked with our standards that our practices are right and wrong depending on how they square with our standards. "And our standards are right or wrong depending on how they square with our practices," as Putnam himself once put it.[32] It is just such transactional linkages that replace transcendental arguments in pragmatism once these frontiers of classical American philosophy have vanished, and the necessity of the dogmas of idealism has been banished from its logic. To paraphrase the quotation from Dewey with which I began: Philosophy will not be emancipated to perform its own task and function until logic is purged, as a whole and in all its special topics, of the last remnants of dualism.

# Notes

1. John Dewey, *The Later Works,* vol. 14, ed. Jo Ann Boydston (Carbondale: Southern Illinois University Press, 1988), p. 167. Hereafter, volumes in this series will be cited as Dewey LW, followed by a volume number, in the standard fashion.

2. Willard Van Orman Quine, "Two Dogmas of Empiricism," in *From a Logical Point of View* (New York: Harper and Row, 1953), p. 46.

3. Willaim Kneale and Martha Kneale, *The Development of Logic* (Oxford: Clarendon Press, 1884), p. 448.

4. Shadworth Hodgson, *The Metaphysics of Experience,* 4 vols. (London: Longmans, Green, 1898).

5. John McDermott, "Spires of Influence: The Importance of Emerson for Classical American Philosophy," in *Streams of Experience* (Amherst: University of Massachusetts Press, 1986), p. 29.

6. Max Fisch, "Peirce as Scientist, Mathematician, Historian, Logician, and Philosopher," in *Foundations of Semiotics,* vol. 1, ed. Achim Esbach (Amsterdam/Philadelphia: John Benjamins Publishing Co., 1983), p. xvii.

7. Ibid., p. xxvii.

8. Charles Sanders Peirce, *Collected Papers,* ed. Charles Hartshorne, Paul Weiss, and Arthur W. Burks, 8 vols. (Cambridge, Mass.: Harvard University Press, 1958), vol. 6, para. 163. Hereafter, this work will be cited as CSP, followed by a volume number and a paragraph number, in the standard fashion. See also Justus Buchler, *Philosophical Writings of Peirce* (New York: Dover Publications, 1955), p. 352.

9. Fisch, "Peirce as Scientist," p. xxviii. See also CSP 6.17ff.

10. CSP 6.14.

11. CSP 5.416–5.434.

12. Peirce's "Platonic forms" and "Scotistic reals" are, as he defines them, general objects (or universals) that are linked up with his objective idealism through the process of "evolutionary love." It is this process, he says, "whereby the existent comes more and more to embody those generals which were just now said to be destined." And, though synechism replaces the Hegelian dialectical logic with the processive logic of "evolutionary love," it was Peirce himself who acknowledged that it is "closely allied to Hegelian absolute idealism" (CSP 5.433–5.434). Responding to this alliance, Charles Hartshorne, whose own reconstruction of Peirce's categorial scheme repudiates it, reflects upon the doctrine of synechism in a piece the

title of which signals its contents: "Charles Peirce's 'One Contribution to Philosophy' and His Most Serious Mistake," in *Studies in the Philosophy of Charles Sanders Peirce,* 2nd ser., ed. Edward G. Moore and Richard S. Robin (Amherst: University of Massachusetts Press, 1964), pp. 455–74. In Peirce's synechism Kant's two dogmas are, of course, on their way out. That is "destined." But they have not yet vanished. It seems that when, in 1937, Dewey reviewed the volumes of Peirce's work put together by Hartshorne and Weiss, he was disposed to neglect the fact that they had not vanished altogether. See Dewey LW 11, pp. 479–84. But by then Dewey had already worked out his reconstruction of synechism in the Logic that he would publish the following year.

13. Robert Burch, "An Unpublished Logic Paper by Josiah Royce," in *Transactions of the Charles S. Peirce Society* 23 (2) (1987), pp. 173–204. Also Robert Burch, "A Transformation of Royce's View of Kant," in *Transactions of the Charles S. Peirce Society* 23 (4) (1987), pp. 557–78.

14. Gerald Myers, *William James: His Life and Thought* (New Haven: Yale University Press, 1986).

15. William James, as Kenneth Ketner points out, was initially in awe of Peirce's enthusiasm for the logicizing of scientific method, but it was doubtless Royce's version of the Kantian dogmas that eventually put him off. For, as Ketner himself quotes James, "I owe more to (Peirce's) writings than to anyone but Royce." See Kenneth Laine Ketner, "Introduction" (to selections from the writings of C. S. Peirce), in *Classical American Philosophy,* ed. John Stuhr (Oxford: Oxford University Press, 1987), p. 20. Peirce, famously, was well aware of this defection and abandoned "pragmatism" to its fate at James's hands, espousing "pragmaticism" instead. What may have put James off — aside from the fact that he detested formal logic altogether — was Royce's startling discovery in 1892 that the laws of physics are determined by the transcendental laws of formal logic as expressed in geometry. Perhaps James simply couldn't stomach this expression of the "Absolute"! (See Burch, "Royce's View of Kant," p. 566.) Like the logics of both Peirce and Royce, Lewis's logic belongs to the history of mainstream developments that stem from Frege and Russell. And his metaphysics remains loyal to the Kantian paradigm of the "metaphysics of experience." Like Peirce and Royce he remained committed to the search for the necessary conditions of experience, and so to a "first philosophy" as the necessary foundation for science. Once again the Kantian dogmas haunt the territory, and distinguish his pragmatism from what Dewey, James, and Mead were working on.

16. It is a moot point whether Dewey's defection from transcendental logic was precipitated by having attended Peirce's lectures at Johns Hopkins or not. Regrettably, Hopkins allowed Dewey "attendance credit" for them and we cannot infer from that much of anything at all — even that Dewey actually attended them. But what is clear is that Dewey's publications on logical matters began soon after his graduation from Hopkins, and continued unabated for the rest of his life. And those writings were uniformly critical of the transcendentalist path in logic that Peirce was following.

17. George S. Morris, *Kant's Critique of Pure Reason* (Chicago: S. C. Griggs, 1886).

18. John Dewey, *The Early Works,* vol. 1, ed. Jo Ann Boydston (Carbondale: Southern Illinois University Press, 1969), pp. 164–66. Hereafter, volumes in this series will be cited as Dewey EW, followed by a volume number, in the standard fashion.

19. Ibid., p. 168.

20. R. W. Sleeper, *The Necessity of Pragmatism* (New Haven: Yale University Press, 1986).

21. CSP 8.243.

22. Dewey LW 12, pp. iii–iv.

23. Dewey's metaphysics does not provide for a completely closed system. Thayer suggests that pragmatism is more of a "metaphilosophy" than a system, but Quine suggests that we should "hold out for a holistic" perspective, despite the fact that it may not apply across the board. See H. S. Thayer, "Pragmatism: A Reinterpretation of the Origins and Consequences," in *Pragmatism: Its Sources and Prospects,* ed. R. J. Mulvaney and P. M. Zeltner (Columbia: University of South Carolina Press, 1981), p. 17. See also, in the same volume, Willard Van Orman Quine, "The Pragmatist's Place in Empiricism," p. 31. In my view Quine resolves this question nicely when he suggests the following: "It is an uninteresting legalism, however, to think of our scientific system of the world as involved *en bloc* in every prediction. More modest chunks suffice, and so may be ascribed their independent empirical meaning, nearly enough, since some vagueness in meaning must be allowed for in any event" (p. 27).

24. Nelson Goodman, *Ways of Worldmaking* (Indianapolis: Hackett Publishing Co., 1978).

25. Donald Davidson, "Mental Events," in *Essays on Actions and Events* (Oxford: Clarendon Press, 1980), pp. 207–228.

26. Putnam actually gives a transcendental argument in "Why Reason Can't Be Naturalized," in *Realism and Reason* (Cambridge: Cambridge University Press, 1983), pp. 228–47. It results in this reflection: "If reason is both transcendent and immanent, then philosophy, as culture-bound reflection and argument about eternal questions, is both in time and eternity. We don't have an Archimedean point; we always speak the language of a time and place; but the rightness and wrongness of what we say is not just for a time and a place." It seems clear to me that there is no need to argue for the "transcendence" of reason in order to reach the conclusion that "the rightness and wrongness of what we say is not just for a time and place" (p. 247). But perhaps that is because I don't know what "eternal questions" are, or how they could possibly be answered. Since Putnam seems to be saying that our reflection and argument is in eternity as well as in time, perhaps all of our temporal questions are also eternal. But, if that is the case, there would be no need for anything like a transcendental argument for the transcendence of reason; its transcendence would simply be analytic.

27. Hilary Putnam, *The Many Faces of Realism* (LaSalle, Ill.: Open Court, 1987), p. 21.

28. Ibid., pp. 20–21, 53–56.

29. Joseph Margolis, *Pragmatism Without Foundations* (Oxford: Basil Blackwell, 1986), pp. 281–307.

30. H. S. Thayer, "Review, *The Necessity of Pragmatism,*" *Canadian Philosophical Reviews* 7 (8) (1987), p. 332.

31. The reference to Goodman's work as a "reminder" is to Putnam's foreword to Nelson Goodman, *Fact, Fiction, and Forecast,* 4th ed. (Cambridge, Mass.: Harvard University Press, 1983), p. ix. The reference to Ruth Anna Putnam's work as a "reminder" is to Hilary Putnam, *The Many Faces of Realism,* pp. 78–y–79.

32. Putnam, *Realism and Reason,* p. ix.

# The Relevance of Philosophy to Life

JOHN LACHS

When the time came for our children to receive their oral polio vaccine, we took them to their pediatrician. Surprisingly, the first question the doctor asked was whether the parents themselves had had their medicine-soaked sugar cubes. Noting the puzzlement in our eyes, he explained that he viewed his job not as the narrow one of taking care of a few children, but as a broader mandate to promote public health. He was convinced, he said, that the well-being of young people is inseparable from the quality of their environment and that it is difficult, therefore, if not impossible, to safeguard their health without taking an interest in their family and in prevailing social conditions.

Not all physicians share this attitude. But I cannot help thinking that those who do, take their responsibility more seriously than doctors satisfied to treat not the socially situated person but the disease. At any rate, I know that the more interested healer is the better one to have.

The contrast between a narrow and a broad conception of responsibility is not unique to medicine. In philosophy no less than in other professions, it is possible to view oneself as a hired hand (or a hired mind?) paid to offer courses or to give lectures. But we may also think of our work as educating young people, as making available to them the skills necessary for a good life. The weight of tradition favors this latter view. The tenor of modern existence, on the other hand, encourages us to focus on professional standards and to be satisfied with a minimalist reading of our responsibilities.

In some fields the distinction between these incompatible notions of the scope of responsibility is of little significance. Even if pharmacists, for example, fail to go beyond the skimpiest demands of their standards of competence, they will not do much harm. To be sure, a broader sense of service could help them do more good: the pharmacist might find a generic substitute for a prescription and save me money. But what is important in such fields is adequately captured by basic competence; beyond that, not a great deal is at stake. In medicine and philosophy, by contrast, the stakes are too high for meeting minimal standards to be enough. By not asking the additional question or not suggesting the innovative treatment, the physician can endanger her patient's life. By failing to connect critical thought with the concerns of daily existence in his students' minds, the philosopher contributes to the impoverishment of personal life and the sustenance of social irrationality.

Philosophy is an ancient instrument whose use is all but forgotten. It sits as mere decoration in the house of learning while the kitchen and the garage buzz with activity. We need to learn to play the instrument again, to remind ourselves of the power of its music. We must go beyond scales and finger exercises until its melody becomes the soul of the house. Our music is the outcome and completion of the constructive noise in the kitchen, but it is also the tool which makes that busyness meaningful and joyous.

Because there is so much at stake in philosophy, we cannot rest satisfied with a minimalist reading of our responsibilities. It is simply not enough to teach philosophy as a set of facts about what people once thought or as a set of verbal or conceptual skills. What Plato and Hegel believed has direct relevance to our lives today. And, as even Groucho Marx knew, verbal skills can have important practical results. Our broader concerns must, accordingly, focus on the application of philosophical knowledge and skills to the pressing problems of personal and social life.

Philosophers today consider themselves academics who offer pure knowledge or, in one view, none at all. The relevance or human significance or concrete result of their work appears distant from their minds. It is important, therefore, to inquire into the grounds of our broader obligations. Of these I see at least five, each powerful but none uncontroversial.

First, the purest source of obligation is fullness of soul. Such generosity used to be called divine; according to one account, God's creation of the world was itself the result of His wanting to share the goodness of existence with as many beings as possible. Stoics who felt no need of worldly goods explained their motivation for teaching their discipline as gratitude for what philosophy had done for them. And even today, those whose life has acquired added meaning as a result of philosophical reflection share the enriching aspects of their field with an authority, enthusiasm, and success rarely seen in the classroom.

The problem here is that in a world that views teaching philosophy as a job, few attain fulfillment through its study. For many today, even the ministry is a calling only in name; in reality, it is something one does for a living. Philosophy has become a profession in just this sense, enabling those who have never profited from its enriching wisdom to profit by telling others about it. The obligation to share the benefits one has received from philosophy cannot amount to much if they come to no more than the pleasure of an occasional argument, steady employment, and modest status in the academic world.

The second source of responsibility is more compelling. Society supports the university as the last and best hope of preparing its young people for life. The aim is emphatically not only, and not even primarily, to equip them with skills necessary for narrow social roles. They are to be acquainted, instead, with the best that human beings have thought and done, with a view to their repeating or improving upon these achievements. There is a tacit contract between the university and its social sponsors for it to be something different from a technical institute and something more than a haven of abstract research. Through its faculty, it is of course to pursue the truth relentlessly and to convey it to its students. But it is expected to do more than this: it is to establish the search for what is true and what is decent as permanent dispositions of young people. Our children are to emerge, accordingly, not only well informed and in possession of important skills, but also with secure habits and character-traits and values. They are to be ready not merely to think straight but to act right, and specifically to act on the basis of what they think and to think about what they do.

There is no doubt that this is what parents who pay for the college education of their children want and need. There is equally little doubt that this is what colleges and universities promise, if the statements of their mission in their catalogues are to be believed. What students actually get is, of course, another matter. When philosophers teach ideas without reference to their historical source, personal relevance, and social consequences, they renege on their responsibility to help students take charge of their lives. When they teach philosophy as a collection of puzzles and mistakes, or as a string of deft verbal moves, they abandon their obligation to make intelligence an effective force in life. Since parents, having been educated by the likes of us, do not know any better, we can get away with this. But it is not something of which we should be proud.

The third source of our broader responsibilities is connected to this last. We are professors, teachers, educators. What we "profess" and teach is not neutral material. We devote our lives to reading, thinking, and writing about it; we convey it to our students without embarrassment, perhaps even with pride. Our posture toward our subject matter is one of interest and devotion; we act as if philosophy mattered and especially as if it mattered to us.

But can it matter if we fail to act on it? Demands for action are by no means unusual in the professions or in specialized fields of knowledge. The French chef who does not eat his own cooking but goes, instead, to a fast-food outlet for dinner is rightly an object of suspicion. The cancer researcher who smokes, the biologist who defends evolution in print but confesses commitment to creation on Sundays, the theorist of democracy who never votes are not cases of charming inconsistency; they constitute failures to live up to the commitments tacit in their professional activities. In just this way, philosophers who fail to embody the principles of their field in their personal lives are suspect: their words ring hollow so long as they remain words only. Devotion to reason in discourse but refusal to honor reason in bringing our actions in line with what we say reveals a basic incoherence, a break in the unity and integrity of the person.

Should our students attend to what we say or what we do? It is reasonable for us to demand of ministers that they not preach what they are unwilling to practice. It is no less sensible for us to require of philosophers who, after all, claim to apply reason to every sphere, that they employ it fully in leading their own lives. The objection that a society ought not to demand that its ministers or its philosophers be better than other people makes a valid point. But it is one that belongs to the realm of excusing conditions or the movement of forgiveness, rather than to the discussion of proper expectations. For the requirement of the unity of theory and practice in our lives is not inflicted on philosophers from the outside. It is the natural result of our self-confessed commitment to the rule of reason.

The fourth fountainhead of our special responsibilities is the very nature of our subject matter. Mathematicians, say, have little obligation to do anything of a practical nature about their reasonings or results. But nearly everything in philosophy repudiates the idea that thinking is a terminal fact. The mathematical properties of infinity neither suggest nor permit physical application. In considering right action, the good society, criteria of justified belief, human rights, duties to our parents, and standards of inference, by contrast, every result cries out for embodiment in our lives. Philosophical reasoning points beyond itself and can gain fulfillment only when it acquires influence over our actions. Those who wish to liberate philosophy from the demand for practical results must restrict its subject matter to the narrowest spheres of logic.

If it is wrong for professors not to act on what they teach, it is absurd for philosophers to disregard the demands their work articulates. Much of philosophy revolves around criteria, standards of what to think, what to believe, what to do. Such standards lay normative claims on our behavior. The claims are of two sorts. The first tells us how properly to do something, if we should care to undertake it — how to reason, for example, if we wish to think. The second decrees what is appropriate or fitting to do, quite apart from whether we want to do it or not. The command that injustice be resisted, freedom preserved, and innocent lives saved falls into this category. Our lives abound in occasions when a claim of one of these sorts makes action of a certain kind mandatory. When such times occur, what philosophers do must be exemplary. Those who know or set the standards must be the first to meet them. People who know the rules of implication must excel at inference; the moral philosopher must lead the moral life.

The fifth and final reason to think that we have special responsibilities derives from a widely accepted analysis of belief. According to this view, whose first great advocate was Plato and which is a hallmark of the American philosophical tradition, to believe something is among other things to have a tendency to act on it. Belief and action are, in this way, organically connected, demonstrating the unity of our cognitive and conative parts. If philosophers believe anything they teach, therefore, they must be prepared to act on it when the occasion arises. Conversely, if they fail to have their principles shape their behavior, we must conclude that they do not believe a word of what they teach. There is something contrived about doubt that does not penetrate to the level of action and something deceitful about beliefs concerning matters of substance that issue only in words. The only alternative to embodying our commitments in our lives is to pursue our profession without commitments and beliefs, as a momentous fraud.

What are the broader responsibilities of philosophers? As with physicians, a full list is neither possible nor appropriate. The first requirement is simply the realization that there are times when we must act. This engenders an alertness to opportunities for putting our principles into action. What we must do clearly depends on circumstances and on what each of us believes. There is, in this way, no ideological demand that philosophers be liberals or conservatives, that they support a free-market economy or welfare-state redistribution, that they love utilitarianism or deontology. Anything intellectually defensible is worthy to guide action, even if others believe differently and I might join them someday. The commitment of physicians to radical mastectomy may change as evidence accumulates and the effects of the procedure are better understood. But that is no reason for failing to implement it so long as it is defensible as the treatment of choice. Seeing what happens when we act on a belief, even a philosophical belief, is one of the tests of its validity; it is, therefore, a fundamental misunderstanding to withhold this trial because the conviction may turn out to be false.

We have two general areas of responsibility. The first is to bring our lives in line with our beliefs. Philosophers have, on the whole, not excelled at this. We tend to be no better, and in our feelings and actions no more rational, than ordinary people. One might even argue, I blush to admit, that in these respects we are below average. In looking over the long list of professional philosophers, we find distressingly many cases of mindless ambition, pettiness, arrogance, insensitivity, and a devastating lack of common sense and good judgment. The absence of even minimal decency lays waste to many colleagues, and makes the lives of their mates and children unbearable. Not many chasms are greater than that between the professed high values and the despicable practice of some philosophers. There is work to be done here by all of us, and by some a staggering amount.

Our personal lives are framed in the context of a community. The second major field of our obligations is, accordingly, the social and political world that surrounds us. The injustice and irrationality of people cannot remain a matter of indifference to us. The inhumanity of large institutions demands a response. The callousness of some who are in power must be exposed. All of these, of course, are my value judgments, and I must be prepared to act them out. Your thoughts may be different from mine, but your responsibility to give them flesh in action is the same. The fact that the social world is so much larger and more powerful than you or I is no excuse for inaction. One's obligation is not to succeed, only to try and to do one's very best. In this way, even if we fail to change the world, at least we point our own souls in the right direction and convert a social defeat into personal victory.

My argument so far has been a plea for what is usually called the unity of theory and practice. What this notion of the integration of human effort actually means, however, is not altogether clear. For at least three different ideas are all referred to by the same phrase, and these three have not been adequately distinguished. The first is what I shall call the unity of theory and practice in theorizing. Perhaps the staunchest proponent of this view, surprisingly, is George Santayana. Dismayed by the discrepancy between what philosophers believe when they act as ordinary human beings and what they find themselves affirming as a result of arcane reasonings, Santayana issued a call for honesty in our intellectual endeavors. Speaking of himself, as he thought the philosopher must, but suggesting universal applicability, he declared, "I should be ashamed to countenance opinions which, when not arguing, I did not believe."[1]

Such honesty yields radical results. Santayana's intention was not to tie philosophical thought to the tangled prejudices of humankind. He believed, instead, that philosophy needs to be the critical explication of what we unconsciously assume in our active moments. There are certain beliefs we enact when we operate in the world, such as that time and space are real and that we are surrounded by mind-independent things which our agency can affect. Our job as thinkers is to discover these tenets of "animal faith" or at least never to let our dialectic carry us to the point where we contradict them. In this way, our life-activities determine or place limits on what we think, and as a result what we believe as active beings and our opinions as theorists always coincide.

This call for the unification of our theoretical and practical lives carries no prescription for broader action. It is explicitly restricted in application to how we ought to think. The second notion of the unity of theory and practice goes beyond it to disclose the full interconnectedness of action and thought. Many philosophers employ some such idea and give eloquent accounts of how our beliefs reflect what we do and our actions express or ought to express our thoughts. Sometimes the unity of the practical and the theoretical means simply the harmony of one's ethics and world view. In other thinkers, it refers to the identity of two forms of consciousness or the equivalence of two different sorts of action. The breakdown of the unity is supposed to cause ruinous inversions or alienation; its recapture promises fulfillment, or the final perfection of the human frame. All of this talk of unity, however, is talk only. This is what I call the unity of theory and practice *in theory,* for very few philosophers who embrace it go beyond writing books. Yet there is something devastatingly hollow about the demonstration that thought without action is hollow, when we find the philosopher only thinking it. We can say all the rights things and we can add that saying them is not enough — but none of this helps us escape the world of words. And words can never encompass the broader forms of action, nor serve as substitutes for them. There can, therefore, be no true unity of theory and practice in theory, in our ideas, in our books. It can exist only through the unified twofold agency of living persons.

What I speak of is the unity of theory and practice *in practice,* where real actions follow real thoughts. This shows, once again, that philosophy inescapably breaks the bounds of thought, seeps out of books to love, embrace, and modify the world. Such unity cannot be found in the words of philosophers but only by comparing their books with what they do. Plato had it because he left for Syracuse, and Mill attained it by running for Parliament. Marx achieved it when he agitated for revolution, and Spinoza reached it by quietly converting his passive emotions into active joy. We can all come near it by acting on what we believe, by making our books the authors of our deeds.

The very fact that we are philosophers burdens us with special obligations. This should present no surprise: a high calling exacts a high price. This means that if we are to be true to our profession, we must be ready for extensive and perhaps even painful action. We must not only lecture our students, but also present ourselves as living examples of what we teach. Those who are after virtue in their philosophical theories should capture some of it in their personal lives.

# Notes

1. George Santayana, *Skepticism and Animal Faith* (New York: Dover, 1955), p. 305.

# George Santayana and the Genteel Tradition

## DANIEL AARON

When George Santayana delivered his lecture, "The Genteel Tradition in American Philosophy," to a California audience in 1911, the word "genteel" had pretty well lost its original meaning. The adjective, a derivative of the French *gentil,* was for a long time synonymous with "polite," "graceful," "decorous," "refined." It distinguished the manners, dress, and tone of the wellborn from those of the commonality. That is the way Jane Austen, for example, understood it. Mr. Darcy in her novel *Pride and Prejudice* is "genteel." The smug and obsequious lower-class Mr. Collins is decidedly not. But by the middle of the nineteenth century, the term had become largely pejorative. "Do you call these genteel little creatures American poets?" Whitman rhetorically asks in *Democratic Vistas.* "To prune, gather, trim, conform, and ever cram and stuff, and be genteel and proper, is the pressure of our days."[1] Today "genteel" is an epithet contemptuously applied to persons (I cite the Oxford English Dictionary) "who are possessed with a dread of being taken for the 'common people,' who attach exaggerated importance to supposed marks of social superiority."[2] To be "genteel" now is tantamount to being both ignoble and socially insecure.

Little of this sense of the word is implicit in Santayana's usage. For him the "genteel tradition" was a descriptive, not an abusive, term. It connoted propriety, correctness, dogmatism, and conservatism[3] — and flaccidity, passivity, and complacence as well. "The subject," he wrote, "is complex and calls for many an excursus and qualifying footnote"; but he did sketch its outlines.[4] Indeed, it's possible to watch his consciousness long before he gave it a name. In time he came to see it as a kind of cultural malady that had afflicted the American mind since at least the end of the Civil War. A consecutive story of its birth, dominion, and decline could be pieced together from his random pieces and casual asides. If it had been, the plot might have run something like this.

The genteel tradition originated abroad, like so many other American phenomena, but became pandemic in Protestant America after Calvinism had ceased to be a vital and dynamic faith and the transcendentalism of an Emerson and Thoreau had atrophied. By mid-century, the citizens of the republic were totally absorbed in building and expanding and accumulating while at the same time internalizing a "hereditary philosophy" that no longer bore any relation to their quotidian activities. The religious and secular priests of a stale idealism represented one half of the national mentality. They were the custodians of a superannuated "high culture." The philistines, cousins of Emerson's Men of Understanding — calculating machines devoid of true emotion or "instinctive piety" — represented the other half. No third party of any size emerged to reconcile them. But science and intellectual and material progress created an inhospitable milieu for the genteel tradition, undermined its shaky foundations, and drove its proponents into academic enclaves. The consequences of this split between the spiritual and material cultures left the nation "half-formed," as Santayana put it, "and groping after its essence" — a nation without a civilization.[5]

Santayana's even-tempered if piecemeal diagnosis of a divided national mentality has been thoroughly aired, and so has the story of its aftermath: how the literary radicals in the early twentieth century made the genteel tradition the target of their antipathies just as it was about to peter out. Santayana had seen in 1911 that the Bohemian insurgents with their "poetry of crude naturalism" were the forerunners of a coming cultural revolution, but he didn't welcome them as allies. The confirmed Tory felt obliged to detach himself from the thirty contributors to Harold Stearn's *Civilization in the United States* when he reviewed that noisy book in 1922. He found the Young Turks "morally underfed" and "disaffected," and he learned more, he drily noted, "about their palpitating doubts than about America or about civilization."[6] Much of what they disliked about the United States he liked; the Americanism they deplored (the genteel tradition excepted) was "simply modernism." He even intimated that the "offended sensibility" emanating from Stearn's book was "itself genteel."[7]

Even so, he felt no hostility toward the young "barbarians" — in his lexicon a term signifying "unevenly educated," "undisciplined," "rebellious against the nature of things." Barbarians were people who despised "that which exists, in language, vocabulary, or morals, and set up the sufficiency of their unchastened impulses." He wasn't put off by their rambunctiousness — that was youth's privilege — but he faulted them for expressing their demands for "self-expression" in appallingly muddy English. Still, no matter how "crude and unnecessarily wasteful" they were,[8] he preferred them to the New Humanists, the last flurry of the New England genteel tradition, who had no wild passions to subdue for all their talk about the "inner check." In his youth he had resisted and resented the moral absolutism of Boston and Cambridge, the essence, he thought, "of the genteel tradition of America."[9] Perhaps this accounts for a certain animus detectable whenever the genteel tradition surfaces in his books and essays. It was more than a topic for the Tocquevillian commentator on American culture; it was a personal matter. Addressing it gave him an excuse to pay back some old scores.

I mention Tocqueville here as the prototypical outsider who came to the United States less than a half century before Santayana arrived, stayed ten months, and wrote his classic study of a democratic state, the advance guard of what he saw as an inevitable tendency. He carried his presuppositions with him and left with most of them intact. He liked the country and its people, but American society didn't appeal to him. America had no literature and no music and was destined by its political system and its social egalitarianism to produce at best a diluted culture.

It would never have occurred to Santayana to make a systematic survey of American ideas and institutions, but his conclusions about American civilization, such as they were, were not all that different from Tocqueville's even though his involvement with America was far more complex and ambivalent.

Both *Persons and Places,* a novelistic autobiography, and *The Last Puritan,* an autobiographical novel, are as much the productions of the "insider as outsider" as they are the reverse. In the former, Santayana makes his marginality the clue to his character and career. He presents himself as the stranger in America, the uneasy guest, the exotic, the spy, the Prince in Disguise. In his public role, he plays the laughing philosopher, the bemused observer of the human menagerie, the tolerant world citizen. Hardly discernible is the not-so-disengaged social critic embedded in the society he is criticizing. Many social critics, Stefan Collini reminds us, tend to dramatize their roles by representing themselves as marginal. "But such a claim need not be taken as an accurate piece of social description: it serves functions of its own, including that of legitimizing the criticisms of indicating the critic's access to some standard of authority denied to those blinkered by or imprisoned in the assumptions of their own society."[10] Santayana was such a critic, I think, and I suspect that he was more affected by the genteel culture he slyly spoofed than he ever let on.

He may have shared some of the traits Thorstein Veblen in a famous essay attributed to the renegade Jew — the hyphenate's "divided allegiance" and skepticism — that made him, in Veblen's terms, an "intellectual wayfaring man" and "a disturber of the intellectual peace."[11] But unlike Veblen, an authentic outsider, Santayana managed to secure his place "in the scheme of conventions" and to remain safely and comfortably ensconced in the society of the well-heeled. He could do this in good conscience, partly because he had no quarrel with American political and economic institutions and accepted (if not necessarily agreeing with) the social prejudices of the establishment, but also because he conveyed his unsubversive opinions with charm and urbanity. However foreign he felt himself to be, his "insider" credentials protected him from the retribution visited upon the genuine outsider.

*Persons and Places,* at once so revealing and evasive, so clearly written and abstract, is instructively different from the autobiographical books of Henry Adams and Henry James, authors with whom Santayana has often been compared. Both belonged to old America. Both Adams and James escaped the contagion of the genteel tradition by distancing themselves from it, Adams through science and historical backtracking, James in what Santayana called "the classic way" — that is to say, by turning it "into a subject-matter for analysis" and "by understanding it."[12] Santayana professed to understand it too, but that did not keep him from coming almost obsessively to its spirit-chilling manifestations long after its knell had sounded. Significantly, he often associated it with his Boston youth.

Two Bostons figure noticeably in his memoirs: the Boston typified by his own shabby genteel household and the Boston of the rich. He made no bones about his preference for the luxurious households of the latter ("if most things were illusions," he decided, "having money and spending money were great realities"), but the Boston he abandoned with relief — the only part of the United States he knew firsthand — emerges in his recollections as the quintessence of the genteel tradition: a compound of tepid refinement and blatant commercialism. "In Boston but not of it." Thus he described his adolescence. His foreignness, his Roman Catholicism (such as it was), and what he refers to tiresomely in his autobiography as his family's "poverty," didn't bar him from fashionable and intellectual circles; they did keep him skirmishing "on the borders of the polite world." At Harvard there were no borders he had to cross, but both in Boston and Cambridge he occupied a middle ground somewhere between that of a native and a "visiting foreigner."[13] So at least the older man remembered his younger self.

The Boston of *Persons and Places* — Santayana's America — is reflected through a glass tinted with sentiment, malice, and humor. His fondness for "the kind and correct Bostonians," those "highly moralised and highly cultivated" types, was unfeigned.[14] But his memoirs were also punctuated with vignettes of drab people not unlike the cranks Henry James mischievously portrayed in his novel *The Bostonians.* There is something curt and

a little spiteful in his recollections of Boston maidens drifting into spinster-
hood and of a society left limp and exhausted in the aftermath of a civil
war about which he had no feeling and little interest. He is particularly
hard on Boston Unitarianism, which seems to have epitomized for him
the hollowness and complacency of the genteel tradition. He associated
it with congratulatory sermons that neither discouraged believers nor an-
tagonized agnostics; with solemn ill-humored and unappetizing breakfasts
—"the improved Unitarian substitute for morning prayers"—and bland
cultural uplift.[15] The personal note that slips into these animadversions
and belies the pose of the bemused outsider he assumes in *Persons and
Places* is even more noticeable in *The Last Puritan.* I read this memoir in
the form of a novel as a sequel to the autobiography and a sustained so-
liloquy (as so much of his writing is) in which the voice of the author re-
sounds not only in the pronouncements of the narrator but also in the
conversation of the disparate characters, mouthpieces for his obiter dicta.
Here the meaning of "genteel" is dramatized rather than spelled out. It is
almost as if under the guise of fiction, he could touch on matters he was
disinclined to probe in his memoirs and essays.

Oliver Alden, the luckless hero of *The Last Puritan,* bears a certain re-
semblance to the type Henry Adams labeled *bourgeois-bostonien.*[16] He
is prefigured in Santayana's *Character and Opinion in the United States*
as one of those gaunt solitary American idealists who "either folds up his
heart and withers in a corner" or flees to foreign shores "to save his soul—
or perhaps not to save it,"[17] and who exhibits, in the words of William
Dean Howells, "that anti-Puritan quality which was always vexing the heart
of Puritanism."[18] Oliver Alden is a throwback to his Calvinist forebears
and lacks, like Captain Ahab, "the low enjoying power." Having convinced
himself that it's wrong to be a Puritan, he's still unable to stifle his "ago-
nized conscience." Neither can he accommodate himself to the "shams and
mummeries" of the genteel tradition.[19] Santayana admires Oliver's integrity and blames him only for not adhering "to his own standard"[20] and
not breaking through to "live victoriously in the spirit."[21] There's a good
deal of Santayana in Oliver, but, as he wrote to a friend, the novel "gives
*emotions* of my experience and not my thoughts and experiences themselves."[22] The author was far readier to compromise "with the mixed loose
world" than was his inflexible protagonist.[23]

Oliver's father, Peter Alden, is more of a Santayana than his son. A
rootless traveler—urbane, skeptical, ironic—he fancies handsome young
men, good food, and agreeable travel, and he is instinctively the gentleman
for all his unconventional habits and ideas. Peter's marriage to Oliver's
mother seems out of character despite the labored authorial explanation,
but the settlement he makes with Harriet Bumstead, the genteel tradition

incarnate, is analogous to Santayana's strategy vis-a-vis America. Peter re-
stores the Bumstead house to its former stateliness and gives over the arrangement of its rooms to his wife while insisting that one upstairs room —
a "Chinese room," he calls it, symbolic of his world elsewhere — be reserved
for himself. Peter Alden soliloquizes: "In walking up and down these dig-
nified stairs, we shall have time to recompose ourselves for the change of
atmosphere in passing from solitude to society, or vice versa: I don't mean
from sincerity to pretence, but from illusions with which he probably doesn't
deceive other people. Let us endeavour to preserve our genteel traditions
for one generation more. If I have a son, I should like him to start from
there. God knows where he will end."[24]

As long as he lived in the United States, Santayana also lived on two
floors, so to speak, with his "Chinese room" to retreat to. Like Peter Alden,
he had been "thoroughly initiated in his youth into a particular circle,"
had found it "too narrow and old fashioned" to endure, and "in slipping
out of it had missed the general movement of national events and national
sentiment."[25] Even so, he took pleasure in the company of an "inner circle" whose members retained something of the social flavor of the old merchant patriciate. He wasn't really of it, as Henry Adams was, or William
and Henry James, or Oliver Wendell Holmes, Barrett Wendell, and John
Jay Chapman, but he felt a kinship with Europeanized Boston cosmopo-
lites, however "genteel" their culture, and enjoyed their cultivated talk and
good dinners.

He felt much closer to the scions of these old families, especially the
gifted minority among his Harvard classmates and students, and brooded
over their wasted lives. Underdeveloped and dissatisfied, gasping for breath
in the thin New England air, they lacked the power of mind to dominate
their circumstances. He differentiated himself from this traditionless rem-
nant (he could fall back, he claimed, on Old World resources unavailable
to them in spite of their frequent sojourns abroad), yet they all vibrated
in the same aesthetic string. Santayana succeeded where they failed, because he was driven by practical necessity and more skilled in the arts of
survival. He was also tougher and smarter.

Martin Green in his book, *The Problem of Boston,* has analyzed the
tastes and temperaments of the aesthete-exiles with particular attention
to what Santayana, Bernard Berenson, Henry James, and Henry Adams
had in common: an aesthetic idealism, a marked feminine component, a
preference for the society of brilliant and mutually enriching "chosen
spirits," a fascination with Roman Catholicism, and a fondness for the
manners and style of the English upper class.[26] Santayana was never more
Bostonian than when playing the anti-Bostonian — ironic, humorous, gen-
tlemanly, temperate, self-contained — observing the proprieties of dress,

distrustful of the French character. The Boston aesthetes, Santayana included, were men of the world and tolerated the forbidden if presented elegantly and without grossness, but in shying away from the experimental, the confessional, the outr), they were no less genteel than their literary contemporaries.

Consider Santayana's lifelong debate over Walt Whitman — one might almost say it was actually a debate *with* Whitman. In "Walt Whitman: A Dialogue," written in 1890, he plays the double role of defender and prosecutor. Van Tender, the tender-minded poet, hails Whitman as "the voice of nature crying in the wilderness," the celebrator of "the beauty of common things." His tough-minded friend, McStout, comes down hard on the vague and indecent pantheist, the "fashionable mountebank."[27] A decade later, Santayana grants Whitman "a wonderful gift of graphic characterization and an occasioned rare grandeur of diction" but sees him as an inspired tramp and poetic demagogue wallowing "in the stream of his own sensibility."[28] He appears to have grown more critical of Whitman as he aged, if Peter Alden speaks for the author in *The Last Puritan*. Alden calls Whitman a "speechifying" rhetorician "as superficial as Rousseau," not a true poet. He pretends (Alden continues) to turn — for it is largely affectation — only from the more refined devices of mankind to a ruder and more stupid existence. "He is like Marie Antionette playing the shepherdess."[29] By disregarding the genteel tradition, he concedes, Whitman performed a valuable service, but because he was lazy, self-indulgent, and undiscriminating, and because he "renounced old forms without achieving a new one,"[30] he laid no foundation for its amendment.

So Santayana pigeonholed the patron saint of the bohemians. And they, having appropriated the "reverberant name" (as Van Wyck Brooks referred to the genteel tradition) conducted a crusade against it and its alleged priests, unaware that they were attacking some of Santayana's cherished values — order, discipline, integration — and encouraging in themselves and others what was for him a sloppy subjectivism. Initially he had confined the word "genteel" to a philosophical tradition. The social and literary iconoclasts of the teens and twenties stretched its meaning to cover the whole of American milk-and-water Anglo-Saxon culture and its (until roughly 1910) influential missionaries. Santayana was no democrat. He accepted class distinctions as a matter of course, along with the social prejudices and preferences of the genteel bookmen. He didn't anticipate an American Renaissance. It would have seemed to him an oxymoron.

The radicals did. What is more, they advocated a melting-pot culture which to Santayana was no culture at all. Van Wyck Brooks's little book, *America's Coming-of-Age,* published a few years after Santayana left the United States for good, is an expression of this cultural nationalism. Brooks is the link between Santayana and the unharnessed apostles of the New who came of age during the presidency of Woodrow Wilson. In his Harvard years (1904–1907), Brooks had belonged to the company of college aesthetes, some of them Santayana's friends and protegés, and had shared (in the words of his biographer) their "weary languor and mild fin-de-siècle passion."[31] Brooks's *Wine of Puritans* (1908), written in the form of a dialogue, was published one year after his graduation and three years before Santayana's "Genteel Tradition in American Philosophy." Its title and theme are embodied in the remark of one of the speakers: "You put the old wine in new bottles . . . and when the explosion results, one may say the aroma, or the ideal, turns into transcendentalism, and the wine, or the real, becomes commercialism. In any case, one doesn't preserve a great deal of well-tempered wine."[32] Brooks's metaphor of a transported culture and of a country deprived of a cultural childhood is echoed in Santayana's observation: "The country was new, but the race was tried, chastened, and full of solemn memories. It was an old wine in new bottles."[33]

Eventually Brooks discovered treasures in America's "usable past," enthusiastically espoused a cultural nationalism, and grew testy with expatriates like Eliot and Pound. Santayana never changed his mind about a country he was delighted to leave and about which he came to know less and less. When he quit the United States in 1913, the genteel tradition was virtually defunct, doomed, he believed, by an unlovely modernist counterculture—itself the product of triumphant industrialism. Like Matthew Arnold, G. Lowes Dickinson, and H. G. Wells—but perhaps with fewer misgivings—he beheld the United States as a promise or threat of what was to come. He took a lot of America with him when he left, especially the genteel New England he had anatomized and laughed at and half despised. For this New England he retained the kind of respect and covert affection one has for a persistent and familiar enemy.

# Notes

1. Walt Whitman, *Complete Poetry and Collected Prose* (New York: The Library of America, 1982), pp. 955, 961.

2. Also see John Tomsich, *A Genteel Endeavour: American Culture and Politics in the Gilded Age* (Stanford, Calif.: Stanford University Press, 1971), pp. 2–3.

3. G. W. Howgate, *George Santayana* (Philadelphia: University of Pennsylvania Press, 1938), pp. 186–87.

4. George Santayana, *Winds of Doctrine: Studies in Contemporary Opinion* (New York: Charles Scribner's Sons, 1913), p. 212.

5. George Santayana, *Persons and Places: Fragments of Autobiography* (Cambridge, Mass.: MIT Press, 1986), p. 195.

6. James Ballowe, ed., *George Santayana's America: Essays on Literature and Culture* (Urbana: University of Illinois Press, 1967), pp. 161–62.

7. Ibid.

8. Daniel Cory, *Santayana: The Later Years: A Portrait with Letters* (New York: G. Braziller, 1963), pp. 29–30.

9. George Santayana, *The Genteel Tradition at Bay* (New York: Charles Scribner's Sons, 1931), p. 28.

10. Stefan Collini, "Speaking from Somewhere," *The Times Literary Supplement,* April 15–21, 1988, p. 427.

11. Max Lerner, ed., *The Portable Veblen* (New York: Viking Press, 1970), pp. 474–75.

12. Santayana, *Winds of Doctrine,* p. 204.

13. Santayana, *Persons and Places,* pp. 85, 224, 354.

14. Ibid., p. 254.

15. George Santayana, *The Last Puritan* (New York: Charles Scribner's Sons, 1937), p. 27.

16. Newton Arvin, ed., *The Selected Letters of Henry Adams* (New York: Farrar, Straus and Young, 1951), p. 239.

17. George Santayana, *Character and Opinion in the United States* (New York: W. W. Norton, 1967), p. 170.

18. W. D. Howells, *The Landlord at Lion's Head* (New York: The New American Library, 1964), p. vii.

19. Santayana, *The Last Puritan,* pp. 6–7.

20. John McCormick, *George Santayana: A Biography* (New York: Alfred J. Knopf, 1987), p. 337.

21. Irving Singer, ed., *Essays in Literary Criticism of George Santayana* (New York: Charles Scribner's Sons, 1956), p. 251.

22. McCormick, *George Santayana,* p. 330.

23. Singer, *Essays,* p. 252.

24. Santayana, *The Last Puritan,* p. 63.

25. Ibid., p. 113.

26. Martin Green, *The Problem of Boston: Some Readings in Cultural History* (London: Longmans, Green and Co., 1966), pp. 142–63.

27. Ballowe, *Santayana's America,* pp. 97–104.

28. Singer, *Essays,* p. 157.

29. Santayana, *The Last Puritan,* pp. 180–81.

30. Ballowe, *Santayana's America,* p. 149.

31. James Hoopes, *Van Wyck Brooks: In Search of American Culture* (Amherst: University of Massachusetts Press, 1977), p. 47.

32. Claire Sprague, ed., *Van Wyck Brooks, The Early Years: A Selection from His Works, 1908–1921* (New York: Harper Torchbooks, 1968), p. 6.

33. Hoopes, *Van Wyck Brooks,* p. 62.

# The Promise of Process Philosophy

NICHOLAS RESCHER

In recent years, "process philosophy" has virtually become a code word for the doctrines of Alfred North Whitehead and his followers. But of course, this cannot really be what process philosophy is ultimately about: If there indeed is a "philosophy" of process, it must pivot not on a *thinker* but on a *theory.* What is at issue must, in the end, be a philosophical position that has a life of its own.

Whitehead himself fixed on "process" as a central category of his philosophy because he viewed time and change as salient metaphysical issues. Invoking the name of Bergson, he adopted "Nature is a process" as a leading principle and saw temporality, change, and passage as fundamental facts to be reckoned with in our understanding of the world.[1] This view was underpinned by Whitehead's appreciation of Leibnizian *appetition* — the striving through which all things endeavor to bring new features to realization.[2] And in back of this lay the Heracleitean doctrine that "all things flow," and the rejection of a Parmenidean/atomistic view that nature consists in the changeable interrelations among stable, unchanging units of existence.[3]

As Whitehead himself thus emphasized, process philosophy does not represent the doctrine of a particular thinker, but reflects a major tendency or line of thought that traces back through the history of philosophy to the days of the pre-Socratics. Its leading exponents were Heracleitus, Leibniz, Bergson, Peirce, and William James, and it ultimately moved on to include Whitehead and his school (Charles Hartshorne and Paul Weiss, as well as Andrew Paul Ushenko), and also others such as Samuel Alexander and C. Lloyd Morgan.

As is often the case in philosophy, the position at issue is best understood in terms of what it opposes.

From the time of Aristotle, western metaphysics has had a marked bias in favor of *things.* Aristotle's insistence on the metaphysical centrality of ostensively indictable objects (with *tode ti* as a pointable-at *this*) has made an enduring and far-reaching impact. The Aristotelian primacy of substance and its ramifications (see *Metaphysics* IV, 2; 10003b6–11) — with its focus on mid-size physical objects on the order of a rock, a tree, a cat, or a human being — has proved decisive for much of western philosophy.

However, another line of thought was also current. After all, the concentration on perduring physical *things* as existents in nature slights the equally good claims of another ontological category, namely processes, events, occurrences — items better indicated by verbs than nouns. Clearly, storms and heat waves are every bit as real as dogs and oranges. Even on the surface of it, verb-entities have as good a claim to reality as noun-entities. For process theorists, *becoming* is no less important than *being* — but rather the reverse. The phenomenology of change is stressed precisely because the difference between a museum and the real world is seen as crucial to our understanding of reality.

Moreover, processes are not in general a matter of the doings of things. The fire's heat causes the water to boil. But it is clearly not a *thing*. To be sure, some events and processes relate to the doings or undergoings of things (the collapse of a bridge) or of people (Smith's breaking a leg). And other events and processes relate to the coordinated doings of things (an eclipse of the sun) or of people (a morning rush hour). But many events and processes are patently subjectless in that they do not consist of the doings of one or more personal or impersonal agents (a frost, for example, or a magnetic field). At work in these self-subsistent or subjectless processes are not "agents" but "forces."

The progenitor of this rival tradition was Heracleitus. For him reality is not a constellation of things at all, but one of processes. The fundamental "stuff" is not material substance but process, namely "fire," and all things are products of its workings (*puros tropai*). Process is fundamental: the river is not an *object,* but a continuing flow, the sun is not a *thing,* but an enduring fire. Everything is a matter of process, of activity, of change (*panta rhei*)! Not stable things but fundamental forces and the fluctuating processes they produce constitute the world. We must at all costs avoid the fallacy that Bergson characterized as "spatializing time."

The principal standard bearer of this line of thought into the domain of modern philosophy was Leibniz, who maintained that all of the "things" that figure in our experience (animals alone grudgingly excepted) are mere phenomena and not really things at all. The world in fact consists of clusters of processes he calls "monads" (units), which are "centers of force" or "bundles of activity." For Leibniz, processes rather than things furnish the basic materials of ontology.

Against this historical background, it seems sensible to understand "process philosophy" as a doctrine committed to, or at any rate inclined towards certain basic propositions:

1. That time and change are among the principal categories of metaphysical understanding.

2. That process is a principal category of ontological description.

3. That processes are more fundamental, or at any rate not less fundamental, than things for the purposes of ontological theory.

4. That several of the major elements of the ontological repertoire (God, nature-as-a-whole, persons, material substances) are best understood in process terms.

5. That contingency, emergence, novelty, and creativity are among the fundamental categories of metaphysical understanding.

Process philosophers, then, are those for whom temporality, activity, and change — of alteration, striving, passage, and novelty-emergence — are the cardinal factors in our understanding of the real. Ultimately it is a question of priority. Process philosophers view the time-oriented aspects of the real as constituting its most characteristic and significant features. For them, process has priority over product — both ontologically and epistemically.

This general process-oriented approach is historically too pervasive and systematically too significant to be restricted in its bearing to one particular philosopher and his school. Indeed, one important task for the partisans of process at this historical juncture is to prevent the idea of "process philosophy" from being marginalized through a limitation of its bearing to the work and influence of one single individual or movement.

## Process Ontology

To be sure, one perfectly plausible way of downgrading processes is to question not their reality, but rather their fundamentality. On this approach, it is conceded that nature is indeed replete with many and varied activities and processes, but insisted that they are simply the doings of a substantial agent. Every verb must have a subject, and every event or occurrence is a matter of the agency of things. Denying the ontological autonomy of processes, this process-reducibility doctrine insists that all there is in the world are things and their properties and actions. This perspective reasserts an orthodoxy that maintains the ontological substance-bias of western philosophy.

But in fact it represents a rather problematic position. The world is full of processes that do not represent the actions of things (save on a rather naive and obsolescent atomist/materialist model of nature). When water freezes or evaporates, it is not a "thing" (or collection thereof) that is active in producing this result. The freshening of the wind, the forming of waves in the water, the pounding of the surf, the erosion of the shoreline are all processes that are not really the machinations of identifiable "things."

Consider such a process as "a fluctuation in the earth's magnetic field" or "a weakening of the sun's gravitational field." Clearly such processes will make an impact on things (magnetic needles, for example). But by no stretch of the imagination are these processes themselves the doings/activities of things/substances. There is not a *thing* "a magnetic field" or "a gravitational field" that *does* something or performs certain actions. The idea that processes *can* be the doings of things represents a plain truth. But the idea that processes *must* be the doings of things is nothing but an unhelpful prejudice. Where is the thing that is being active when we have a fall in barometric pressure? For process philosophers, the classical principle *operari sequitur esse* is reversed: their motto is *esse sequitur operari,* since being follows from operation because what there is is in the final analysis the product of processes.

But can processes really get on without things to give them existential embodiment? Traditional metaphysics sees processes (such as the rod's snapping under the strain when bent sufficiently) as the manifestation of dispositions (fragility), which must themselves be rooted in the stable properties of things. It takes processes to manifest dispositions that are themselves products of the categorical (nondispositional) features of things. Process metaphysics involves an inversion of this perspective. It takes the line that the categorical properties of things are simply stable clusters of process-engendering dispositions.

But can these process-dispositions avoid the need for rooting in the categorical properties of things? Is the dispositional realm autonomous — that is, can dispositions be self-activating? After all, dispositions are matters of if-then. If this is all we have, can we then *ever* move to the categorical sphere?

The answer is affirmative. We can do this provided we have *nested* dispositions. If all we have are dispositions of the form

When and where p, there q

then of course we would need a categorical input (namely *p*) to have a categorical output. But with nested dispositions of the form

When and where (when and where p, there q), there r

we can in fact get a categorical output from hypothetical inputs. Where dispositions are sufficiently complex (i.e., nested), a transition from the dispositional to the categorical sector is possible. Mere dispositions can combine to engender categorical actualities. And so processes (rod-snappings) can occur in the framework of a process ontology that has no recourse to processual substances with categorical properties that underwrite the dispositions (such as rodfragility) that processes actualize.

In this connection, an important asymmetry is often lost from sight. Processes can make do without things. As the example of "it is getting colder" shows, there can be "subjectless" processes — processes which to all appearances are not, like sneezing or dissolving, encompassed in the activities of things.

On the other hand, no workable substance ontology can operate without a heavy reliance on processes. A substance, after all, is determined (individuated) as such by its properties, and there are just two major types here, namely the dispositional and the absolute (nondispositional, categorical). But the dispositional ones are crucial — at any rate from an epistemic point of view. For all that we can ever *observe* about a substance is what it does — what sorts of impacts (changes, effects) it produces in interaction with others — that is, what sorts of processes it engenders. The absolute (nondispositional) properties that we attribute to things are always the product of a theory-bound conjecture — features imputed to things to provide a causal explanation for their impacts upon others. As Leibniz insisted, a substance is primarily a center of force, a bundle of dispositions to exert impacts of various sorts upon the others. Substances can come upon the stage of consideration only through the mediation of processes.

One must not forget that even on the basis of an ontology of substance and property, dispositional properties are *epistemologically* fundamental. Without them, a thing is inert, undetectable, disconnected from the world's causal commerce, and inherently unknowable. Our only epistemic access to the absolute properties of things is through inferential triangulation from their dispositional properties — or better, from the processes through which these manifest themselves. Accordingly, a substance ontologist cannot get by without processes. If things are totally inert — if they *do* nothing — they are pointless. For without processes there is no access to dispositions, and without dispositional properties, substances lie outside our cognitive reach. One can only observe what things *do,* via their discernible effects — what they *are,* over and above this, is a matter of theory projected on this basis.

A process ontology simplifies matters. Instead of a two-tier reality that combines things and the inevitable processes, it settles for a one-tier ontology of process alone. It sees things not just as the *products* of processes (as one cannot avoid doing) but also as the *manifestations* of processes — as complex bundles of coordinated processes. It replaces the troublesome ontological dualism of *thing* and *activity* with a monism of activities of varying sorts. In its sight, things simply *are* what they *do*. Even as thought itself is a cognitive process, we cannot understand its products without seeing them too as products of processes.

## Process and "The Problem of Universals"

Let us now turn from particulars to universals. Recourse to process is also a helpful device for dealing with the classical problem of universals. We are surrounded on all sides by instances of types more easily conceived of as being processes rather than substantial things, not physical items like a magnetic field or an aurora borealis, but also conceptual artifacts like words or letters of the alphabet, let alone songs, plays, or poems.

Processes can, do, and must have patterns and periodicities that render them in-principle repeatable. After all, to say that an item (be it a thing or a process) has a *structure* of some sort is to attribute something to it that other items can in principle have.[4] But of course, structure, though repeatable ("abstractable"), is itself not an abstraction—it is something that a concrete item concretely exhibits. Abstraction does not *create* structure, but presupposes it.

Classically, there are three rival theories of "universals," which see them, respectively, as: (1) *made by minds* (nominalism), that is, imputed to things by minds in virtue of their (the minds') operation; (2) *found (by minds) in things* (Platonic realism), that is, perceived by minds in preexisting aspects of things; (3) *generated in mind-thing interaction* (conceptualism). Now a substance ontology, which is bound to see universals as simply being the properties of things (Aristotelian secondary substances), encounters difficulties here. For on its basis one is driven inexorably towards Platonism. We want universals to be objective, but can only secure this status for them on the basis of a Platonic realism. And when we look more closely at the sorts of things at issue—letters of the alphabet, say, or poems—this doesn't really seem to be such an attractive option.

But with process universals (processual structures) there are fewer difficulties. Processes are inherently universal and repeatable—to be a process is to be a process of a certain sort, a certain specifiable makeup. What concretizes processes is simply their spatiotemporal emplacement, their positioning in reality. And so a process as such is by its very nature a concrete universal—any actual process is *at once* concrete and universal. There is, presumably, little or no problem about process types because these can be accounted for in terms of a commonality of structure.

In particular, colors, say, or numbers or poems lend themselves naturally to a process account. Take phenomenal colors, for example. A *mental* process such as perceiving or imagining a certain shade of red is simply a way of perceiving redly or imagining redly (in a certain particular way). That putative universal — the shade of phenomenal red — ceases to be a mysterious *object* of some sort and becomes a specifiable feature of familiar processes (perceivings, imaginings). How distinct minds can perceive the same universal is now no more mysterious than how distinct walkers can share the same limp. Otherwise mysterious-seeming universals such as odors or fears are simply shared structural features of mental processes. Universals are pulled down from the Platonic realm, to become structural features of the ways in which we concretely conduct the business of thinking. Recourse to a process approach is once again a useful problem-solving device.

## Process Philosophy of Nature

Let us move on from matters of ontology to some issues in the process philosophy of nature.

A classical atomism whose ontology consists only of atoms and the void is the ultimate contrary to a process philosophy. A physics of fields and forces that operate on their own, without an embedding in things, is the quintessence of a process philosophy of nature. But wherein lies the appeal of such a view?

A substance ontologist is committed to seeing the physical world (nature) as a collection of *things* or *objects*. And on this basis, she immediately faces the problem of accounting for *laws* that coordinate the behavior of things. (How do all hydrogen atoms learn how to behave like hydrogen atoms?)

But by seeing the world as a matrix of processes — by viewing nature as the substantiation of a family of operative principles (taken in their all-inclusive systemic totality) — we secure straightaway a coherent conceptualization of nature in a way that removes such difficulties. For the idea of law is inherent in the very concept of a process. And we can *understand* the world's processes — precisely because we ourselves are a party to them, seeing that we ourselves, in our own makeup and being, participate in the operation of nature.

A process approach thus simplifies greatly the problem of securing a coherent view of nature. Modern physics teaches us that at the level of the very small, there are no ongoing *things* (substances, objects) at all in nature — no particulars with a continuing descriptive identity of their own — there are only patterns of process that exhibit stabilities. (The orbit-jump of an "electron" is not the mysterious transit of a well-defined physical object at all.) Only those stability waves of continuous process provide for any sort of continuity of existence. The development of stable "things" begins at the sub-submicroscopic level of the buzzing proliferation of "events" that have no fixed nature in themselves but only exist in reciprocal interaction with each other, and which have no stable characteristics in and of themselves, but only exhibit stable aspects at the level of statistical aggregates.

It was unfortunate for them that the founders of process philosophy did not witness the rise of the quantum theory. The classical conception of an atom was subject to the principle that "by definition, atoms cannot be cut up or broken into smaller parts," so that "atom splitting" was a *contradiction in terms.* The demise of classical atomism brought on by the dematerialization of physical matter brings much aid and comfort to a process-oriented metaphysics. Matter in the small, as contemporary physics concerns it, is not a Rutherfordian planetary system of particle-like objects, but a collection of fluctuating processes organized into stable structures (insofar as there is indeed stability at all) by statistical regularities — that is, by regularities of comportment at the level of aggregate phenomena. Twentieth-century physics has thus turned the tables on classical atomism. Instead of very small *things* (atoms) combining to produce standard processes (windstorms and such), modern physics envisions very small processes (quantum phenomena) combining to produce standard things (ordinary macro-objects) as a result of their modus operandi.

The quantum view of reality throws classical atomism on the trash heap. For it holds that, at the microlevel, what was usually deemed a physical *thing,* a stably perduring object, is itself no more than a statistical pattern — a stability wave in a surging sea of process. Those so-called enduring "things" come about through the compilation of stabilities in statistical fluctuations, much like gusts of wind. Processes are not the machinations of stable things; things are the stability patterns of variable processes. All such perspectives of modern physics at the level of fundamentals dovetail smoothly into the traditional process approach.

Neither the logic of object and predicate nor even the grammar of subject and verb prevail in the language of nature, but the language of differential equations, the language of process. In this regard as in so many others, Leibniz had insight far beyond his time. Important though logic and language are (and he stresses that they are *very* important), it is the mathematical language of process — of transformation functions and differential equations — that is of the greatest help in depicting the world's physical realities. (This is something of which Whitehead, himself a first-rate mathematician, was keenly aware.)

## Process Psychology: Difficulties of the Self

Next, let us briefly consider the utility of the process approach in philosophical psychology.

The self or ego has always been a stumbling block for Western philosophy because of its recalcitrance to accommodation within its favored framework of substance ontology. The idea that "the self" is a *thing* (substance), and that whatever occurs in relation to "my mind" and "my thoughts" is a matter of the activity of a thing of a certain sort (a "mind" substance) is no more than a rather blatant sort of fiction, a somewhat desperate effort to apply the thing paradigm to a range of phenomena that it just doesn't fit.

It is, after all, rather repugnant to conceptualize *people* (persons) as *things* (substances) — oneself above all. Aristotle already bears witness to this difficulty of accommodating the self or soul into a substance metaphysic. It is, he tells us, the "substantial form," the entelechy of the body. But this accommodation strategy raises more problems than it solves, because the self or soul is so profoundly unlike the other sorts of entelechy examples that Aristotle is able to provide.

People instinctively resist being described in thing-classificatory terms. As Sartre said, a wrongdoer may say "I did this or that act" but will resist saying "I am a thief," "I am a murderer."[5] Such attributions indicate a fixed nature that we naturally see as repugnant to ourselves. People tend to see themselves and their doings in processual terms as sources of teleological, agency-purposive activities geared to the satisfaction of needs and wants as they appear in the circumstances of the moment. In application to ourselves, at any rate, static thing-classifiers are naturally distasteful to us.

If one is committed to conceiving of a *person* within the framework of a classical thing-metaphysic, then one is going to be impelled inexorably towards the materialist view that the definitive facet of a person is the body and its doings. For of everything that appertains to us, it is clearly one's *body* that is most readily assimilated to the substance paradigm. Think here of David Hume's ventures into self-apprehension: "From what (experiential) impression could this idea (of *self*) be derived? This question is impossible to answer without a manifest contradiction and absurdity; and yet it is a question which must necessarily be answered, if we would have the idea of self pass for clear and intelligible. . . . For my part, when I enter most intimately into what I call *myself,* I always stumble on some particular perception or other, of heat or cold, light or shade, love or hatred, pain or pleasure. I never can catch *myself* at any time without a perception, and never can observe anything but the perception."[6] Here Hume is perfectly right. Any such quest for *observational* confrontation with a personal core substance, a self or ego that constitutes the particular person that one is, is destined to end in failure. The only "thing" about ourselves we can get hold of *observationally* is the body and its activities.

However, from the angle of a process metaphysic, the situation has a rather different look. We have difficulties apprehending what we *are* but have no difficulty experiencing what we *do*. Our bodily and mental activities lie open to experiential apprehension. There is no problem with experiential access to the processes and patterns of process that characterize us personally: Our doings and undergoings, either individually or patterned into talents, skills, capabilities, traits, dispositions, habits, inclinations, and tendencies to action and inaction are, after all, what characteristically define a person as the individual he or she is. What makes my experience mine is not some peculiar qualitative character that it exhibits but simply its forming part of the overall ongoing process that defines and institutes my life.

Once we conceptualize the core "self" of a person as a bundle of actual and potential processes — of action and capacities, tendencies, and dispositions to action (both physical and psychical) — then we have a concept of personhood that renders the self or ego experientially accessible, seeing that experiencing itself simply *consists* of the exercise of such processes. In a process-oriented approach, the self or ego (the constituting core of a person as such, that is, as the particular person he or she is) is simply a megaprocess — a *structured system of processes,* a cohesive and (relatively) stable center of agency. The crux of this approach is the shift in orientation from substance to process — from a unity of hardware, of physical machinery, to a unity of software, of programming or mode of functioning.

Miguel de Unamuno says that Descartes got it backwards, that instead of *cogito, ergo sum res cogitans* it should be: *sum res cogitans, ergo cogito.*[7] But this is not so. Descartes' reversal of scholasticism's traditional substantialist perspective is perfectly in order, based on the sound idea that activity comes first (*Im Anfang war die Tat*) — that what we do defines what we are. The fundamentality of psychic process for the constitution of a self was put on the agenda of modern philosophy in Descartes.

Leibniz went even further in generalizing the view that agency defines the agent. Along Cartesian lines, he saw the unity of the self as a unity of process, taking its individuality to consist in a unified characteristic mode of acting (of perceiving the world). But in this regard the self was, for Leibniz, paradigmatic for substance in general. In effect, Leibniz's monadology took the Cartesian process approach to the personal self and *universalized* it to encompass substance in general. A substance, like a self, is just so much a "thing" as a center of action.

The salient advantage of this process-geared view of the self as an internally complex process of "leading a life (of a certain sort)" — with its natural division into a varied manifold of constituent subprocesses — is that it does away with the need for a mysterious and experientially inaccessible unifying substantial *object* (on the lines of Kant's "transcendental ego") to constitute a self out of the variety of its experiences. The unity of self comes to be seen as a unity of process — of one large megaprocess that encompasses many smaller ones in its makeup. We arrive at a view of mind that dispenses with the Cartesian "ghost in the machine" and looks to the unity of mind as a unity of functioning — of *operation* rather than *operator*. A "self" is viewed not as a *thing* but as an integrated process.

On this basis, the Humean complaint — "One experiences feeling this and doing that, but one never experiences *oneself*" — is much like the complaint of the person who says, "I see him picking up that brick, and mixing that batch of mortar, and troweling that brick into place, but I never see him building a wall." Even as "building the wall" just exactly is a complex process that is *composed* of those various activities, so — from the process point of view — one's self just is a complex process *composed* of those various physical and psychic experiences and actions in their systemic interrelationship.

The process-based approach in philosophical psychology doubtless has difficulties of its own. But they pale into nothingness compared to those of the traditional substantival approach.

## Process Theology

Let us now move on to another theme, process theology.[8] The neo-Platonic sympathies of the church fathers impelled the theology of the western monotheistic religions to the orthodox philosophical stance that to see God as existent we must conceive of Him as a being, a *substance* of some (presumably very nonstandard) sort. And to the pleasure of philosophers and the vexation of theologians, this has opened up a host of theoretical difficulties. For example: (1) On the classical conception of the matter, a substance must always originate from substances. Q: Whence God? A: From himself; He is *causa sui*. (2) Substances standardly have contingent properties. Q: Does God? A: No; He is in all respects (self-) necessitated. (3) Substances standardly have spatiotemporal emplacement. Q: Does God? A: No; He, unlike standard substances, exists altogether outside place and time. And so on. No sooner has western theology made God a substance in order to satisfy its ontological predilections than it has to break all the rules for substances, and take away with one hand what it seemed to give us with the other.

But in conceptualizing God in terms of *process* — as a characteristically unified family or system of transcendent processes bearing *ab extra* on humankind and world — we overcome many such difficulties at one blow. For it now becomes far easier to understand how God can be and be operative. To be sure, conceiving of God in process terms involves recourse to various processes of a very special kind. But extraordinary (or even supranatural) *processes* pose far fewer difficulties than extraordinary (or let alone supranatural) *substances*. After all, many sorts of processes, are in their own way unique — or, at any rate, very radically different from all others. It is not all that hard to see that processes like the creation of a world or the inauguration of its nomic structure are by their very nature bound to be unusual. But in the world of processes, that is not all that strange.

Moreover — crucially — God is a *person*. And so, once we have an account of personhood in process terms as a systemic complex of characteristic activities, it is no longer strange to see God in these terms as well. If we "processify" the human person, then we can more readily conceive of the divine person in process terms as well. God is now understood as a complex system of characterized processes that creates and sustains the world and endows it with law, beauty (harmony and order), value, and meaning.

The process approach accordingly affords a framework for the conceptualization of God that not only removes many of the difficulties inherent in the thing-oriented, substantival approach of traditional metaphysics, but also makes it vastly easier to provide a philosophical rationale for the leading conceptions of Judeo-Christian religiosity.

## The Agenda for Process Philosophy

As these deliberations indicate, the process approach has many assets. But it has some significant liabilities as well. For it is by no means unfair to the historical situation to say that process philosophy at present remains no more than a glint in the mind's eye of certain philosophers. All that we have so far are suggestions, sketches, and expressions of confidence. The work of developing the process doctrine to the point where it can be compared with other major philosophical projects like materialism or absolute idealism still remains to be done. Many writers have hinted at a process philosophy, but nobody has yet developed one—not even Whitehead, though he has perhaps gone further in this direction than anyone else.

Take an example. What is it that makes *"this* typing of *and"* and *"that* typing of *and"* two instances of the same process? Obviously it is not the sameness of the product—identical *ands* can in principle be produced in very different ways by very different processes. Rather it is that the two concrete processes invoked are simply two different spatiotemporal instances of the same generic procedure—that exactly the same recipe is followed in either case. Clearly the theory of process individuation and reidentification needs to be carefully worked out. The issue is complicated. For processes *are* sometimes collected together not through processual sameness but merely a sameness of product. Take Aristotle's example of "building a house." Clearly, house building is not really a single sort of process at all but a family of processes linked only by a sameness of product. What this sort of complexity is needs to be worked out carefully.

Moreover, we need a more detailed theoretical analysis of the interrelationships of processes. It is clear, for example, that two such relationships are fundamental.

1. The process/subprocess relation that makes one process into a subsidiary component or constituent of another.

2. The concrete-process/process-type relationship that renders two given concrete processes instances of a common type—presumably under the aegis of a principle of commonality of structure.

The character and connection between these modes of process relationship is something that very much needs to be clarified.

To develop an adequate groundwork for process philosophy we need:

—An analysis of the conception of process in its various manifestations and an explanation of which of its features have primary importance for metaphysical purposes

—A survey of the major sorts of processes that bear importantly in metaphysical issues

—A thoroughgoing examination of the nature of emergence, novelty, innovation, and creativity

—A clear scheme for distinguishing the salient features of diverse processes: living versus inert, conscious versus unconscious

—A classifying taxonomy of processes of various sorts

—Provision of a cogently developed line of argument for the primacy of process

—An integrated and coordinated presentation of the scientific and philosophical ideas relating to processes

—A systematic survey of the pivotal issues from a process point of view to show how the process approach can avert difficulties

— A reasoned schema for distinguishing and characterizing natural processes in a hierarchical format (proto-physical, physical, chemical, biological, social), suitably distinguishing each level from and yet relating it to the next

This list is only the starting point. To provide an adequate account of process philosophy we need cogent and integrated series of well-developed expositions and arguments to articulate and substantiate the central theses of this position. A great deal of work remains to be done before process philosophy becomes anything like a well-defined philosophical doctrine. Perhaps, as Andrew J. Reck has shrewdly noted, "the unfinished and never-to-be-finished quality of [processual] flux has seduced many adherents to the metaphysics of process away from systematic theory-building."[9] Be this as it may, the fact remains that at this state of the historical dialectic, process philosophy is not a developed *doctrine* but a projected *program.* All that can be said at this time — though said with a considerable degree of confidence — is that this program is well worth pursuing. On all indications — and there are a good many of them — the process approach to philosophical issues offers good promise of engendering a substantial philosophical doctrine that has much interest in itself and can overcome various serious defects of the available alternatives. But we stand at the frontier here precisely because there is still so much to be done.[10]

## Appendix: Process Semantics

The idea of *nonexistent individuals* has long troubled subject-predicate theorists. How can there possibly be a nameable individual — such as the winged horse Pegasus — that does not actually exist?[11] In standard logic, after all, "... a ..." is equivalent to "$(\exists x)(x = a \, \& \, \ldots x \ldots)$." But how are we then to avert the awkward consequence that the truistic premise

winged horse (Pegasus)

does not yield the patently false conclusion:

$(\exists x)$ x is a winged horse.

Bertrand Russell's well-known theory of descriptions endeavored to resolve the issue within the framework of subject-predicate logic, but ran into various difficulties which need not be rehearsed here.

In the middle years of this century, W. V. O. Quine suggested the interesting idea of dispensing with named individuals altogether in semantical theory, replacing them with suitable "adjectives."[12] Dismissing the substantive *Pegasus,* we are to resort to the object-description *pegasizes.* For Quine's approach we are to rephrase the equation "x = a" as a predication where " = a" is taken as a general term, so that "Pegasus is a winged horse" becomes the harmless truism: "Whatever pegasizes (i.e., nothing) is a winged horse." In such cases the singular term or name "comes to play the role of the 'F' in 'Fa' and ceases to play that of the 'a'."[13] In this vein, Quine speaks of an "artificial and trivial-seeming device (which creates) the *ex hypothesi* unanalysable, irreducible attribute of *being Pegasus,* . . . . The noun 'Pegasus' itself could then be treated as derivative, and identified after all with a description: 'the thing that is-Pegasus', 'the thing that pegasizes.'"[14] The singular term for a nonexistent such as Pegasus is thus switched to a predicative position, so as to become a general term. We trade that noun in for a less problematic adjective. Pegasus simply vanishes as a "nonexistent *individual.*"

But Quine is left standing in an anomalous position. For his elimination of singular terms in favor of adjectives does not, as he himself recognizes, involve the actual elimination of objects to which the *ex hypothesi* noninstantiated predicate is (nominally) attributed: "the objects stay on as values of the variables though the singular terms be swept away."[15]

This uncomfortable halfway house can be abandoned, however, if we shift to a process semantics. On such an approach, one would look at "pegasizing" not as a characteristic attribute that represents a *property of individuals,* but as a *process* that can transpire at coordinate positions.[16] There is now a shift from *adjectives* to *verbs.* Pegasizing is now a very particular sort of process, and the object-neutral conception of "it pegasizes" is analogous to "it rains" or "it is hot." The (false) statement "Pegasus exists" will be glossed as

$$(\exists p)(\text{pegasizing at p})$$

and the (true) statement "Pegasus does not exist" would be glossed as its denial

$$(\forall p) \neg (\text{pegasizing at p})$$

where "p" is a *positional* variable in a space-time framework. After all, what concretizes a particular instance of a physical process of a certain generic sort as a part of the world's activities is precisely its locatability in the space-time framework. It is particularized through the operation of a certain sort of process of location placement (be it ostensive or descriptive in terms of a locational system such as coordinates). Every particular physical process conjoins a "positional" placement aspect with a "structural" type-classification aspect: it is both a *this* and a *what*. (Note: "adding 2 and 2" is not a physical process, but Smith's adding 2 and 2 here and now is.)

This approach, which dispenses with singular object/substance terms altogether and uses quantification as a merely positional device, can be carried over uniformly to existents as well. By parity of reasoning one eliminates not only nonexistents such as Pegasus as (mysterious) objects, but Quine's object-descriptions as well. For, in this approach, one goes beyond seeing pegasizing as an *adjective* to insisting on seeing it as a genuinely process-indicative *verb*.

But now a process semanticist can carry the preceding idea one step further. For one can proceed to adopt a uniform approach to existents and nonexistents, putting quining ("to quine") along with pegasizing ("to pegasize"). There is no longer any need for a shadowy variable-range of nonnameable individuals because one can straightforwardly operate with instances of verb-application. "It quines here" does duty for "Quine is here," and "it quines somewhere" replaces "Quine exists." "Quine is a philosopher" — that is, "Quine sometimes philosophizes" — does not now represent the subject-predicate claim:

philosopher (Quine)

but rather the process-relating claim that Quine sometimes philosophizes, namely:

some philosophizings are (parts or aspects of) quinings

or more fully

($\exists$p)(it philosophizes at p & it quines at p & (it philosophizes at p @ it quines at p)).

(Here @ represents *containment* or *inclusion* among processes.) Accordingly, the process semanticist treats *nonexistent* particulars and *actual* particulars alike — both are reflected in processes that may or may not be realized at coordinate reference positions.

In general, a process semantics must accomplish with verbs and adverbs what a semantics of individuals accomplishes with properties and relations. When the one says "X has the property F" the other says "X functions F-ly" for some suitably F-corresponding process. (Thus "X is triangular" becomes "X disports itself triangularly.") And where the one says "X bears the relation R to Y" the other says "X functions R-ly towards Y." (Thus "X is north of Y" becomes "X locates itself to-the-north-of Y-ly.")

Further refinements suggest themselves. For example, one can now also introduce process/action variables. For this purpose we might as well use the convenient x, y, z, . . ., now freed from their previous role as individual-object variables. And we shall further adopt the notation "T(x)" for "the process x is of type T," as a mechanism of process-description in the place of object-characterization.

This variant semantics makes it possible to overcome some well-known difficulties that affect the standard thing-property semantics.

Consider, for example, Donald Davidson's well-known complaint of that standard subject-predicate logic has difficulty in coming to terms with:

(1) X buttered the toast slowly and deliberately.

As he sees it, the closest one can come to formulate this by standard means is:

(2) X buttered the toast slowly and X buttered the toast deliberately.

And Davidson now objects: "The trouble is that we have nothing here we would ordinarily recognize as a singular term. Another sign that we have not caught the logical form of the sentence is that in this last version there is no implication that any *one* act was both slow and deliberate."[17]

But recourse to a semantics of processes serves to avert these difficulties. To render (1) we first move to:

(3) (∃y)(y is an action of buttering toast & y is an X-performed action & y is a careful action & y is a deliberate action).

The final step in the rendition is to gloss that individual-object reference to X processually by making use of the equivalence:

y is an X-performed action = (∃p)(it y's at p & it X's at p & (it y's at p @ it X's at p)).

We then arrive at:

(4) (∃y)((toast buttering (y) & (∃p)((it y's at p & it X's at p) & (it y's at p @ it X's at p)) & deliberate action (y) & slow action (y))).

Observe (a) that there is now indeed something in this statement that "we would ordinarily recognize as a singular term," namely, "a (certain particular) toast buttering," and (b) that the formulation of (4) makes it transparently clear that a single action is at issue throughout. Thus in the language of processes, the formalization of (1) presents no great problems. Its truth-conditions can be formulated more effectively in terms of processes and their relations than in terms of things and their properties.

As this brief sketch indicates, a semantics of processes is a useful resource that affords means for overcoming some of the characteristic limitations, problems, and difficulties of a semantics of objects-and-attributes.

# Notes

1. A. N. Whitehead, *The Concept of Nature* (Cambridge: Cambridge University Press, 1920), chap. 3.

2. A. N. Whitehead, *Process and Reality* (New York: Macmillan, 1929), pp. 47, 124.

3. Ibid., pp. 318, 471.

4. The events that constitute a process must be temporally coordinated. But they need not be causally connected. The king's morning toilette is a process. He arises, and then washes, and then brushes his teeth, and so on. The unifying linkage of this complex process is "and this." But there is no causal connection. (He does not brush his teeth *because* he has washed.) In consequence, specifically *causal* processes constitute a particular sort of process.

5. "Bad Faith," in *Being and Nothingness,* trans. Hazel Barnes (New York: Pocket Books, 1966), pp. 107ff.

6. David Hume, *A Treatise of Human Nature,* book II, part IV, sect. 6, "Of Personal Identity." In the "Appendix," Hume further elaborates: "When I turn my reflection on *myself,* I never can perceive this *self* without some one or more perceptions; nor can I ever perceive anything but the perceptions. It is the composition of these, therefore, which forms the SELF."

7. Miguel de Unamuno, *Del sentimiento tragico de la vida,* ed. P. Felix Garcia (Madrid, 1982), p. 52.

8. For a useful anthology on the topic, see *Process Theology: Basic Writings,* ed. Ewert H. Cousins (New York: Macmillan, 1971), which seeks to integrate the tradition of Whitehead with that of Teilhard de Chardin.

9. Andrew J. Reck, "Process Philosophy: A Categorical Analysis," in *Studies in Process Philosophy II,* ed. R. C. Whattemore, *Tulane Studies in Philosophy* 24 (New Orleans: Tulane University Press, 1975), p. 59.

10. I am indebted to Johanna Seibt and David Carey for constructive comments on a draft of this paper.

11. On the history of the issue see chap. 4, "The Concept of Nonexistent Possibles," in Nicholas Rescher, *Essays in Philosophical Analysis* (Pittsburgh: University of Pittsburgh Press, 1969), pp. 73–109.

12. W. V. Quine, "On What There Is," *The Review of Metaphysics* 2 (1948), pp. 21–38; rpt. in *From a Logical Point of View* (Cambridge, Mass.: Harvard University Press, 1953), pp. 1–19.

13. W. V. Quine, *Word and Object* (Cambridge, Mass.: Harvard University Press, 1980), p. 179, sect. 37.

14. Quine, "On What There Is," p. 8.

15. Quine, *Word and Object,* sect. 40, p. 192n.1.

16. On the logic of position see chap. 13, "Topological Logic," in Nicholas Rescher, *Topics in Philosophical Logic* (Dordrecht: D. Reidel, 1968), pp. 229–49.

17. Donald Davidson, "The Logical Form of Action Sentences," in *The Logic of Decision and Action,* ed. Nicholas Rescher (Pittsburgh: University of Pittsburgh Press, 1967), p. 81.

# WHITEHEAD AND MEAD

# Whitehead and Dewey on Experience and System

### DONALD W. SHERBURNE

Whitehead has generally been viewed as just a bit apart from the mainstream defined by the so-called "classical" American philosophers, so in this paper, in an effort to counteract this impression, I shall begin by drawing out and emphasizing the extensive similarities between Whitehead and Dewey before looking at, and responding to, Dewey's main criticism of Whitehead. I will argue that Dewey's criticism is wide of the mark, and wide of the mark in part, I suspect, because of a rather unusual circumstance surrounding the writing of the one major study of Whitehead's thought undertaken by Dewey. That study is Dewey's contribution to the Library of Living Philosophers volume on Whitehead, and the unusual circumstance surrounding its writing will emerge as my study progresses.

Early in the Library of Living Philosophers article, Dewey stresses that "what I have called the background and point of departure seems to be the same for both of us, no matter what deviations may occur later." These deviations will occupy us eventually, but first it is interesting to note Dewey's characterization of the shared beginnings. He isolates three and describes them on the same page: "the ideas that [1] experience is a manifestation of the energies of the organism; [2] that these energies are in such intimate continuity with the rest of nature that the traits of experience provide clews for forming 'generalized descriptions' of nature — the especial business of philosophy according to Whitehead — and [3] that what is discovered about the rest of nature (constituting the conclusions of the natural sciences) provides the organs for analyzing and understanding what is otherwise obscure and ambiguous in experiences directly had"[1]

We must now look harder and more carefully at the account Dewey gives of the "background and point of departure" he shares with Whitehead. In the second section of his paper Dewey elaborates upon his understanding of Whitehead's version of their shared insight that "the traits of ex-

perience provide clews for forming 'generalized descriptions' of nature."
Noting Whitehead's well-known denial of the bifurcation of nature, Dewey
goes on to comment that "no doubt the denial has its completion in the
express sense that physical nature must be such as to account for the specialized peculiarities of human experience, while the latter provides clews
to be used in expanding to their full significance that which physical science discovers."[2] Then, quite on his own, Dewey goes on to make the point
central to Whitehead's whole project. Whereas as long as Newtonian physics dominated science dualism was enormously tempting (because there
was such a huge difference between the traits exhibited by the objects that
populated Newtonian nature on the one hand, and the features of human
experience, on the other), once Newtonian physics was surpassed, then the
door was open to a denial of a difference between the traits of nature and
the traits of human experience. In a gesture of genuine respect Dewey observes, "The genius of Whitehead is exhibited in the earliness of his perception that the new mathematical physics did away with the supposedly scientific foundations, upon the physical side, which gave obvious point to
the separation."[3]

I will take one more paragraph to emphasize as strongly as possible the
extent to which Dewey shares in Whitehead's fundamental project. Dewey
goes on, immediately following this quotation, to present three passages
from Whitehead that Dewey sees as presenting the very heart of the "point
of departure" the two men share. All three of the passages from Whitehead that Dewey selects are from *Adventures of Ideas* and they read: "It
is a false dichotomy to think of Nature *and* Man. Mankind is that factor
*in* Nature which exhibits in its most intense form the plasticity of nature.
. . . An occasion of experience which includes a human mentality is an
extreme instance, at one end of the scale, of those happenings which constitute nature. . . . The direct evidence as to the connectedness of one's immediately past occasions can be validly used to suggest categories applying to the connectedness of all occasions in nature."[4] Dewey's summary
reflection on these passages marks him as being in a most profound sense
a card-carrying Whiteheadian. He concludes:

> The idea that the immediate traits of distinctively human experience are highly
> specialized cases of what actually goes on in every actualized event of nature
> does infinitely more than merely deny the existence of an impassable gulf
> between physical and psychological subject-matter. It authorizes us, as
> philosophers engaged in forming highly generalized descriptions of nature,
> to use the traits of immediate experience as clews for interpreting our obser-
> vations of non-human and non-animate nature. It also authorizes us to carry
> over the main conclusions of physical science into explanation and descrip-
> tion of mysterious and inexplicable traits of experience marked by "conscious-
> ness." It enables us to do so without engaging in the dogmatic mechanistic

materialism that inevitably resulted when Newtonian physics was used to account for what is distinctive in human experience.[5]

I have not forgotten those deviations Dewey alluded to, but before I turn to them, I want to back away from both Whitehead's and Dewey's language to give my own version of the significance of these "shared beginnings," this shared "point of departure." Dewey wanted philosophers to put more emphasis on understanding their discipline as a historical phenomenon, wanted a genetic-functional account rather than an ontology built out of stiff, unbending categories. What follows is, in the briefest of nutshells, my version of such an account. It uses as a diagnostic tool a casual remark once made by Paul Weiss, who opined that three philosophers have succeeded in doing justice to man as a part of nature — Aristotle, Hegel, and Whitehead. That observation, for me, sets the parameters in terms of which one can grasp the history of philosophy in its deepest significance. The aim of philosophy, if one takes the accomplishments of the giants in the tradition seriously, is to give an account of nature, and of human being, that is such that human being can be seen to be an integral part of nature. Aristotle is still "the Philosopher" from this perspective, and one justifies this term of praise because of the way he was able to shape a vocabulary that was able to understand the crucial aspects of human being in just those terms that he used to understand the crucial aspects of nature. Richard Rorty, of course, would roll his eyes at this point. He has written that a post-Philosophical culture "would contain nobody called 'the Philosopher,'"[6] and this swipe at Aristotle is expanded by the claim that in his *Metaphysics* Aristotle is "solemnly laying down dicta which are utterly irrelevant to the kind of work he was really good at, the kind of thing we get in the *Historia animalium.*"[7] I would certainly not want to deny that Aristotle was good at what he did in the *Historia animalium,* but Rorty's expression "really good" speaks worlds about his genetic analysis of Philosophy (with a capital *P*). But I would be willing to bet that when St. Thomas and Dante, a millennium and a half after the death of Aristotle, thought about what Aristotle was good at, the *Historia animalium* was not what leaped to mind!

But back to my genetic analysis, not Rorty's. When the Copernican revolution knocked the props out from under Aristotle's vocabulary for talking about nature, and replaced it with a very different vocabulary, the task of philosophy became finding a way to complete the Copernican revolution by generating a way of doing justice to human beings as a part of nature as it was now understood. Hobbes is the fascinating figure of this post-Copernican era, for he failed in that, while he clearly saw humankind as a part of nature, the concepts at his disposal did not permit him to do justice to that human being he was putting in the new version of nature. (In my own view, Rorty is Rorty just because he accepts a Hobbesian account of humankind, a materialist, behaviorist account that cannot do justice to the character of human experience any more than can the account found in the first one hundred fifty pages of *Leviathan.*) Descartes' dualism or some form of idealism seemed to be the only alternatives, but Descartes' bifurcation removed human being from nature while Hegel's idealism, brilliant as it was, was a big fudge in that the nature in which it placed human being was the peculiarly human "nature" of human history and not the nature of Galileo and Newton. (Kant, in contrast, had the real nature in view but failed to reach it because he insisted on trying to do justice to nature as a part of humankind, rather than humankind as a part of nature.) This genetic account of philosophy sees the scientific revolution of the twentieth century as ushering in the possibility of finally completing the Copernican revolution precisely because the notion of nature has been modified in ways that invite the possibility of seeing human being as a part of that nature while still doing justice to the nature of human being and its experience. Whereas Dewey and Whitehead are in the forefront of those struggling to complete the Copernican revolution, they are by no means alone — one need only think of Teilhard de Chardin, Polanyi, and Merleau-Ponty to realize that they have a lot of company bringing a variety of perspectives to the completion of the self-same task.

But now it is time to turn to Dewey's disagreements with Whitehead, for in spite of the enormous overlap in terms of background and point of departure, "deviations," as Dewey says, do occur later. The criticisms of Whitehead all spin out of a reference to, as Dewey says, "a mathematical strain [which] dominates his cosmological account."[8] Or again, in referring to Whitehead's aspiration to construct a "coherent, logical, necessary system of general ideas in terms of which every element of our experience can be interpreted," Dewey claims that this aspiration suggests "the kind of structure exhibited in pure mathematics. It seems to go much further than the mere statement — to which no exception can be taken — that the different portions of any philosophical scheme must hang together."[9] And again, we find Dewey condemning in Whitehead's work "the abstract formalization that defines systematization upon the model provided by mathematics."[10]

These comments, as the basis of Dewey's uneasiness with Whitehead's metaphysics, rest on a mistaken understanding, which in turn follows, I strongly believe, from that "unusual circumstance" to which I have referred. It emerges in the first footnote in Dewey's article, where, after citing a passage in *Adventures of Ideas,* he adds: "The fact that my further references and quotations are limited to this particular book of Whitehead's is partially due to the limitations under which this essay is written."[11] My hunch is that Dewey wrote his article at his summer place and had not brought along *Process and Reality* or any other work by Whitehead. But in any case, it is in the very first section of the first chapter of the first part of *Process and Reality* that we find the extraordinary passages where Whitehead, one of the great mathematicians of his time, condemns any attempt to foist the method of mathematics off on philosophy. Let's attend to Whitehead:

> Philosophy has been misled by the example of mathematics. . . . The verification of a rationalistic scheme is to be sought in its general success, and not in the peculiar certainty, or initial clarity, of its first principles. . . . Philosophy has been haunted by the unfortunate notion that its method is dogmatically to indicate premises which are severally clear, distinct, and certain; and to erect upon those premises a deductive system of thought.

> But the accurate expression of the final generalities is the goal of discussion and not its origin. . . . The primary method of mathematics is deduction; the primary method of philosophy is descriptive generalization. Under the influence of mathematics, deduction has been foisted onto philosophy as its standard method, instead of taking its true place as an essential auxiliary mode of verification whereby to test the scope of generalities.[12]

My conclusion is that had Dewey studied *Process and Reality* with the same care he obviously lavished on *Adventures of Ideas,* he would have realized not only that he and Whitehead shared "background and point of departure," but that they went much further down the path of philosophy together than Dewey had ever realized. Dewey was concerned that philosophy not consider itself as an intellectual report from the outside upon a subject matter that it looked upon as complete and finished in itself. He fought against the idea that philosophy is a finished set of meanings, a formal, static product of intellectual analysis. Rather Dewey, while he does see philosophy as engaged in the search for generic traits of experience, and realizes that this involves a "purification" of experience, that is, some sort of systematization of experience, nevertheless wants a systematization that remains close, close, close to the ground, so that it is ready at every turn to loop back to primary experience to reform and direct it. Dewey knows that you have to have secondary discourses derived from primary experience, and he knows that science is one such secondary discourse. But the systematization of science is close to the ground, involving a sort of horizontal type of abstraction rather than building straight up into a sharply vertical abstraction of the Hegelian or Platonic sort. Dewey's reconstruction in philosophy is deeply suspicious of system and abstraction, but he knows you cannot get at the generic traits of primary experience without some abstraction and some systematization. He distrusts system, and he needs system — that is his problem. Whitehead has a system, and Dewey thinks it is the bad kind, too final, too mathematical, too vertical, too removed from primary experience to admit the looping return to experience that lights up the values that might be brought about in the culture. And here Dewey is wrong. It might have helped him to see this if he had read in *Process and Reality* not only the passages on mathematics and method already quoted, but the following passage from the end of the preface: "There remains the final reflection, how shallow, puny, and imperfect are efforts to sound the depths in the nature of things. In philosophical discussion, the merest hint of dogmatic certainty as to finality of statement is an exhibition of folly."[13]

Finally, Dewey should have sensed from his reading of *Adventures of Ideas* that Whitehead has a low, horizontal systematization that easily loops back to impact upon primary experience. It is there, in the introduction, that Whitehead introduces the famous opposition of Steam and Barbarians on the one hand, and Democracy and Christians on the other. The insight is that as a culture moves from one age to another, that movement is brought about by the impact of senseless agencies on the one hand, and formulated aspirations on the other. In the world of the Roman Empire the senseless agency, beyond the range of philosophy, was the brute force of the barbarians, while the formulated aspirations also shaping the cultural transition were found in the beliefs and values of the Christians. The analogous elements shaping the development of the European Renaissance were Steam, the senseless agency, and Democracy, the formulated aspiration. The formulated aspirations that mold cultures emerge from philosophical understandings. The whole point of *Adventures of Ideas* is to show that the scientific developments of the twentieth century require new philosophical understandings, to adumbrate Whitehead's version of those understandings in a less technical form than they were given in *Process and Reality,* and then to tease out of these understandings new formulated aspirations capable of shaping the future development of our culture. The famous part IV of that book, titled "Civilization," which generates and explores the notions of Beauty, Zest, Peace, and Adventure, is a laying out of a set of formulated aspirations apt for guiding cultural development now, here, today. This is a looping return to primary experience if there ever was one. I think Dewey never got a sense of the structure of that volume; if he had, I think he might have seen that Whitehead had worked out a mode of systematization that avoided certainly many, if not all, of the problems Dewey had with traditional metaphysics, and at the same time looped back again and again to the very practical, concrete issues that shape the character of a culture.

# Notes

1. Paul Schilpp, ed., *The Philosophy of Alfred North Whitehead* (New York: Tutor, 1951), p. 645; numbers added.

2. Ibid., p. 646.

3. Ibid., p. 647.

4. Alfred North Whitehead, *Adventures of Ideas* (New York: Macmillan Co., 1933), pp. 99, 237, 284.

5. Schilpp, ed., *Philosophy of Whitehead,* pp. 647–48.

6. Richard Rorty, *Consequences of Pragmatism* (Minneapolis: University of Minnesota Press, 1982), p. xxxix.

7. Richard Rorty, "Comments on Sleeper and Edel," *Transactions of the Charles S. Peirce Society* 7 (Winter 1985), p. 44.

8. Schilpp, ed., *Philosophy of Whitehead,* p. 646.

9. Ibid., p. 657.

10. Ibid., p. 661.

11. Ibid., p. 644.

12. Alfred North Whitehead, *Process and Reality,* corr. ed. (New York: Free Press, 1978), pp. 8, 10.

13. Ibid., p. xiv.

# Mead and the Social Self

MITCHELL ABOULAFIA

Through the haze of our postmodern times, it is a rather difficult task to catch a glimpse of the "self" as it has wandered down the highway of despair that Hegel called history. It has been battered, torn asunder, and semipermanently deconstructed; no lesser foes than those who view Nietzsche as a kindred spirit have been ready and willing to provide the dialogue for the final self-destructive act. Can G. H. Mead offer us anything in times such as these? As a grandchild of the Enlightenment, Mead must be a mind for a different age. And even if it is true that some sociologists or social psychologists have managed to use his ideas over the years, what can this marginalized pragmatist and so-called social behaviorist offer philosophers, whether they be analytically fine-tuned or continentally inspired, in the late twentieth century?

Mead provides a model of the ontogenesis of the self and self-consciousness that is worthy of further attention, not only for what it actually accomplishes, but for the avenues it opens up. There has been noteworthy recent work on Mead; Habermas, for example, has attempted to show how Mead represents a turning point in modern thought because of the manner in which he moves beyond philosophies of consciousness with a theory of communicative action.[1] I would like to address several of the more striking features of Mead's model of the self, organizing the material in a manner intended to shed some light on a few of the more troubling features of his approach. For instance, I employ his notion of sociality to assist in clarifying the relationship between his well-worn concepts of the "I" and "me." In a larger sense, I address the still vital ideas of a classic figure of American philosophy and suggest some paths for their further development.[2]

Mead stands behind his claim that the self is a social and essentially a cognitive phenomenon with a theory of linguistic and normative development. The genesis of the self, and of what he calls mind, are intimately connected; so we turn first to mind. To understand the development of mind, he asks us to consider the gesture. Animals use gestures to bring about certain consequences. The wolf bares its fangs and another wolf reacts by turning tail or growling back. Gestures of this sort call out specific behaviors, and following a rather functionalist line in this context, Mead wants to claim that meaning is to be understood as the response of the second organism to the behavior of the first.[3] The baring of fangs means here: run or growl. Human beings, however, can respond to their environment in a self-conscious manner; that is, they can be aware of meanings, not merely as third parties labeling the specific responses of other organisms, but as generators of intersubjective meanings, meanings they can recall in the absence of the other.

Human beings develop this capacity through what Mead calls the significant symbol. The significant symbol is a gesture that means the same to me as it does to you, a gesture we both understand. How do significant symbols arise? Mead claims that verbal gestures — speech — yield significant symbols. Unlike the gestures of animals, verbal gestures allow those who employ them to become aware of the gestures as they are being made. As you and I drive down the highway, I suddenly say to you, "watch out!" in order to get you to brake the car before it hits the above-mentioned wolf in the road. I also hear the words "watch out," and I may very well feel my foot beginning to move to hit my nonexistent passenger's brake. The verbal gesture allows an organism to hear and to respond to itself as if it were responding to the gesture of another. It is conceivable that hand gestures could substitute for verbal gestures, and even function as a fully developed sign language, for it is the reflexive capability that Mead is interested in. Nevertheless, while the hand as a manipulator of objects was of crucial importance for the evolution of the species — and still is in the development of the individual — in terms of mind the verbal gesture clearly occupies a unique place in Mead's account.[4] Mead summarizes his position when he says, "Mentality on our approach simply comes in when the organism is able to point out meanings to others and to himself. This is the point at which mind appears, or if you like, emerges."[5]

Mead attempts to account for both ontogenetic and phylogenetic development with his model. Mind originated when a species arose that had the capacity to make and respond to verbal gestures. Presumably such a skill would have provided a survival advantage for the species as a whole and for social groups that used it. We, on the other hand, have no such concerns, for each of us develops a mind in the context of an already evolved language and in a society that maintains itself by employing this language to teach us its norms. It is worth noting that Mead does not deal with the phylogenetic or ontogenetic development of grammatical language, and that commentators have argued that one cannot move from Mead's functional definition of meaning, grounded as it is in the similarity of responses, to sameness of meaning, without a modification of his approach.[6] To address the question of the sameness of meaning, we would have to pay closer attention to the nature of language and to the intricacies of interaction between ego and alter. Habermas actually attempts to modify Mead along these lines by drawing on Wittgenstein, claiming that in return Mead offers Wittgenstein the possibility of accounting for the genesis of rules that govern the use of symbols.[7] In any case, to do full justice to Mead's approach we would have to address his views on how meaning is constituted in and through human activity.[8]

That I can hear myself as if I were the other provides the key for understanding the development of the self. In being able to anticipate the response of the other to my verbal gesture, without explicitly responding as the other does, I show that I have learned to take the attitude of the other. By taking the attitude of the other, I can present myself with the other's responses when the other is not present. I can talk to myself, that is, respond to myself. The term "response," then, refers not only to simple behavioral reactions to stimuli, but also to the answers that one gives to others and to oneself.[9] But what is the self one learns to talk to?

For Mead the self does not arise with the first use of significant symbols, either phylogenetically or ontogenetically; however, through the use of these symbols the skill of taking the attitude of the other is honed. I learn to respond not only to specific gestures, but also to a wide variety of verbal and nonverbal behaviors, as if I were other, which in a sense I am. Eventually human beings respond to sets of integrated behaviors that we call roles. The child learns these roles by taking the attitudes of others, and responding to them from alternative perspectives. The alternative perspectives are themselves sets of behaviors known as roles. In playing the role of doctor, teacher, police officer, the child must also implicitly, or even explicitly, play at being patient, student, and criminal. Clearly we have covered considerable ground in moving from significant symbols to the complex roles just mentioned. But Mead would argue that the mechanism for being able to realize these roles is built into the organism, so to speak, in its capacity for linguistic interaction. It is without a doubt true that for Mead the grasping and manipulation of physical objects is of considerable importance in the development of the child's cognitive skills, such as the skill of being able to delay a response, which is required for the solving of problems. Nevertheless, the constitution of the self presupposes the above-mentioned linguistic and behavioral interactions, and is primarily a result of them. Still, we have not said what the self is for Mead.

Individual roles cannot give us a self, in Mead's view. To merely have a repertoire of roles is just that, a repertoire of roles. It is not a self. The self should be seen as organized, unified, and cognitively accessible. So, instead of thinking of the individual as playing one-on-one roles, we must move to the level of *the game*. Mead likes to use baseball as his example of the game. A game can be thought of as requiring an organized set of responses from its participants. To play third base one must know how the pitcher, catcher, and first baseman, are expected to respond. This organization requires that the individual have some comprehension of the whole game, a whole that has implicit rules, which presumably can be made explicit. To have a self we must participate in social wholes, which are to be viewed not only in terms of formally organized games, but in terms of any social group that can be analyzed systemically. A family could be seen as a social group of this sort. For such social groups the other that is present is not a specific other, but a *generalized other.* Mead writes, "The organized community or social group which gives to the individual his unity of self may be called 'the generalized other.' The attitude of the generalized other is the attitude of the whole community. Thus, for example, in the case of such a social group as a ball team, the team is the generalized other in so far as it enters — as an organized process or social activity — into the experience of any one of the individual members of it."[10]

How helpful is this? In spite of the numerous difficulties that arise with a conception as pliable as the generalized other, we can see that Mead has a genuine insight here. There must be a level at which the integration of the "facets" of the self takes place, if there is to be the unity that we usually associate with the term "self," and it is the net of our social interactions that provides us with this unity. The facets may be seen as repertoires of gestures, nonverbal behaviors, and roles. Further, since for Mead the self is a phenomenon of cognition, we presume that we can be aware of these unified facets, that is, we presume that we can be self-conscious. I should note here an ambiguity in Mead's use of the term "self-conscious." For Mead the term can refer to any awareness of meaning, as when one knows the meaning of a specific significant symbol, or it can refer to being aware of the self. We develop an awareness of self, a self-consciousness, only after we have internalized a generalized other that unifies our responses, that is, frames and organizes sets of responses known as the self.

Yet all of this must indeed sound rather silly if we remain with Mead's baseball-team self. Groups, however, vary in diversity and complexity, and Mead tells us that different groups may have different generalized others; examples of such groups are "concrete social classes or subgroups, such as political parties, clubs, corporations, which are all actually functional social units, in terms of which their individual members are directly related to one another. The others are abstract social classes or subgroups, such as the class of debtors and the class of creditors."[11] If there are potentially so many generalized others providing the organizing frame for the self, have we not arrived back at a self that is a mere plenum of selves or even of roles?

In some sense we do have such a self before us, although Mead has other insights that qualify his position and make it more interesting. For example, he appears to suggest that there may be a generalized other for society as a whole. Where would such a generalized other be found? It would be found in the normative sphere, that is, in the claims that a society makes on individuals to act or live in a certain manner, in the complex and interconnected rules that individuals must learn in order to be active members of a moral community. Mead notes, "There are what I have termed 'generalized social attitudes' which make an organized self possible. In the community there are certain ways of acting under situations which are essentially identical, and these ways of acting on the part of anyone are those which we excite in others when we take certain steps. If we assert our rights, we are calling for a definite response just because they are rights that are universal — a response which everyone should, and perhaps will, give."[12]

Although in this section of *Mind, Self, and Society* Mead goes on to speak of common responses in terms of the institutions of society, I think it safe to assume that Mead not only viewed a societal generalized other as possible, but also actually hoped for an increase in the scope of such a generalized other. I say this in part because of Mead's internationalism, which is reflected in his notion that the self will enhance itself as societies become more internationally minded. So, for example, he goes on to declare, "We all belong to small cliques, and we may remain simply inside of them. The 'organized other' present in ourselves is then a community of a narrow diameter. We are struggling now to get a certain amount of international-mindedness. We are realizing ourselves as members of a larger community. The vivid nationalism of the present period should, in the end, call out an international attitude of the larger community."[13] In another section he tells us that "the only way in which we can react against the disapproval of the entire community is by setting up a higher sort of community which in a certain sense out-votes the one we find."[14] The higher community Mead hopes for is one that is more rational and universal than the nation-state. On the one hand, there is present a Kantian cosmopolitanism in Mead regarding the possibilities of human development in the direction of a moral world order. On the other hand, there is also a Herderesque or Romantic sensibility towards community, for there are indeed specific generalized others and these are grounded in particular social and historical communities, ones that need to be understood in terms of specific institutions. Mead's cosmopolitanism, with its hopes for greater universality through science and reason, must make room for the particular and unique.

As a matter of fact, the unique plays a crucial role in Mead's thought. In spite of what has been said thus far, Mead does not reduce the self to a mere reflection of a given generalized other, nor does he see the self as fixed and unchanging. Mead insists that there is genuine individuality. One of the ways he approaches individuality is to see each self as unique in the manner in which it mirrors the community. Mead refers to Leibniz's monads in this context, for each of us reflects a or the social whole, as each of Leibniz's monads mirrors the universe from a unique vantage point.[15] But Mead is not satisfied with this sort of uniqueness. He thinks the universe a place in which truly novel events take place, and human beings are clearly part of this universe. He claims that in addition to the social self as object, which he at times calls the "me," there is also the "I."[16] In traditional terms one might say that the "I" is the transcendental ego, while the "me" is the empirical ego. For Mead, however, they are functional distinctions, and as such he sees the "I" not only as that which is aware of the "me," but as that which originates responses. Mead declares, "The 'I' is the response of the organism to the attitudes of the others; the 'me' is the organized set of attitudes of others which one himself assumes. The attitudes of the others constitute the organized 'me,' and then one reacts toward that as an 'I'."[17] While the responses of the "I" do relate to the history of previous learned behaviors, its responses are not reducible to this past, for it can act in novel ways.

Once again complications arise. We have seen the self treated as that which mirrors the generalized other. Now it is also clear that if we extend the term self to include the tendency to respond in novel ways, the "I" dimension must be included for a full account of the person. Further, Mead tells us that the actions of the "I" become known only in retrospect, that is, after they are transformed into the "me." He states, "If you ask, then, where directly in your own experience the 'I' comes in, the answer is that it comes in as a historical figure. It is what you were a second ago that is the 'I' of the 'me'."[18] This appears to imply that the "me" should not be understood solely as "the organized set of attitudes of others which one himself assumes," because it also appears to be the home of the memory images of previous responses made by the individual. So, while the structure of the "me" has on first sight an impersonal quality to it, its actual character is to be personalized by specific responses of the individual, responses that are in varying degrees unique.

But how can a single organism be seen as having a unified or unifiable "self" if it is responding in new and unique ways, which are not a part of the "me-self" until they happen, and yet are part of the individual? This is one way of stating the notorious problem of the relationship between the "I" and "me" phases of the individual. I would argue that a full answer to this question calls for a substantial modification of Mead's approach, but we can begin to address the issue here by turning to his concept of "sociality."[19]

For Mead the term "sociality" refers to the capacity to exist betwixt and between two systems. His idea is readily accessible if one thinks of an eco-system before and after the introduction of a new organism or after the mutation of an already existing one. Before the new organism is introduced the ecosystem has one set of relationships that constitute it as a system of interdependent organisms. If we assume that the new organism is suc-cessfully integrated into the original system, we must now speak of a new ecosystem. But before the new system emerges there is a stage of transi-tion. Mead refers to this stage as one of sociality. And, while it occurs throughout nature, when sociality occurs in the world of human beings, it brings with it a new dimension. "But the animal could never reach the goal of becoming an object to itself as a whole until it could enter into a larger system within which it could play various roles. . . . It is this development that a society whose life process is mediated by communica-tion has made possible. It is here that mental life arises — with this con-tinual passing from one system to another, with the occupation of both in passage and with the systematic structures that each involves. It is the realm of continual emergence."[20]

This passage — which is from one of Mead's last projects, *The Philoso-phy of the Present* — provides a rather interesting avenue for coming to terms with the relationship of the "I" and "me." Mead thought of the self as a system of social relations, organized in relation to both specific general-ized others and what we have called the societal generalized other. But he also thought of the self as that which can encompass a personal history, a history generated in the integration of novel responses and the previously organized constellation of responses called the "me." As we have seen, the "I" can respond in novel ways; for example, the role an individual plays may modify his or her prior responses. The individual may then experience a state of sociality — a betwixt and between the old and the new. If the novel is integrated into the prior system, in this case the "me" system, a "new" and coherent self that is rooted in the past self will be formed. I might note in passing that Mead sees time, like history, as being a function of novel occurrences. Without novel events, there would be no direction to time. Novelty is not merely a psychological phenomenon for Mead, it is part and parcel of the fabric of the universe.

Leaving aside Mead's metaphysics of the novel, can his approach tell us anything further about how one learns to be a self that encompasses the novel? It can begin to, if we take a closer look at the process of how sociality becomes part and parcel of one's relationship of oneself. On the one hand, in order to learn verbal gestures and roles we come to expect certain responses from others; on the other hand, from very early on we learn that the other doesn't always meet our expectations. We learn to expect that the other may respond in novel ways, even as we learn to anticipate the typical. In taking the attitude of the other we pass back and forth between perspectives, until being between perspectives becomes, shall we say, second nature. Taking the attitudes of others forces us into states of sociality, both in terms of having to take on the novel responses of others and in terms of the alterations we must face in taking the perspectives of self and other (in roles that we are familiar with but which vary situationally). The individual anticipates the possibility of novel responses, and the need to adjust to them as well as to typical ones. This anticipation of the novel, in turn, encourages the generation of novel responses. One anticipates what the other might do, and acts on it, even when the other has never so acted, and has no intention of doing so. We learn to become our own novel others by having to live with the otherness of the other.

From what has been said, it can well be imagined that the consistency of response by the other must play a crucial role in the child's development. The child must learn to anticipate and make certain responses in order to take on certain roles. The adult assists in this process by recognizing the appropriateness of the child's responses and by acknowledging the child for being able to make them. As a matter of fact, Mead's ideas open up an interesting avenue for addressing the question of recognition, which has remained an important category for interpreting human experience ever since Hegel focused on it in his master-and-slave dialectic. Hegel declares in his *Phenomenology of Spirit* that "self-consciousness exists in and for itself when, and by the fact that, it so exists for another; that is, it exists only in being acknowledged."[21] Being fully human depends on being recognized by others. How does it come to pass that recognition can mean so much to us? I would like to make a few comments on the subject here, comments that will sidestep the intricacies of the process of the development of meaning, as well as the question of mutual recognition.

We have seen that for Mead the verbal gesture allows for the possibility of taking the attitude of the other and making it one's own. We have also noted that in a world in which the other responds both in novel and in typical ways, anticipation is part and parcel of our experience. The child must learn to deal with it and looks to the other to confirm the anticipated. If the child could speak with the voice of an adult, he or she would say the following: "Do my verbal gestures mean what I expect them to mean? As I speak I hear a verbal gesture and I am aware of a meaning, or I should say that I anticipate a meaning. In order to be certain of the meaning the other must respond in a fashion that allows me to confirm my anticipatory understanding. This confirmation entails a response from the other that allows me to know that I know (or at least believe that I know). In other words, I may be cognizant of the anticipated meaning of my verbal gesture when I speak, but I only become certain of it through a second cognitive act, that is, through a re-cognition that depends on the other."

Early in life we look to the consistency of the other's response to assure us of meanings, or perhaps we should say proto-meanings. Eventually direct statements of understanding and sophisticated verbal and nonverbal cues from the other can be substituted for mere consistency of response. In this light, we should call the response of the other that allows me to re-cognize my own anticipatory understanding, the recognition of the other.

At first glance this may appear to trivialize what it means to be recognized by an other, but much hangs on what one means by the other. For Mead we move from gestures to roles to selves, and selves exist in relation to the or a generalized other. In each case I continue to look to the other to affirm what I anticipate, and confirm what I know, as what I claim to know becomes increasingly complex. I remain dependent on the other as the other becomes increasingly abstract and general. Instances of recognition move from the mere recognition of certain words and acts by specific others, to the possibility of being recognized by a much wider community, for example, the scientific community or the moral community, through a generalized other. One can then be recognized not only for specific acts or achievements, but also for just being a certain sort of person, a certain sort of unified self.

# Notes

1. Jürgen Habermas, *The Theory of Communicative Action, vol. 2, Lifeworld and System: A Critique of Functionalist Reason,* trans. T. McCarthy (Boston: Beacon Press, 1987).

2. Mitchell Aboulafia, *Philosophy, Social Theory, and the Thought of G. H. Mead* (Albany: State University of New York Press, 1990). The introduction, as well as several of the pieces in the volume, expand on ideas and themes I outline in this paper.

3. G. H. Mead, *Mind, Self, and Society, from the Standpoint of a Social Behaviorist,* ed. Charles W. Morris (Chicago: University of Chicago Press, 1934), pp. 77–78.

4. Ibid., pp. 67–69.

5. Ibid., p. 132.

6. Ernst Tugendhat, *Self-Consciousness and Self-Determination,* trans. P. Stern (Cambridge, Mass.: MIT Press, 1986).

7. Habermas, *Theory of Communicative Action,* pp. 15–22.

8. Hans Joas, *G. H. Mead: A Contemporary Re-examination of His Thought,* trans. R. Meyer (Cambridge, Mass.: MIT Press, 1985).

9. Habermas, *Theory of Communicative Action,* pp. 13–14.

10. Mead, *Mind, Self, and Society,* p. 154.

11. Ibid., p. 157.

12. Ibid., pp. 260–61.

13. Ibid., p. 265.

14. Ibid., pp. 167–68.

15. Ibid., p. 201.

16. G. H. Mead, "The Social Self," reprinted in *Selected Writings: George Herbert Mead,* ed. A. J. Reck (Chicago: University of Chicago Press, 1964), p. 142.

17. Mead, *Mind, Self, and Society,* p. 175.

18. Ibid., p. 174.

19. Mitchell Aboulafia, *The Mediating Self: Mead, Sartre, and Self-Determination* (New Haven, Conn.: Yale University Press, 1986).

20. G. H. Mead, *The Philosophy of the Present,* ed. Arthur E. Murphy (Chicago: Open Court, 1932; Chicago: University of Chicago Press, 1980), p. 85.

21. G. W. F. Hegel, *Phenomenology of Spirit,* trans. A. V. Miller (Oxford: Clarendon Press, 1977), p. 111.

# TECHNOLOGY
# AND THE PUBLIC GOOD

# Philosophizing as a Public Good: The Many Faces of Philosophical Public Service

## PAUL T. DURBIN

*Vital and courageous democratic liberalism is the one force that can surely avoid . . . a disastrous narrowing of the issue[s]. . . . The question[s] cannot be answered by argument. Experimental method means experiment, and the question[s] can be answered only by trying, by organized effort. The reasons for making the trial are not abstract or recondite. They are found in the confusion, uncertainty and conflict that mark the modern world.*

*It has been stated [here] that philosophy grows out of, and in intention is connected with, human affairs. . . . [This] means more than that philosophy ought in the future to be connected with the crises and the tensions in the conduct of human affairs. For it is held [here] that in effect, if not in profession, the great systems of Western philosophy all have been thus motivated and occupied.*

— John Dewey

*But there are some reasons for optimism emanating from actual developments among liberal and Left [activists] in recent years. The most notable fact is that, throughout the nation, myriad progressive groups have been mobilizing and acting on behalf of crucial issues . . . [including] the legions of intellectuals committed to progressive economic and social policy formulation.*

— Michael W. McCann

Three epigraphs may seem too many, but I include all three in order to set up a clear contrast between academicism and anti-academicism in philosophy. Dewey seems to have expressed the anti-academic ideal for philosophy about as well as anyone. At the opposite extreme, Bertrand Russell can be cited on the ideal of analytical philosophy—an ideal that quickly became transformed into an ideal for *academic* analytical philosophy. In a popularized statement of his ideal, Russell claims that analytical philosophy, with its reliance on logical techniques, is "able, in regard to certain problems, to achieve definite answers." In this, he says, its methods "resemble those of science."[1]

Hans Reichenbach has provided what is perhaps the clearest statement of another aspect of this ideal—its close connection to the empirical sciences. Reichenbach says it is up to "the old-style philosopher to invent philosophical systems, for which there still may be a place assignable in the philosophical museum called the history of philosophy"; in place of this, Reichenbach says the "scientific philosopher" goes to work at serious analysis of the findings of science.[2]

## Academic Philosophy and Social Issues

For decades, this analytical ideal remained dominant—and mostly restricted to academia. But recently it has been proposed that, without violating academic rigor, the analytical philosopher ought to venture outside academia into the public arena. In a posthumously published book, *Professional Philosophy: What It Is and Why It Matters,* Thomas Perry includes a discussion of the "special qualifications which analytic philosophers can bring to the clarification of public issues."[3]

Perry is clear about what his ideal is: "Philosophers are not content to leave the great metaphysical questions to poets, dramatists, and novelists, who examine them *primarily* for the purpose of art rather than for the pursuit of literal truth."[4] He also has his heroes: Russell, Quine, Keith Donnellan, and Saul Kripke, who, he thinks, have produced the purest attempts to use the latest findings of science together with logical techniques to arrive at the literal truth. Though Perry seems to think this goal requires no definition, one of his heroes, Quine, provides a clear explication Russell would have approved of. Quine says that particle physics might offer the clearest example: "Two sentences agree in objective information, and so express the same proposition, when every cosmic distribution of particles that would make either sentence true would make the other true as well." But of course Quine adds that we "can never hope to arrive" at this ideal, so empiricists have substituted for particles the "introspection of sense data," or if they are "more naturalistically inclined, . . . neural stimulation."[5] And, again as everyone knows, Quine does not think even these latter, lesser goals can be achieved.

Perry goes on to count as "serious" philosophers those who recognize that some traditional philosophical problem areas — he lists ethics, aesthetics, political philosophy, and philosophy of law — can only be dealt with in terms of "elucidations," not "exact analyses"; and here he lists more heroes: R. M. Hare, Kurt Baier, William Frankena, and John Rawls.

Furthermore, Perry even admits that "there is more than one way to be serious in philosophy," and here he sets up a contrast with philosophers "in the speculative tradition . . . [of] continental Europe." About the latter he says nothing on the score of whether they can contribute anything to the clarification of public issues.

Perry's precise examples of elucidations — which, because they build on one another with the quality of scientific discourse, therefore contribute to the clarification of public issues — are not actually drawn from his heroes, either the Russellians or those espousing "the moral point of view," but from younger followers in the latter tradition. "Do people have a moral and political right to privacy? Philosophers have recently contributed to public discussion of this and many other practical questions by exploring the conceptual issues and doubts which sometimes make policy choices more difficult." Under this heading, Perry deals with a series of arguments by Judith Thomson, Thomas Scanlon, James Rachels, and Jeffrey Reiman, which "throw increasing light on the privacy problem."[6]

What Perry maintains, in short, is that we are now seeing the analytical tradition bear fruit in contributions to public debate which analytical philosophers are uniquely qualified to provide.

## Anti-Academicism

This view is opposed by many anti-academic philosophers. In *One-Dimensional Man,*[7] Herbert Marcuse accuses analytical philosophers of being reactionary guardians of the status quo; in *The Technological Society,*[8] Jacques Ellul views analytical philosophy as a quintessential example of "technicism" or academicism with absolutely no potential for dealing with the urgent public issues of our technological world; and, of course, in *Philosophy and the Mirror of Nature*[9] and *The Consequences of Pragmatism*[10] Richard Rorty, once himself a leading analyst, has declared that philosophy in the analysts' sense (and perhaps in any sense) is dead.

What I want to discuss here is in this anti-academic tradition — namely, the great variety of contributions that philosophers of all persuasions could and indeed should make to the discussion of urgent contemporary problems.

It was the view of John Dewey — most notably in *Reconstruction in Philosophy*[11] and *Liberalism and Social Action*[12] — that philosophy grows out of and must contribute to the solution of urgent social problems. If a particular approach to philosophy does not contribute to the solution of social problems, Dewey brands it as academic, in a pejorative sense, or blames particular philosophers for contributing to the problems that block progress by clinging to outworn dogmas or persisting in the "quest for certainty." Dewey would invite all philosophers to join with other intellectuals in organizing to employ the "experimental method" to deal with "the confusion, uncertainty and conflict that mark the modern world."

George Herbert Mead certainly shared this view with Dewey, but in at least one place he gave it explicit expression in a way that Dewey did not. According to Mead, the progressive creative problem solving of a community is, by the very fact of its being progressive, an ethical endeavor. Indeed, in his quite early delineation of the various philosophical disciplines as parts of the social *praxis* of a progressive community, Mead defines ethics in just that way. Elsewhere, Mead says, "The order of the universe that we live in *is* the moral order. It has become the moral order by becoming the self-conscious method of the members of a human society. . . . The world that comes to us from the past possesses and controls us. We possess and control the world that we discover and invent. And this is the world of the moral order."[13] For both Dewey and Mead — and, before them, William James — this necessarily ethical, progressive, social problem solving involves the sort of openness to and tolerance of all points of view in a democratic society that is usually associated today with civil-liberties advocates of a progressive sort.

For James and Mead and Dewey, it was enough to define a social movement as progressive if it aimed at the improvement of society by democratic means. Today, we have become more skeptical, perhaps even cynical, about progress.[14] Still, I think the pragmatists' view of social movements as progressive if they help to remove particular "problems that block progress" in the broad historical sense is clear enough, if vague. And perhaps their optimism is preferable to our current mood of cynicism.

That philosophers ought to contribute to this progress was Dewey's main point in *Reconstruction in Philosophy* and *Liberalism and Social Action*. Like all intellectuals facing the urgent crises of the day, we philosophers have our contribution to make — and that includes philosophers of all persuasions. The only condition is that we seek to contribute to progress, to

the solution of real problems that vex not only our own society but humankind world-wide.

Here it may be helpful to provide a note on the activism of James, Mead,
and Dewey. Gary Bullert's *Politics of John Dewey,*[15] contrary to the impression it might give, is really about the most significant philosophical
work Dewey did—as becomes clear by the time one gets to the last two
chapters of Ralph Sleeper's admirable intellectual biography of Dewey,
*The Necessity of Pragmatism.*[16] Of the small number of books on Mead,
I think Hans Joas's *G. H. Mead: A Contemporary Re-Examination of His
Thought,*[17] is the most successful in conveying Mead's activist orientation
and hostility toward academicism. Recent interpretations of James do not
seem to me successful on this score, with the exception of the treatment
of James as a central figure in philosophy before it came to be professional-
ized in Bruce Kuklick's *Rise of American Philosophy.*[18]

## Arguments against Academicism in This Venture

Before turning to what I have in mind that philosophers of various persuasions might offer, I would like to pause a moment to challenge Perry's
proposal about the unique qualifications of analytical philosophers to contribute to the clarification of social problems.

My first reaction, when I read Perry's book, was somewhat petulant,
perhaps even dyspeptic. Like Dewey's and Mead's reactions to the epistemologists of those times (Mead called epistemology "riffraff"), I am inclined to say that much of what Perry praises amounts to academic nit-
picking without the slightest chance of contributing to the solution of
social problems. But, more substantively and objectively, I believe that
there is a problem with Perry's proposal that the pursuit of "the literal
truth"—or even of "conceptual reorganization" as a stopgap on the "serious" philosophical way to literal truth—will be helpful in solving urgent
social problems.

I see several objections that can be raised against Perry.

The first and most devastating comes from empiricist philosophy itself
—"serious" philosophy if there ever was such. Perry praises the literal pursuit of truth, at least as an ideal, and he echoes Russell in saying that analytical philosophy is progressive in the same way that science is. But long
before Thomas Kuhn and other anti-empiricists came on the scene, the
narrowest of logical empiricists had given up on the *achievement* of truth
as the ideal of science; Karl Popper's *Objective Knowledge*[19] can be taken

as the last gasp of the old positivist tradition, and all Popper can offer as an ideal is ever greater *approximation* to the truth. For philosophy, and *a fortiori* for other intellectual disciplines, practitioners must be satisfied with much less.

Less serious philosophers by Perry's standards — and he lumps these under the broad heading of "continental European philosophers" — would object equally strenuously to the claim that the pursuit of literal truth or of conceptual clarification will, in a unique way, help us solve social problems. Philosophers in the existentialist tradition, of whatever stripe, do not even worry about literal truth; if problems are to be solved, it will be by authentic decisions, not the overly cerebral lucubrations of analytical philosophy.

From another perspective, philosophers indebted to Hegel — whether left- or right-wing Hegelians or their descendants — have not generally repudiated his claim that the pursuit of literal truth is not even a human goal; "comprehensive truth," the only thing worthy of the name, belongs to some ideal state that can at best beckon us in a mysterious way toward its pursuit. (In a Marxist version of the dialectic of history, there may be a claim that the ideal state is this-worldly, not otherworldly, but it is still off in the future and cannot be known now as our guide along the way.) But Hegelians of both the left and the right think that they have solutions, if not salvation, to offer to the modern world.

Philosophers still less serious by Perry's standards — and I think here he would list, among others, religious ethicists, neo-Thomists, members of the Society for Christian Philosophy — may actually be the ones today who would say they can contribute to contemporary problem solving from a perspective of the literal truth. Their objection to Perry would be that so often academic purists rule them out *a priori* from even being considered as contributors to the search for solutions of urgent social problems. (Too often, Dewey also seemed to reject help from this quarter, as inherently antiprogressive; but his and Mead's and James's principle of tolerance should have left open the door to religious thinkers if they genuinely want to look for progressive solutions.)

## Contributions of Philosophy
## to Contemporary Social Problem Solving

Now to my main point. The sermon I want to preach here is not just a general admonition to philosophers that they should become involved in progressive, organized, public-interest efforts to solve the major social problems of our technological age. It is not even the negative inverse of this, that (by Dewey's standards) if they do not, they are not doing "real" philosophy — and may even be contributing to the problems that block progress. What I want to emphasize here — when now, at last, I get to my main point — is the variety of specific ways in which philosophers trained in *all* these traditions can make concrete contributions.

1. I do believe, though my negative remarks earlier might suggest the contrary, that analytical philosophers can make something of a contribution. I think it is less likely to be to policy discussions (such as Perry's example of clarifications of the meaning of privacy) than it is to issues involving science and technology. I believe, for instance, that analytical philosophers interested in such topics as artificial intelligence may actually contribute to developments in information technology, in cognitive science, even in the understanding of brain physiology. If I had to choose one example here, it would be Fred Dretske's *Knowledge and the Flow of Information.*[20]

From another perspective, applied ethicists may also contribute to the solution of ethical and social problems. However, under the broad heading of applied ethics, many things are done other than strict conceptual analysis. My favorite example of a contribution applied ethicists have made to the solution of current social problems is the work of philosophers such as Tom Beauchamp on the President's Commission for the Study of Ethical Problems in Medicine and Biomedical and Behavioral Science in the early 1980s.[21]

2. Philosophers can also make contributions of other sorts out of their academic backgrounds. As much out of favor as he may be in philosophical circles today, a philosopher such as Mortimer Adler, in his work with the *Encyclopaedia Britannica* publishers, can contribute significantly to the systematizing and summarizing of knowledge that is so urgently needed to counterbalance the fragmentation of knowledge in the modern world. Indeed, philosophers may be uniquely qualified (not in Perry's sense) to help in encyclopedia publishing, in putting together comprehensive bibliographies and handbooks, and in general, in *organizing* knowledge. Similarly, philosophers of a variety of persuasions can contribute to academic *interdisciplinary teaching* teams and programs that have the same integrative aims — here, to help students integrate their fragmented and specialized knowledge already at the undergraduate level. Even within academia, philosophers can do a public service by joining other faculty members — as John Dewey did — in the fight to protect academic freedom, so often under attack today.

3. Stepping outside the ivory towers of the academy, philosophers can make genuine and creative contributions to public commissions, to tech-

nology assessment boards, to ethics committees for various professions, and so on. In point of fact, it is often, today, religious ethicists who are invited to serve in such capacities. And, in my experience, they seem to do the job quite well, without having the benefit of rigorous analytical training. Of course, applied ethicists are also invited, and some of them do seem to be able to contribute significantly to public discourse, even by way of conceptual analysis of controversial issues — for example, in the Warnock Commission report in Great Britain several years ago. In the United States, I think Christopher Stone's book, *Earth and Other Ethics,*[22] makes a similar contribution in advocating pluralism as a way to justify animal rights, environmental rights, and the rights of future generations.

4. The final way contemporary philosophers can contribute to the modern world is as what I would call secular preachers — advocates of *vision* in the solution of social, political, and cultural problems. Here I think of philosophers like Albert Borgmann in *Technology and the Character of Contemporary Life.*[23] Bruce Kuklick, in *The Rise of American Philosophy,* maintains that this role came largely to be scorned by academic philosophers after the rise of professionalism in the discipline. I believe Kuklick is, for the most part, correct. But I also believe that the small number of philosophers who still feel called upon to play this role — perhaps larger numbers in countries other than the United States — are not necessarily out of the philosophical mainstream, even when their preaching is covertly religious rather than completely secular. The need for vision is so great in a world of fragmented specialized knowledge that it may even be time to welcome religious thinkers back into the philosophical mainstream. Or, if that is too much to swallow, it seems correct to say that academic professionalism in philosophy would be missing an opportunity if no one today were willing to play the role of visionary secular preacher.

## Conclusion

This volume deals with frontiers in American philosophy. What I have claimed here is that there are many ways to advance those frontiers in addition to the academic. For my part, I would side with Dewey and Mead, and maintain that the most important frontiers are not academic; a philosophy true to its traditions from the time of Socrates on will be concerned primarily with urgent real-life problems and only secondarily with academic concerns. If the latter are legitimate at all, it is *only* because they help solve social problems. I recognize that this is a debatable view, but

I think it is as defensible now as it was in Dewey's day — or for that matter in the days of Socrates.

# Notes

1. Bertrand Russell, *A History of Western Philosophy* (New York: Simon and Schuster, 1945), p. 834. The epigraphs are drawn respectively from John Dewey, *Liberalism and Social Action* (New York: Putnam, 1935), p. 92; Dewey, *Reconstruction in Philosophy* (Boston: Beacon Press, 1920; 2nd ed., 1948), pp. xi–xii; and Michael W. McCann, *Taking Reform Seriously: Perspectives on Public Interest Liberalism* (Ithaca, N.Y.: Cornell University Press, 1986), p. 261.

2. Hans Reichenbach, *The Rise of Scientific Philosophy* (Berkeley: University of California Press, 1951), pp. 123–24.

3. Thomas D. Perry, *Professional Philosophy: What It Is and Why It Matters* (Dordrecht: Reidel, 1986), p. xiii.

4. Ibid., p. xiv.

5. W. V. Quine, *Philosophy of Logic* (Englewood Cliffs, N. J.: Prentice-Hall, 1970), pp. 4–5.

6. Perry, *Professional Philosophy,* p. xiii

7. Herbert Marcuse, *One-Dimensional Man* (Boston: Beacon Press, 1964).

8. Jacques Ellul, *The Technological Society* (New York: Knopf, 1964; French ed., 1954).

9. Richard Rorty, *Philosophy and the Mirror of Nature* (Princeton, N.J.: Princeton University Press, 1979).

10. Richard Rorty, *The Consequences of Pragmatism* (Minneapolis: University of Minnesota Press, 1982).

11. John Dewey, *Reconstruction in Philosophy* (Boston: Beacon Press, 1920; 2nd ed., 1948).

12. John Dewey, *Liberalism and Social Action* (New York: Putnam, 1935).

13. George Herbert Mead, "Scientific Method and the Moral Sciences," reprinted in *Selected Writings: George Herbert Mead,* ed. A. Reck (Indianapolis: Bobbs-Merrill, 1964), pp. 248–66.

14. Gabriel A. Almond, Marvin Chodorow, and Roy Harvey Pearce, eds., *Progress and Its Discontents* (Berkeley: University of California Press, 1982).

15. Gary Bullert, *The Politics of John Dewey* (Boston: Beacon Press, 1983).

16. R. W. Sleeper, *The Necessity of Pragmatism: John Dewey's Conception of Philosophy* (New Haven, Conn.: Yale University Press, 1986).

17. Hans Joas, *G. H. Mead: A Contemporary Re-Examination of His Thought* (Cambridge, Mass.: MIT Press, 1985; German ed., 1980).

18. Bruce Kuklick, *The Rise of American Philosophy: Cambridge, Massachusetts, 1860–1930* (New Haven, Conn.: Yale University Press, 1977).

19. Karl R. Popper, *Objective Knowledge: An Evolutionary Approach* (Oxford: Clarendon Press, 1972).

20. Fred I. Dretske, *Knowledge and the Flow of Information* (Cambridge, Mass.: MIT Press, 1981).

21. President's Commission for the Study of Ethical Problems in Medicine and

Biomedical and Behavioral Science, *Compensating for Research Injuries* (Washington, D.C.: U.S. Government Printing Office, 1981); several other studies are on such issues as nonresuscitation, defining death, and access to health care in subsequent years.

22. Christopher D. Stone, *Earth and Other Ethics: The Case for Moral Pluralism* (New York: Harper and Row, 1987).

23. Albert Borgmann, *Technology and the Character of Contemporary Life* (Chicago: University of Chicago Press, 1984).

# Dewey and the Technological Context of Directed Practice

WEBSTER F. HOOD

John Dewey has a theory of technology. American historian Richard D. Mosier contends in *The American Temper* that the history of American ideas culminates in Dewey's philosophy and, even more interesting, that his philosophy can be interpreted as a technological theory of knowledge. He informs us that "ideas are definitions of operations, plans of action, not the mere flow of phenomena in the subjective consciousness; and this development, known as the instrumental theory of knowledge, is in fact a theory of technology as well."[1]

That Dewey had a continuing interest in technology is surely true. We find numerous remarks, in his great volume of writings, on the role of tools in experience, the meaning of work, and the instrumental basis of knowing, as well as frequent references to railways, power stations, and laboratories. Indeed, unlike most of his contemporaries in philosophy, he was keenly aware of the emerging context of technology and its growing importance to philosophic discussion. But nowhere in his writings do we find an extended discussion of technology as such, comparable to his reflections on aesthetics and education, nor anything that approaches an explicit theory of technology.

Nonetheless, Dewey was among the very first contemporary philosophers to recognize that people cannot be understood outside of their principal contexts, one of which is definitive of twentieth-century culture, namely, the context of technology. He clearly recognized that technology presents genuine philosophic problems, requiring analysis and interpretation. Along with a few other philosophers, he made the understanding of technology a central concern throughout his career and argued that the main crises of our times resulted from our failure to address the many problems posed by its rapid growth.

The thesis I explore in this paper is that some of Dewey's chief ideas on technology can be used to understand the pervasive context of technological practice and its relationship to science. Dewey was among the first thinkers to grasp the impossibility of conceiving of contemporary science outside of technology, declaring that scientific investigation was culturally embedded in its instrumentation and special techniques. "The work done (in the laboratory) could no more be carried out without its special equipment of apparatus and technical operations than could the production of glass or electricity nor any one of the great number of industrial enterprises that have taken over as integral parts of *their* especial work processes originating in the laboratory."[2]

We have, in fact, developed a culture that has institutionalized the industrial patterns of regularity and effectiveness and the compelling ideal of human mastery, both of which are projected by scientific research and the technological mode of human action. Take, for instance, an advertisement in *Scientific American* extolling the powers of the Questar visible-data-managing system, a multiple-purpose instrument capable of making distant noncontact measurements and alignments that are extremely precise.[3] The Questar is virtually a "self-contained little laboratory" that can be employed in projects as different as documentation of crystal growth, crack propagation assessment, measurement of thermal expansion of metals in real time, or any problem whatsoever that requires measurement, imaging, and recording. Or consider the widely publicized installation of tiny electrodes in people's mouths to measure differences in plaque acid levels after chewing sugared and sugarless gum following meals. Whatever the project facing us, specially designed instruments, like the Questar and electric probes, stand ready and await our command. Clearly, present science is embedded in technology and supports and cultivates its growth. Ernest Gellner succinctly describes this technological institutionalization of science when he makes the same contention as Dewey: "Modern science is inconceivable outside an industrial society; but modern industrial society is equally inconceivable without modern science. Roughly, science is the mode of cognition of industrial society, and industry is the ecology of science."[4] Following Dewey, it is this technological context that provides "the ecology of science" to which we must now attend.

The question of the technological foundation of scientific praxis is my major problem in all that follows. I have in mind the familiar "hard" sciences as well as science-based professions such as engineering, medicine, and meteorology. Many other science-based professions also come to mind — mineralogy, agronomy, dentistry, radiology, architecture — all of which are professional forms of directed practice. Taking their cue from the dominant context of technology, practitioners of these professions see themselves primarily as problem solvers. Ophthalmologists, for instance, correct vision problems using diagnostic techniques based on optics, neurology, and the physiology of diseases of the eye. Astronautical engineers employ physics, design theory, and electronics to solve problems of the construction and operation of space satellites. Pharmacologists use biochemistry, statistical techniques, and other allied disciplines to control diabetes. My task will be one of constructing a model, based largely on Dewey's *Logic: The Theory of Inquiry,* for analyzing scientific and science-based practices. It will be a model only in the sense of uncovering the interrelations of different concepts and questions, suggested by the *Logic,* that have a bearing on technologically directed practices. Since I can provide here only a sketch for a very large and complex issue, my model must necessarily be provisional. In addition, I will develop my model along phenomenological lines. But first we need to reacquaint ourselves with Dewey's theory of experience and then see how it can be used to understand technologically directed practices.

Human experience, first of all, can be characterized as a growing pattern of transactions with things in our environment, an extensive pattern of doing and undergoing something, at some place and time, *with* something; for instance, trying to light a fire, compose a letter, or drive an automobile across town for groceries. Experience is composed of two moments, which Dewey analytically terms "trying" and "undergoing," each of which corresponds to an active as well as a passive side of conduct. "On the active hand, experience is trying—a meaning which is made explicit in the connected term 'experiment.' On the passive, it is *undergoing.* When we experience something we act upon it, we do something with it; then we suffer or undergo the consequences. We do something to the thing and then it does something to us in return."[5] The prototypical situation always consists of some person standing in some relationship to the surroundings, most commonly assisted by tools and other artifacts.

Second, trying and undergoing are also characterized by one dominant feeling, tone, or mood, one pervasive quality that makes them "*an* experience"—for example, the felt satisfaction of landing a trout, reading a poem, or returning home from a day's work. All the components of an experience for Dewey, no matter how unlike they may be to one another, are pervaded by a unifying quality that renders it "the one qualitatively unique experience which it is."[6] Later we will examine the contribution of felt quality to our understanding of directed practices.

A third defining characteristic of experience is that there is always a centered focus occurring within an unarticulated context or horizon. Experience does not consist of a disordered array of things. When a person has transactions with things in his environment, he finds himself located within a multiplicity of things that stand out from a common background; the surroundings and the items in it, whether they be trees, buildings, or tools, come to be contextual, that is, emerge from a more or less implicit horizon. For instance, I might find myself focusing on one thing in my surroundings — I am chopping wood with an ax — while in subsequent transactions the wood, or whatever I was concerned with, passes into the background or context and other items emerge. Done with splitting the cords, for example, I now find myself cleaning out the log bin before the fireplace. In this manner, there is a shifting focus as I continue to deal with the emerging items present in my field of activity; such activity in its background and foreground discloses vital connections with future items and aspects of experience of which I am not yet aware.

When Dewey refers to forms of technologically directed practices, he normally has in mind "scientific technique," that is, activities that employ instruments, appliances, and techniques of experimentation, whether this occurs in industry and engineering or in the laboratory of the physicist, chemist, or biologist.[7] Both science and technology are culturally developed forms of directed practice: there is planning ahead, noting what happens, relating what happens to what is attempted — all of which involve a governing conception of the desired result and the free search for, and flexible adaptation of, material means to achieve it. In his view, what is essential in knowing and making, or theory and production, is the understanding of relations, especially the relations between our actions and their experienced outcomes. Underlying directed practices, there is the "peculiar combination" of trying and undergoing; or, as he writes, "experience as trying involves change, but change is meaningless transition unless it is consciously connected with the return wave of consequences which flow from it."[8] When we acquire this kind of understanding — Heidegger calls such basic understanding "circumspection"[9] — our actions and their context become more meaningful. Experience is more than a passive adjustment to our surroundings or a mere recording of information; it involves positioning ourselves in such a way that we can deliberately have transactions with things, whose consequences we intelligently register and feed back into the control of future action. Such understanding of relations or intelligence makes directed practices possible.

We have at last reached the point where we can analyze the technological context of scientific and science-based practices. If we interpret Dewey's *Logic: The Theory of Inquiry* as a way of understanding what scientists, engineers, and other professionals actually *do* — exactly what sorts of doings and undergoings occur in the laboratory, the factory, and the test site — we shall better understand the culturally pervasive context of technological practices. Dewey outlines a number of stages that inquiry takes for the researcher-practitioner and critically discloses the *full context* or *situation* as it unfolds in experience. He provides us with a deep appreciation of the open-textured features of technologically directed practice, rather than focusing on the formal features of proof, confirmation, and falsification.

Contrary to what one might expect, he wrote the *Logic* because he was interested, not in the theory of proof, the subject matter of advanced logic, but in the supporting cultural background of inquiry and what it implied for the present. I believe he saw rather clearly the challenge posed by the new cultural praxis created by technology, and admonished us also to recognize it. For, as he put it, "failure to examine the conceptual structures and frames of reference which are unconsciously implicated in even the most factual inquiries is the greatest single defect that can be found in any field of inquiry."[10] Consequently, if my interpretation of the *Logic* is on the right track, its principles are not propositions that are true or false but proposals that grow out of his theory of experience and are relevant or irrelevant in the sense that they help or fail to help us understand the conditions set by technological culture.

This takes us to Dewey's definition of inquiry: "Inquiry is the controlled or directed transformation of an indeterminate situation into one that is so determinate in its constituent distinctions and relations as to convert the elements of the original situation into a unified whole."[11] Dewey expands this initial definition into various stages — the indeterminate situation, the institution of a problem, the determination of a problem-solution, and reasoning — each of which discloses the context relativity of inquiry and the office of experience. The stages constitute a kind of scaffolding that permits us to see the various relationships holding between experience and technologically saturated contexts. We now turn to each of the stages.

First there is *the indeterminate situation: the genesis of the context of inquiry.* The process of inquiry arises only insofar as it is created by responding to an indeterminate situation. According to Dewey, to transform an indeterminate or problematic situation into a significant problem (and for Dewey there is always more than one way to do this), the researcher-practitioner needs to appreciate fully the demands of the situation, making sense of difficult materials that initially make little sense. Since it is always the whole situation that is indeterminate or doubtful, Dewey says that "we are doubtful because the situation is inherently doubtful."[12] And, if we are to comprehend the situation in its initial demands, we need to work with it, freely undergo transactions with its obscure materials, and actively engage it with present intellectual and technical resources. Diagnostic effort must be expended to work out well-defined tasks presumably having determinate solutions. Ingenuity is required by the researcher-practitioner not only to find solutions but also (at this orienting stage) to state the problem. When civil engineers, for instance, deliberate over the construction of a new municipal airport on the outskirts of a large metropolitan area, they find themselves immersed in a complex, confused situation created by a tangle of financial, topographic, and political issues. The problem of building the airport takes the shape of these encompassing issues. After it has been decided where the airport is to go and how to construct it, that is, after the situation has been comprehended by having transactions with it, the engineers now have a problem amenable to their inventory of theoretical and technical resources. But should it appear that the airport they are constructing is leading to the elimination of valued farmland, or to the creation of noise pollution and permanent traffic congestion, the engineers again find themselves thrust into an indeterminate situation. While there are no *a priori* ways to anticipate types of indeterminacy, Dewey points out that this situation might be considered indeterminate in its projected outcome should it appear confused, obscure, or conflicting.[13]

Although it is a truism that problem setting is necessary for problem solving, this does not imply that the conditions for problem setting are themselves a problem — they must somehow *be allowed* to become a problem. If inquiry is basically a matter of problem solving, this does not mean we need feel obliged to accept any question or imagined problem whatsoever as a candidate for consideration. Problems are not simply given or made up in advance by the mind. Dewey has been much misunderstood on this score: problem setting is not the same as problem solving. What his critics have overlooked is his correct emphasis on the lived occasions for problem setting. If it is true that experience is not primarily cognitive, problems must first be allowed to be, to become determinate, and be framed out of the situation in which they arise. At this stage, indeed, problems are determinate only if they can be framed. "Any belief as such is tentative, hypothetical; it is not just to be acted upon, but is to be *framed* with reference to its office as a guide to action. . . . When it is apprehended as a tool and only as a tool, an instrumentality of action direction, the same scrupulous attention will go to its formation as now goes to the making of precision in technical fields."[14]

But what does it mean to claim that problems can be stated only if they can be framed? What does framing have to do with technology? The researcher-practitioner is in the fullest sense an actor, and not a mere spectator, who creatively forms surroundings by selecting and reconstructing materials out of experience. Problem setting is a form of constructive activity in which trying and undergoing are fundamental. When the researcher-practitioner sets or states the problem, he selects what he will treat as its significant materials, fixes the boundaries of his attention to it, and thereby establishes a frame for the problematic materials that allows him to say what needs to be done and what path should be followed. In short, framing the situation makes it possible to say what is wrong and indicate the direction inquiry ought to take. Just as for Hegel, inquiry can be an enriching affair where there is direction; as Dewey writes, "We live forward."[15] Therefore, the activity of problem setting should be understood as an uncovering affair by which the researcher-practitioner, through having transactions, *designates* the things that warrant his attention and *frames* the situation so that he can deal with them.

It is worth noting here that the antecedent conditions of inquiry, the pretechnical and pretheoretical dimensions of experience, are not themselves anything technical or theoretical. Framing or problem setting is possible because something has been already undergone by someone in a living situation, characterized by a unifying quality that makes "the one qualitatively unique experience which it is."[16] In other words, problem setting finds its roots in unique, local situations, where we experience a complex of particulars united by a pervasive quality, which could be confusion, conflict, frustration, curiosity, or some other felt meaning. All antecedent conditions of inquiry are concrete disclosures made possible by undergoing. In Dewey's own words, "the peculiar quality of what pervades the given materials, constituting them a situation, is not just uncertainty at large; it is a unique doubtfulness which makes that situation to be just and only the situation it is."[17] Moreover, "it is this unique quality that not only evokes the particular inquiry engaged in but that exercises control over its special procedures."[18] A chemist, for example, when given a strange substance, might playfully examine it and develop a "feel" for the substance through his instruments; and this could in turn suggest specific directions for investigation and exercise control over the full course of his study.

We have now arrived at the second stage of inquiry—the statement of a problem: the articulation of a frame and its completion. Pasteur's classic experiments demonstrating the existence of microorganisms are a good example of what Dewey had in mind for this phase of inquiry. Pasteur began to state a problem, or articulate and project a frame, when he hypothesized that very small particles of living matter (germs) had to be present before the fermentation of sugared yeast water could begin.[19] Since these living particles were too small and too few to be seen, the experiment of course had to be indirect. Pasteur articulated and constructed a frame capable of embodying his hypothesis by employing glass flasks, a vacuum pump, tubing, a source of heat, and a few artifacts. He showed that air that had been passed through a red-hot tube (calcined air) could be introduced into a vessel (first suitably sterilized by boiling) containing fermentable material, without fermentation occurring. On the other hand, when ordinary air was passed into an identical vessel containing the same material, fermentation soon started. An essential element in the construction of his frame was his manufacturing a reliable nutrient (extract of yeast, nitrogenous substances, mineral salts, and sugar) which could repeatedly be made available without starting to ferment on its own. He had now completed his frame and was ready to conduct his experiment. Simple as Pasteur's arrangement of instruments and materials was by comparison to present laboratories, it was not just that fermentation depended on instrumentation and standardization; rather, the phenomenon of fermentation had been largely constituted by the completion of the frame supported by the technological setting of the laboratory. Recalling Dewey's definition of inquiry, the transformation of a problematic situation into a more determinate one in the direction of constituting a "unified whole" had begun.

The construction of Pasteur's frame for his experiment takes us to Dewey's third stage of inquiry — *the determination of a problem-solution: the progressive development of a problem.* When Dewey declares that the statement of a problem "has no meaning save as the problem instituted has, in the very terms of its statement, reference to a possible solution, he is not to be taken fully literally."[20] He does not mean to imply that a bare inspection of the statement of the problem will automatically yield a solution or guarantee its resolution. A statement has meaning only if it refers to a conceivable solution or solutions made possible by a referential complex of instruments and skillful operations. The expression "determination of a problem-solution" depends not only on the availability of equipment, instruments, and uniform procedures, but also on the presence of a special configuration of equipment purposefully designed (as we saw with Pasteur) to carry out specific tasks. The determination of the problem-solution refers to the area of planned activity, opened by naming or designating and framing problematic materials so that testing can take place. Returning to Pasteur, he collected dust from ordinary air by sucking a large quantity of air through a cotton filter.[21] He then carefully inserted the cotton filter into the first flask containing sugared yeast water and proceeded to introduce heated air. In the second or control flask containing sugared yeast water, no cotton filter was inserted; but, just as with the first flask, heated air was introduced. After these transactions, the necks of both flasks were drawn down and sealed with flame. As Pasteur had predicted, the flask containing the filter was found vigorously fermenting, while the one without the filter was dormant. Therefore, Pasteur supported his hypothesis that if germs from the atmosphere and elsewhere were not destroyed or kept out of the flasks, fermentation would result.

The germ hypothesis had to be framed before it could serve as a candidate for a "problem-solution"; it took on significance only insofar as it could be operationally understood and tied into the instrumental context of a developing frame. Inquiry for Dewey solves a problem if and only if research entails both a statement of the problem and future restatements — thus the conjoining of the term "problem" with "solution" in the expression "problem-solution," indicating the tentativeness of any solution. A problem for inquiry is always progressively disclosed, deliberately framed and reframed in a sustaining technological context. For example, Pasteur reframed his problem and conducted a second set of experiments.[22] He substituted asbestos for the cotton, and the outcome was the same: fermentation. Obviously, since two different filters produced the same results, the presence of the filter was not responsible for the fermentation. A third and even more striking reframing, marked by a single change in one operation in his field of planned activity, further developed the problem. He showed that introducing a dust-filled, asbestos filter into the flask in the usual way *after it had been heated* produced no fermentation. On the other hand, the same filter filled with dust *but not heated* caused fermentation.

In addition to calling our attention to the progressive development of problems, Dewey argues that there is no real distinction between the context of discovery and the context of justification. If he is correct in holding that we are dealing with the instrumentally staged development of *one* problem, no real or important distinctions can be made between discovery and justification. We misunderstand directed practices when we focus exclusively on the logical relations of statements after research has ended, for we lose sight of their context-dependency and thereby miss the truly revealing phases and distinctions created in the process of inquiry itself.

The last stage in the *Logic* is *reasoning: thinking as action and planning for action.* When Dewey discusses reasoning as a specific stage of inquiry, he employs the notion in a special sense which I will shortly make clear. Hypotheses are introduced as candidates for answers to research questions. While a suggested hypothesis might be relatively clear, it becomes significant for the researcher-practitioner only when it discharges its function in a developing instrumental context, opened and sustained by his transaction. There, Dewey states, it is "*framed* with reference to its offices as a guide to action."[23] More precisely, the meaning of a hypothesis is its use as a plan for action: Like an instrument or tool, it is used to probe, guide, and shape the situation. Dewey writes, "An hypothesis, once suggested and entertained, is developed in relation to other conceptual structures until it receives a form in which it can instigate and direct an experiment."[24] Reasoning, in this unconventional and liberal sense, has to do with the formation of a hypothesis as a plan for action, and itself incorporates the constraints and opportunities of directed practice. It is not Dewey's intention to elaborate on the logic or necessary interrelations of theoretical ideas entertained by the researcher-practitioner, but rather to show him these ideas link up with the demands of a problem and help direct its resolution. Reasoning, or planning for action, involves designing experiments and keeping track of what is going on, not just observing anticipated outcomes. It is more like managing ongoing tasks than constructing proofs, and it is displayed in our knowing our way around the laboratory, where the use of hypotheses is reflected in a guiding sense of how what we are dealing with can disclose itself. We normally do not test hypotheses or theories in our everyday practices; rather, we use them. Hypotheses guide us in forming well-defined tasks that require skillful consideration and organized instrumentation to complete. In these ways, reasoning helps transform a problematic situation into a more determinate one.

Donald A. Schon offers an interesting description of a case of inquiry into product design that illustrates Dewey's conception of reasoning. I will follow Schon's presentation throughout the illustration.[25]

A team of design engineers were presented with the problem of improving the performance of a new kind of paintbrush made of synthetic bristles. They observed that, compared to the older kind of brushes, made out of natural bristles, the new brush spread paint over a surface in a lumpy and uneven way, which Schon described as "gloppy." After trying out a number of improved versions, they noted that natural bristles had solid ends, but synthetic bristles did not. They tried splitting the ends of the synthetic bristles, and created bristles with various diameters, but all to no avail. A hypothesis or plan of action was needed.

Someone offered an ingenious hypothesis: Assume that a paintbrush is a kind of pump. This hypothesis was proposed by observing that when a person presses a paintbrush against a surface, the paint is forced to flow through the spaces between the bristles onto the surface. Like a pump, the painter creates a flow through the enclosed passages created by the bristles. Moreover, while painting a surface, painters often vibrate their brush at the same time as they bend it. Vibrating seemed to increase the flow of paint.

The engineers tested both the natural and synthetic brushes, conceiving of them according to the pump hypothesis. Through suitable instrumentation and operations, they found that when natural bristles were applied to a surface, they formed a gradual curve. On the other hand, synthetic bristles made a shape closer to an angle. These differences in the transmission of the paint onto the surface might explain the poorer performance of the synthetic fiber brush. The pump hypothesis (which had served as a probe and guide up to this point) was reformulated: If a paintbrush is a kind of pump and delivers paint to a surface in a gradual curve, then the performance of the synthetic brush can be improved by forming its bending shape into the desired curve.

A number of changes in the design were made. Successive approximations to the desired curve were proposed and implemented. Fibers were grouped so as to engender more density in the region of the curve; they were fused together in that region. And so forth. This line of reasoning proved correct, for these changes in design significantly improved performance. Not only was this innovation made possible by reasoning, but the basic understanding of the phenomenon of painting and its description were greatly improved as well. The end product of reasoning finally emerges, Dewey tells us, when "through a series of intermediate meanings, a meaning is finally reached which is more clearly relevant to the problem in hand than the originally suggested idea."[26]

To conclude: I have sought to show how Dewey's ideas may be used to understand the encompassing context of technological practices where the sciences and science-based professions find their new abode. My effort has consisted in a phenomenological style of thinking about technology that focused on Dewey's *Logic: The Theory of Inquiry*. I have argued that the *Logic* can be read as one of the first texts in contemporary philosophy that attempts to make sense of the pervasive technological setting of the sciences and science-based professions. The *Logic* helps us grasp the new cultural dimensions of technological praxis and can guide future philosophic investigation into people's deep involvement with technology. People play an important role in the development of technology—the stages of the *Logic* I briefly examined show people's central concern with the creation of technological contexts. The genesis of contexts of inquiry, the building of frames and their completion, the progressive development of problems, and the role of reasoning were all presented as ways in which people fashion the technological context of directed practices. I interpreted these technological stages of professional practice through the primacy of experience. Human beings, as Dewey views them, are involved with technology in a way that reflects their concern to move beyond any fixed idea they might have of themselves and the particular circumstances in which they now find themselves. Human transactions with technical problems and scientific projects can be shown to reflect our capacity for growth and wholeness: They suggest an increasing awareness of the expanding context of human action, an ever recurrent growth in fundamental meaning through the enlargement of intelligent activity. If we share such vision with John Dewey, science and technology take on meaning and ultimate significance. Dewey remains one of the few philosophers to have offered us this kind of vision.

# Notes

1. Richard D. Mosier, *The American Temper* (Berkeley: University of California Press, 1952), p. 300.

2. John Dewey and Arthur Bentley, *Knowing and the Known* (Boston: Beacon Press, 1949), p. 280.

3. *Scientific American* 258 (1) (Jan. 1988), p. 10.

4. Ernest Gellner, *Thought and Change* (Chicago: University of Chicago Press, 1965), p. 179.

5. John Dewey, *Essays in Experimental Logic* (Chicago: University of Chicago Press, 1916), p. 139.

6. Ibid., p. 5.

7. John Dewey, *Problems of Men* (New York: Philosophical Library, 1946), p. 173.

8. Dewey, *Essays in Experimental Logic,* p. 139.

9. Martin Heidegger, *Being and Time,* trans. John Macquarrie and Edward Robinson (New York: Harper and Row, 1962), p. 98.

10. John Dewey, *Logic, The Theory of Inquiry* (New York: Henry Holt and Co., 1938), p. 507.

11. Ibid., p. 104.

12. Ibid., pp. 105–106.

13. Ibid., p. 106.

14. John Dewey, *The Quest for Certainty* (New York: Paragon Books, 1929; New York: G. P. Putnam's Sons, 1979); pp. 277–78.

15. John Dewey, "The Need for a Recovery of Philosophy," in *John Dewey on Experience, Nature, and Freedom,* ed. Richard J. Bernstein (New York: Liberal Arts Press, 1960), p. 27.

16. Dewey, *Essays in Experimental Logic,* p. 5.

17. Dewey, *Logic: The Theory of Inquiry,* p. 105.

18. Ibid.

19. James B. Conant, *Science and Common Sense* (1951; New Haven, Conn.: Yale University Press, 1967), pp. 248–49.

20. Dewey, *Logic: The Theory of Inquiry,* p. 272.

21. Conant, *Science and Common Sense,* pp. 249–50.

22. Ibid., pp. 250–51.

23. Dewey, *The Quest for Certainty,* pp. 227–28.

24. Dewey, *Logic: The Theory of Inquiry,* p. 112.

25. Donald A. Schon, *The Reflective Practitioner* (New York: Basic Books, 1983), pp. 184–87.

26. Dewey, *Logic: The Theory of Inquiry,* pp. 397–98.

# The Principle of Continuity in C. S. Peirce and Contemporary Decision Support Technology

MARJORIE C. MILLER

Contemporary decision support systems (DSS), broadly considered, involve comprehensive sets of integrated functions supporting all phases of the decision-making process, including problem recognition, problem definition, information gathering, strategy generation, outcome prediction, model generation, and post-hoc evaluations. Such systems are being used with increasing frequency, increasing range (applying to very large, complex systems and available to users with access to microcomputers), and increasing impact on decision processes and decision formation in public life — affecting governmental, financial, industrial, commercial, and academic institutions.[1] Philosophers have been involved in the formulation of DSS primarily through their role in the development of decision theory.[2] Curiously, however, there are some significant lacunae in the move from bounded, decision-theoretic analyses to the integrated applications of DSS. Because of the enormous impact of the aggregate use of DSS, and because of the complexity of the metaphysical, logical, and ethical issues involved, the subject of DSS is worthy of some direct philosophic attention. In this paper I shall argue that several of Peirce's conceptions, interrelated through his principle of continuity, provide us with a particularly useful approach for undertaking such an analysis. Further, I shall suggest that such a distinctively late twentieth-century analysis may shed valuable light on the conceptions developed by Peirce nearly a century ago.

The significant conceptions to be addressed include the architectonic of the sciences, the nature of inquiry, habit, logic as semeiotic, and synechism. To begin with Peirce's architectonic: logic, it will be remembered, follows aesthetics and ethics in the order of the normative sciences (the second order within philosophy, between phenomenology and metaphysics).[3] For all the sciences of the architectonic there are a number of ways in which the sciences are interrelated; thus Peirce does not make logic a derivative of aesthetics and ethics in all senses. Rather, as Peirce defines the relation, "ethics, or the science of right and wrong, must appeal to Esthetics for aid in determining the *summum bonum*. It is the theory of self-controlled, or deliberate conduct. Logic is the theory of self-controlled, or deliberate, thought; and as such must appeal to ethics for its principles."[4]

The logic governing deliberation meant to result in action (hence, clearly, the logic involved in decision theory and, especially, the logic involved in DSS) is at least partly dependent on a theory of action and value; and that, in turn, is dependent on a theory of ultimate value. There is a continuity that obtains between valuational principles, both logical and ontological. But, as has often been noted,[5] traditional decision theories — either Bayesian versions or probabilistic versions — tend to founder precisely on the inability to formulate a satisfactory account of "self-controlled, or deliberate, conduct," that is, of *rationality*. While much current work has attempted an end-run around the problem (by focusing on descriptive statistical approaches to decision logic, by adopting various "weaker" definitions of Maximum Expected Utility, etc.), the Peircean development of the architectonic (merely summarized here) supports the claim that the development of the logic of deliberation must remain inadequate unless it takes into account the *continuity* that obtains between the theoretical enterprises of logic and the broader systematic investigation of the theory of action and the theory of value.

Again, the complex interrelation of the sciences requires us to look at the architectonic not only in terms of those sciences *above* a given science, but also with respect to those that are below. The other dimension of Peirce's view of the architectonic is that the more concrete sciences provide "data" for generalization and abstraction.[6] As Pritchard points out, "since metaphysics is that more concrete science closest to logic, its general principles would be eminently relevant to logic. If 'objective logic,' or the processes of thought that are realized in the universe, have *continuity* as a general character, it is encumbent upon general logic to discern the relationship between this constitutive character and the regulative principles of thought."[7] Hence, continuity figures in a logic of deliberation both as a regulative and, in some sense, a constitutive principle.

Having arrived at the principle of continuity by several routes, let us put it aside for the moment and turn to Peirce's conception of inquiry. A decision, after all, is distinguished from a random choice by being that choice which follows a process of deliberation — and deliberation is surely a mode of inquiry.

It is crucial to remind ourselves that for Peirce it is not the case that all inquiry is for the sake of action. Nevertheless, all inquiry has an active dimension, and all inquiry terminates in belief, which is interpretable by a habit, which (so far as the inquiry has been successful) serves as a reliable mode of activity. In designing or instituting DSS one is aiming, ultimately, at the production of reliable modes of activity (i.e., at generating information, models, and strategies that will produce decisions embodying habits of action which, if the inquiry/deliberation has been successful, will not require us to reconsider the beliefs that they interpret). Hence, Peirce's view of the nature of the process ought to prove quite relevant.

Thinking, in its roughest and in its most sophisticated forms, is essentially an attempt to get rid of a state of doubt, and this irritation does not cease, according to Peirce, until one has reached a state of belief.[8] The live doubt is usually one *related* to a decision problem: "Most frequently doubts arise from some indecision, however momentary, in our action."[9] Of course Peirce points out that, especially in scientific inquiry, "doubt . . . is not usually hesitancy about what is to be done then and there. It is anticipated hesitancy about a fictitious state of things."[10] Nevertheless, the connection between doubt and decision is central to the delimitation of a process of inquiry.

Inquiry, for Peirce, must begin with a foreground of live doubt against a background of indubitable beliefs. The background of beliefs about which we cannot "feign hesitancy" forms a crucial dimension of every inquiry. Decision theories usually acknowledge this background as the set of beliefs decision maker (DM) has about the world at the time of deliberation, as well as incorporating some of those beliefs into the formulations of DM's utilities. A look at the application of the theories to the DSS problem, however, points up some interesting shortcomings in this approach.

Decision theory begins with a notion of option paths: of branchings only one of which the DM may decide to pursue. But when we translate this to DSS, we discover that not every DM is faced with a clear situation of branching. In fact, one might argue that the first task of a DM is always to *identify* a given situation as one requiring a decision, that is, the recognition (or the early recognition) that one is *at* (or coming to) a significant fork in the road may indeed be that which separates the creative and effective DM from one more mechanical, plodding, and inadequate. Given Peirce's analysis of inquiry as that which begins in doubt, and given his claim that *some* (though not all) beliefs may be doubted in a "feigned" way, we are required to recognize the role of hypothesis generation (which Peirce calls abduction) in the very earliest stages of the decision situation: We can regard as problematic situations only those situations within which we can hypothesize about alternative possibilities with respect to some beliefs. We begin not with the *presentation* of options, but with our ability to *imagine* them — and this ability applies not to every belief held by a given DM in her or his unique situation, but rather only to those beliefs the DM may (or may be *made to*) living-ly doubt.

This analysis tends not to undermine any claim of traditional decision theory but rather to point up an inadequacy with regard to scope. Given the aims and structures of DSS, it becomes clear that current decision theory begins at an arbitrarily advanced point in the process: no characterization of a given DM, at time t, holding beliefs S, facing choices Ca-n will help us to discover just how DM *identified* a given situation as presenting just choices Ca-n. Nor will it suggest how we might encourage, or make available, a recognition of either *prior* situations that might have presented broader and more promising choices, or more subtle discrimination of options such that the current situation holds a greater range of choices than initially perceived. Either of the latter two cases requires a logic of abduction (or of hypothesis generation) rooted in a theory of inquiry encompassing a field broader than that currently addressed in decision-theoretic literature.

Turning to Peirce's conception of "habit": At one point he defines it as a rule of action established in our nature.[11] In the same paragraph he notes that the having of such a habit is "involved" in the having of a belief. While the significance of habit is obviously relevant with respect to the conclusion of inquiry (i.e., with respect to the fixation of belief), it is equally relevant at every stage of the process. That body of indubitable beliefs mentioned above, including normative maxims governing both the goals and methods of inquiry, "leading principles" of logic — all are, for Peirce, habits, or dispositions to act in certain ways. Habits have, among others, "energetic interpretants."[12] They are interpreted by the actions they guide. The entire decision process, then, involves a multitude of habits: those structuring a DM's ways of identifying situations; those organizing the specification of options; governing the preferred approach to the collection of data; governing the weighting of preferences, utilities, expected outcomes; organizing the modeling of the decision process; articulating the regularities of the behavior that may be determined by the process. While some of these habitual horizons of decision making are taken into account in such contemporary DSS literature as the discussion of decision styles,[13] the overly psychologistic dimension of these accounts fails, to some extent, to give due weight to the objective, public, assertorial nature of such habits. Neither the traditionally atomistic manipulation of beliefs, preferences and probabilities, nor the psychologistic, impressionistic discussion of decision styles captures the unique Peircean category of "habit."

Although this is not the place to provide a detailed analysis of Peirce's notion, I suggest that it is promising in its ability to respond to at least two difficult dimensions of traditional theory: (1) the necessity to account for the meta-dimensions of interpretation, preference, and weighting; and (2) the need for a more adequate account of the connection between holding a belief and taking an action.

Habit is distinguished from volition, by Peirce. A volition, the outcome of deliberation, is the result of an essentially deductive process. Habit formation, the development of a rule, is the result of an inductive process — requiring, "both logically and psychologically," multiple repetitions of instances. It is abduction, or hypothesis generation, that is responsible for the development of a *case,* of an individual instance, of a recognizable decision situation. [14] A habit, as a rule — a "would-be," in Peirce's words, — is a "how" a person would "be led to behave and upon what sort of occasion." [15] Such a habit, the meaning of a belief, is itself the expression of a "resting place" of thought — a resting place, because the irritation of doubt is soothed, thought pauses in the establishment of the habit; but Peirce recognizes that the habit itself, as "a rule for action, the application of which involves further doubt and further thought, at the same time that it is a stopping-place, . . . is also a new starting-place for thought." [16] Habit, as belief, as rule for action, as the expression of regularity which can be understood as the continuity of a probability function — the "would-be" considered as the actuality of the possibility contained in a probability function — is a conception rooted in continuity. It involves the continuity of the process that produces the habit, the continuity of the regularity that is the habit-as-rule, and the continuity of the actions and further thoughts that interpret the rule. Finally, habits both governing and generated by the process of inquiry embody a rationality that rests on the continuous process of meaning and interpretation. Such a rationality is rooted not only in the describable regularity of the deliberative behavior but also in the perceived continuity of consciousness. [17]

While this discussion of habit certainly does not resolve the decision theorist's problem of formulating an adequate algorithm of rationality, it does suggest that a solution will require a more effective focus on the continuity of process: current time-slice analyses break the continuum into arbitrary units which necessarily distort it. The paradoxes of rationality, I suspect, have much in common with Zeno's paradoxes of motion.

Having looked at the architectonic, at the conception of inquiry, and at the conception of habit, let us turn to Peirce's view of logic as semeiotic. As semeiotic, logic is the positive-theoretical analysis of the sign function as meaningful, which is also — in the broadest view — the normative-theoretical dimension of how thought ought to be conducted to develop meaning and truth.

To analyze thinking is to analyze a process conducted within an interpretive community (a community that may be composed of different moments or dimensions of the life of a single person). The many processes of decision making (information gathering, assessment, problem definition, strategy generation, evaluation, etc.) severally and together involve problems of logic understood not only as "critic," but also as semeiotic — sign interpretation, or meaning. The interpretive activity is, of course, not limited to the DM herself: interpretation functions *interactively* at each phase of the decision-making process, and hence must be taken into account at every phase of the design, development, installation, and evaluation of DSS. Like the process of inquiry itself, the process of sign translation must be "endless."[18] Since every sign determines an interpretant, and since every interpretant functions as a sign, the "idea of representation involves infinity."[19] The endlessness of interpretation and intrepretability here, however, does not involve us in a hopeless morass — one in which conclusions or decisions would be theoretically impossible to reach. Rather, as we know, Peirce argued that meaning is adequately captured, a living definition provided, when an inquirer can describe the habits "which that concept is calculated to produce." Habit and meaning are interdefined; action under particular circumstances is the "energetic interpretant" of the sign whose meaning is precisely the habit or rule of such action under such circumstances. Thus it is only an adequate theory of *meaning* which can provide us with (1) an understanding of the continuities of the logical processes involved in DSS, and (2) an emphasis on the continuous ramifications of each stage of the process in terms of interpretive interactions between the DM, the information base, the unique circumstances, and the habits presupposed, used, and produced.

Peirce's notion of logic as not merely methods of reasoning (though this is the subject of "critic," the central member of his tripartite division of logic) but more broadly as semeiotic illuminates the centrality, the primacy of a theory of meaning for a theory of choice. Real decision makers are enmeshed not in atomistic, isolable, bound situations but rather in a meaningful world: one preferred, hoped for, anticipated, sorted, evaluated, and imagined in terms of the meanings with which it is fraught.

Further, the centrality of continuity or synechism as a regulative principle of logic illuminates the ramifications of the triadic elements of the sign relations, of the place of logic in the architectonic of the sciences, and of thirdness as not only a regulative but also a constitutive principle. It is the latter point that encourages the investigation of signification, of continuity as the essence of thought, and of synechism as constitutive principle, to lead us to an understanding of that rationality which is the necessary foundation of both decision theory and any decision aid (or DSS).

Peirce wrote, "Three elements are active in the world: first, chance; second, law; and third, habit-taking."[20] Further, he argued with respect to persons that the teleology that regulates action must be understood as "a developmental teleology." "This reference to the future is an essential element of personality. Were the ends of a person already explicit, there would be no room for development, for growth, for life: and consequently there would be no personality. The mere carrying out of predetermined purposes is mechanical."[21] Current decision theory incorporates a response to chance in its evaluation of probable outcomes; it incorporates a response to law in its attempt to develop algorithms including valid methods of reasoning relating probabilities to beliefs, relative desires, and stated preferences for given decision makers. But when these decision-theoretic results are applied to complex mechanical, electronic, and organizational structures they often fail to provide reliable DSS. Perhaps the failures may be understood as failures to incorporate an adequate understanding of habit taking: Habit taking is that solidification of meaning which has a mediating function between chance and law. It is the evolutionary progress of regularity which does not preclude the "developmental teleology" of human decision makers; it is the energetic interpretant of the Peircean principle of synechism: "that tendency of philosophical thought which insists upon the idea of continuity as of prime importance in philosophy and, in particular, upon the necessity of hypotheses involving true continuity."[22]

Continuity again. Continuity is the principle encountered in our discussions of the architectonic, the nature of inquiry, habit, logic as semeiotic, and here in the central principle of synechism. Much has been written in the twentieth century about the shattering of the continuum through quantum mechanics: discontinuities and quantum leaps must serve as the constitutive elements to be drawn from physics to metaphysics to the regulative functions of logic. Curiously, in the necessarily integrated functions of complex DSS, the Peircean concepts, rooted in synechism and its insistence on the regulative value as well as the constitutive significance of the principle of continuity, appear to be effective in illuminating fruitful directions for further inquiry. Additionally, I would like to propose that the distinctive practical problems emerging in the institutionalization of DSS shed some interesting light on the reasons for a certain degree of danger and sterility in the rapidly expanding field of decision theory. That is, decision-theoretic analyses have been too narrowly focused in logic as critic; Peirce's contribution to the field of logic as semeiotic can be fully appreciated only if one takes seriously the injunction to "insist upon the prime

importance of continuity" — in all the guises in which we have encountered
it here, and in its developed meaning as system.

## Notes

1. See Stephen J. Andriole, ed., *Microcomputer Decision Support Systems: Design, Implementation, and Evaluation* (Wellesley, Mass.: QED Information Sciences, 1986). See also John E. Fleming, "A Suggested Approach to Linking Decision Styles with Business Ethics," *Journal of Business Ethics* 4 (April 1985), pp. 137–44.

2. See Patrick Suppes, "Decision Theory," in *Encyclopedia of Philosophy* (New York: Macmillan Publishing Co., 1972).

3. Charles S. Peirce, *Collected Papers of Charles Sanders Peirce,* 8 vols., ed. Charles Hartshorne, Paul Weiss, and Arthur Burks (Cambridge, Mass.: Harvard University Belknap Press, 1958), vol. 1, paras. 180–92. Hereafter, references to this work will be written as CSP, followed by a volume number and a paragraph number, in the standard fashion.

4. CSP 1.191.

5. Suppes, "Decision Theory," p. 313.

6. CSP 6.1.

7. Illona Kemp Pritchard, *A Critical Examination of the Role of Continuity in Peirce's Thought,* Ph.D. diss., SUNY Stony Brook, 1976, p. 7; emphasis added.

8. CSP 5.375, 5.400.

9. CSP 5.394.

10. CSP 5.373, n.1.

11. CSP 5.397.

12. CSP 5.491.

13. See, for example, Fleming, "Decision Styles," pp. 137–44.

14. Charles S. Peirce, *Philosophical Writings of Peirce,* ed. Justus Buchler (New York: Dover Publications, 1955), pp. 197–98.

15. CSP 2.665.

16. CSP 5.394–5.395.

17. See CSP 6.182: "My notion is that we directly perceive the continuity of consciousness." Although Manley Thompson (*The Pragmatic Philosophy of C. S. Peirce* [Chicago: University of Chicago Press, 1953]) argues that Peirce later modifies this view in important ways, I would argue that Thompson's version misses some important continuities in Peirce's own thought. While the view cannot be defended here, an interested reader is referred to Pritchard, *Examination of Continuity,* for further discussion of the point.

18. CSP 7.357.

19. CSP 8.268; see also Pritchard, *Examination of Continuity,* p. 67.

20. CSP 1.409.

21. CSP 6.160.

22. CSP 6.169.

# METAPHYSICS AND EPISTEMOLOGY

# Making Categories or Making Worlds, II

## KATHLEEN WALLACE

There have been many challenges to the possibility of metaphysics in recent and perhaps not so recent memory. It has been claimed that metaphysics is dead because its epistemological foundations are bankrupt. If there cannot be a perspectiveless perspective, then metaphysics meets the same fate as foundationalism — it must be given up because it cannot justify its claims to universality and necessity.[1] It seems clear that the impossibility of perspectivelessness poses a special difficulty for philosophy in general and metaphysics in particular. The question is why? Is it because the aim and achievement of perspectivelessness is endemic to metaphysics and therefore, if it is impossible, then so, too, is metaphysics? Or, is it because in identifying metaphysics with this view of its purposes and goals we fail to envision other possibilities? If the former, then metaphysics is indeed impossible. But, if the latter, then the burden falls on us. What then are the limiting assumptions?

To identify these, we have to backtrack for a moment. Why does the charge of perspectivalism pose such a challenge to intellectual work and thought in general? Because it raises the specter of unbridled relativism. Relativism can take many forms. One would be the view that there is no way of *validating* one or some perspectives as true or superior to any other because one can never get out of a perspective. Another, Goodman's, is that since we seem to construct perspectives and facts, we in effect make the world or worlds we know and encounter. The "fit" between our constructions and "the world" is a matter of practice or convention.[2]

These versions of relativism are driven by one or more of several assumptions:

1. That there is a way the world is which we can never know because we can never get out of our perspective.

2. As a corollary to this, that the world either has no determining influence on the perspectives we occupy, or if it has some, we can't determine

what that influence would be. The former disjunct would include a Kantian position since the *a priori* forms of understanding *qua a priori* are, by definition, not "natural," not determined by the world. Either would entail that there is no possibility of evidence.

3. Relevance — or relation — is not an ontological category. So, for example, in Goodman's case, we relate "things" to one another in our world constructions and symbol systems, but "in themselves" "things" are radically individual (Goodman's nominalism) or just are what they are, or perhaps have no nature at all.

The consequences of any of these assumptions when combined with perspectivalism is either to reduce all objects of knowledge to objects of our own making or to render always suspect, or even worse impossible, validation or justification of knowledge claims, beliefs, and categories. The consequences for metaphysics are just that much worse, because, even if we were to give up the claims of universality and necessity, we can't specify what the level of generality in metaphysics amounts to. Moreover, other disciplines can at least identify what would count as evidence, even if they can't know whether they've got it or not. In metaphysics, on the other hand, validation seems an even more remote possibility because the range of evidence cannot be specified. Therefore, not only could evidence never be exhausted, but we could never know what would count as decisive.[3]

But this is an unsettling conclusion to which we come. As Peirce would put it, we crave the fixation of belief. Validation is not a dimension of experience or metaphysics we can evade. There is a human compulsion to seek it. It matters to us whether we get it right or not, whether our choices are right or wrong, whether our professed goals and allegiances are good or not. If this craving is legitimate, then we have to reconceptualize the terms in which we frame the issues. Is there a way to account for legitimate perspectivalism (and therefore, at least some legitimate diversity in our understandings of the world) *and* for the evidentially compulsive effects of the world, without which validation would reduce to psychological need or cultural agreement and understanding? I refrain from defining validation at this point except to say that I am not equating it with standards of truth, logical validity, or empirical verification. While these may be species of validation, I think the concept of validation is broader than these options would suggest.

As long as we maintain that knowledge is perspectival, but the "independently real" is not, then either the object of knowledge seems to be of our making, or validation or justification of any knowledge claims will always be suspect. For if knowledge is always perspectival and "reality" is by definition "mind-independent," that is, not of our making, and therefore non-perspectival, then the consequence is not that our beliefs are underdetermined by the evidence, but that there is no evidence. On the other hand, if we say that knowledge has to transcend perspectives and conform to "reality," we abandon the task of explaining how it is possible for reality — the world — to tolerate diverse perspectives, let alone categorial or metaphysical theories. So, how *do* we account for at least some *legitimate* diversity *and* the evidentially compulsive effects of the world?

Now it seems to me that one way to capture both the evidential compulsion of the world and the "perspectival" character of our knowledge of it is to give up the assumption that the world or the "independently real" is nonperspectival. Let me hasten to add, as realists blanch with horror, that this does not entail that the world reduces to *our* perspectives. Rather, in order to make sense of this point, we would have to abandon the terminology of perspective and reformulate the ontological point. It seems to me that this is the thrust of the Buchlerian category of ordinality.[4] "Ordinality" means that the determinateness of any being is a function of relation in some respect. If "being," nature, or the world is ordinal, what would that commit us to?

In relation to the earth my body weight is one thing, but in relation to the moon, other things being equal, it would be something less. Each would be my weight in a given respect, but neither is more *really* my weight than the other (except in so far as I am here rather than there). We can also measure the different weights by different standards — pounds or kilograms, say — neither of which may be more or less "true" than the other. Likewise, a length of wood is *really* 1 meter *and* 39.37 inches.

Now, to extend the principle, in relation to physical location, railroad tracks do not converge, while in relation to (in the order of) vision they do. We may not be able to abandon the terminology of saying that they only *appear* to converge, but don't *really* do so, but I see no reason ontologically if the different weights are equally admissible as real, why the railroad track differences should not also be. Thus, it is the railroad tracks themselves which converge in one respect and do not in another. Each is just as real a trait of the tracks as the other is, because each is a trait of the tracks in a given respect ("order"). This is not a violation of the law of noncontradiction because we have specified the relevant respects.

There are several points to be drawn from this. First, relevance or relation is an ontological category. Things, events, processes, have the determinate traits they have in virtue of constitutive relations. They *are* their unique integrity of relations. Second, perspective is to be understood as a relation or "order," not a mental, linguistic, or other container. The visual order, as one example of a perspective, is not just of our own making, but is a relation between us and objects in a given respect. Therefore, we can't make the world to be whatever we want it to be, because our perspectives are not merely or solely ours. We cannot weigh whatever we want to on either the moon or the earth. Nor can we see the tracks as forming a circle as they recede into the distance, even though we can imaginatively construct *other* objects that have traits the physical railroad tracks do not.[5] That a being can have different traits in different (ordinal) respects does not entail that it can have *any* traits or relations whatever. Ordinality is qualified by commensurations; a being may acquire or actualize traits in relation to us, but our perspectives are also constrained by the other constitutive traits of a being.

Objectivity is not jeopardized because we are not locked into any one perspective and can discriminate the mediating traits between perspectives. Objectivity has to do with the breadth or range of perspectival location, not absolute certainty or freedom from our interpretive influence. Objectivity is possible because while we cannot have no perspective, we can occupy and move between perspectives. This is so because perspectives themselves have ontological status; they are a species of order or relation. If we know both traits of the railroad tracks — both their convergence and nonconvergence — it is because we know in virtue of occupying many orders (perspectives), or being in many relations, such as orders of vision, travel, and mathematics, to name a few.[6] Evidence becomes evidence within a perspective, but its compulsiveness *qua* evidence is not the exclusive function of our particular contribution to the perspective. Thus, we would be able to satisfy the requirement of evidential compulsion, while preserving the perspectival nature of knowledge without apology. We preserve the independence of the world, *and* allow that the world in relation to us as knowers, or anything else for that matter, is no less the world for being known.

So what follows for metaphysics if we admit that relevance is an ontological category and that to have or to be in a perspective is to be in a relation that is not merely made by us? Are we now in a better position to say anything worthwhile about metaphysics? Why even call "it" metaphysics, especially if that only connotes what it is impossible and illegitimate to attempt? To meet this objection, the alternative would have to be one that aims for and claims sufficient generality (even if not perspectiveless universality) to justify calling it metaphysics, but which, at the same time, avoids the pitfalls of "foundationalism" and the perspectiveless spectator syndrome. In a more chastened philosophical spirit, then, perhaps we could think of metaphysics as the shaping of categories with which to orient ourselves to understanding the world at a very general level. Generality can't be empty or uninformative. "Being is" is very general, but, Parmenides notwithstanding, very uninformative. Generality has to be qualified by aptness or relevance. "Human beings are featherless bipeds" is a true statement, but philosophically and metaphysically a failure because it does not formulate or identify traits relevant to making "human being" understandable philosophically, even if it were true that it served a biological classificatory function.

But the problem seems to be that metaphysical categories involve our bringing a lot more of our perspectives to the world than the other way around. It is surely right to be concerned about uncontrolled speculative tendencies, but there is a legitimate constructive aspect to metaphysics. How could there not be? We make or construct categories. We don't discover them ready made. Does this mean that we make the/a world or that we erect an impenetrable veil between us and the world itself? Not at all. If we backtrack for a moment to an earlier example, we construct standards of measurement without which we would not and could not know weight. Each designation—in kilograms, pounds, or stones, or with respect to length, meters or inches—may be correct or apt in relation to the body in question, and each may allow us to make true (and false) assertions about bodies. However, one standard may be superior to another relative to the purposes of inquiry, practice, the context of national location, and so forth. It doesn't seem to me that to admit this commits us to abandoning objectivity. For in shifting between perspectives we can determine where and how they are equivalent and not, and we can determine which is better and why. We are also constrained. We don't make physical and gravitational relations, even though we can be and are related, cognitively and noncognitively, to those relations. And we can't attribute to a length *qua* length weight, liquid volume, and a multitude of other standards of measurement of physical properties.

Likewise—although, following Hume's advice, we have to exercise caution in any inference based on analogy—we construct and invent concepts and categories. Plato invented the divided line and the allegory of the cave. They function to orient us to dimensions of the world, for example, to the being of ideals, the nature of knowledge, the process and purposes of education, to name a few. These conceptual constructions have cognitive, even if not literal or exhaustive, value. The respects in which they are right or not may be "tested" by the dialectical processes they engender as well as by their reference as "fit" to discrete "facts" or "concrete experience." Aristotle, too, invented what we are more accustomed to calling categories, for example, substance or *ousia*. As part of a system of categories, they, too, orient us to the world at a very general level. While both an allegory and a category may be apt (or not), neither is true or false, and here I agree with Goodman. But each allows us to make—it "frames" or orients us so that we can make—assertions that can be assessed as true or false. But what are we aiming for when we shape categories? I think that the aim metaphysically is to push the terms of conceptualization at a very general level in one direction rather than another. It seems to me that's exactly what Aristotle achieved relative to his predecessors. Plato's myths and allegories also function in this way, namely, to transform the terms of conceptualization and, as with the divided line and the allegory of the cave, to introduce new concepts, like the idea of the Good, which reanimate and redirect the dialogue or inquiry.

If there is any meaning to the notion that metaphysics is "foundational" or fundamental, it can't hinge on some claim that we have identified *the* "really real" aspects of nature or the world. "Fundamental" could not mean absolute, presuppositionless or perspectiveless. "Fundamental" or "foundational" marks a functional and relative distinction. Some distinctions or categories are more fundamental than or are foundational to others. So, for example, Aristotle's category of *ousia* is more fundamental than that of soul or psyche because it is more widely applicable and because it is presupposed by the latter, but not vice versa. Likewise, Buchler's category of "contour" (or "gross integrity") is more fundamental than the category "proceptive domain" and both are foundational to the concept of "guiding moral tone."[7] But none of these distinctions is presupposition-less because each is a function of and helps to articulate a set of theoretical commitments, again none of which is presuppositionless. We can make cross-system comparisons and evaluations as well. So, for example, we can assess Aristotle's system as superior to Anaximenes' in terms of its generality, scope, and the judiciousness of its distinctions. Whitehead's category of prehension is broader than Buchler's category of proception, but Buchler's allows us to make more judicious distinctions. These are not merely "technical" advantages, but ones that have consequences for the movement of inquiry, or to use Buchler's term, "query." The relative superiority of one over another can be assessed, just as the relative superiority of standards of measurement can, without in either case foundering on the Scylla and Charybdis of presuppositionlessness and mere subjectivity or relativism.

So metaphysics (particularly, general ontology) instead of being a perspective that *includes* all perspectives — an impossible claim to validate since we'd have to be able to transcend all perspectives in order to determine this — would rather be a perspective that is presupposed and exemplified in or by other perspectives. The latter is testable because determination of whether the relation of generality obtains would not require the perspectiveless standpoint. Rather, the scope of generality is determinable because (a) perspectives themselves may overlap; and (b) we can shift between perspectives. Instead of aiming for "universality" or a perspectiveless foundation, the aim would be comprehensiveness (apt or relevant generality) and pervasive exemplification. Exemplification would be subject to evidential and "exhibitive" validation; aptness or relevance would mean that metaphysics, or a system of categories, too, is *a* perspective, albeit a very general one, and therefore, that it is not universal in the sense traditionally supposed.

"Foundational" more usually means necessary, determinative of every other distinction or always relevant. Universality typically means all-inclusiveness, distributively or collectively. But in the view I am here suggesting, distinctions made in a metaphysical sense are not *necessary* to the making of every other cognitive, conceptual, or theoretical determination, although sometimes metaphysics can be helpful in revising or making new concepts or principles. (Contemporary discussions aroused by developments in physics concerning the nature of causality would be a good example of a context in which metaphysical distinctions could be helpful.) Theoretical entities as defined in physics are not determined by some prior metaphysical distinctions, even though they may implicitly exhibit them. In fact, if a metaphysical system is right or apt, physical distinctions should exemplify the metaphysical distinctions. Quark *qua* quark and quark *qua* natural complex, for example, are two different traits of the same being and the former also exemplifies the latter, but not vice versa. I am both a sister and a sibling. The former, "sister," exemplifies "sibling," but not vice versa, since the latter could also be exemplified by "brother." So, the latter is more general and admits of more pervasive exemplification, even though both are traits of the same being, me. "Sibling" is "foundational" to the extent to which it helps to articulate the wider meaning of the former. "Sister" can help to articulate the meaning of "sibling," too, but it does so by specifying its scope and exemplifying the general relation in a particular context.

Back to our more abstract example, quark and natural complex, the former a physical designation, the latter a metaphysical one. Neither distinction is more important or better or foundational in any sense. The integrity of the concept "quark" does not derive from the broader metaphysical concept. In some respects the intelligibility of "quark" may be enhanced by the metaphysical categorization, for example, by enabling us to see similarities with other beings in virtue of the broader classification; traits we would not otherwise be able to identify. In other respects, for example, for the experimenting physicist, it may not be very helpful. Likewise, sister-ness may be enhanced by understanding it as a sibling relation, but there are also traits of sister-ness which are not derivable from or based upon the broader distinction, such as the way sisters relate to one another as opposed to brothers. That we move back and forth between levels of conceptual distinction does not undermine the merit or integrity of the distinctions.

What makes a categorical distinction valid or not is a much more complicated matter than the validation of my sister-sibling example or the standards of measurement mentioned earlier because the standards and the goal of conceptual orientation admit of greater latitude.[8] Standards of measurement and concepts may be, at least in part, conventions, but none is necessarily any less valid for being so. Not every metaphysical system is valid or right, but it may be possible that more than one metaphysical theory is valid, albeit in different respects — I hesitate to say "true" because a system of categories as such, like the standards of measurement, may be neither true nor false, although the more false assertions a system would tolerate or entail, the weaker its validity. I have, of course, not addressed the more difficult issue of why metaphysics in particular seems to tolerate or at least result in a diversity of theories or systems. But that it does is not because there is *no* evidence or possibility of validation. What I have been trying to show is that we do not have to give up the possibility of validation in the face of persistent diversity. Rather, we want to be able both to preserve perspectivalism *and* to account for legitimate diversity. So, my aim has been a more modest one of trying to explore how to reconcile the perspectival and constructive character of knowledge and experience with the possibility of validation. I have suggested that one fruitful way of doing so would involve reorienting the way we look at the issues. First, we should admit that relevance is an ontological category, as I think the Buchlerian category of ordinality does. If there is indeterminacy of evidence and the lack of finality in validation, it is because there is indefinite relatedness and diversity in the world. Second, our perspectives are not merely ours, and therefore, to have a perspective does not necessarily mean that what one "sees" or experiences or whatever is not "really" a trait of the world. Rather, it means that the world, in relation to a perceiver, experiencer, or knower really has some trait in that respect. Objectivity, then, has to do with the range of perspectival location, not certainty or conformity to some otherwise "mind-independent" or "nonperspectival" trait.[9] Finally, I have suggested that we redefine metaphysics as being concerned with apt generality and conceptual orientation, nor foundationalism, universality, and perspectivelessness. If there is diversity in metaphysics, it is, at least in part, because the world, as well as our own experience, demands that we keep starting over again. If more than one metaphysical theory has validity, and if we can know the world in a variety of ways, it is both because the world *is* in a variety of ways (principle of ordinality) and because we can construct concepts, categories, and the like, which create new possibilities for knowing the ways of the world.

# Notes

1. See, for example, Richard Rorty, *Philosophy and the Mirror of Nature* (Princeton, N.J.: Princeton University Press, 1979); also Rorty, *Consequences of Pragmatism* (Minneapolis: University of Minnesota Press, 1982).

2. Nelson Goodman, *Fact, Fiction and Forecast,* 4th ed. (Cambridge, Mass.: Harvard University Press, 1983); also Goodman, *Ways of Worldmaking* (Indianapolis: Hackett Publishing Co., 1978). In my view, and in spite of his asseverations to the contrary, Goodman's nominalistic ontology stands in the way of his developing an adequate account of the "fit" or "rightness" of theories, categories, and art. If only individuals are "real," then it would be difficult to define what the "fit" of constructions, which necessarily are constituted by relational traits, is to the real world of individuals.

3. I think that this is the crux of Rescher's "orientational pluralism." See Nicholas Rescher, *The Strife of Systems: An Essay on the Grounds and Implications of Philosophical Diversity* (Pittsburgh, Pa.: University of Pittsburgh Press, 1985). There is no way to judge the superiority of one philosophical view to another, except on purely technical grounds, because there is no access to decisive evidence.

4. Justus Buchler, *Metaphysics of Natural Complexes* (New York: Columbia University Press, 1966).

5. Thus, take a painting in which railroad tracks do not converge as they supposedly recede into the distance. These are not the physical tracks now in a different location. Rather, the painted tracks and the physical tracks resemble one another in some obvious respects, but in this example they are not the same object. If they were, we would be implicated in a violation of the law of noncontradiction, that is, it would be possible for the railroad tracks to converge and not possible for the railroad tracks to converge as they recede into the distance. Of course, in other instances it may be that a painting or a photograph represents the physical railroad tracks; it depends on the particular art object. The art object, too, is in and of the world, since the perspective(s) and relation(s) that constitute it are.

6. Knowledge is not limited to true or justified belief or assertion. We also know in virtue of acting, doing, and making.

7. These categories and concepts are introduced by Buchler as follows. "Contour" is introduced in *Metaphysics of Natural Complexes;* "proceptive domain" in *Toward a General Theory of Human Judgment,* 2nd rev. ed. (New York: Columbia University Press, 1951; New York: Dover Publications, 1979); and "guiding moral tone" in "Russell and the Principles of Ethics," in *The Philosophy of Bertrand Russell,* ed. Paul Arthur Schilpp (Evanston: Northwestern University Press, 1944).

8. I borrow the notion of conceptual orientation or reorientation from Buchler. See Justus Buchler, "Reply to Anton: Against 'Proper Ontology'," *Southern Journal of Philosophy,* vol. 14 (1) (1976): 89. It is to be distinguished from Rescher's

"orientational pluralism." See Rescher, *The Strife of Systems;* also see Nicholas Rescher, "Aporetic Method in Philosophy," *The Review of Metaphysics,* vol. 41 (2) (Dec., 1987): 283–97. Buchler's notion, and mine as I propose it here, is meant to identify a kind of conceptual and theoretical function. Rescher's is the claim that psychological, cultural, sociological, in short, "value commitments," antecedently determine our attitudes or "orient" us to accept or be receptive to ways of looking at the world. Hence, the diversity of philosophical theories rests on diverse underlying "value commitments." "Conceptual [re-]orientation" as I am using it here does not necessarily involve the resolution of what Rescher would call "apories." Rather, it may involve transcending the terms of the debate. Transcendence need not involve resolution or the introduction of qualifying distinctions, but may consist in abandonment. Not in a vacuum, of course, as if one could have no presuppositions, but abandonment of the traditional terms and starting in a sense all over.

9. Error can arise through a variety of ways, not the least of which would be failure to identify the relevant evidence, or overgeneralization when the evidence warrants something less.

# The Underdetermination Thesis

MURRAY G. MURPHEY

The Underdetermination Thesis is a fundamental claim concerning the nature of scientific knowledge. Its principle advocate, W. V. Quine, makes his most considered statement of it in his 1975 paper, "On Empirically Equivalent Systems of the World." Although Quine has made subsequent modifications in his position, none of them touches the argument to be made here, and I shall therefore base my comments on the 1975 paper.

The Underdetermination Thesis concerns the relation of scientific theories to observations or, more exactly, to observation sentences. Quine gives two criteria for a sentence being an observation sentence: (1) "witnesses will agree on the spot in    assenting to an observation sentence"[1] or in dissenting from it, and (2) the application of such sentences can be learned by ostention,[2] although it can also be learned in other ways. The sentence "it is blue" is an observation sentence in Quine's sense, but so also are "lo, a rabbit," "that's a ball," and "this is water." Thus, observation sentences for Quine are not limited to protocols or phenomenal reports such as "red patch here now"; sentences including terms such as "ball" or "rabbit" or "water" also may qualify.[3]

Observation sentences so specified are occasion sentences — that is, they are true if uttered on some occasions but false if uttered on some others. These are not the sort of observation sentences derivable from scientific theories. In order to bring them into a form usable in science, they must be converted into "standing sentences" whose truth or falsity is independent of the occasions of utterance.[4] Quine proposed to do this by pairing observation occasion sentences to space-time coordinates, as, for example, "at a point having space-time coordinates w, x, y, z, there is a rabbit." The observation sentences actually derivable from scientific theories would then be conditionals having a standing observation sentence as antecedent and another standing observation sentence as consequent[5] — for example, "if at a point w,x,y,z, this ball is dropped, then after t seconds the ball will be at point $w + t$, $x'$, $y'$, $z'$."

This formulation of what constitutes the observatio sentences of science is critical to Quine's argument for the Underdetermination Thesis. It is obvious that observation sentences so defined are not *purely* observational; certainly talk of rabbits, balls, and water involves conceptual elements that are not "given" in experience. In fact, Quine does not think that there is a "pure given" in experience, so that for him even terms like "blue" and "red" involve some conceptualization. But sentences can be ordered as more or less observational, and what Quine calls "observation sentences" lie at the observational end of the continuum.[6] Despite the fact that they do involve some conceptual elements, such observation sentences are taken by scientists as purely enough observational to be used as data against which scientific theories are tested.

By a theory we normally mean some set of logically consistent sentences. Such a theory may be axiomatized, and it is well known that if a theory can be axiomatized in one way, it can also be axiomatized in many other ways. A particular choice of axioms may be called a theory formulation, and the axioms may be treated as a single sentence — the conjunction of the axioms. All formulations of the same theory are of course logically equivalent.[7] If the number of axioms in the conjunction is finite, the formulation is termed a "finite theory formulation."

Suppose we take a theory formulation and switch two of its nonobservational terms — say, "electron" and "molecule." Would the theory formulation resulting from this switch be equivalent to the formulation before the switch? It would not be logically equivalent to it, since the two formulations would say different things about electrons and molecules. Yet it is obvious that the one formulation would be merely a notational variant of the other; it is just that what we call an "electron" in one we call a "molecule" in the other, and vice versa. Such notational variants should not be allowed to count as different theory formulations; accordingly, Quine rules that "two formulations express the same theory "if they imply the same observation sentences and there is "a reconstrual of predicates that transforms the one theory into a logical equivalent of the other."[8]

Given this apparatus, it is possible to state the Underdetermination Thesis as follows: For any one (finite) theory formulation there is another that is empirically equivalent to it but logically incompatible with it, and that cannot be rendered logically equivalent to it by any reconstrual of predicates.[9] This thesis can be stated in two different forms, which may be termed for convenience the weak and the strong forms of the thesis. The weak form is this: Consider a given infinite set of heterogeneous observation sentences and some finite theory formulation T that accounts for all the observation sentences in the set. Then there must exist a second finite theory formulation T' that also accounts for all those observation sentences and is logically incompatible with T and irreconcilable with T by any reconstrual of predicates. Such would be the situation of a given theory of physics P at a specified time t, and the claim would be that we could find an alternative theory P' that accounts for exactly what P accounts for yet is both incompatible and irreconcilable with P. This claim may be true, although I know of no general proof for it, but I think it would not strike most scientists as revolutionary.

There is, however, a much more radical claim involved, which I shall call the strong form of the Underdetermination Thesis. Suppose we have a spatiotemporal coordinate system for the universe. Then let each observation occasion sentence "expressible in our language" be paired to each combination of space-time coordinates, and form all the observational conditionals that can be generated from the combination of those sentences. Some of these conditionals will be true and some will be false, but they will be all the observation conditionals there are or ever can be — they will be all possible observation conditionals. Let T* be a finite theory formulation accounting for all of the true observation conditionals. Then the strong form of the Underdetermination Thesis says that there exists a finite theory formulation T! which also accounts for all possible observation conditionals, and that T! is both incompatible and irreconcilable with T*. If this were so, there would then be no way to know which of the two incompatible theory formulations, T* or T!, was true, for, since both account equally well for all the observational data there are or ever can be, there remains no observation that could possibly discriminate between them. Thus we could never tell which picture of the world — that given by T* or that given by T! — was true, even though, since they are logically incompatible theories, they cannot both be true. Given such a situation, the whole notion of truth, and so of reality, is called into question — at least if it is assumed that either truth or reality is knowable. It should now be clear why the strong form of the Underdetermination Thesis is of such fundamental importance.

Is the Underdetermination Thesis true? Not in its full generality, as Quine shows, since it is possible to specify cases where it fails — for example, where the number of observation conditionals is finite, or where the observation conditionals are embraced in a finite number of universally quantified conditionals. [10] To meet such problems, Quine is forced to restrict the thesis to the case of an infinite set of observation sentences, which are to be accounted for by a finite theory formulation where the heterogeneity of the observation sentences is such that the finite formulation cannot be equivalent to some finite conjunction of universally quantified conditionals.[11] But even this "tempered version" must be qualified.

> We might study two incompatible theory formulations, trying in vain to imagine an observation that could decide between them, and we might conclude that they are empirically equivalent; we might conclude this without seeing a reconciling reconstrual of predicates. This we might; but there could still be a reconciling reconstrual of predicates, subtle and complex and forever undiscovered. The thesis of underdetermination, even in my latest tempered version, asserts that our system of the world is bound to have empirically equivalent alternatives that are not reconcilable by reconstrual of predicates however devious. This, for me, is an open question.

> Failing that, a last ditch version of the thesis of underdetermination would assert merely that our system of the world is bound to have empirically equivalent alternatives which, if we were to discover them, we could see no way of reconciling by reconstrual of predicates. This vague and modest thesis I do believe. For all its modesty and vagueness, moreover, I think it vitally important to one's attitude toward science.[12]

One notes, with some surprise, how exceedingly qualified Quine's assertion of the "last ditch version" of the Underdetermination Thesis is. Quine does not claim that this version of the thesis is proven, or even provable, for given two empirically equivalent but logically incompatible theory formulations, there is no way to prove that no reconstrual of predicates is possible that will transform one theory formulation into a logical equivalent of the other. Thus the status of the Underdetermination Thesis as Quine asserts it is that of an unproven hypothesis he believes to be true, although he admits that it is unprovable. Nevertheless, there is, as Quine emphasizes, good reason to believe it. Scientific theories imply their observation sentences; they are not implied by them. But a given set of observation sentences can be implied by many alternative theories. It seems plausible therefore to say that alternative theory formulations can imply all observation sentences. Whether the alternative theory formulations that imply these observation sentences can also be incompatible and irreconcilable with each other is not obvious and is perhaps less plausible, but I know of no proof to the contrary. It is therefore the nature of the logical relation between scientific theories and scientific observations — more strictly, between finite theory formulations and observation sentences — which gives the Underdetermination Thesis its persuasiveness.[13]

Despite the seeming plausibility of the Underdetermination Thesis, there are very serious problems with it. There is first the problem of specifying just what the members of the set of observation sentences are. Putnam has pointed out that "when Quine speaks of the totality of all *possible observations*, he means the totality of *all true observation sentences*, i.e.

of the totality of all *ordered pairs consisting of an observation sentence and a point in space-time at which that observation sentence could have been truly uttered,* whether or not someone was present at that point in spacetime to truly utter it. He does not count counterfactual observation sentences . . . and *a fortiori,* he does not count sentences about what the outcomes of various experiments would have been if those experiments had been performed."[14] But Putnam rightly objects that "as long as the theories imply different predictions about what *would* have happened *if* the experiment *had* been performed, then they are inequivalent, as most physicists understand the matter."[15] Putnam is, I think, right to insist that such counterfactuals must be included in the set. But this does not end the matter, for there are further difficulties in specifying the membership of this set. In the Strong Form of the Underdetermination Thesis, Quine talks of "all possible observations,"[16] or equivalently, as Putnam notes, of all possible observation sentences, treated as if they formed a determinate set like the set of natural numbers. But as I emphasized above, Quine's notion of an observation sentence is not that of a phenomenal report but of a sentence that may include terms such as "rabbit" or "ball" or "water"— terms which, although perhaps intended by Quine without ontological commitment, we normally think of as object terms. Clearly, many observations of science are made with the aid of instruments or upon instruments, and it is hardly news that scientific instrumentation changes constantly, with new instruments being invented and old ones being discarded. Moreover, scientific instruments are themselves the product of scientific theories, so that changes in theory produce changes in instrumentation, which generate new observations, which in turn compel changes in theories, and so on endlessly. Thus in a real sense, scientific theories create their own observations, and the relation between theory and observation is a dynamic process. And as new terms are introduced for new instruments, and often for the observations made with them, so of course the language of science constantly changes, and with it the set of observation sentences supporting the theories also changes. Yet when Quine talks of pairing every space-time point with "each observation sentence expressible in our language"[17] to yield the determinate set of all possible observation sentences, he seems to assume that the language is fixed, unchanging, and independent of the scientific theories to be considered. In other words, he is taking the "language" as it is at a given time and projecting it over all times as an adequate medium in which all possible observation structures can be stated. If he were talking in phenomenalist terms, this might conceivably be so, but as he has defined observation sentences, the language in which observation is couched will change continually and unpredictably with variations in instrumentation and so of theory. There is no fixed totality of possible observation sentences, except at a given time; over any extended period the set will show a highly variable membership.

Quine could reply that since, under the strong form of the Underdetermination Thesis, all final theories of the world imply the same observation sentences, there could not be a difference in observation sentences between such theories due to instrumentation or anything else. But this puts the cart before the horse, for it assumes we have already reached theories that account for all observation sentences. But how can we know that unless we already know what the set of all observation sentences is? Without such an antecedent specification of the membership of the set, the Underdetermination Thesis becomes circular. And no such antecedent specification is possible.

Quine might claim that the criteria he gave for observation sentences — agreement of witnesses and learnability for ostention — are independent of such changes in the language and uniquely determine the set. But surely after all that Quine has written about the problems of ostention, such as deferred ostention, that claim is implausible.[18] Moreover, the role of hypotheses in perception is now well known, and Kuhn among others has pointed out their role in scientific observation. Two witnesses, receiving the same sensory stimuli, but having different perceptual hypotheses, may not agree on what observation sentence applies to the situation.[19] It is then doubtful that these criteria are sufficient to save the day.

This objection — that Quine treats the set of all possible observation sentences as a determinate totality when in fact it is not — leads to a more fundamental problem. Quine presents the Underdetermination Thesis as a thesis about science. But science consists of something more than theories and observations; as C. S. Peirce was fond of pointing out, science is a process of inquiry in which theories are tested and revised in the light of the outcomes of experiments and observations based on predictions derived from those theories.[20] The role of theories as generators both of new observations and of manipulations of natural phenomena leading to predicted results is fundamental to science, as scientists understand that term. More precisely, most scientists would agree that for a fixed body of observational data, it will always be possible to devise alternative explanations that, however arcane, will account for those data. But there is a fundamental difference between a theory's ability to explain a given set of observations and a theory's ability to predict correctly the occurrence of new observations. Granted that for some set of n observation sentences we can "cook up" a theory that will explain them, it does not follow that such a theory can correctly predict the outcomes of new experiments or that it can correctly predict the existence of observations not included in the original set of n observation sentences at the time the theory was created.

This is precisely the reason that scientists have always insisted that the real test of a scientific theory is its ability to predict something new, something not hitherto observed, or to account for some already known phenomenon that was not considered relevant when the theory was created. For example, the discovery that relativity theory could account for the long known but hitherto unexplained behavior of the orbit of Mercury was taken as confirming evidence for that theory because its ability to account for that phenomenon was completely unexpected by Einstein when he devised it.[21]

Seen from this point of view, it is clear that the situation Quine proposes in the strong form of the Underdetermination Thesis is one to which science — understood as a process of inquiry — does not apply. For in setting up the strong form of the thesis, Quine converts the indefinitely extended process of scientific inquiry into a finished state in which all possible observations have been made. Clearly, there can be no test among alternative theories in this situation on the basis of their predictive power or their ability to account for hitherto unrelated data, since the definition of the situation as given by Quine is such that all possible observational outcomes are already included in the explained data and there are no unexplained data. Quine's "limiting case" of scientific knowledge is not really a case of scientific knowledge at all, but a case of postscientific knowledge in which all inquiry has ceased, all possible observations have been made, all possible observation sentences have been explained, and we have a fixed totality of data to which no additions can be made — just the sort of case in which multiple theories would be expected to proliferate because the possibility of deciding among them has been ruled out by definition.

To put the point somewhat differently, from the claim that multiple theory formulations that are incompatible and irreconcilable can explain n observation sentences equally well, it does not follow that all of these theory formulations will be equally successful in correctly predicting new observations or in accounting for new data not hitherto considered relevant. This is why the weak form of the Underdetermination Thesis would not arouse much scientific opposition; the scientist's response would be to look for new observations that could discriminate between the formulations. It is just this possibility of further tests that is ruled out by the strong form of the thesis, and it is the ruling out of further inquiry that makes impossible a decision among the competing theory formulations. But ruling out further inquiry is illegitimate: it supposes the completion of an indefinitely extended process of scientific inquiry in a finite time; it supposes that a time will actually come when we have a complete explanation of every observable aspect of the universe; and it supposes that there is a determinate set of all possible observation sentences that can be expressed in our language despite the fact that the language itself is constantly changing as a result of scientific inquiry. For these reasons, I think that the Underdetermination Thesis in its strong form must be rejected.

If these arguments are sound, there is no reason to hold that science cannot or will not lead to a single true theory. The characterization of such a theory does not, it should be noted, require the notion of scientific progress in the sense so tellingly critiqued by Kuhn. All that it does require, as C. S. Peirce pointed out long ago,[22] is the characterization of scientific inquiry as such a process that at some point a theory will emerge that will ever after be affirmed. This way of putting the matter involves no reference to a completed totality of observation sentences; the process of inquiry goes on indefinitely, and that theory, if any, is best that will always meet the tests that arise in the course of inquiry. But whether or not the process of scientific inquiry has that character is a question that cannot be pursued here.[23]

# Notes

1. W. V. O. Quine, "On Empirically Equivalent Systems of the World," *Erkenntnis* 9 (1975): 313–28.

2. Ibid.: 316.

3. Ibid.

4. Ibid.: 316–17.

5. Ibid.: 317.

6. W. V. O. Quine, *Word and Object* (Cambridge, Mass.: MIT Press, 1960), pp. 42ff.

7. Quine, "On Empirically Equivalent Systems of the World," p. 318.

8. Ibid., p. 320.

9. Ibid., p. 322.

10. Ibid., p. 323.

11. Ibid., p. 324.

12. Ibid., pp. 326–27.

13. Ibid., p. 313.

14. Hilary Putnam, *Mind Language and Reality* (Cambridge: Cambridge University Press 1984), p. 180.

15. Ibid., p. 181.

16. W. V. O. Quine, "On the Reasons for Indeterminacy of Translation," *Journal of Philosophy* 67 (1970): 179.

17. Quine, "On Empirically Equivalent Systems of the World," pp. 316–17.

18. W. V. O. Quine, *Ontological Relativity and Other Essays* (New York: Columbia University Press, 1969), p. 40.

19. Jerome Bruner, *Beyond the Information Given* (New York: W. W. Norton, 1973), part 1; also Arnold Glass et al., *Cognition* (Reading, Mass.: Addison-Wesley, 1979), chaps. 2–3.

20. Charles S. Peirce, *The Collected Papers of Charles Sanders Peirce,* 8 vols., ed. Charles Hartshorne, Paul Weiss, and Arthur Burks (Cambridge, Mass.: Harvard University Press, 1958), vol. 1, paras. 233ff; vol. 5, para. 311. Hereafter cited as CSP, followed by volume number and paragraph number, in the standard fashion.

21. Philipp Frank, *Einstein: His Life and Times* (London: Jonathan Cape, 1953), pp. 164–65.

22. CSP 5.311, 7.327, 8.12.

23. George Pappas has pointed out to me that Quine could answer the objections I have raised as follows. Let there be a coordinate system for the universe with t representing the time coordinate. Then define the series of languages Lt1, Lt2, . . . . "All possible observation sentences" could now mean (1) all observation sentences in the sum set of the series, (2) the observation sentences in Ltx when T (our theory of the world) succeeds in explaining all the observation sentences in Ltx, or (3) all observation sentences in language Ltx for all x. Clearly, (1) will not do, since by t some observation sentences in the sum set would have been abandoned. Now (2) would do the job Quine wants it to do, if there were reason to say that after tx no new observation sentences, and so no new observation terms, could be added to the language. But this is utterly implausible; it supposes an end to the process of inquiry, for which supposition no grounds whatever are given. Finally, (3) has more to recommend it. It says that at any time tx, if a theory T explains all observation sentences expressible in Ltx, there is another theory T* that is incompatible and irreconcilable with T and explains all the same observation sentences. But since there is no final state here, one can equally assert that if at any time tx there are theories T and T*, which account for all observation sentences in Ltx and which are incompatible and irreconcilable, then there exists some new observation sentence true at some space-time point tn,w,y,z, which can be added to Ltx to form Ltx + 1 and which is such that either T or T*, but not both, can predict the new sentence, or that neither T nor T* can predict the new sentence but that a new theory T! can be created which will. In short, (3) reduces the strong form of the Underdetermination Thesis to the weak form, and so renders it relatively harmless.

# Explanatory Coherence and Data Sentences

## GEORGE S. PAPPAS

A theory of epistemic justification specifies conditions that must be met if a belief is to be epistemically justified. Such a theory does not attempt to supply an analysis of the concept of epistemic justification; instead, that concept is left undefined but taken as reasonably well understood intuitively, understood at least well enough so that the matter of the correct account of the concept is not an impediment to theory construction.

Among extant theories of epistemic justification, those that receive the greatest attention sort fairly smoothly into three major categories: foundationalism, reliabilism, and coherentism. I think there are plausible theories of epistemic justification within each of these three categories; however, in this paper I will concentrate attention on coherentist theories. My primary interest here concerns explanatory coherence theories, but to provide some idea of what such theories come to, it will be helpful to begin by looking a bit more closely at the general category of coherence theories.

## Subjective and Objective Coherence Theories

Traditionally coherence theories have been what we might term "objective" theories. By this I mean, roughly, that a subject's belief may qualify as justified, according to the theory, provided it stands in certain formal or quasi-formal relations to other beliefs of that subject. This is all that is needed; it is not further required that the subject have any cognitive attitude towards his justified beliefs or towards the quasi-formal or formal relations that such beliefs have to one another. By contrast, subjective coherence theories *do* require that the subject have a belief expressly about each belief that is to be counted as justified.

To bring out this distinction, we may note following Lehrer[1] that the key idea ingredient in all coherence theories, both objective and subjective, is this:

(CT) A belief *b* had by a person *S* at a time *t* is epistemically justified at *t* if and only if: *b* is a member of a system of beliefs had by *s* at *t* and this system of beliefs is coherent at *t*.

The concept of coherence, in turn, is defined in various ways. On one proposal, prominent in the idealist tradition since Hegel, coherence is essentially a logical relation between the propositions believed by the person. So, minimally such a theory would incorporate *CT* as above and then add that

A person *S*'s system of belief *K* is coherent at *t* *iff*: the system *K* is logically consistent, and each of the beliefs in *K* is logically related to each of the other beliefs in *K*.

Strictly, of course, such logical relations obtain between the propositions believed and not between the beliefs in *K*. However, for ease of exposition I will discuss coherent systems of beliefs.

A logical coherence theory along these lines was defended by Blanshard.[2] A different account was proposed and partly defended by C. I. Lewis, as follows:[3]

A system of beliefs *K* is coherent *iff*: *K* is logically consistent and each of the beliefs in *K* is inductively supported by the remaining members of *K*.

The latter sort of theory we might regard as an inductive coherence theory. Notice that with each of these accounts of the concept of coherence, a system of beliefs is coherent provided only that some objective relations hold between the members of the systems in question, in the one case logical relations, in the other some (unspecified) inductive relations. Thus there is no requirement that a subject whose system of beliefs is coherent in either sense should also believe that, for example, the members of the system stand in the relevant logical relations to one another, or believe that one belief in the system is inductively supported by the other beliefs in that same system. In general, the subject need have no beliefs about the coherence of the system of coherent beliefs, nor about the members of the system, nor about the ways in which those members are interrelated. Of course, it might be a psychological truth that a typical subject would have beliefs of this sort; but that is not to the point.

The preceding two theories are objective coherence theories; a subjective theory, along the lines of one defended by Lehrer, can be stated this way:[4]

A system of beliefs *K* is coherent *iff*: *K* is logically consistent, and each member of *K* is such that it is believed to have a better chance of being true than its denial and than every statement with which it competes.

We need not enter into the details of the concept of competition; the important point for present purposes is to note that this account of coherence requires no actual, objective relations between the members of the system of beliefs other than consistency. Instead, the requirement is that the subject believes, *of* the individual members of the system, taken one at a time, that each is more likely to be true than its denial and than any competitor of that belief. It is this factor which makes this a subjective account of the notion of coherence, and quite different from the logical and inductive objective theories, despite the fact that all of these theories incorporate *CT.*

## Explanatory Coherence

Among the objective coherence theories, the logical version has not fared well, and it is easy to see why by consideration of an example. A great many people know and are justified in believing both that Memphis is north of New Orleans and that Jimmy Carter was once president of the United States. Now these two propositions stand in no logical relations to one another. So, a logical coherence theorist would have to say either that these respective beliefs are not justified, and thus do not qualify as knowledge; or, that their justifiedness consists in the fact that though they are logically independent of one another, each is logically related to some subset of propositions contained in the coherent system. To see that the latter option is not plausible, consider a person whose historical and geographical knowledge and justified beliefs vis-a-vis the United States is quite impoverished; she is just now learning American history and geography and presently her beliefs in these two areas are limited to those mentioned above regarding Memphis and Jimmy Carter. Such beliefs would not, or at least need not, be logically related to other justified beliefs in the person's coherent system of beliefs. On the other hand, the first option is not plausible either, for in its general form it would mean that in no case where a person has some newly acquired beliefs in an area with which she was till then totally unfamiliar would those newly acquired beliefs count as justified no matter what else is true of the person or of the manner in which the beliefs were acquired. Better to give up the logical coherence theory than to pay this price for keeping it.

Theoretically, there are many variants of inductive objective coherence theories, depending on which concept or concepts of inductive support are used. However, the variant that has received the greatest amount of attention, both by critics and by those who would defend the theory, is one in which the inductive relation is construed as an explanatory one. It is this sort of theory that one associates with the work of Sellars and perhaps Quine, and I think, with many philosophers who have been influenced by such authors.[5]

I know of three ways in which the notion of explanatory coherence might be analyzed. The first, which is sometimes attributed to Quine, can be expressed this way:[6]

(1) A system of statements $K$ understood and believed by person $S$ is coherent just in case $K$ is consistent and each member of $K$ is explained by the conjunction of the remaining members of $K$.

Another, once endorsed but later rejected by Keith Lehrer, is this:[7]

(2) A system of statements $K$ understood and believed by person $S$ is coherent just in case $K$ is consistent and each statement in $K$ is either (a) a member of some subset of $K$ that serves to explain some member of $K$ not in that subset, or (b) is a statement that is explained by some subset of $K$ but that is itself not a member of any subset of $K$ that explains other members of $K$.

These claims are complex in wording but simple in content. Statement (1) just amounts to saying that in addition to consistency, each member of $K$ must be an *explainer* in order for $K$ to be coherent; and (2) merely says that in addition to consistency, each member of $K$ must be either an explain*er* or an explain*ee* in order for $K$ to be coherent. We thus have two versions of an explanatory coherence theory of justified belief, resulting from conjoining $CT$ and either (1) or (2).

The first of these variants, that which combines $CT$ and (1), is not promising as an account of justified belief. Imagine that $T$ is some well-established and especially fruitful scientific theory, and that it is noticed that $T$ explains some hitherto unsuspected conjecture $p$. Then, given that $T$ is itself justified for appropriate scientists, it would seem that $p$ is justified for those same scientists in virtue solely of the fact that it is explained by $T$. The conjecture that $p$ is justified, in other words, is in virtue of being merely an explainee.

The second variant, the conjunction of $CT$ and (2), fares better, at least concerning the example just presented. However, another example causes trouble for this second variant. Imagine that $S$ knows, and thus is justified in believing, that she is standing thirty feet from the base of a forty-foot-high flagpole, atop which sits an owl. Suppose, too, that next to $S$'s foot is a mouse. $S$, knowing the height of the flagpole and the distance from the mouse and the base of the flagpole, computes that the mouse is fifty feet from the flagpole top. In doing this, she utilizes the Pythagorean Theorem, something she also knows. Hence, $S$ is fully justified in believing that the owl is fifty feet from the mouse. However, the statements she uses in this deduction do not explain why the owl is at that distance from the mouse. Nor need any other beliefs in $S$'s coherent system of beliefs explain this since, we may safely assume, $S$ need know nothing of the dietary propensities of owls. Finally, the statement that the owl is fifty feet from the mouse does not itself explain or figure essentially in the explanation of other beliefs in $S$'s coherent system of beliefs. We thus have a case in which $S$ is fully justified in believing that the owl is fifty feet from the mouse, but this statement neither explains nor is explained by other justified beliefs had by $S$.[8]

A third sort of explanatory coherence, one that probably escapes this sort of counter-example, can be stated this way:

(3) A statement $p$ is justified for a person $S$ *iff:* either (a) $p$ is a member of a system of statements, $K$, understood and believed by $S$, and $K$ has maximal explanatory coherence among the systems of statements understood by $S$; or (b) $p$ is explained by the members of $K$.

Maximal explanatory coherence, in turn, can be explicated this way:

(4) A system of statements, $K$, has maximal explanatory coherence for $S$ just in case among the consistent systems of statements understood and believed by $S$, $K$ explains more of what is to be explained than does any other system of such statements.[9]

The idea behind (4) can be illustrated by noting that a person will typically believe a great many different statements, and that the total number of believed statements can be broken up into different systems or subgroups, each of which is consistent. That subgroup explaining more of whatever is to be explained has maximal explanatory coherence for that person.

It should be clear that we cannot avoid talking of what is to be explained. Maximal explanatory coherence is intuitively the idea that one system of statements does a better job of explaining than some other system or systems. But this way of putting things immediately invites the question of just what it is that one system explains better than another, or more of than another. If system $K$ explains more, or does a better job of explaining, than another system $L$, but only insofar as $K$ explains statements that are not in need of explanation, then no real "victory" over system $L$ is thereby achieved. Explanatory competitiveness between systems of statements makes clear sense only relative to some agreed-upon pool of potential explainees.

Let us call statements to be explained "data statements." Such statements are not data in any sense that recalls the notion of the given; to be a datum is merely to be in need of explanation, relative to some system of beliefs or statements. Then we need to ask how these data statements are selected. That is, we want to know how, given the explanatory coherence theory, any given statement, Si, is justifiably selected as a statement to be explained. Only if there is some way to make such a justifiable selection from within the confines of the explanatory coherence theory is such a theory apt to prove plausible.

A natural answer to the question of the justified selection of data statements is that we select those statements that are individually confirmed by experience. Thus, statements to be explained would be observation statements such as "I see small spots before my eyes." Other statements believed by a person would be justified for that person provided they serve to explain the statement about the small spots. However, it is plain that this option is closed to the defender of the explanatory coherence theory. For this approach would allow some statements to be justified on extra-systematic grounds, while the guiding principle behind all coherence theories is that all justification derives from systematic considerations.

Another approach is "social"; statements to be explained are those that would be assented to by nearly everyone under specific circumstances. The statement concerning the spots would be affirmed by nearly anyone in the right circumstances—when spots are present. Thus, what would serve to justify such an observation statement would be community agreement rather than experience.

To see a problem here, let us label the spot statement "X." Now consider the further statement "The statement 'X' would be assented to by nearly everyone in appropriate circumstances." The foregoing method of picking data statements is adequate only if we are justified in believing the latter statement; but what would its justification be? Either it would be an explaining member of a maximally coherent system of statements or it, too, would be a statement to be explained. Presumably it is not the latter, so it would have to be an explaining member of the system. But what does it explain? We can *give* it an explanatory role. First we label it,

Y: The statement "X" would be assented to by nearly everyone in appropriate circumstances.

and then we note that Y helps to explain another statement, namely

Z: Person A assents to statement "X."

Of course, now our problem breaks out again regarding Z; why should we assume that *it* is a statement to be explained, a data statement? We could solve this problem by stipulating that another statement, Y2, is true,

Y2: The statement "Z" would be assented to by nearly everyone in appropriate circumstances.

The truth of Y2 makes Z a data statement; but what justifies Y2? Presumably it, too, is an explaining member of the maximally coherent system, so perhaps it would explain

W: Person B assents to statement "Z."

It should be clear from just this fragment that the method of community agreement for selecting data statements leads to an infinite regress. That is, this method requires an infinite number of explaining statements and an infinite number of data statements, each of which is justified in order for "X" to be justified. Thus, this regress seems to be vicious, an excellent reason for rejecting the method of community agreement for selecting data statements. [10]

Another method for nonarbitrary selection of data statements has been proposed by Lycan. [11] He thinks that a principle of conservatism is acceptable, one which holds that "the bare fact of one's holding a belief renders that belief justified to some degree; any belief at all is at least minimally justified."[12] Applied to spontaneous beliefs, that is, to beliefs one finds oneself forming or acquiring, this principle becomes the Principle of Credulity: "Accept at the outset each of those things that seems to be true. That is, I hold that each of the spontaneous beliefs I have mentioned is *prima facie* justified, and therefore available as a candidate for explanation in order to get our explanatory enterprise off the ground."[13]

Lycan goes on to note that spontaneous beliefs may not survive as justified (though they may well be kept as beliefs). For they may not form a consistent set at any moment of acquisition, or some may be inconsistent with other previously justified beliefs in one's system of beliefs. Those beliefs that do survive and are explained by one's background justified beliefs are justified fully just because they have been thus explained.

The further details of Lycan's theory need not be examined here. For our present purposes, we need only note three relevant aspects of Lycan's view. First, as he is quick to concede, even emphasize, neither the conservation principle nor the credulity principle is itself epistemically justified. They function, rather, as ultimate principles in support of which very little can actually be said. "They are not . . . justified in the epistemological sense by anything at all."[14] Given this concession, it is hard to see what reason has been given for thinking that spontaneously formed beliefs have any prima facie justification, however slight. Second, even if we waive the first point, Lycan's procedure does not pick out data statements on purely systematic grounds. For these data statements gain their limited degree of justifiedness in virtue of being spontaneously formed. True, Lycan could retreat and claim that all *fully* justified statements gain that status in virtue solely of systematic considerations — in virtue, that is, of explaining or being explained. So one might say that all full justification derives solely from systemic matters, but leave it open that lesser degrees of justification may be conferred in extra-systematic ways. Such a retreat, however, has the ring of a foundational theory, for it abandons the usual coherentist general contention that all justifiedness derives from and only from systemic matters.

These two problems are somewhat minor, but a third is more important. Even if the principle of credulity were epistemically justified, spontaneous beliefs are not justified, even weakly, *as data statements.* They each have some individual justification, given the credulity principle. But this fact does not imply that they are *to be explained.*

Suppose, to illustrate, that *S* forms spontaneously the belief that a tree is in front of her. Then, on Lycan's account, this belief has some minimal degree of justification for *S.* He then takes it for granted that this belief constitutes data, something to be explained. Recall what he says: "I hold that each of the spontaneous beliefs . . . is *prima facie* justified, *and therefore* available as a candidate for explanation in order to get our explanatory enterprise off the ground."[15] From the fact that some belief is thus weakly justified, however, it does not follow that it is to be explained, a belief that stands in need of explanation. And it is the latter sort of claim that one needs to justify, however minimally, if one is to nonarbitrarily select data statements.

I know of just one other attempt to provide a method for selecting data statements—that provided by Rescher.[16] Actually he provides a number of different methods, but I will restrict attention here to just one of them. Rescher uses the abbreviation "m.c.s." for "maximal consistent subset." We suppose that we have a set of inconsistent statements and the task, adapting Rescher's project to present purposes, is to provide a nonarbitrary method for selecting just those m.c.s. that are to be counted as data statements, statements to be explained. Here is what Rescher says:

Assume . . . that the data providing the starting-point are statements put forward by a certain source, and that these form an inconsistent propositional set S. Let it be the case that some (consistent) subset of these propositions yields a particular consequence P. And let us now suppose further that we have external grounds for postulating that P is something that this source could not possibly have intended or could not possibly have accepted. Then we would be in a position to "disqualify" all of those m.c.s. of S that yield P as a consequence—or, equivalently, all those that are incompatible with not-P. Accordingly, we should "prefer" the rest of the m.c.s. over these not-P-incompatible ones.[17]

This idea leads to two rules, which jointly make up the method; the second of these rules is this: "Given an inconsistent propositional set S, to prefer those m.c.s. of S that yield as consequence (i.e., entail) certain 'designated' (or postulated) theses. Thus, if p is 'designated,' Si is preferred whenever: P is deducible from Si."[18] But what are these designated theses? They are the the ones for which one has "external grounds," where such grounds lie outside the system of statements being considered or on hand. Thus, the same problem confronts Rescher's method as we found caused trouble for Lycan's: Data statements are selected only by the assumption of some source of justification that is extra-systematic, justification that is gained in some way other than in virtue of being an explaining or explained member of a coherent system of statements. This strategy is one that strictly abandons coherentism.[19]

I know of no other nonarbitrary method of selecting data statements that does not also depart from coherentism in favor of certain extra-systematic factors. However, it does seem clear that an explanatory coherence theory is the most plausible version of an objective coherence theory one might have; and, if earlier remarks are correct, such a theory must make reference to statements that are to be explained. Lacking a method for justifiably selecting such statements, and lacking, too, any real prospects for finding one, we should draw the conclusion that no objective coherentist theory is apt to prove plausible.

# Notes

1. See Keith Lehrer, *Knowledge* (New York: Oxford University Press, 1974), chap. 7.
2. See Brand Blanshard, *The Nature of Thought* (London: Allen and Unwin, 1939); and Lehrer, *Knowledge,* pp. 157–59.
3. See C. I. Lewis, *Analysis of Knowledge and Valuation* (LaSalle, Ill.: Open Court, 1946), chaps. 11, 12.
4. See Lehrer, *Knowledge,* chap. 8.
5. For example, William Lycan, Conservatism and the Data-Base," in *Reason and Rationality in Natural Science,* ed. Nicholas Rescher (Lanham, Md.: University Press of America, 1985), pp. 103–125.
6. For support of this reading, see Quine's essay, "Posits and Reality," in W. V. O. Quine, *The Ways of Paradox and Other Essays* (Cambridge, Mass.: Harvard University Press, 1966), pp. 233–242.
7. For the endorsement, see Lehrer's essay in *Induction, Acceptance, and Rational Belief,* ed. Marshall Swain (Dordrecht: Reidel, 1970), pp. 100–133; for the rejection, see Lehrer, *Knowledge,* chap. 7.
8. This example derives from Lehrer, *Knowledge,* pp. 166–67.
9. This theory derives from James Cornman, "Foundational versus Non-Foundational Theories of Empirical Justification," in *Essays on Knowledge and Justification,* ed. George Pappas and Marshall Swain (Ithaca, N.Y.: Cornell University Press, 1978), pp. 229–252.
10. This criticism is adapted from Cornman, "Foundational versus Non-Foundational Theories of Empirical Justification."
11. See Lycan, "Conservatism and the Data-Base."
12. Ibid., p. 108.
13. Ibid., pp. 110–11.
14. Ibid., pp. 105–106.

15. Ibid., pp. 110–11; emphasis added.

16. See Nicholas Rescher, *The Coherence Theory of Truth* (New York: Oxford University Press, 1973).

17. Ibid., p. 99.

18. Ibid., p. 100.

19. Rescher's other four methods are considerably more complex and sophisticated, each worthy of detailed investigation. However, space limitations rule out such an examination. I should note, however, that Rescher's other methods for selecting data statements require that certain probability or plausibility claims be established, and I think that some of each are established only on the basis of considerations that lie outside the scope of coherence theories.

# SOCIAL CRITIQUE

# Charles Sanders Peirce's Sociology of Knowledge and Critique of Capitalism

KENNETH W. STIKKERS

"Besides the French and German traditions . . . the literature of American pragmatism is replete with unexploited suggestions for sociology of knowledge." What C. Wright Mills claimed in 1940[1] remains true today. Ironically, though, American pragmatism exerted a profound influence on two of the pioneers of that discipline: Wilhelm Jerusalem and Max Scheler.

From 1900 William James carried on a warm and sympathetic correspondence with Jerusalem, sharing his evolving thoughts on pragmatism and radical empiricism.[2] In 1908 Jerusalem published a German translation of James's *Pragmatism,* and in the introduction he proclaimed himself a pragmatist but mildly criticized James for ignoring the social nature of human knowledge. After reading James's *Pluralistic Universe* Jerusalem wrote to him, and in that letter the term "sociology of knowledge" first appears in English:

> What has struck me most is the compenetration and interpretation of our mental events (we say in German "*Erlebnisse*") and his [Bergson's] conception of "pure drives."

> To place myself inside the events has been the main purpose of my psychology of knowledge. Not only the sensational place of events but truly the process of thinking gets another aspect when considered from within.

> That Life exceeds Logic, as you formulate it, that is one of my fundamental convictions.

> I hope to send you, in a few weeks, an article where the outlines of my future sociology of knowledge are given. I am very eager to hear what you think of this new way.[3]

The article to which Jerusalem refers, "*Soziologie des Erkennes,*" is his seminal work on the subject, outlining those very social conditions of knowledge that he charged James's pragmatism and radical empiricism had ignored.

Max Scheler, who offered the first comprehensive theory of a sociology of knowledge, was also greatly influenced by the American pragmatists. (He was perhaps the first to recognize the significance of Jerusalem's essay, reprinting it as the lead article in the *Koelner Vierteljahrshefte fuer Sozialwissenschaften,* which he edited.) Indeed, his lengthy commentary on American pragmatism, *Erkenntnis und Arbeit,*[4] which focused on Peirce, was intended to complement his *Probleme einer Soziologie des Wissens,* and throughout his writings Scheler speaks positively of the American pragmatists, especially James.[5]

One purpose of this essay is to elucidate some of those "unexploited suggestions for sociology of knowledge" to which Mills refers, as found in the philosophy of Peirce.

Furthermore, although Peirce has been interpreted in a variety of lights — as the founder of pragmatism, a philosopher of science, a mathematician, a logician, a metaphysician — he has never been considered primarily a social philosopher, although much has been written about his notion of community.[6] Indeed, Peirce wrote relatively little explicitly about the nature of society and contemporary social issues. He did, however, think the problem of the relationship between the individual and the community to be a central one for philosophy. "The question whether the *genus homo* has any existence except as individuals, is the question whether there is anything of any more dignity, worth, and importance than individual happiness, individual aspirations, and individual life. Whether men really have anything in common, so that the *community* is to be considered as an end in itself, and if so, what the relative value of the two factors is, is the most fundamental practical question in regard to every public institution the constitution of which we have it in our power to influence."[7] Underlying his thought is a fundamental concern for the whole social dimension of human life, not just for the social nature of human knowing, and scattered throughout his writings are numerous comments highly critical of American capitalism and its Gospel of Greed. A further purpose of this paper, then, is not to transform Peirce into a social thinker — for this he was not — but to elucidate this underlying social concern, demonstrate its significance for Peirce's epistemology, and explain his criticisms of capitalism in light of it.[8]

As John Dewey observed, Darwinism severely challenged philosophy on several fronts.[9] It challenged the history of epistemology as a search for eternal, unchanging verities, suggesting that "truth" is as much in the making as is any other element of nature, and it challenged the history of social theory, which, for the most part, had attempted to build human institutions upon some fixed, eternal laws, for example, the "laws of nature and nature's God" of which the Declaration of Independence speaks. Might the rules governing society, too, be evolving as part of the processes of natural selection? Peirce was among the first to respond to the challenge of Darwinism in his early efforts to establish a new foundation for human knowledge. In his essay "The Fixation of Belief," Peirce suggested that the primary aim of intellectual inquiry is to relieve "irritation," or doubt, which arises when an old habit meets with unfamiliar circumstances, by forming a new belief that will allow us to adapt to the new situation.[10] Thus, Peirce suggested, the formation of new ideas closely parallels the process of natural selection, described by Darwin.

Peirce outlined four methods by which people try to overcome doubt and fixate beliefs in new habits, three of which are essentially social: the method of tenacity, whereby one clings firmly to old beliefs and simply resists the irritations of doubt; the method of authority, whereby an institution determines what constitutes correct belief and enforces it by whatever means it has available; the *a priori* method, based merely upon the subjective whims and fancies of people interacting within a society; and the method of science.

Peirce finds serious fault with each of the first three methods.

The method of tenacity must ultimately fail because it ignores the essentially social character of human existence. "The social impulse is against it," Peirce claims. Inevitably we find that others hold views different from ours, and sooner or later the strength of our tenacity is worn away. Hence, Peirce observes, "Unless we make ourselves hermits, we shall necessarily influence each other's opinion; so that the problem becomes how to fixate belief, not in the individual merely, but in the community."[11] The fixation of belief must be a social rather than an individual process.

Despite its historical successes, the method of authority, too, must eventually fail. To begin with, "no institution can undertake to regulate opinions upon every subject," and once people begin to formulate ideas of their own in areas left uncontrolled by the institution, it will not be long before the ideas begin to affect areas of thought that are so controlled. In addition, every society produces exceptional individuals who see through the arbitrariness of the institutional rules that govern them. These problems within the method of tenacity increase as communication among societies increases and knowledge of past ages becomes more widely available. Thus the method of authority cannot long continue to repress irritations and maintain belief.

The *a priori* method, while appearing to allow great freedom of thought, "does not differ in a very essential way from that of authority." In the free flow of opinions that the *a priori* method permits, "sentiments in their development will be greatly determined by accidental causes" — indeed, as accidental as the method of authority — and, as in the societies dictated by authority, there will arise certain individuals who will not be content with such arbitrariness, but seek a stronger footing for belief.[12] Hence, "the shock of opinions will soon lead men to rest on preferences of a far more universal nature" than those found within the *a priori* method.[13]

Moreover, Peirce criticizes each of these first three methods as being self-verifying and nonfalsifiable. "If I adopt the method of tenacity, and shut myself out from all influences, whatever I think necessary to doing this, is necessary according to that method. So with the method of authority: the state may try to put down heresy by means which, from a scientific point of view seem ill-calculated to accomplish its purposes; but the only test *on that method* is what the state thinks; so that it cannot pursue the method wrongly. So with the *a priori method. The very essence of it is to think as one is inclined to think.*"[14] In other words, none of these methods provides a criterion for distinguishing between right and wrong, correct and incorrect beliefs: *All* views that they assert are deemed uncritically "correct," by virtue of their being so asserted.

To overcome such arbitrariness, Peirce suggests that we seek a criterion for belief that transcends our individual thought. "To satisfy our doubts, therefore, it is necessary that a method should be found by which our beliefs may be determined by nothing human, but by some external permanency — by something upon which our thinking has no effect. . . . Our external permanency would not be external, in our sense, if it was restricted in its influence to one individual [as in mysticism, for example]. It must be something which affects, or might affect, every man."[15] The method of science provides such a criterion. Indeed, "scientific investigation has had the most wonderful triumphs in the way of settling opinion," Peirce proclaims. Its unique contribution to thought is its introduction of the notion of the independently Real. Such a concept is universal and not arbitrary. "Nobody, therefore, can really doubt that there are Reals, for, if he did, doubt would not be a source of dissatisfaction. The hypothesis, therefore, is one which every mind admits. So that the social impulse does not cause men to doubt it."[16]

The scientist thus keeps a constant eye on the Real; rather than being governed by arbitrary, personal feelings and purposes, as the other methods allow,[17] the beliefs of the scientist are made "to coincide with the fact."[18]

But Peirce's formulation of the scientific method in this essay makes it sound much more rigid and impersonal than his writings as a whole would have it.

First, the phrase "the fixation of belief" is misleading: The goal of the scientist, as Peirce suggests in other writings, should not be to fixate belief but rather to keep thought in a constant state of evolutionary process. "The struggle of the scientific man is to try to see the error of his belief — *if he can be said to have any beliefs*. . . . The scientific man is above all things desirous of learning the truth and, in order to do so, ardently desires to have his present provisional beliefs (and *all his beliefs are provisional*) swept away."[19] Moreover, because of the evolving nature of truth,[20] Peirce proclaims that "on the whole, then, we cannot in any way reach such perfect certitude nor exactitude"[21] and suggests that indeed the greatest barriers to science are the efforts to fixate knowledge once and for all.[22]

Second, Peirce introduces a subjective element into his notion of the Real, thereby ridding it of some of its absolutist character. He still maintains that the Real is "that whose characters are independent of what anybody may think them to be,"[23] but this is qualified to mean that "reality is independent, not necessarily of [human] thought in general, but only of what you or I or any finite number of men may think about it, and that, on the other hand, though the object of the final opinion depends on what that opinion is, yet what that opinion is does not depend on what you or I or any man thinks."[24] Reality thus is rooted neither in any sort of purely objective world nor in individual subjectivity, but in human *inter*subjectivity (cf. Edmund Husserl). This socializing of reality, moreover, augments the fallibility of our individual understandings of the Real and makes it all the more essential for us to refrain from fixating our beliefs. "But the scientific spirit requires a man to be at all times ready to dump his whole cartload of beliefs, the moment experience is against them. The desire to learn forbids him to be perfectly cocksure that he knows already. Besides positive science can only rest on experience; and experience can never result in absolute certainty, exactitude, necessity, or universality."[25]

Thus Peirce expanded the social character of reality: Initially the "social impulse" leads us to believe *that* there are such things as "Reals," but then it also tells us something about *what* those Reals are. Reality unfolds in the evolution of human intersubjectivity; it is a social process rather than something to be possessed once and for all by any individual. Such a view is still no Jamesian pluralism: Peirce was not yet ready to "damn the Absolute." Rather, Truth, although no longer identified with hard objective facts, to which the scientist merely conforms her opinions, was now seen as the definite telos of an evolutionary process, which he described in this way:

> Different minds set out with most antagonistic views, but the progress of investigation carries them by a force outside themselves to one and the same conclusion. This activity of thought by which we are carried, not where we wish, but to a fore-ordained goal, is like the operation of destiny. No modification of the point of view taken, no selection of other facts for study,

no natural bent of mind even, can enable a man to escape the predestined opinion of truth and reality. *The opinion which is fated to be ultimately agreed to by all who investigate is what we mean by the truth, and the object represented in this opinion is the real.* That is the way I would explain reality.[26]

Thus, Peirce continues, "all the followers of science are animated by a cheerful hope that the processes of investigation, if only pushed enough, will give one certain solution to each question to which they apply it." This, then, is the definition of truth that emerges: it is what the community of scientists will ultimately agree upon, given sufficient, even infinite, time. His prime example illustrating this evolution of truth is the effort to discover the speed of light. Different scientists using different methods, "may at first obtain different results, but, as each perfects his method and his processes, the results are found to move steadily together toward a destined centre. So with all scientific research."[27]

Scientific knowledge, then, resides in an asymmetrical reciprocity between community and the Real. On the one hand, the Real presupposes community. Recall that earlier we noted that the Real, as a potentiality, arises from the "social impulse" and this impulse allows us "to distinguish between absolute truth and what we do not doubt."[28] The Real thus resides in a vision of a future, ideal society.

> The real, then, is that which, sooner or later, information and reasoning would finally result in, and which is therefore independent of the vagaries of me and you. Thus the very origin of the conception essentially involves the notion of a COMMUNITY, without definite limits, and capable of an indefinite increase of knowledge. . . . What anything real is, is what it may finally come to be known to be in the ideal state of complete information, so that *reality depends on the ultimate decision of the community;* so thought is what it is, only by virtue of its addressing a future thought which is in its value as thought identical with it, though more developed. In this way, the existence of thought now depends on what is to be hereafter; so that it has only a potential existence dependent on the future thought of the community. . . . Reality consists in the agreement that the whole community would eventually come to. . . .[29]

Moreover, since the quest for Truth is a collective effort, the disruption and fragmentation of a society is but the exterior manifestation of the loss of a vision of and/or will to Truth among the individuals of that society. Truth escapes us when our society lacks unity and stability, and, reciprocally, communal harmony dissipates with the loss of our vision of or will to Truth. Truth is correlative with social stability and unity. "When society is broken into bands, now warring, now allied, now for a time subordinated one to another, man loses his conceptions of truth and reason. If he sees one man assert what another denies, he will, if he is concerned, choose his side and set to work by all means in his power to silence his adversaries. The truth for him is that for which he fights."[30] Thus social stability is essential for scientific investigation and progress. Furthermore, insofar as communication is foundational for community, it also is an essential prerequisite for arriving at Truth. Therefore, it is of utmost importance to establish the rules of "How to Make Our Ideas Clear": The hope of the great scientific community rests upon this effort.

On the other hand, a stable society depends upon a collective desire and will to seek the Real — that is, upon the method of science. The method of authority and the *a priori* method cannot adequately deal with dissenting opinions; they merely provide continual, internal irritations, which break up communal solidarity. Ultimately, then, social habits — custom, tradition — must bow before the Real.

Logic occupies a key position in this reciprocal relationship between community and the Real, and hence Peirce's preoccupation with its study. Not only does logic provide us with a method for searching out Truth, it also provides us with the rules of communication, which are so essential to the life of the community. Thus logic is essentially social: Logicality and sociability are two sides of the same coin.

> Logicality requires that our interests should not be limited. They must not stop at our own fate, but must embrace the whole community. This community, again, must not be limited, but must extend to all races of beings with whom we can come into immediate or mediate intellectual relation. It must reach, however vaguely, beyond this geological epoch, beyond all bounds. He who would not sacrifice his own soul to save the whole world, is, as it seems to me, illogical in all his references, collectively. *Logic is rooted in the social principle.*
>
> But all this requires a conceived identification of one's interests with those of an unlimited community.[31]

Logic demands that all selfish interests, all personal claims to Truth, be abandoned. "To be logical men should not be selfish."[32] There is no room for individuality in logic; in fact, "the sole function of . . . logical deliberation," Peirce claims, "is to grind off the arbitrary and the individualistic character of thought."[33] Thus to be logical means to be thoroughly social. "This complete self-sacrifice in man, and the belief in its saving power, will serve to redeem the logicality of men. For he who recognizes the logical necessity of complete self-identification of one's own interests with those of the community. . . . And that ideal perfection of knowledge by which we have seen that reality is constituted must then belong to a community in which this identification is complete."[34] In short, Logic and Love for the community are interdependent.[35]

In the final analysis, though, the Real is more fundamental than society and is what anchors Peirce's system. Science should never surrender to the interests of society. "I must confess," states Peirce, "that I belong to that class of scallawags who propose, with God's help, to look the truth in the face, whether doing so be conducive to the interests of society or not."[36] He condemned traditional wisdom which placed loyalty to the community above loyalty to Truth. "It is noticeable that where different faiths flourish side by side, renegades are looked upon with contempt even by the party whose belief they adopt; so completely has the idea of loyalty replaced that of truth-seeking. Since the time of Descartes, the defect in the conception of truth has been less apparent. Still, it will sometimes strike a scientific man that the philosophers have been less intent on finding out what the facts are, than on inquiring what belief is most in harmony with their system."[37] Community and Reality, although interdependent, are not equally important nor equally foundational to scientific inquiry.

True science, therefore, is of no necessary practical value to the community, and it should not apologize for this. "True science is distinctly the study of useless things. For the useful things will get studied without the aid of scientific men. To employ these rare minds on such work is like running a steam engine by burning diamonds."[38] The true scientist is always viewed as a "radical" by the society in which she lives. "Conservatism — in the sense of a dread of consequences — is altogether out of place in science — which has on the contrary always been forwarded by radicals and radicalism, in the sense of eagerness to carry consequences to their extremes. Not the radicalism that is cocksure, however, but the *radicalism that tries experiments.*"[39] Furthermore, insofar as "morality consists in the folklore of right conduct," according to the standards of society, it is essentially conservative and contrary to the principles of science. Science, for Peirce, must be amoral, if not outright immoral: "Yet in more ways than one an exaggerated regard for morality is unfavorable to scientific progress."[40] "A scientific man must be single-minded and sincere with himself. Otherwise, his love of truth will melt away at once."[41]

It is in light of his insights into the social nature of reality that Peirce's diatribes against modern political economy, that is, capitalism, take on new significance. Generally these attacks have been treated as tangential comments, unrelated to Peirce's larger system of thought, to his metaphysics, epistemology, and logic. But if our analysis is accurate, then they are indeed valid conclusions drawn from his theories and integral, not peripheral, to his central doctrines.

Peirce contended that the nineteenth century was marked by its domination by political economy. "The nineteenth century is now fast sinking into the grave, and we all begin to review its doings and to think what character it is destined to bear as compared with other centuries in the minds of future historians. It will be called, I guess, the Economical Century; for political economy has more direct relations with all the branches of its activity than has any other science." Political economy has built itself upon modern science's findings and principles of logic in its development and organization of the means of production, but the morals governing the distribution of goods in the market economy are fundamentally opposed to those of science. Science and logic are dependent upon the "social impulse." This means that to be scientific and logical is to place "public spirit" above personal gain. But the marketplace of capitalism operates upon an opposite morality. "Well, political economy has its formula of redemption, too. It is this: Intelligence in the service of greed ensures the justest prices, the fairest contracts, the most enlightened conduct of all the dealings between men, and leads to the *summum bonum*. . . . The great attention paid to economical questions during our century has induced an exaggeration of the beneficial effects of greed . . . , until there has resulted a philosophy which comes unwittingly to this, that greed is the great agent in the elevation of the human race and in the evolution of the universe."[42] Indeed, the influence of political economy in the modern age has been so profound that ethical systems have emerged within philosophical circles to accommodate and to rationalize its growth and development, for example, utilitarianism.

Surely, then, for Peirce, the political economy of capitalism is antiscientific and hence a most despicable creature: it leeches upon the discoveries of science but then undermines science's very foundations in community by using such discoveries for the promotion of personal gain — all the while acknowledging "that society could not exist upon a basis of intelligent greed alone."[43] "The old-fashioned political economist adored, as alone capable of redeeming the human race, the glorious principle of individual greed, although, as this principle requires for its action hypocrisy and fraud, he generally threw in some dash of inconsistent concessions to virtue, as a sop to the vulgar Cerberus. But it is easy to see that the only kind of science this principle would favour would be such as is immediately remunerative with a great preference for such as can be kept secret, like the modern sciences of dyeing and perfumery."[44] Neither community nor science can prosper and grow under such conditions of greed and secrecy, and the history of political economy has thus been a history of the systematic destruction of human society and simultaneous dismantling of human reason — for, remember, community and logic are two sides of the same coin. If for no other reason, political economy is to be condemned because it is a self-destructive system, as Peirce prophetically warned. "Soon a flash and quick peal will shake economists quite out of their complacency, too late.

The Twentieth Century, in its latter half, shall surely see the deluge-tempest burst upon the social order,— to clear upon a world as deep in ruin as that greed-philosophy has long plunged it into guilt."[45]

Modern America, for Peirce, is thus in the middle of a conflict between its Christian tradition, which teaches that redemption occurs in communal love, on the one hand, and the demands of political economy, which preaches the virtues of self-interest and personal gain, on the other. "Here, then, is the issue," Peirce summarized. "The gospel of Christ says that progress comes from every individual merging his individuality in sympathy with his neighbors. On the other side, the conviction of the nineteenth century is that progress takes place by virtue of every individual's striving for himself with all his might and trampling his neighbor under foot whenever he gets a chance to do so. This may accurately be called the Gospel of Greed."[46]

Thus I have suggested that, although Peirce was not primarily a social philosopher, a deep social concern permeates his thinking. In particular, Peirce offered numerous important contributions to the sociology of knowledge, insights into the fundamentally social nature of human cognition and of reality itself. On the one side, to be reasonable means to be social; on the other side, reality resides only in communal inquiry, in human intersubjectivity. Moreover, these insights formed the basis for Peirce's sharp attacks on American capitalism, attacks that are not tangential to his theories but valid conclusions drawn from his metaphysical doctrines, epistemology, and logic.

# Notes

1. C. Wright Mills, bibliographical appendix to *Contemporary Social Theory,* ed. Harry Elmer Barnes, Howard Becker, and Frances Bennett Becker (New York: D. Appleton-Century, 1940), p. 892. See also C. Wright Mills, "Language, Logic, and Culture," *American Sociological Review* 4 (1939): 670–80; Mills, "Methodological Consequences of the Sociology of Knowledge," *American Journal of Sociology* 46 (Nov., 1940): 316–30.

2. Ralph Barton Perry, *The Thought and Character of William James,* 2 vols. (Boston: Little, Brown and Co., 1935), vol. 2, p. 580.

3. Letter of Wilhelm Jerusalem to William James, May 2, 1909, in Papers of William James, Houghton Library, Harvard University, MS 450. See also William James, *Der Pragmatismus: Einer neuer Name fuer alter Denkmethoden,* trans. Wilhelm Jerusalem (Leipzig: W. Klinkhard, 1908); and Wilhelm Jerusalem, "Soziologie des Erkennes," *Die Zukunft* 67 (May, 1909): 236–46; rpt. in *Koelner Vierteljahrshefte fuer Sozialwissenschaften* 1 (1921): 28ff.

4. Max Scheler, *Gesammelte Werke,* vol. 8: *Erkenntnis und Arbeit* (Bern:

Francke Verlag, 1979), pp. 191–382. In the same volume, see also *Wissensformen und die Gesellschaft,* ed. Manfred S. Frings.

5. For additional information on the relationship between American pragmatism and Scheler's sociology of knowledge, see Kenneth W. Stikkers, introduction to Max Scheler, *Problems of a Sociology of Knowledge,* ed. Kenneth W. Stikkers, trans. Manfred S. Frings (London: Routledge and Kegal Paul, 1980), pp. 24–26.

6. See, for example, John E. Smith, "Community and Reality," in *Perspectives on Peirce: Critical Essays on Charles Sanders Peirce,* ed. Richard J. Bernstein (New Haven, Conn.: Yale University Press, 1965), pp. 92–119; rpt. in John E. Smith, *Themes in American Philosophy: Purpose, Experience, and Community* (New York: Harper and Row, 1970), pp. 80–108. See also R. Jackson Wilson, "Charles Sanders Peirce: The Community of Inquiry," in *In Quest of Community: Social Philosophy in the United States, 1860–1929* (London: Oxford University Press, 1970), pp. 32–59; Murray G. Murphey, *The Development of Peirce's Philosophy* (Cambridge, Mass.: Harvard University Press, 1961); Vincent G. Potter, S.J., *Charles S. Peirce: On Norms and Ideals* (Amherst: University of Massachusetts Press, 1967); Joseph P. DeMarco, "Peirce's Concept of Community: Its Development and Change," *Transactions of the Charles S. Peirce Society* 7 (Winter, 1971): 24–36; Mary B. Mahowald, "Peirce's Concept of Community: Another Interpretation," *Transactions of the Charles S. Peirce Society* 9 (Summer, 1973): 175–86; Jacob Liszka, "Community in C. S. Peirce: Science as a Means and as an End," *Transactions of the Charles S. Peirce Society* 14 (Fall, 1978): 305–21.

7. Charles Sanders Peirce, *Collected Papers,* ed. Charles Hartshorne, Paul Weiss, and Arthur Burks (Cambridge, Mass.: Harvard University Press, 1958), vol. 8, para. 38. The passage is also reproduced in Charles Sanders Peirce, *Writings of Charles S. Peirce: A Chronological Edition,* vol. 2, ed. Edward C. Moore (Bloomington: Indiana University Press, 1984), p. 487. The emphasis in the passage is in the original. Hereafter, reference to Peirce, *Collected Papers,* will be given as CSP followed by a volume number and a paragraph number, in the standard fashion.

8. To the best of my knowledge, no one has yet related Peirce's scattered critical comments on capitalism to his philosophical system as a whole: Such comments are generally viewed as tangential and unrelated to Peirce's main doctrines. Megill observes some superficial similarities between Peirce and Marx but fails to connect Peirce's criticisms of capitalism with the whole of his *Weltanschauung;* see Kenneth A. Megill, "Peirce and Marx," *Transactions of the Charles S. Peirce Society* 3 (Fall, 1967): 55–65.

9. John Dewey, "The Influence of Darwin on Philosophy," in *The Influence of Darwin on Philosophy and Other Essays in Contemporary Thought* (New York: Henry Holt, 1910), pp. 1–19.

10. CSP 5.358–5.387.

11. CSP 5.378.

12. CSP 5.383.

13. CSP 5.382.

14. CSP 5.385; emphasis in the original.

15. CSP 5.384.

16. Ibid.

17. CSP 5.385.

18. CSP 5.387.

19. CSP 6.3; emphasis added.

20. CSP 1.107–1.109.

21. CSP 1.147; see also 1.120.

22. CSP 1.135–1.140.

23. CSP 5.405.

24. CSP 5.408.

25. CSP 1.55.

26. CSP 5.408; emphasis added. John Dewey referred to this as "the best definition of *truth* from the logical standpoint which is known to me." See John Dewey, *Logic: The Theory of Inquiry* (New York: Henry Holt, 1938), p. 345n.

27. CSP 5.407; see also Max Fisch, "The Classic Period in American Philosophy," general introduction to *Classic American Philosophers* (New York: Appleton-Century-Crofts, 1951), p. 14.

28. CSP 5.421.

29. CSP 5.311, 5.316, and 5.331; emphasis added.

30. CSP 1.59.

31. Emphasis added.

32. CSP 2.654.

33. CSP 1.178.

34. CSP 5.356.

35. I am reminded here of Frederick Soddy's observation: "Amid all the sneers at the impracticality and visionary character of communist schemes, let it not be forgotten that science is a communism neither theoretical nor on paper, but actual and in practice. The results of those who labour in the fields of knowledge for its own sake are published and pooled in the general stock for the benefit of all. Common ownership of all its acquisition is the breath of its life. Secrecy or individualism of any kind would destroy its fertility." See Frederick Soddy, *Science and Life,* Aberdeen Address (New York: E. P. Dutton, 1920), pp. 2–3.

36. CSP 8.143.

37. CSP 5.406.

38. CSP 1.76.

39. CSP 1.148; emphasis in the original.

40. CSP 1.50.

41. CSP 1.49.

42. CSP 6.290.

43. CSP 6.291.

44. CSP 1.75. Cf. Adam Smith's use of dye manufacturing as a prime example of trade secrets and their effects in commanding "extraordinary profits" for the manufacturer: Adam Smith, *An Inquiry into the Nature and Causes of the Wealth of Nations,* ed. Edwin Cannan (Chicago: University of Chicago Press, 1976), book I, pp. 68–69. See also Soddy's remarks above in note 35.

45. CSP 6.292.

46. CSP 6.294; see also Henry Steele Commager, *The American Mind: An Interpretation of American Thought and Character Since the 1880's* (New Haven, Conn.: Yale University Press, 1950), pp. 228, 232.

# Emma Goldman and the Spirit of Artful Living: Philosophy and Politics in the Classical American Period

### LYNNE M. ADRIAN

Emma Goldman is an important, though neglected, figure of the classical period of American philosophy. Though she was almost entirely self-educated and regarded herself as an anarchist agitator, her impact on the thought of American intellectuals was wide ranging and profound. Goldman's thinking covered a multitude of subjects; this essay will focus on a singular area that may be among the most ignored but most important aspects of her thought aesthetics. Unique historical conditions during this modernizing era allowed Goldman to construct an aesthetic that shifted the concept of art from a *product* to a *process*. Because of this shift all creative human endeavors, and indeed life itself, could be regarded as artful. Moreover, the concept of artful living is a necessary insight into much of the intellectual activity of the period, and through her writing and speaking Emma Goldman did much to vitalize this concept in the intellectual and artistic world. During the years from 1906 to 1916 Goldman lectured from 120 to 320 times a year. She "later estimated that she had spoken to between 50,000 and 75,000 people every year."[1] Many of her contemporaries credited her with introducing them to the modern drama, particularly in its connection to developing industrial society and not merely as an isolated aesthetic variance, and her drama lectures often inspired the formation of drama study groups. "According to one observer, as Goldman spoke she burned 'with the flaming ardor of an apocalytic vision' that she found expressed so eloquently in Whitman, Neitzsche, Gorky and Hauptmann."[2] She also provided both the funds and the sustaining vision for her magazine *Mother Earth* (circulation three to five thousand), which was one of the first important pre-World War I "little magazines" with readers ranging "from Italian immigrant silkworkers and Philadelphia pharmacists to Alfred Stieglitz, Eugene O'Neill, and the painter Robert Henri."[3]

During the fin-de-siecle years, the conception of art was changed radically. Previously art had been defined in terms of the beautiful—a product only of those human endeavors directed into certain traditionally approved channels, such as classical music, drama, poetry, novels, painting, sculpture, and ballet. Between 1890 and 1915 American intellectuals and artists began to regard other forms as artistic. For these Americans, art had ceased to be a *product* and had become instead a *process* through which something whole and richly satisfying was produced. With this shift one could now think of living life not only in a beautiful way, but *artfully* as well, making life itself part of one's artwork. These beliefs opened for the first time the prospect that anyone engaging fully in a human occupation might be an artist. If the painting was merely the trace left by the artistic process of living, as Henri maintained, then it could be regarded as no more inherently a work of art than a well-made table, a freely educated child, or a labor union improving the ability of many to live wholly.

Artful living became the process of living all of one's life in an artful manner, of creating a unity and meaning out of all the experiences of life. It was in part derived from a central anarchist principle that "the goal of the ethical life was to live in harmony with one's principles and to reduce inconsistency so that one could be an inspiration to others."[4] It differed from "beautiful living" in that it did not consist of merely appreciating the beautiful things around oneself. It was rather an active, synthetic principle involving the process of conscious human creation. As a process it was a rich, wholistic concept, which could never be reduced to a set of first principles offering a pattern to be followed; instead it was an idea or direction that must be individually synthesized.

Artful living, then, with its view of art as a process, seems perfectly suited to someone like Goldman, whose life and thought were almost one. One of the most striking features of Emma Goldman's writing is the extent of her knowledge. She quoted diverse sources, from the Bible to Marx, Whitman to Goethe, Kropotkin to Jefferson, and all with equal fluency. Such literacy is particularly amazing when one pauses to remember that Goldman completed only one year of education in a German *Realschule* and some technical training in nursing. Though grounded in European philosophical anarchism, Goldman's use of organism and creativity in her aesthetics related more directly to the American tradition, particularly that of the Transcendentalists. In addition to the European sources of anarchism (Bakunin, Proudhon, Kropotkin, and Nietzsche—and, for Goldman, Freud as well), she was also versed in the American philosophical tradition of Jefferson and the Transcendentalists.[5]

Shortly after Goldman's arrival in New York City and her active entrance into the anarchist movement, she became acquainted with Justus Schwab, an anarchist and the owner of an inn where east side radicals often met. He introduced her to the writings of Whitman, Emerson, Thoreau, Hawthorne, Spencer, Mill, Jefferson, and other English and American authors, all of which she eagerly absorbed. She noted in her autobiography the importance of her intellectual affinity to these figures, stating that simultaneous attempts to interest her in spiritualism failed completely.[6] After a brief period of intense review of thinkers such as Jefferson, she turned increasingly to the Transcendentalists. She was influenced by these thinkers, and they were incorporated into both Goldman's concept of anarchism and her political activism. "As time went on she drew rather on other figures in the American background, on Emerson, Whitman, and especially, Thoreau. Contrary to uncritical thinking on this subject, there was in America a native radical tradition that meshed nicely with anarchist theory. . . . Thus while the content and form of her dream came primarily from Russian sources, this dream could put down roots in the hospitable soil of a native tradition."[7]

The clarity with which this synthesis of thought occurred was remarkable. American and European traditions are no longer differentiated, and concepts are not drawn from one or the other. Instead, Goldman blended the two into her own use of the terms. A key instance of this blending is her use of the concept of "organicism." Use of organic metaphors to explain both individual persons and social constructs are common in both European anarchist thought and American Transcendentalism. Organic metaphors occur throughout Goldman's writing as well, often in crucial places in her discussion of aesthetics and education. In fact, Goldman used organic metaphors to bridge the two key contradictions within anarchist theory. One of these perennially problematic contradictions is the question of whether the intellectuals or the workers will be the guiding force in developing anarchism. Goldman followed both European anarchist theory and the example of Thoreau in advocating a unity between intellectual and manual labor, noting that "intellectual and physical labour are as closely related in the social body as brain and hand in the human organism. One cannot function without the other."[8] The other tension within anarchism is between the individual and the mass as the locus of social change and regeneration. This tension is expressed in the problematic relationship between individual and communistic anarchism. Here also, Goldman was dependent on an organic metaphor to demonstrate that in her anarchist theory individualism could be blended with working-class consciousness and commitment and eventually be revolutionarily enacted through syndicalist economic practices. "Anarchism is therefore the teacher of the unity of life; not merely in nature, but in man. There is no conflict between the individual and the social instincts, any more than there is between the heart and the lungs; the one the receptacle of the precious life essence, the other the repository of the element that keeps the essence pure and strong. The individual is the heart of society, conserving the essence of social life; society is the lungs which are distributing the element to keep the life essence — that is, the individual — pure and strong."[9]

Despite Goldman's frequent references to the Emerson-Whitman tradition, it is important to note several critical differences in her use of terms such as "organicism." For Emerson and Thoreau, organic unity was given by a deistic Oversoul. For these men the world was a wholistic, unified "garden" in which problems of discord were caused by human unwillingness to assume the proper place in nature and to perceive the overriding organic unities of the universe. For Goldman, however, this organic unity in the individual and society as a whole was created through growth in consciousness and in greater freedom of individual expression. As she wrote in *Anarchism and Other Essays,* "I begin with an admission: Regardless of all political and economic theories treating of the fundamental differences between various groups within the human race, regardless of class and race distinctions, regardless of all artificial boundary lines between woman's rights and man's rights, I hold that there is a point where these differentiations may meet and *grow* into one perfect whole."[10] Thus, social unity and harmony mimic nature, but they were arrived at not from imitation of a preexisting pattern in nature, but through conscious human growth and free choice.

Because of Goldman's atheism, this rooting of both creativity and good and evil in humankind is especially emphatic. Creativity is internal and thus artful, rather than being a derivative of the Oversoul as it is for Emerson. One creates art through an active process rather than from becoming Emerson's transparent eyeball, seeing nature whole. While Emerson emphasizes process in art (the vision over the picture produced), it is still a process *towards* a fixed ideal which both the philosopher and the artist seek. Since Transcendentalism often drew on Hegelian idealism, such an emphasis is not surprising. For Goldman, however, any preexisting categories are deadening and process is ongoing — not fixed by being a process *towards* an ideal, but rather one that is an end in and of itself. Thus, living can be considered *artful* rather than *beautiful* because it is a creative process, the artistry residing in the individual's own efforts toward unity and growth rather than in living in harmony with a universal plan of God or Nature. The Transcendentalists, in this view, have only the potential for *beautiful* living in harmony with nature, rather than *artful* living.

This different attribution of the source of unity also creates very different interpretations of good and evil. For Emerson evil is not really terribly "bad," because once it is thoroughly understood evil can be seen as united with good in the Oversoul. For Goldman, however, evil is situated within the province of humanity. Either it is the result of present conditions (as she maintains is 90 percent of all crime), or it is inherent in the individual, in which case no amount of legislation would eradicate it. Thus, evil is real and not merely human failure to understand the ultimate order of the universe. Goldman would further credit much of the Transcendentalists' desire to explain evil as the lack of understanding of the underlying order of the universe to Nietzsche's concept of transvaluation, whereby people turn a vice that cannot be overcome into a virtue, rather than admit their impotence. Emerson unified evil with good in the glorified Oversoul because of an inability to eradicate it; if evil cannot be eliminated it must instead be converted into a part of the good. Goldman herself uses a similar process when she locates organicism in human creativity; since she no longer finds human beings impotent, bound to follow unknown, greater powers, she reverses the previous transvaluation. The resulting end of human impotence renders possible *artful* rather than merely *beautiful* living.

Emma Goldman's artful living is lucidly demonstrated by her concern for the artist's position in society. Though she tended to focus her attention upon drama, she was familiar with many artists, and other art forms, and always believed that a large part of her success in the United States was due to her refusal to limit herself solely to subjects in political economy.[11] Even during tense political situations, she deemed the modern drama an appropriate subject, for example, choosing to lecture on Ibsen's *Enemy of the People* during a particularly violent free-speech fight.[12] For her, "the modern artist is, in the words of August Strindberg, 'a lay preacher popularizing the pressing questions of his time.'"[13] The work of such artists was essential, for Goldman believed that political harangues alone could never reach sufficiently large audiences to revolutionize social conditions. "An adequate appreciation of the tremendous spread of the modern, conscious social unrest cannot be gained from merely propagandistic literature. Rather must we become conversant with the larger phases of human expression manifest in art, literature, and, above all, the modern drama — the strongest and most far-reaching interpreter of our deep-felt dissatisfaction."[14]

Having accepted such a vital role for the artist in the regeneration of society, Goldman was nonetheless unstinting in her criticism of those who failed to speak honestly of daily life and instead chose material success. In an article entitled "Intellectual Proletarians" she referred to the artists who chose to become successful in contemporary social terms as "dead souls upon the intellectual horizon. The uncompromising and daring spirits never 'arrive.' Their life represents an endless battle with the stupidity and the dullness of their time. They must remain what Neitzsche calls 'untimely,' because everything that strives for new form, new expression or new values is always doomed to be untimely."[15] For Goldman, many members of the bohemian art community fit into the same category. In an address to them in 1909 she clearly outlined her position on artful living and its importance in her aesthetic.

> The majority of the (artist) Guilders impressed me as people to whom "bohemianism" was a sort of narcotic to help them endure the boredom of their lives. Of course there were others, those who knew the struggle that is the lot of every sincere and free person, whether he aspires to an ideal in life or in art. To them I addressed my talk on "Art in Life," pointing out . . . that *life in all its variety and fullness is art, the highest art.* The man who is not part of the stream of life is not an artist, no matter how well he paints sunsets or composes nocturnes. It certainly does not mean that the artist must hold a definite creed, join an anarchist group or a socialist local. It does signify, however, that he must be able to feel the tragedy of the millions condemned to a lack of joy and beauty.[16]

Alfred Stieglitz, whose "291" art gallery and *Camera Work* magazine introduced both art photography and abstract art to the United States, considered himself an anarchist and helped support *Mother Earth,* as did the noted photography critic Sadakichi Hartmann.[17] However, the most influential convert Goldman made to her aesthetics was probably the painter Robert Henri, who defined himself as an anarchist from the 1890s until his death in 1929. He became one of Goldman's personal friends who regularly attended her art and drama lectures and held long discussions on aesthetics with her while he painted her portrait. Henri is particularly significant because he influenced an entire generation of artists through the art classes Goldman persuaded him to offer at the Modern School of the Francisco Ferrer Center in New York City. Henri trained not only the so-called Ashcan painters, but also Arthur B. Davies, the organizer of the Armory Show in 1913, and other important figures in the American abstract art movement, including Stuart Davis and Man Ray.[18] Rockwell Kent referred to Henri as "possibly the most important figure in our cultural history."[19]

Henri is perhaps the clearest example of this shift from product to process and from beautiful life to artful living in the thought of the artistic community. In *The Art Spirit,* a compilation of notes, articles, fragments of letters, and talks to students, he opens by stating: "Art when really understood is the province of every human being. It is simply a question of doing things, anything, well. It is not an outside, extra thing."[20] Thus, art is no longer a separate enterprise, but has become a part of all life. It is no longer the province of a select few who can paint or sculpt, but includes the doing of anything well, by anyone. This position leads Henri to state later in his work that "I am not interested in art as a means of making a living, but I am interested in art as a means of living a life. It is the most important of all studies, and all studies are tributary to it."[21] Still later in the work, he states that "to be an artist is to construct, and to whatever degree one shows the genius for construction in work of any sort, he is that much an artist. The *artist* life is therefore the desirable life, and it is possible to all."[22]

Goldman's links to new movements in art were not restricted to the visual arts. If anything, her impact was clearer in the drama, which was her particular forte as a critic and popularizer. The Free Theater at the Ferrer Center "held a pioneering place in the 'little theater' movement which emerged in New York during the war. Links between the Free Theatre and drama groups in Greenwich Village were numerous. . . . The Provincetown Players, launched in 1916, emerged from the same circles, with Floyd Dell, Hutchins Hapgood, Eugene O'Neill, William Zorach, and Stella Balantine (Emma Goldman's niece) among the founders. Harry Weinberger, a close friend of Emma and Berkman, became the group's attorney, and M. Eleanor Fitzgerald, Berkman's companion, its manager and most vital figure. Among its first productions were works by Mike Gold and John Reed, as well as Dell and O'Neill, all of whom attended the Ferrer Center."[23] In turn, in her role as drama critic in Goldman was "one of the first to recognize [O'Neill's] importance as a modern dramatist, and she afterwards lectured on him in England."[24]

While her magazine *Mother Earth* is not noted for its innovative aesthetic choices, it seems possible that other related magazines reaped the artistic benefits *Mother Earth* missed because Goldman personally tended to prefer realistic writers. *The Masses* opened its pages to many of the anarchists connected with the Ferrer Center and Goldman, her friend Theodore Dreiser wrote an article for *Revolt* (published by fellow *Mother Earth* editor Hippolyte Havel); and the Ferrer Center's in-house magazine *The Modern School* regularly published works by innovative artists such as Hart Crane, Wallace Stevens, and Mike Gold.[25]

I would further maintain that Emma Goldman's concept of artful living had an impact on the aesthetics Dewey develops in *Art as Experience*. "Emma Goldman . . . was a friend of John Dewey's and 'had a high regard for his ideas.'"[26] In turn, Dewey was publicly defending her as early as 1901, when he responded to the press attacks that followed McKinley's assassination by insisting "that Emma Goldman's 'reputation as a dangerous woman was built up entirely by a conjunction of yellow journalism and ill-advised police raids. She is a romantically idealistic person with a highly attractive personality.'"[27] Throughout her lifetime, Dewey continued to be a personal friend and correspondent of Goldman's; he was one of the sponsors of her 1934 visa request, and gave one of the addresses at a welcoming dinner in New York.[28] Given their friendship, it does not surprise me that Dewey's assertion in the opening chapter of *Art as Experience* that "the intelligent mechanic engaged in his job, interested in doing well and finding satisfaction in his handiwork, caring for his materials and tools with genuine affection is artistically engaged"[29] echoes Goldman's comparison of making a table to an artist painting. Dewey begins with the strong belief that art is not separate from life, and that "*theories* which isolate art and its appreciation by placing them in a realm of their own, disconnected from other modes of experiencing, are not inherent in the subject-matter but arise because of specifiable extraneous conditions."[30] In fact, as George Axtelle observed, "Dewey greatly expanded the common usage of the term 'art': any activity carried on with loving care for its outcome is by definition art."[31] While more systematically developed as philosophy, Dewey's aesthetics seem to echo Goldman's concept of artful living.

It is certainly suggestive to see Emma Goldman as a key connection between "artful living" as an aesthetic concept, innovative arts, art educators, and philosophers of aesthetics. In her drama lectures, in her life itself, and in the art she created in her autobiography *Living My Life,* Emma Goldman developed, articulated, and helped popularize the aesthetic concept of "artful living," which is, I believe, crucial to understanding the temper of the classical period of American philosophy.

## Notes

1. Alice Wexler, *Emma Goldman: An Intimate Life* (New York: Pantheon Books, 1984), p. 166.

2. Martha Solomon, *Emma Goldman* (Boston: Twayne Publishers, 1987), p. 26.

3. Wexler, *Emma Goldman,* p. 124.

4. Blaine McKinley, "'The Quagmires of Necessity,' American Anarchists and Dilemmas of Vocation," *American Quarterly* 34 (1982), p. 504. See also David DeLeon, *The American as Anarchist: Reflections on Indigenous Radicalism* (Baltimore: Johns Hopkins University Press, 1978).

5. In regard to the influences of American thinkers, it is important to note that Emma Goldman considered herself to be more an American than of any other nationality. After having established deep roots in the United States, her deportation in 1919 was a personal tragedy mitigated only by her belief that in Russia she could help in building the revolution. After leaving Russia in 1921, she became virtually a woman without a country, and to the end of her life Goldman felt a deep bond with the United States. As she noted in her autobiography, "There still

was a large place in my heart for my erstwhile country, regardless of her shabby treatment. My love for all that is ideal, creative, and humane in her would not die. But I should rather never see America again if I could do so only by compromising my ideas." Emma Goldman, *Living My Life,* 2 vols. (1931; New York: Dover, 1970), vol. 2, p. 988.

6. Goldman, *Living My Life,* vol. 1, p. 145.

7. Richard Drinnon, *Rebel in Paradise: A Biography of Emma Goldman* (New York: Bantam, 1973), pp. 41–42n.

8. Emma Goldman, *My Further Disillusionment in Russia* (Garden City, N.J.: Doubleday, Page and Co., 1924), p. 166.

9. Emma Goldman, *Anarchism and Other Essays* (Port Washington, N.Y.: Kennikat Press, 1910), p. 52.

10. Ibid., p. 213.

11. Goldman, *Living My Life,* vol. 2, p. 527.

12. Goldman, *Living My Life,* vol. 1, p. 495.

13. Emma Goldman, *The Social Significance of Modern Drama* (Boston: Richard G. Badger, 1914), p. 3.

14. Goldman, *Anarchism and Other Essays,* p. 241.

15. Emma Goldman, "Intellectual Proletarians," in *Red Emma Speaks: Selected Writings and Speeches by Emma Goldman,* ed. Alix Kates Shulman (New York: Vintage Books, 1972), pp. 177–78.

16. Goldman, *Living My Life,* vol. 1, pp. 463–64; emphasis added.

17. Paul Avrich, *The Modern School Movement: Anarchism and Education in the United States* (Princeton: Princeton University Press, 1980), pp. 153, 125–26.

18. Donald Drew Egbert, *Socialism and American Art: In the Light of European Utopianism, Marxism, and Anarchism* (Princeton: Princeton University Press, 1967), p. 96; Avrich, *The Modern School Movement,* p. 157; Diane Kelder, ed., *Stuart Davis: Documentary Monographs in Modern Art* (New York: Praeger, 1971), pp. 3–4.

19. Avrich, *The Modern School Movement,* p. 150.

20. Robert Henri, *The Art Spirit,* comp. Margery Ryerson (Philadelphia: J. B. Lippincott Co., 1923), p. 15.

21. Ibid., p. 158.

22. Ibid., p. 221.

23. Avrich, *The Modern School Movement,* p. 143.

24. Ibid., p. 145.

25. Ibid., pp. 130, 141, 164.

26. Ibid., p. 38.

27. Drinnon, *Rebel in Paradise,* p. 106.

28. Ibid., p. 344.

29. John Dewey, *Art as Experience* (New York: G. P. Putnam's Sons, 1934), p. 5.

30. Ibid., p. 10. See also Max Eastman, "John Dewey," *The Atlantic Monthly* (Dec., 1941), pp. 671–85.

31. George Axtelle, "John Dewey and the Genius of American Civilization," in *John Dewey and the World View,* ed. Douglas E. Lawson and Arthur E. Lean (Carbondale: Southern Illinois University Press, 1964), p. 55.

# Contradictions in American Culture

## JOHN J. RYDER

Cultures are rich and variegated phenomena, and a society with any complexity at all can expect its broad cultural aspects to be characterized by diversity, ironic relations and connections, conflict, and even contradiction. The range of relevant social differences is wide. Ethnic diversity embodies cultural differences, gender distinctions and relations are significant, class divisions have as constituent phenomena various cultural traits and ideological commitments, and even far less fundamental aspects of people's lives, such as personal taste in art or recreation, are not irrelevant. Cultural diversity and even conflict is to be expected of any society not yet atrophied to the point of near extinction.

American society and culture are not exceptions to this generalization. Our history is replete with the diversity, irony, and conflict characteristic of a society in the complex process of development. The Puritan flight from religious and political repression before long produced a society characterized by witch hunts, repression, and ostracism of its own dissidents. Puritan culture in the century or so of its preeminence saw the remarkably ironic slide from an otherworldly emphasis typical of religious utopianism, a New Canaan and a City on a Hill, to a distinctive commitment to mercantile and business success.[1] In the nineteenth century Thoreau would focus his attention on a pervasive contradiction of American culture and ideology. While committing itself to freedom and the value of human individuals, the nation was quite prepared to comply with the Fugitive Slave Law and with the existence of slavery itself. Thoreau was particularly outraged by the willingness of the political leaders and citizenry of his own state of Massachusetts to return runaway slaves to their masters. "The remembrance of my country," he said, "spoils my walk."[2] More recently, Dewey commented at length and insightfully on three central and pervasive components of American culture and ideology: freedom, individuality, and intelligence.[3] Some of Dewey's themes have been taken up again by John McDermott, particularly his discussion of cynicism and meliorism in American life.[4] And the enduring theme of the tension between individuality and community in our culture has received fresh treatment by Robert Bellah and his associates.[5]

Dewey had a fairly sharp eye for disharmony, perhaps because he was so deeply committed to the pursuit of community and shared interests. He argued that the longstanding faith in freedom central to the American identity and to our history had by this century resulted in a situation in which in the name of freedom most Americans were dominated by a system and policies distinctly incompatible with free development. Similarly, in the name of individuality we had allowed the individual activity of some to crush the conditions necessary for the individual growth of the many. And in the name of intelligence we had erected a stultifying cultural dogmatism. Dewey explained these contradictions in terms of a conflict between the content of our cultural and ideological values on the one hand and the material conditions that have resulted from the evolution of American society on the other. The basic problem, in Dewey's view, is that the values we generally endorse are no longer appropriate given the characteristics of an advanced industrial society. Our conception of freedom, for example, is inherited directly from the eighteenth century. In the centuries of struggle against feudal and monarchist fetters, a conception of freedom as the absence of constraint was a powerful revolutionary weapon. But material and social conditions have so thoroughly changed in two hundred years that the very same conception is now an obstacle to freedom. The problem, Dewey argues, is that the content of our values is anachronistic. The contradiction can be overcome, in this view, by revising our understanding of freedom, individuality, intelligence, and other central values, so that they accord more directly with the conditions of contemporary life. Such a revision would in turn allow for the social policy necessary to achieve those values in fact.

Dewey's analysis of such contradictions as these recognizes that the evaluation of the adequacy of values cannot be undertaken in a mythical and rarefied realm in which values are isolated from material and social life. It does not, however, take into account the ways and extent to which values and our commitment to them are themselves grounded in material conditions and the process of their development. This latter aspect of values has been more clearly and systematically acknowledged by others. Edel, for example, has emphasized the importance of social, economic and other factors in the historical process of fashioning value commitments by individuals and groups in any given place or time. He says of an adequate treatment of values that "it insists on the continuous testing of goals in the light of their social functioning, on the deep roots of values in the practices and institutions of a society, on the necessity of altering institutions and social forms as part of the process of achieving and redirecting values."[6] While both Dewey and Edel see that there is a relation between values and social conditions, Edel understands far more clearly that the former reflect in more or less complex ways the latter.

By arguing that our cultural malaise is primarily a conflict between material conditions and an outmoded ideology, Dewey tacitly assumes that each term of the conflict is largely homogenous, and thus the difficulty is in their relation to each other. As he presents it, our ideology is more or less of a piece, as are the needs and interests associated with our material conditions. Dewey's mistake here is actually twofold. First, he fails to see the significance of the fact that in crucial respects our values are themselves contradictory, and that the same is true of material interests. Second, a failure to see these more intrinsic contradictions leaves Dewey with no adequate way to understand the relation between values and material reality. To suggest that it is the first necessity to restructure our ideology is to put the cart before the horse. Our material reality, both its successes and failures, is not primarily the result of the content of our values. The actual relation, as Edel suggests, is the other way around.

This brief study of some of the prevalent ethical and ideological commitments of American culture is situated in part in the tradition of Dewey and Edel. Like Dewey I propose to bring into relief some of the contradictory characteristics of American social life, and like Edel I will suggest that an understanding of these phenomena requires that we look beyond the sphere of values themselves to the more encompassing complex of social and economic factors in which they arise and develop. With respect to Dewey's first mistake, I will suggest that both the material relations of contemporary American life and our ideological commitments are intrinsically contradictory. With respect to his second mistake, I will offer the alternative view that the roots of our cultural difficulties lie not simply in an insistence on anachronistic values, but in the material contradictions of American social life. The adequacy of this general perspective can be illustrated through a discussion of several salient aspects of American culture.

There is a wide range of cultural phenomena on which one could focus, any of which would provide adequate illustration of the contradictory character of our values and ideology. Even a superficial glance at several of them will help to indicate the breadth of cultural contradiction. In the sphere of political activity, for example, several incompatible values are often expressed simultaneously. Even something as fundamental as the nature and justification of the national state is not exempt from the phenomenon of contradiction. On the one hand, our society is historically rooted in the view that the state is a means to a morally more significant end. Jefferson, you recall, argued that all men are equal, and that each individual possesses certain natural rights. The state is obliged to respect those rights, and in some sense its function is precisely to protect them. If the state fails to respect the natural rights of its citizens it relinquishes whatever entitlement it might have had to continue to exist. Jefferson's defense of the right of revolution presupposed the view that the state is a means. What was important for Jefferson and at least some of his colleagues was not the state itself, but rather the values and ideals to which the state must be subservient. Such a supremacy of values and ideals is a cornerstone of what has been called the "Democratic Faith" that has characterized Americans' opinion of ourselves for over two hundred years. We are a people, it is often argued, that recognizes above all else the intrinsic significance of all people, and we trust the ability of the people to rule themselves. The state, then, is only justifiable to the extent that it serves the same end. Though American political ideology is grounded in this view, it must be contrasted with another view of the state that is not uncommon in our recent experience. While we pay homage to the tradition of Jefferson and Madison, we often act as if the state is not a means to an end, but an end in itself. We might recall being told on more than a few occasions that whether the state's actions are right or wrong is irrelevant; the state must be supported either way. We are exhorted to support the "national interest," which in turn is understood in terms of the decisions and action of the state. Thus we hold our society in high esteem precisely because of the Jeffersonian tradition, and at the same time we endorse and often act on the basis of the more technically fascistic conception of the state as a moral end in itself.[7]

A second contradiction in the values and ideology of American political life concerns the nature and possibility of democracy itself. Even in its barest political sense, in which "democracy" means nothing more than more or less mass participation at some point in the electoral process, it requires a faith in the ability of people to organize and govern themselves. Such a faith has been a longstanding feature of American political culture, and it has also been taken for granted that for the most part the structure of our political organization is adequate to democratic government. This faith in democracy is to be contrasted with a deep rooted political despair that has become an increasingly prevalent feature of American political life. While we praise democracy in the abstract, a growing number of us are coming to regard participation in the political process as largely futile. This sense of futility is expressed in a number of ways, from relatively small participation in the electoral process to the growing sentiment that the machinations of political figures and bodies have little to do with the concerns of our lives. We seem, then, both to endorse democracy and to reject its possibility; we are both proud of our nation and suspicious of a good deal of what it does.

A final political contradiction worth mentioning has to do with the nature of political activity itself. One of the fundamental justifications of the democratic political process has long been that it is a necessary forum in which to deal with the many problems of social life. It has been argued, and rightly, that this forum, the actual process of political life, is the appropriate sphere in which ideas and social policy are developed, debated, analyzed, modified, improved, rejected, and endorsed. It is the substance of political activity that has been taken to be its justification and its virtue. The primary problem is that even if such a process ever did exist on a large scale, which is doubtful, it no longer does. What has been understood and valued as a forum for the discussion and analysis of public policy has become a process of image making. This can be seen in the interest of political commentators in the process of "selling" candidates, and in the media's nearly exclusive interest in how political "products" are "packaged" and "advertised." One of the consequences of this is that candidates for public office are more and more concerned with how they are perceived by the public than they are with clearly stating and defending their positions. Here, as in the other areas of political theory and practice that have been mentioned, there is an inherent contradiction among the values to which we are committed, or between what we say in general and what we actually do.

One can turn to areas of American life other than the political and encounter other conflicts of values. One of the more glaring concerns the nature of social ideals. In some respects Americans tend to be committed to an ethical system that rests on principles of community and self-sacrifice. We claim to take seriously the admonitions to love our neighbors as ourselves, and to treat others as we would have them treat us. At the same time many of us will claim that people are by nature, which is to say necessarily, self-serving even to the point of virtual disregard for the interests and welfare of others. The general theoretical foundation of this view is the atomism of the early modern period, which was stretched to its logical extreme by Leibniz. For many Americans we are all Leibnizian "monads," albeit saved from preestablished harmony only by the Newtonian conception of natural law expressed socially by Adam Smith's laws of the marketplace. The ethics of private interests and profit presupposes the necessity of activity that is uninterested in the relative well-being of those around us. To be sure, Smith and other theoreticians of this perspective believed that a social system based on the pursuit of individual self-interest would redound to the greater good, but it is common today to say that the general outcome is unimportant, the crucial thing is the "realistic" recognition that individuals are inherently self interested.

The social atomism of at least one side of American ideology finds expression in other ways as well. We tend to insist, for example, on the virtues of competition and on its necessity in social and economic life. We learn in our schools that competitiveness is an inherent characteristic of human beings. The ideology of individual competition, however, must be contrasted with the values required by the realities of "corporate" life, resting as it does on the process of mass production. One does not need to look hard to find corporate executives, for example, extolling the virtues of loyalty and "team playing." In many respects this is perfectly reasonable. It makes little sense to expect to run a large, complex economic organization if its members refuse to corporate. But despite the fact that the necessity of cooperation is readily apparent to anyone who participates in the economic life of society, we continue to regard the spirit of individual competition as one of the greatest of human virtues.

This survey of contradictory values in political and social life indicates the breadth of the phenomenon in American culture. The picture can be filled in further by turning to a more detailed consideration of two essential components of American ideology: freedom and the individual. The extent to which Americans are committed to freedom needs no commentary. Our heritage is rich with evidence from the Puritans through the Revolutionary period, from the Civil War to the modern movements for civil rights. I will propose, though, that while freedom has been and continues to be a fundamental value of Americans, it lives side by side with a remarkably strong tolerance and even propensity for domination.

The concept of "freedom" is a philosophically difficult one, and it is rarely handled with sufficient care in American political theory. The founders were inclined to understand freedom as the absence of constraints, and they tended to divorce the concept of freedom from any consideration of material conditions. The two are related only with respect to the ownership of property. Aside from the important civil liberties articulated in the Bill of Rights, the only material implication of this concept of freedom is a defense of the relatively unrestricted pursuit of the unlimited private accumulation of capital. The nearly exclusive association of freedom with civil liberties has led to a traditional situation in which the possibility is rarely considered that freedom in any legitimate sense requires at least the fulfillment of the necessary material conditions for leading a fully human life — work, housing, education, food, health care, and material security. If the latter conception of freedom were to be endorsed, then American society, since it does not sufficiently fulfill any of these requirements, has a way to go before it can count itself free.

But this point aside, the contradiction here is between domination and even the traditional "civil libertarian" conception of freedom. While Americans will appeal to freedom as a fundamental value of our society, many of us at the same time allow and even endorse the domination of individuals and whole cultures. In fact this has been a feature of American society from its inception. While extolling the virtues of freedom, even if only as the absence of constraint, we for many years strengthened the legal basis of slavery, imposed property qualifications on participation in the electoral process, refused to allow women to participate in political life, destroyed the cultures of the various Native American societies, and pursued a policy of political, economic and military domination throughout the world. Even many of us who are not proud of U.S. policies in the past are perfectly content to pursue contemporary policies that have many of the same characteristics.

It is sometimes suggested that the reason for the apparent discrepancy is that many of us simply do not know the consequences of our own national policies. There is some truth in this. Successive administrations have found it more and more necessary to lie to the American people about what they were doing and why, presumably because they have felt that if they were to tell us the truth we would withdraw our support. While there is some basis for such a perception, the fact remains that to a large and disturbing extent we are prepared to endorse the politics of domination, provided of course that we are the dominant ones.

One of the prominent characteristics of contemporary American culture is its cynicism, and among the many examples of it is the willingness of many Americans to accept the proposition that the interests and welfare of peoples around the world, or even among their neighbors, are inherently antagonistic. When the often outrageous consequences of economic domination both at home and abroad are pointed out to people, one sometimes hears in response the tried, and false, cliche "It's either us or them," which is to say that if some of us are to have the "good life," then others must pay the price. Such a view is usually based on some version of social Darwinism, and is irreconcilable with an emphasis on freedom. One of the interesting features of this contradictory situation is that while we tend to be content to allow domination, we are often too embarrassed to say so. A rare example of someone who was not too embarrassed is Garrett Hardin, who rejects what he refers to as the "Christian and Marxist" principle of altruism and defends an "us or them" mentality by cloaking it in pseudoscientific garb, cut largely from the outworn and moth-eaten principles of Malthus.[8] But Hardin is an exception. The more common practice is outright deception. "The purpose of America is never to take freedom, but always to return it," Lyndon Johnson said as he announced the Marine invasion of the Dominican Republic in 1965.

The incompatibility of freedom and domination, whether domestic or among nations, has a correlative contradiction in the American approach to the individual. For all its emphasis on the supreme value of the individual and human dignity, American culture betrays an extraordinary talent for various degrees of human degradation. The significance of the human individual for Jefferson and other figures in the American Enlightenment has already been mentioned. Indeed it was the perceived value of individuals as moral ends in themselves that informed much of the revolutionary fervor of the period. And the ethical significance of individuals underlies at least one strain in the tradition of social ideals that has already been discussed. One of the reasons for values to be grounded in the significance of social relations is that the constituents of such relations are themselves ethically significant. The moral importance of the human being has been subject to something of a perversion in the fascination with "self" in recent American culture. But even without such a perversion, it is not at all clear that Americans would or could consistently comply with a principle of human dignity. While we claim to believe that all people are "created equal" and are inherently valuable, we have a heritage of racism and sexism second to none in its virulence. Americans find it remarkably easy to organize our world, and diagnose its shortcomings, on the basis of racial slurs and stereotypes. Even many of our school textbooks will teach the Declaration of Independence in one chapter and in another describe how lazy the people of Latin America are. And despite our self-proclaimed faith in the value of human individuals, we are able to dismiss whole populations from the human race with mere political or racial labels. Nazi war criminals, for example, whose crimes were directed largely against communists found after the war that they had quite a few friends, and jobs, in the United States. And we are certainly aware of the relative ease with which the military and others can acclimate us to killing the enemy if the enemy is considered to be a member of a given race first and a person only second. The point is not that Americans have invented such attitudes. They have been all too common in many societies throughout history. The contradiction lies in their predominance in a society that prides itself on its recognition of the inherent worth of all people.

We have already mentioned the extent to which a dominant American conception of the individual is conditioned by a more general atomism. The view that individuals are essentially discrete, unrelated particulars has its social expression in the ideological myth of the "self-made" individual. We are inclined to think that people can make of their lives whatever they wish, and that they can do it more or less on their own. The dual conceptions of the pioneer and the commercial or industrial entrepreneur embody this view. Whether it is a farm in Kansas or a business in Boston, all someone has to do is want it enough, and work sufficiently hard, and he or she can have it. The actual conditions of contemporary life make it clear, however, that this is all mythological. First, modern communities reflect a vast and complex network of interrelations. The self-made individual would have no electricity, no heat, no automotive transportation, no electronics, and no food in the stores. Second, the vast majority of Americans will not and indeed cannot privately own the means of production, and thus we necessarily function in a network of social relations. It is sometimes suggested that the myth is redeemed because anyone who wishes to become a small merchant or producer can do so. This view, however, rests on a confusion between the terms "anyone" and "everyone." It is certainly true that anyone can try his or her hand in the market in the sense that there are no legal restrictions to prevent it. This is in part what distinguishes the current from previous modes of production. There are, of course, social factors involved in success in the marketplace, but even if it were true that will alone were sufficient, it would still not follow that since anyone can enter the market, everyone can. The material conditions of modern life require large-scale production and distribution, which in turn require a large labor force. If everyone were privately to own a portion of the means of production there would be no labor force at all. Despite the fact, then, that the actual conditions of modern life require cooperative interaction, the myth of the self-made individual continues to flourish.

Two sorts of cultural contradictions have been discussed, one that involves contradictions among values or ideological commitments themselves, and another in which the important contradiction is between values endorsed and life as it is actually lived. The latter phenomena are the ones on which Dewey focused in his analyses. The conception of the individual that leads to both the myth of individuality and the emphasis on competitiveness is an ideal that directly confronts the complexity and inherent community of social life. On the other hand, our commitment to freedom in relation to our toleration or even endorsement of domination represents a contradiction at the level of values and ideology itself. The same is true of the equivocation in our conception of the state as a means or as an end in itself. Both kinds of cases are grounded in the complexity and contradictions of social life. While Dewey was correct in seeing that in several respects the values we endorse derive from a much earlier period in our history, he failed to see the incompatible characteristics of our material conditions which they reflect. Many of the cultural contradictions we have discussed represent a conflict between one set of ideological categories grounded in the revolutionary character of the American tradition and another that represents the interests of those who dominate American society by virtue of control of its wealth and productive capacity. To consider the state as a means to a greater moral end, for example, objectively represents interests of those whom the state can and should serve, while to see it as an end in itself serves no other function than to perpetuate the interests of those who already dominate the political, economic, and social life of the country. In much the same way, a system of ethical principles that takes seriously the dignity of human individuals and the moral significance of their social relations embodies valuable ideals and represents the objective interests of the majority. An ethic of private profit, on the other hand, pits us against each other in ways that benefit those who stand to profit the most, that is, those who control the bulk of the society's wealth. These cultural conflicts, then, point to contradictory material interests inherent in the society. These latter antagonisms also generate cultural contradictions in that they have created a material situation that is incompatible with the expectations raised by and the commitments grounded in one strain of our heritage. While we say that in our democracy the majority holds the power, that same majority must confront the fact that the necessary material conditions of security and progress are in others' hands. As a result, we tend to resort to contradictory values, to a general cynicism, or to a situation in which in material respects we endorse one set of principles and ideologically we support another.

# Notes

1. Harold A. Larrabee, "Naturalism," in *Naturalism and the Human Spirit,* ed. Yervant H. Krikorian (New York: Columbia University Press, 1944), pp. 326–27.
2. Henry David Thoreau, *Anti-Slavery and Reform Papers* (Montreal: Harvest House, Ltd., 1963), p. 40.
3. John Dewey, *Individualism Old and New* (New York: G. P. Putnam's Sons, 1929); Dewey, *Liberalism and Social Action* (New York: G. P. Putnam's Sons, 1935); Dewey, *Freedom and Culture* (New York: G. P. Putnam's Sons, 1939).
4. John J. McDermott, *The Culture of Experience* (New York: New York University Press, 1976), pp. 118–49.
5. Robert Bellah et al., *Habits of the Heart* (New York: Harper and Row, 1985).
6. Abraham Edel, "Naturalism and Ethical Theory," in Krikorian, ed., *Naturalism and the Human Spirit,* pp. 65–95.
7. University of Colorado Philosophy Department, eds., *Readings on Fascism and National Socialism* (Chicago: Swallow Press, 1952).
8. Garrett Hardin, "Living on a Lifeboat," *BioScience* 24:10 (Oct., 1974), pp. 561–68.

# LOGIC AND METHODOLOGY

# Necessity and Truth in Dewey's Logical Theory

## H. S. THAYER

In the preface to his *Logic: The Theory of Inquiry,* Dewey states an idea of fundamental importance to his logical theory. He refers to the "principle of the continuum of inquiry"—a principle, he says, that evidently "only Peirce had previously noted." He then remarks, "Application of this principle enables an empirical account to be given of logical forms, whose necessity traditional empiricism overlooked or denied while at the same time it proves that the interpretation of them as *a priori* is unnecessary."[1] It is a skillfully condensed expression of a major objective of Dewey's work. It aptly presages the extensive critical argument and scrupulous development of the theory of logical forms elaborated in detail and with much originality in the *Logic.*

The present paper demands a similar effort at compressed statement. My comments must be prefatory and promissory: at best, if successful, the pithy sketch.

As the title of his book makes clear, Dewey regards the subject matter of logic as *inquiry:* logical forms, distinctions and terms, propositions, inference, and implication originate and function in inquiry. Inquiry is the deliberate transformation of a problem situation into one that is determinate and resolved. Simply put, it is how a certain method turns the facts of a problem into those of a solution.

This is a novel interpretation of the subject matter of logic and logical locutions and operations. The major novelty is in the contention that the structural schemes and techniques of reasoning which had become classified and codified in a plentiful literature on logic—and which had gained the status of *the* subject matter of logic—were in fact a kind of residue and repository and offshoot of a more fundamental subject matter. The latter subject matter is a species of behavior: It consists of ways of responding and acting that have proven effective when, under widely different circumstances, a course of human action is arrested by an obstacle and some modification or redirection of behavior is required and eventually attained. The rhythm of behavior is arrest, readjustment, and restoration of equilibrium. In the fullness of time that rhythm and the pattern inherent in it is itself subject to reflection and wonder.

Concentrated reflection in turn eventuates in theory. The pattern of conduct is generalized and denoted as "inquiry"; the theory is a theory of inquiry. One of the aims of Dewey's theory is to account for the emergence of logical forms and techniques from the pattern of living practices. Recognition of the fact that the formal structures of logic as it is now studied have evolved from biological and cultural conditions of the more fundamental subject matter, namely, the process of inquiry, increases our understanding of how and why logical forms have acquired their distinctive characteristics and regulative uses and their authority in reasoning. We thus gain deeper appreciation of the meaning of logical forms by ascertaining how they reflect and inherit an inseparable connection with controlled activities for promoting inquiry and producing warranted conclusions or knowledge. It is not that the study of formal logic is in some basic respect misguided. It is rather that the subject of study remains incomplete and conditional. Just as a holiday may be suffused with an adventitious, intrinsic value, still its relative significance and its very existence will be unaccountable without reference to connections with the daily labors of the working week.

There is a further critical shortcoming to limiting the conception of logic as the symbolization of syntactical structures of statements and implications. Dewey argues that some of the difficulties in classical and contemporary logical theory are due to the failure to take note of and develop important distinctions that have served as indispensable and invaluable in the procedures of successful inquiries.[2] One source of difficulties is the recurrent influence of unwarranted metaphysical and psychological doctrines on the language and interpretation of the logical subject matter.

The roots of logic, then, are lodged in our animal past; their germination was in simple and gradually more complex organic functions and dispositions for the maintenance of life. I suppose the first logicians were the first humans. It was they who invented and exploited a kind of "logic" or rationale implicit in the emergence of the arts of using materials of experience and nature to control and enrich future experience. The evolutionary history here is one with the evolution of tools. The primitive method of trial and error in making tools was also the making of inquiry; to revise a simile of Aristotle's, inquiry is a tool of tools. In the fuller fullness of time came culture and with its language; or perhaps this came as a mutual coalescence: language being ripe with culture and culture fertile with language. Perhaps language is culture.

With language the rudimentary art of inquiry could be given voice. It could be shared socially, and its disciplinary procedures could be articulated independently of their actual employments. The overt manipulation of materials involved in any inquiry receives formulation; operations with the maximum survival value and use become defined as forms and instilled as norms. With language inquiry becomes *logos.*

The point of these speculations about origins is to suggest what Dewey had in mind in the passage quoted where he speaks of offering an "empirical account" of logical forms. But questions of origins aside, it is also to suggest that logic is neither self-born, nor autonomous, nor ingeniously self-circumscribed; its place is in the fundamental subject matter of inquiry whenever and wherever inquiries occur in innumerable human and social manifestations. My purpose here has also been to stress the main line guiding the ensuing sketch.

# I

I turn somewhat abruptly to the topic of necessity and truth in Dewey's logical theory. I do so because these have been matters of considerable critical controversy.

One of the important logical forms for Dewey is the proposition. And of the several different kinds of propositions one is the *general,* affirming of *all* or *everything* something to be (or not be) the case; as in "All men are mortal." General propositions divide into two distinct types: *generic* and *universal.* The distinction of types is not always evident from the linguistic form in which the propositions are stated; they may look alike, a point that has troubled some of Dewey's readers. The distinction is propounded in various ways by Dewey as one of "content,"[3] "logical force,"[4] "operational application,"[5] "logical movement."[6] In short, the difference is one of *meaning.*

Generic propositions state connections between spatiotemporal kinds of existing traits and things. The selected traits as conjoined form a kind. Thus, *warm-blooded* and *lung-breathing* form a kind, *mammalian;* and this kind falls within another kind, *vertebrate;* and is marked off from other kinds, such as *fishes.*[7] These propositions are results of observation and experimental investigation: They embody perceptual operations in inquiry and provide the means of *inference*. They are distinct from conceptual or ideational materials formulated in universal propositions stating possible operations related by *implication*.

Universal propositions do not express conjunctions of existing traits; they formulate certain relations of abstract characters.[8] They serve as "definitions of conceptual or ideational meanings."[9] The form of the proposition in such cases is hypothetical and necessary. As Dewey states it, the form is: "*If* certain contents *then* necessarily certain other contents."[10] One of his examples is: "If a plane figure is a triangle, then the sum of its interior angles is equal to two right angles." He thus comments that the "universal hypothetical has the form of a definition in its logical sense."[11]

It is here, if anywhere (and also in his treatment of mathematical reasoning in chapter 20), that Dewey assigns a role to logical necessity in the theory. But this role does not have much in common with logical necessity as usually understood. A few words must be said by way of clarification.

1. While universal propositions have the form of definitions, they also formulate possible ways of acting, possible operations that might be performed. Hence, their function in inquiry is to prepare and order existential materials as means to possible solutions of a problem. The necessary relation of the contents enclosed in the "if-then" form are put to use. And brought into use, the proposition becomes a *hypothesis* whose value and relevance depend on its capacity in relation to other propositions to indicate and effect ways to the solution of the problem that initiated inquiry.[12]

2. It is to be observed that when Dewey speaks of universal propositions as possessing the form of definitions, we are not to think of the definition as a mere notational convenience whereby a shorter expression is substituted for a longer one. For, according to Dewey, the definition constitutes "an analysis of a conception into its integral and exhaustive contents."[13]

3. Dewey has been criticized for overlooking the fact that universal and generic propositions cannot be distinguished by means of the linguistic form in which they are stated. But he frequently acknowledges the point and emphasizes that the meaning of terms and propositions is not conveyed by linguistic form apart from their functions in inquiry.[14] He offers a number of examples, of which I will cite two. First, there is the venerable assertion that "all men are mortal." This cheerless pronouncement is capable of two interpretations: (a)"All men have died or will die." In this sense we have a generic proposition expressing an existential connection between the kinds, *human* and *mortal*. (b)"If anything is human then it is mortal." In this case it is a universal proposition that expresses a necessary relation of the contents of the "if" and "then" clauses. It has no direct reference to existent facts since it purports to be valid whether or not human beings exist. It states a necessary relation between the abstract char-

acters of *being human* and *being mortal;* and it is partly a definition of what it means to be human.[15]

A second example is the Newtonian law of gravitation: "If anything is a material body, it attracts other material bodies directly as its mass and indirectly [inversely] as the square of the distance."[16] As a universal proposition this is a partial definition of "being a material body."[17] But here a question arises. While the formal or mathematical statement of the law can be regarded as expressing a "necessary relation" between its contents and thus as a partial definition of "material body," it is also a law of physics with a significant empirical meaning accruing from its use in certain experimental contexts. Regarded this way it is surely more than a definition. It is quite doubtful that Newton thought of the law as a definition. The law, for Dewey, asserts a necessary and atemporal relation among its contents. But it also states that in fact a certain way of behaving obtains among material bodies. Are we to take Dewey, then, as believing that the law ascribes a necessary relation among material bodies? Is he espousing a version of synthetic *a priori* propositions in his theory of logic? The answer is no. Dewey's *Logic* is not a contribution to rationalist epistemology. But since these dogmatic assurances of mine may fail to eliminate all lingering suspicions that Dewey is a rationalist wolf in empirical sheepskin, let me explain.

The difficulty we have encountered here results from confusing the meaning of a universal hypothetical proposition with an existing subject matter and existential propositions through which it has been given an "operational application." This last phrase is Dewey's. I think we can say more simply that the confusion is over *meaning* and *reference* in the following way. For Dewey, the universal proposition states a relationship between ideal or "abstract characters."[18] But there are no such abstract characters or relations in nature. The contents of the proposition have no existential reference. There are indeed sequences of events among particular existing things. The universal proposition in conjunction with other propositions (among them existential and singular) serves to locate and distinguish the behavior of actual sequences of material objects. But it is a mistake to identify or equate the necessary relation between abstract characters formulated by the law with the conjunctions and sequences of events found in nature. The propositional order of meanings is not an ontological order of existences.[19]

4. There is another kind of question that has arisen over Dewey's conception of universal propositions. Could the necessary relation expressed in these propositions be analytic? Are Dewey's universal propositions analytic statements? Although the notion of analytic statement enjoyed considerable prestige when Dewey's *Logic* appeared in 1939, the identification

cannot be made. The reason it cannot is because of the way analytic statements have been defined and understood. They are characterized as statements that are true, and "necessarily true," by virtue of the meanings of
their terms. The notions of analytic statement, necessary truth, or logical
truth, all based on an idea of truth by meaning, have no relation to Dewey's
theory, however. The decisive factor prompting this conclusion is fairly
simple. In Dewey's view, propositions are neither true nor false.[20] Propositions are means or instruments for the conducting of inquiry; they are
analogous to the tools of a craft. They have a use-value but no truth-value.
Truth, or warranted assertion, is a feature only of the conclusion of inquiry — the conclusion warranted by inquiry. It has been objected that Dewey
is guilty of defying common usage on this matter; logicians and diction-
aries have alike proclaimed that propositions must be true or false. But
that protest is aside from the point here. For if Dewey has elected to construe the nature of propositions in his own way, there is little sense in trying to project doctrines of analyticity or logical truth into idioms where
they have been effectively excluded.

5. Something should be said about Dewey's empirically oriented interpretation of logical forms once more with respect to the necessary relation
contained in universal propositions. While the latter have the form of definitions, they do not enjoy the status of infallibility. On this score also they
differ from logical truths. Universal propositions are subject to criteria of
relevance and efficiency in contributing to the progress of inquiry; they must
also satisfy conditions of consistency with other propositional forms and
observational findings in inquiry. Dewey points out that while the Newtonian and Einsteinian conceptions of gravity are both to be stated as hypothetical universal propositions, "each is an empirically significant contrary of the other."[21] Thus, universal propositions are subject to revision
and even replacement by others in inquiries and advances of knowledge.

## II

The question is sometimes asked whether Dewey's theory of logic entails
ontological commitments. The question is not only broad but diffuse
and so provokes qualifications and various kinds of answers. Logic is not
grounded in or outside of ontology; it is grounded in inquiry. But since
inquiry is throughout an existential transformation of subject matters,
one could reasonably conclude that logic has an ontology. Furthermore,
if one regards logical forms as integral to an evolution of less to more refined instruments in the genesis of simpler to more complex physical and

biological activities—so that the logical operation is a distant lineal descendant of the organic adaptive function—then ontological considerations pervade the theory. On the other hand, if by "ontology" is meant a fixed categorical order of being, which logical principles reflect and depend on for their validity, then Dewey's theory of logic is nonontological. For he does not subscribe to the idea of a fixed or completed order of being or to some correspondence theory of the truth of logical principles.

If we grant that there is a sense in which logic and ontology meet in Dewey's theory, we should recognize that there are also reaches of thought —or better, language—unconditioned by any ontological limitations. There are universal propositions whose contents have no existential reference, namely, propositions of pure mathematics. Purely formal systems of such propositions are determined not by factual subject matters but by what Dewey calls "conditions of abstract transformability."[22]

A brief comment by Dewey in the *Logic* suggests a way of seeing the relation of logic to ontology in a new light. He says, "Existence in general must be such as to be *capable* of taking on logical form."[23] Since the word "capable" is italicized, the dispositional construction is unmistakable: Existence is of such a kind as to be able to be transformed by inquiry. And it is inquiry that is the active agency of transformation of those potentialities in existing things to become logical subject matters. This is the controlled use of real things by freeing uses from them and giving to them other uses. So the distinction or disparity of logic and ontology receives a functional reinterpretation: Ontology stands to the logical movement of inquiry as potentiality to actuality.[24] The formal and material factors are not two halves of a whole, but reciprocal and transacting conditions of tensions and integrations in phases of a temporal process. Such is the case of the growth of any natural thing: There is the outer simplicity of its asserted presence and the exceeding intricacy of the inner workings and energies sustaining it.

From the least personal and most universal point of view—say, one that might be assumed as nature's rather than as one's own—the ontological order of things is implicated in and contributory to its own alterations and transformations; and inquiry is one way that reality makes changes in itself.

But such recondite speculation ill becomes the kind of sketch I have attempted in these pages. And it well becomes drawing to an end.

## Notes

1. All references in this paper are to John Dewey, *Logic: The Theory of Inquiry,* in *The Later Works,* vol. 12, ed. Jo Ann Boydston (Carbondale: Southern

Illinois University Press, 1986). Hereafter cited as LW 12, followed by a page number, in the standard fashion.

2. For example, Dewey argues that the barber paradox is due to confusion of "the existential and the conceptual" specifications of terms (LW 12, p. 361). The liar paradox is generated by confusing the difference between generic and universal propositions (LW 12, p. 381). See also the critique of the notion of "propositional function," (LW 12, p. 376). In these and other cases, the critical distinctions necessary for resolving a number of recalcitrant problems in logical theory are derived, Dewey contends, from analysis of actual procedures involved in the conduct of inquiry.

3. LW 12, p. 288.
4. LW 12, p. 304.
5. LW 12, pp. 263, 276.
6. LW 12, p. 276.
7. LW 12, pp. 267–68.
8. LW 12, p. 259.
9. LW 12, p. 260.
10. LW 12, p. 270.
11. LW 12, p. 271.

12. The following is a helpful statement of the issue: "While scientific method is not possible without non-existential, *if-then* propositions, and while such propositions are necessary conditions of scientific method, they are not its *sufficient* conditions. An hypothesis concerns what is *possible,* and a proposition regarding possibles is indispensable in inquiry that has scientific standing. The hypothesis is formulated in an abstract *if-then* proposition. It then formulates a rule and method of experimental observation. Consequences of the execution of the indicated operations define *application* in the only logically coherent sense of that conception. One indispensable *condition* of application in the case of method in natural science is, therefore, that the *contents* of the hypothetical proposition be themselves determined by prior existential inquiries in such a way that the contents are capable of directing further operations of observation." LW 12, pp. 378–79.

13. LW 12, p. 270.

14. Thus after distinguishing four senses of the one word "all" Dewey remarks: "that 'all' has these four meanings in a warning against using words as a clew to logical form apart from their context in inquiry." See LW 12, pp. 209, 304.

15. LW 12, pp. 254–55.
16. LW 12, p. 270.
17. LW 12, p. 271.
18. LW 12, p. 438.
19. On this point see especially LW 12, p. 438.
20. LW 12, p. 287.
21. LW 12, p. 395.
22. LW 12, pp. 394, 406.
23. LW 12, p. 387.

24. There is a second order and sense of *potentially* when we think of the logical forms of inquiry as having developed from rudimentary practices.

# Necessity in Dewey's *Logic*

## DOUGLAS BROWNING

In his *Logic: The Theory of Inquiry* John Dewey proposes to defend three hypotheses regarding forms, namely, that all logical forms, with "their characteristic properties," are disclosed in inquiry into inquiry, originate in primary inquiries, and are "concerned with control of inquiry so that it may yield warranted assertions."[1] Though it seems to me that each of these hypotheses confronts difficulties that are peculiar to it, in what follows I will raise an objection only to the last.

Dewey provides us with the following careful statement of this hypothesis (*FH*): "All logical forms, such as are represented by what has been called *proximate logical* subject-matter, are instances of a relation between means and consequences in properly controlled inquiry, the word 'controlled' in this statement standing for the methods of inquiry that are developed and perfected in the processes of continuous inquiry."[2] I will not elaborate upon this. It is important, however, to see that Dewey's reference to *logical forms* in this passage is to be taken as indicating a certain more or less commonly recognized range of items about which rival hypotheses or theories, including his own, have been proposed. In presenting a hypothesis about these items, then, he should not be taken as begging the question by employing the term "logical form" to mean only, as Nagel suggests in his introduction to the *Logic,* "the way in which selected features of a situation in which inquiry occurs *function* in it."[3]

Now, the point I wish to make is this: Though Dewey supports *FH* throughout the *Logic* by a careful and patient appeal to cases, he in fact considers an important set of cases of logical form that resists interpretation in this functionalist way. The resistant cases at issue are those which exhibit, on Dewey's own account of them, the distinctive feature of a certain sort of necessity. More specifically, it is Dewey's view that certain logical forms in inquiry are such as to exhaust and be exhausted by the content of what he calls *reasoning* in the narrow sense, that is, in the sense in which it represents a phase or strand of an inquiry considered as a whole. Such reasoning is carried forward only by means of propositions of the logical form that he calls *universal* and the development involved is ordered by the formal relation among these propositions of *implication*.[4] These universal propositions, he maintains, are such as to propose a necessary connection between the "meanings" (in some sense) of their terms. The expression "All triangles have three sides" may be so understood and, if so, it would exemplify a logical form in which this necessity was ingredient. As Dewey would say, what is proposed would have the form of indicating a necessary connection between the two symbol-meanings or characters of "being a triangle" and "being three-sided" or, in a different language, between the categories *triangularity* and *three-sidedness*.[5] A proposition *expressed linguistically* in these terms but which did not purport (or function) to indicate such a necessary connection would have a different *logical* form. Similarly, a case of reasoning that involves a number of such propositions would itself exemplify a logical form of necessary implication between those propositions taken in a certain order. The difficulty, then, is this. In support of *FH* Dewey must provide a functionalist interpretation of these necessary connections. But it doesn't seem that he can.

We need at this point to clarify the sort of necessity Dewey believes to be exhibited by universal propositions and the implications among them. There is a traditional distinction drawn between what might be called existential (or actual or physical or causal) and logical necessity. Existential necessity is taken to hold between things or events in the actual world, whereas logical necessity is taken to hold between meanings, propositions, or perhaps other such conceptual or linguistic entities. It is clear that, were Dewey to accept the distinction, he would take the necessity that concerns us to be logical. In fact, he does not accept the traditional distinction, for, on the one side, he does not believe that a case can be made for any such thing as existential necessity at all. In the *Logic* he echoes a position which he had held throughout most of his career, certainly since the publication in 1893 of the article "The Superstition of Necessity," to the effect that what is taken as a necessary connection between events consists of the misapplication of that which serves the logical function in inquiry of achieving a certain result, namely, an ordering of means to consequences, to an existential sequence which in fact constitutes that result.[6] On the other side, though he uses the term "logically necessary" sparingly, when he does, he often uses it either more broadly than or differently from the traditional use which is tied to the merely conceptual. Typically, and in accordance with his view that the theory of inquiry constitutes logic in the large sense, he uses the term "logical" to cover whatever has to do with inquiry *qua* inquiry, from its initiation in confronting an indeterminate situation as problematic through the final judgment achieved. Thus, all such elements in their actual inquirential functioning have, he maintains, *logical* status,[7] and nothing has this status except in that context and role.[8] On such a use of "logical," then, the term "logically necessary" would indicate that whatever is required in an inquiry in order for that inquiry to be properly controlled and successful in achieving warranted judgment is indeed *required.* For example, according to Dewey both existential propositions and abstract or universal propositions are logically necessary constituents of properly controlled inquiry. This certainly does not represent the traditional use of "logically necessary." In order to avoid confusion, let us adopt for this Deweyan use the term "inquirentially necessary."

Consider now Dewey's general claim that it is inquirentially necessary to institute and employ universal propositions which are serially ordered by implication. Since each of these propositions, as well as each case of the relation of implication, must itself exhibit a feature of necessity, it would seem that any inquirential necessity for them is to be understood as a necessity for a necessity. This reference to an additional, embedded necessity is, of course, relevant only to universal propositions. Thus, existential propositions, which, according to Dewey, are equally inquirentially necessary, do not exhibit it.

The two sorts of cases that involve such an embedded necessity are indicated by Dewey in the following passages:

> In a universal proposition, possibility of a mode of operation is expressed in an *if-then* form. *If* certain contents, *then* necessarily certain other contents.[9]

> ... propositions may be so ordered in discourse that subsequent ones follow necessarily from antecedent ones.[10]

There is, then, a necessity that holds between the contents within a single universal proposition and a necessity that may hold between such propositions. Let us call these (for reasons derived from the next quoted passage) *analytic* and *implicative* necessity, respectively, and let us group them together under the general label *conceptual necessity.* The point at issue, then, is that Dewey would, it seems, have to agree to something like the following:

Where $A$ and $B$ are variables for conceptual contents and $p$ and $q$ are variables for conceptual (i. e., universal) propositions, it is inquirentially necessary to employ propositions of the form "if $A$, then necessarily $B$" and it is inquirentially necessary to employ an ordering of propositions of the form "if $p$, then necessarily $q$."

We see that in each of these theses there are two instances of reference to necessity, one of which lies within the scope of the other.

That Dewey makes a distinction between these two *applications* of a conceptual necessity is clear from the following important passage. After giving two examples of universal if-then propositions, he remarks:

> In neither of the two cases cited does one clause *follow* from the other. For in their necessary interrelation they present the analysis of a conception into its integral and exhaustive contents. Hence it is misleading to say that one clause *implies* the other; not only because implication holds between propositions, not between clauses, but because such a statement obscures from view the primary logical consideration — namely, that the two clauses represent the analysis of a single conception into its complete and exclusive interrelated logical constituents. For this reason a universal hypothetical proposition has the form of a definition in its logical sense.[11]

Now the critical issue for us is this. How can Dewey argue, as adherence to *FH* would seem to demand, that inquirential necessity is sufficient to account for the conceptual necessity involved in certain logical forms? I will now attempt to show that he does not and indeed cannot, at least with consistency, so argue.

I will, in what remains of this paper, concentrate attention on the issue of analytic necessity. Let me begin with an examination of a passage from the *Logic* which might be taken, though mistakenly as we shall see, to make the claim that the analytic necessity of universal propositions may be fully accounted for solely on the basis of an inquirential necessity for them. The passage is from chapter 17, "Formal Functions and Canons," in which, under the section titled "Formal Relations of Terms," Dewey considers the ordering relations of transitivity, symmetry, and correlation.

> The list, just given, of different types of relations sustained by terms to other terms, is one found in all modern logical treatises. The usual doctrinal interpretation is, however, quite different from that here given. For in current treatment, it is assumed that terms sustain these relations in and of themselves by the inherent nature of their own content. If this assumption is not always explicitly stated, it is implicit in failure to interpret terms on the ground of their functional force in satisfaction of the logical conditions of order that are imposed by the demands of valid inference and discourse. Stated positively, the doctrinal position expounded demands that formal *relations* of terms be interpreted as conditions which terms must satisfy in any inquiry that yields warranted conclusions, not as their inherent possession.[12]

Though this passage does not speak directly to the status of the relation of necessity between the terms of a universal proposition, it may be assumed that such analytic necessity is taken by Dewey to be a relation or at least a feature of the relations indicated insofar as they are found in discourse or reasoning and thus in universal propositions. On this understanding, the passage is critical for a consideration of the grounds of analytic necessity, for it not only appeals to the conditions on properly controlled inquiry (or, at least, inquiry in which warranted judgment is achieved) for a proper interpretation of the inquirential necessity of such necessity, but it also seems to repudiate any appeal to what is the "inherent possession" of these terms or their contents for an interpretation of analytic necessity.

There is, however, an ambiguity involved in Dewey's reference to the "inherent possession" of terms which needs to be clarified before we can assess the claim made. He may be taken, on one interpretation, to be using the term "inherent possession" to indicate what purportedly belongs to each term considered by itself, in isolation from a system of meanings, or he may be taken, on a second interpretation, to be using it to refer to what belongs to a term given its employment within such a system.[13] Fortunately, the context of the passage makes it perfectly clear that it is only the former appeal to terms considered in isolation that he has in mind as unacceptable. Thus, he begins the chapter, two paragraphs before the passage above, by reminding us that, according to what he has already said,[14] "every term (meaning) is what it is in virtue of its membership in a proposition (its relation to another term), and every proposition in turn is what it is in virtue of its membership in either the set of ordered propositions that ground inference or in the series of propositions that constitute discourse."[15] It is clear that, in these passages at least, Dewey is intent, first, on denying that a term considered in isolation from other terms in a system provides a sufficient ground for determination of its logical relation to another term and, second, on affirming that the ground which is sufficient for the determination of these relations is one that derives from an ordering of a number of terms which, whether borrowed or constituted and imposed in the context of present inquiry, serves to satisfy conditions that are inquirentially necessary.[16]

But nothing whatsoever in this serves to indicate that a system of meanings, *once instituted,* does not then possess those relations which are inquirentially necessary. Indeed, what is inquirentially required would seem to be, not just a collection of terms, but a system of terms that exhibits an embedded necessity of an analytic sort. To put it another way, once a system of terms is proposed for use in reasoning, it may be (and should be) independently examined to determine whether it does in fact exhibit of itself, inherent to it, the requisite ordering relations. And these relations, however much inquirentially required, are not to be confused with or assimilated to their being inquirentially required.

That Dewey sees this and accepts it seems to me to be plain. One support for this conclusion lies in his discussion of how the analytic necessity of a universal if-then proposition is to be understood. The point is indicated in remarks already quoted in which Dewey insists that "the primary logical consideration" is "that the two clauses represent the analysis of a single conception, into its complete and exclusive interrelated logical constituents."[17] What is significant is that an attempt at such an analysis can be correct or incorrect, can be a proper analysis or a misanalysis. "Implication holds between propositions, not between constituents. The necessary relation obtaining between 'antecedent' and 'consequent' in the universal hypothetical is an expression of the fact that there is but one and the same meaning involved, the 'antecedent' and 'consequent' being taken to be its constituent parts. If the 'taking' is correct the relation is (truistically or tautologically) *necessary*."[18] And it is clear that only a correct analysis can function in warranting a judgment, interim or final, in the course of inquiry. Only that which is *correctly* understood is *fitted* for functional validity.[19]

There is another problem regarding a "correct analysis" which we cannot avoid considering here, even though it is somewhat tangential to our issue. It affects, that is, not the claim of an appeal to a necessity inherent in meanings considered as such, but Dewey's denial, already belabored in our discussion above, that such inherence is a possession of isolated meanings. The problem is that of understanding how this analysis of a conception into two constituents could be so understood as to depend upon a larger body of meanings in which that original conception may be found. It would appear, to the contrary, that some such analysis of single conceptions considered in isolation is a necessary condition for the very institution of a properly ordered system of meanings. Dewey's language sometimes suggests this. "Because the universal hypothetical propositions which constitute ordered discourse arise from analyses of single meanings or conceptions, their constituents sustain a necessary relation to each other."[20] I take it that one thing Dewey wishes to deny is that a universal proposition of the form "if $A$ then $B<D$" *could be generated merely by considering either the conception $A$ or the conception $B$ in isolation. Rather, both $A$ and $B$ represent "analytic" constituents of an "encompassing" conception $C$, and this must be taken to be the single meaning or conception at issue. This is mysterious enough. But perhaps what he wished to maintain was that $C$ can be fixed in its meaning only in a system that is, that $C$ is intelligible only as $C$-relative-to-$S$, but that, once so understood, it now becomes subject to a correct analysis into $A$ and $B$. If this were Dewey's view, it would seem to follow that the comprehension-providing system $S$ will be logically (functionally) different in its terms and their relations from the system $S'$ which is generated from such analyses. There is no reason I can think of that would disallow Dewey's acceptance of this.

Let me now return to the main course of our discussion. If Dewey does accept the presence among meanings of an analytic necessity as an inherent possession of them, then it would seem to follow that, insofar as such a necessity is to be made inquirentially available, an inquirer must have the ability to discern that necessity merely by consideration of meanings and apart from the further consideration of the role they might play in inquiry. Such discernment would constitute something that sounds suspiciously like *a priori* and perhaps even immediate knowledge. To many this will sound so very un-Deweyan as to indicate a compelling reason for denying the claim of inherent possession altogether. But in fact Dewey explicitly held such a view in the *Logic*. What is important to him is that we keep this sort of knowledge distinct from the sort that is existential and achieved through inquiry.

> A certain ambiguity in words has played a very considerable role in fostering the doctrine of immediate knowledge. Knowledge in its strictest and most honorific sense is identical with warranted assertion. But "knowledge" also means understanding. . . . I can *understand* what the word and the idea of centaur, sea-serpent, transmutation of chemical elements, mean, without thereby knowing them in the sense of having grounds for asserting their existence. No intelligent search for a new invention, no controlled inquiry to discover whether a certain conception of, say, the nature of atoms is or is not borne out by the facts, can be conducted without a direct grasp or understanding of the meaning-content of some idea. As the very description of this kind of "knowledge" shows, it is not knowledge in the sense of *justified assertion* that a state of existence is thus-and-so. It is easy, however, as the history of philosophy illustrates, to carry over the first meaning into the second. Since the first is direct or immediate when it occurs, it is assumed that the second also has the same properties.[21]

These observations make clear that this admission into Dewey's theory of inquiry of the possibility of grasping an analytic necessity is the admission of something that cannot itself be explained by or reduced to the determination of its inquirential necessity. The seeing of analytic necessity as characterizing a proposition is not a seeing of it or the proposition as an instance of a relation between means and consequences in properly controlled inquiry. Thus, though a case of understanding that discloses analytic necessity may arise only in inquiry, itself be disclosed only in inquiry, it presents us with what would appear to be a "property" of a logical form which can in no respect be identified with an inquirential function.[22]

It seems to me, then, not only that Dewey is forced by his own considerations to the conclusion that cases of analytic necessity exemplify a logical form that is distinguishable from an inquirential function, but also that these considerations are compelling. The field of entities exhibiting conceptual necessity, even if present only in primary inquiry and disclosable only in inquiry into inquiry, is neither reducible to nor explainable by reference to the field of inquirential functions or operations. Moreover, it seems to me that such conceptual necessities (as we may call such entities) are, if any are, deserving of the status of having logical form. If this is so, *FH* must be amended to read that every logical form, except one of a conceptual necessity, is identical to some inquirential function. Whether this qualified version is acceptable or not is still, of course, a matter for consideration, but Dewey defends it ably and, so far as I am concerned, persuasively.

## Notes

1. John Dewey, *Logic: The Theory of Inquiry,* in Dewey: The Later Works, vol. 12, ed. Jo Anne Boydston (Carbondale: Southern Illinois University Press, 1986), p. 11. Dewey's *Logic* is hereafter cited as LW 12.

2. LW 12, p. 19.

3. LW 12, p. xi.

4. Cf. LW 12, pp. 60, 301.

5. Cf. LW 12, pp. 255, 259, 377.

6. Neither his repudiation of existential necessity nor his avowal of the sort of necessity that belongs to universal propositions could be more clearly stated than in the following passage from Dewey, p. 438: "The *functional* force of the propositions whose contents are necessarily related to each other (functional in determining an existential sequence), is mistakenly ascribed to the sequence it serves to determine, as if it were the content of the law, while to the sequence in turn is ascribed the necessary relational property which belongs only to the abstract *if-then* hypothetical universal proposition, by which it is instituted." Cf. also Dewey, pp. 440, 444–45.

7. LW 12, p. 188.

8. LW 12, pp. 152, 223–24, 261, and 284.

9. LW 12, p. 270.

10. LW 12, p. 329.

11. LW 12, pp. 270–71.

12. LW 12, pp. 327–28.

13. So long as we concentrate on this passage alone, the issue is muddied by Dewey's reference to "terms" in the plural. Consider the claim he attributes to the opposition that "terms sustain these relations in and of themselves by the inherent nature of their own content." The final phrase in this might be read "by the inherent nature of *each* of them considered in *isolation* from a system which is provisionally adopted in inquiry" or it might be read "by the inherent nature of *their* own content considered *together* in a system which. . . ."

14. Cf., especially, LW 12, pp. 55–56.

15. LW 12, p. 327.

16. The qualification indicated by "sufficient" is important, for Dewey does not deny here or elsewhere that isolated words carry *some* meaning. Cf., for example, LW 12, p. 347.

17. LW 12, p. 270.

18. LW 12, p. 301n.

19. As is clearly indicated in the following remarks from LW 12, p. 156: "The series of propositions which constitute a chain of ordered discourse should be such that the meanings of their constituent terms are as unambiguous and determinate as possible. But fulfilment of this condition does not guarantee the validity of their application in a given problem. Hence *understanding,* like apprehension, is never final. No proposition about a relation of meanings, however determinate and adequate the proposition is, can stand alone logically. Nor is its incapacity to stand alone removed by union with other propositions of the same sort; although the union may result in getting meanings into such a shape that they are fitted for application."

20. LW 12, p. 277.

21. LW 12, pp. 145–46.

22. One might attempt to save *FH* by interpreting it as proposing, not that every "characteristic property" of a logical form is itself identical to an inquirential function, but that every case of a logical form so understood as to have or include the relevant "properties" is identical to such a function. Thus, for example, it may be said that, though a proposition has the logical form of being universal only if it exhibits analytic necessity, the analytic necessity that is exhibited neither is nor has a logical form. What is to be identified as a *logical* form and, consequently, as an inquirential function (per *FH*) is therefore only the universal proposition as a *logical* whole. And this may indeed be Dewey's own view. But it does not evade the difficulty. For it need not be argued (and has not been argued) that Dewey maintains that the analytic necessity of universal propositions is itself a logical form, or that it is grasped or understood in isolation from the grasping or understanding of an entertained proposition as exhibiting it, in order to make the point that that which is so grasped or understood is not identical to or explainable by the functioning, actual or possible, of it in inquiry. Of course, it remains an issue of exactly what is to count as a "logical" whole or as a bearer of logical form, but at the level of our consideration of and Dewey's defense of *FH* we cannot already assume that something has that status only if it can be identified as an inquirential function. This would be to beg the question. The adjective "logical" as it applies in that context must be taken to be initially presystemic and in any case extrasystemic. And the same must be true of the use of such terms as "proposition."

# James's Natural History Methodology: Empiricist or Phenomenological?

CHARLENE HADDOCK SEIGFRIED

William James often says that he is following a "natural history method," but what this means must, as usual, be reconstructed from his usage. In simplest terms it can be described as originating in his phenomenology of "our nature as thinkers," and means implementing its "triadic structure of impression, reflection, and reaction."[1] It signifies especially that the beginning of investigation must be some factual situation whose existence and description can be mutually agreed upon by everyone, regardless of philosophical persuasions or personal beliefs. The determination of specific facts of experience is the defining characteristic of science, which roots it firmly in concrete life. But he also uses the same model as the correct paradigm for philosophical methodology, which he says is "set by the structural form of the mind. . . . The thinker (1) starts from some experience of the practical world, and asks its meaning. He (2) launches himself upon the speculative sea" before returning to "the *terra firma* of concrete life again" with "some new practical maxim or resolve."[2] Therefore, both science and philosophy seek to unify the phenomena, to weave chaos into order.[3]

They differ, however, in that James never considers scientific theories as speculative, but rather as inductive inferences constructed to explain a set of facts. Science "discriminates the common and essential from the individual and local elements," but never considers these conceptual formulations as anything but approximations.[4] Philosophy, however, "is the science of the most universal principles of reality (whether experienced by us or not), in their connexion with one another and with our powers of knowledge."[5] Philosophy in this broader sense treats questions "in their widest possible connections, amongst the objects of an ultimate critical review of all the elements of the world."[6] On the one hand, James tried to convince philosophers that the more restrained scientific methodology, properly adapted, better suited their goal than the purely rational method and, on the other hand, to convince scientists that the inherent limitations of their subject matter and methodology made it impossible for them to take over the philosopher's task and define the nature of the universe.

## Natural History Methodology Transformed

James sometimes appeals to "the natural history method" as a straightforward recital of the latest findings in physiology or some other delimited scientific field, but more often it refers to his own use of those findings as supporting his phenomenology of the structures of the human appropriation of the world. This transformation is evident already in his earliest writings. In "What the Will Effects" (1888) he says that the new psychology is a result of the reawakening of the human sciences. So far, "the results of this natural-history method of studying human nature" are to add to our store of facts, and it has not yet settled a single issue debated by classical philosophical psychology.[7] But there is one conception developed by the new psychology which he thought had the potential to revolutionize our thinking, and that is its claim that all our activity is really a type of reflex action. The importance of this finding is that it demonstrates that feeling and thinking are "little more than half-way houses toward behavior."[8] Despite the fact that this same conclusion historically paved the way for a reductionistic theory and practice of "behaviorism," James in no way endorsed this development, although there were aspects of behaviorism with which he was in agreement.[9] The reason for his divergence from the psychological school of behaviorism as it subsequently developed lies in his fundamentally different conception of the role of the sciences and of the significance of their findings. The role that the natural sciences play for James is that, through the experimental collection of data about human behavior, they can provide the raw material needed for reflection by philosophical psychologists, that is, those who are concerned with the ultimate questions of human destiny. Furthermore, he holds that behavior does not define meaning apart from intentionality.

Philosophers can draw on the findings of the sciences to provide better explanations and verified empirical evidence for their analyses of metaphysical issues, such as free will and determinism. These important human issues arise in the first place in everyday life, as do their most fundamental descriptions, and their ultimate resolutions. What the empirical sciences can contribute is twofold: an explanatory pattern establishing facts and verifying procedures. These findings can then be taken up and reconstructed in light of issues of ultimate concern. The significance of such findings as that of the reflex arc is that they provide verifiable empirical evidence for the fundamental premise of James's long-range project of overcoming nihilism. He argues that progress in affirming human significance cannot be made by further speculation but only by turning to an examination of our actual experience of being in the world. Far from letting the sciences dictate the boundaries of reality, he confined their role to that of adding a few pieces to a phenomenological explanation developed out of a broad experiential base including the many realms of reality he discusses in *The Principles of Psychology* (1890) and a whole range of beliefs, intentions, feelings, and needs, insofar as they are experienced.[10]

How James incorporates the findings of science without succumbing to its reductionist explanations is illustrated in the way he reconstructs evidence that apparently supports determinism to demonstrate free will, without in any way denying the evidence presented.[11] He does not dispute the finding of experimental psychology, for instance, that all voluntary actions are derived in the first instance from involuntary ones, even though he also agrees that the essence of voluntary action is that the intent to execute an action precedes its execution. The psychological evidence is taken to underscore the fact that human action does not originate in some transcendental realm, but draws on earlier experiences. Far from undermining the possibility of voluntary action, this experiential basis provides an explanation for it that can be further developed to enhance its operation. What is experienced at first involuntarily can be remembered and represented, good and bad feelings recalled, ideas of abstract good and bad brought to bear, and action can then be initiated to repeat or inhibit the original set of circumstances.[12]

In his defense of "the selective pressure of consciousness" in "Are We Automata?" (1879) James concludes by reaffirming "the Common-Sense-Theory."[13] In doing so he defends and explains further his natural history methodology. Its fragmentary findings, though only probable, are at least supported by the study of factual details, whereas the appeal to universal principles satisfies our need for simplicity without adding anything to our "store of facts." Science has risen in contemporary estimation by its careful attention to the details of physical facts at the expense of metaphysics, which has fallen in esteem because of its disregard of them. Science, though, oversteps its bounds when it rules out the possibility of the causality of feelings on the grounds that its effects are not evident in the cause, as if this sort of reasoning would not undermine many beliefs science holds despite the fact that it is unable to satisfactorily account for them, such as how — in light of Hume's critique — physical objects can affect other physical objects or how knowledge is possible at all given our ignorance of the workings of the brain. This admonition to science not to overstep its bounds is said to derive from a level of argument that has itself kept "upon the plane of concrete facts."

"Concrete facts" means in the first place facts as they appear in commonsense, ordinary situations. In everyday life, for instance, we operate as if our actions are under our conscious control. It is this meaning that is being used in the admonition just given to keep on "the plane of concrete facts." But this phrase can also refer to James's phenomenology of the human appropriation of experience, which discloses, for instance, that knowledge is always guided by interests. It is this phenomenologically based distinction of the aesthetic and practical motives for ordering experience that is the relevant meaning for his defense of the natural history methodology as supporting the selective pressure of consciousness. His defense presupposes a knowledge of his phenomenology of interests according to which he subdivides aesthetic interests into "richness," that is, a preference for the diversity of phenomena, and "simplicity," that is, a preference for abstracting the simple essences such phenomena have in common.[14] His failure to carefully distinguish these two meanings of "concrete," as ordinary, unreflective experience and as a phenomenological explanation of such experience, is often a source of confusion. But once a model is constructed that relates them as immediate phenomenal experience and the reflective appropriation of the structures of such experiences, then the explanatory power of James's analysis is freed for further development.

## Observation: "The Primal State of Theoretic and Practical Innocence"[15]

James's own natural history method consists in beginning with some process actually observable in nature, carefully describing it by picking out aspects or "marks" according to his end-in-view, relating these aspects to others found to be similar, and coming up with a general explanation of its cause and nature, which is then proposed as a hypothesis to be tested by his audience or readers. The whole process is predicated on the assumption that the initial set of facts can be clearly observed without any bias and accurately described. The belief in "pure" seeing and transparent description is a tenet of Comtean positivism that became a defining characteristic of science. It is uncritically accepted by James, as it was also by many thinkers of the late nineteenth and early twentieth centuries, because it merely reformulates in scientific terms what he already accepted on empiricist and poetic grounds.

This belief in exact observation and pure description can be found throughout James's writings. In 1887 he writes in a letter to the psychologist, Carl Stumpf, that "of course, the experimental patience, and skill and freshness of observation of the Helmholtzes and Herings are altogether admirable, and perhaps at bottom *worth* more than philosophic ability."[16] In an 1896 speech in honor of Louis Agassiz, delivered to the American Society of Naturalists, James praises him as the paradigmatic student of nature.[17] James's earliest and most striking impressions of the method of natural history were formed in 1865 when he joined the Thayer expedition to Brazil under Agassiz's leadership. They are summed up in a maxim of Agassiz that James liked to quote: "Go to Nature; take the facts into your own hands; look, and see for yourself!"[18] Agassiz is also praised for "the extreme rigor of his devotion to this concrete method of learning," but is said to have an undeveloped "capacity for abstraction and causal reasoning and tracing chains of consequences," which is associated with "reasoning" and the Comtean characterization of the scientific stage, and to instead exhibit a "genius for acquaintance with vast volumes of detail, and for seizing upon analogies and relations of the more proximate and concrete kind," which James associates with "narrative, descriptive, contemplative thinking," characteristic of the poetic.[19]

In favoring the richness of empirical detail over simplification through theory construction Agassiz represented the older natural history tradition. As a student of the new, experimental sciences, James was aware of the importance of abstracting elements out of the whole and using these partial characteristics as the basis for scientific thinking. Nonetheless, he also emphasized that he had "never been able to forget" the priority of living "in the light of the world's concrete fullness" to such abstractions.[20] His own phenomenological approach represented a unique synthesis and transformation of the older and the newer traditions of science. The search for causal elements rather than totality is said to characterize contemporary science, "but the truth of things is after all their living fullness," and someday the elements being discovered will again be gathered up into a "higher and simpler way of looking at nature." It is obvious, then, that although James uncritically assumed the empiricist bias of the priority of gathering facts to reasoning about them or even delineating an experimental program, he critically rejected the empiricist assumption of the experienced world as built up piecemeal out of such bits and pieces. He argues that the elements are abstracted out of the "concrete fullness" of the world, which structures them, and without which they would neither "be" nor "be meaningful." As his phenomenological description of our human interaction within the world of our experience points out, our living in the concrete fullness of the world conditions any experimental selectivity, whether or not we advert to it. James wants to make explicit this concrete world within which and according to which all particular human projects take place to demonstrate the falsity of the positivist claims of a purely disinterested observation and access to primal units of sense data on a foundationalist building-block model. To the first he opposes the necessarily interested character of all human appropriation of the world and to the second he opposes a holistic view, according to which we are an irreducible part of any investigative field.

James does share the empiricist bias against the necessity of an explicit conceptual framework to a recognition of facts. The concrete fullness of the world provides a sufficient setting within which facts can be experienced. It is enough if the conditions that set up and make possible the recognition of particular facts are only implicitly operative. In everyday life we need not advert to them. James has made a lasting contribution to the way we understand ourselves in his substitution of a phenomenology of our concrete, living world of experience, which emphasizes temporality and the fortuitous origin of our predispositions, for the traditional, speculatively generated system of categories, which emphasizes essential invariance and necessity. But it is difficult to see how the naturalist gathering facts partakes only of the world of everyday experience and not also of an experimental project with explicit protocols.

Because Agassiz never explicitly reflected on the scientific interests that guided his picking out of a phenomenon those structures which were worth reporting, much less adverting to the more general structures of human experience that allowed him to recognize and describe a particular phenomenon as an object of interest to a naturalist out of the phenomenal totality with which it was continuous, it is understandable that he naively assumed that he was merely describing exactly what was present as it was in itself. He was infamous, for instance, for preventing students from entering into a course of studies with him if they could not intuitively observe and describe the very same features of an organism that he did. But James did reflect on the shared structures and subjective interests that make it possible to disengage an object as an object out of the big blooming buzzing confusion of phenomenal continuity, and he insisted on the teleological conception of essence according to which the fact of the being of a thing cannot by itself determine how we will apprehend it, which depends upon our interests. How can he nonetheless claim that we have direct observational access to facts that can be exactly described as they are? He never explicitly resolves this issue, but some insights follow in the next section as to why he never even recognized the discrepancy between his assumption of a naive direct access to things in themselves and his explanation that we cannot know objects except as they are related to us.

James also seems to systematically confuse the transcendentalist claim that there are conditions according to which experience operates, which can be reflectively delineated, with the claim that experience cannot take place unless we are explicitly aware of these structures while we are experiencing something.[21] Why, then, does James seek to make explicit the human structures of our experience? This is not straightforwardly obvious. He usually does so to disprove what he takes to be the extremes of the overconceptualized, transcendentalist position and the atomism of the empiricist and positivist positions. But he draws a sharp distinction between what is available to us on reflection and the way in which we originally experience the world. He seems to assume that if the structures only become obvious on reflection, then they cannot be assumed to be operating when we are not aware of them. In this he relies uncritically on the Berkleyan *esse est sentire* doctrine.

## Bare Facts in a "Real" World versus Interpreted Facts of Experienced Phenomena

James expressed his ideal in 1879 as "the union of the mathematician with the poet, fervor with measure, passion with correctness."[22] In *The Principles of Psychology* of 1890, he characterized the philosopher, physicist, and psychologist, Gustav Theodor Fechner, as instantiating such an ideal: "Fechner himself indeed was a German *Gelehrter* of the ideal type, at once simple and shrewd, a mystic and an experimentalist, homely and daring, and as loyal to facts as to his theories."[23] This conjunction of science and poetry, of fact and theory, of exact description and flights of fancy, of accuracy and passion describes both the ideal that guides his own work and the reconciliation he wants to achieve as his most lasting contribution to the debate over how to resolve the challenge positivist science posed to traditional beliefs and values.[24] Some have taken James's critiques of science and praise of art as evidence of an animosity to science as such.[25] They are rather his attempt to balance the contributions of both in our organizations of experience by detaching the genuine contributions science can make to our understanding of the world from those illegitimate positivist claims made in the name of science which would make it the sole avenue to truth and not one contributor among others.

James says that according to "the modern mechanico-physical philosophy" of positivism facts are merely motions of primordial solids and the only laws that are truly scientific are those that express these changes of motion.[26] Future states can be predicted from our knowledge of present states by considering only "the necessary geometrical, arithmetical, and logical implications." Nature becomes a "bare world" for science so construed, consisting only of atoms and ether with no properties but masses and velocities expressible by numbers and analytic formulas. James reiterates this accepted view of science as positivistic at the end of his *Principles,* which was a sustained argument for including those "sensible phenomena" which are considered to be "pure delusions for the mechanical philosophy." He is treading a thin line between helping psychology to become an exact science by distinguishing in the literature what has been determined as the result of strict laboratory procedures and what is ungrounded speculation, and then criticizing these same procedures for being unduly reductionistic and taking for pure description of phenomena what is actually constrained by theoretical presuppositions.

He denies that science simply replicates reality, arguing instead that its world is as much a construct as that of "sentimental" philosophy, since both activities originate in the belief that nature conforms to mental relations, that is, we constrain the phenomena to make them answer to our subjective interests.[27] Scientific facts are not simply impressed on the mind from without, but are constructed according to our interests: "The craving to believe that the things of the world belong to kinds which are related by inward rationality altogether, is the parent of Science as well as of sentimental philosophy, and the original investigator always preserves a healthy sense of how plastic the materials are in his hands."

This would seem to indicate that James, already by 1890, believed that all perception is "theory laden," or at least, interest-dependent, and that, therefore, there can be no appeal to an irrefutable level of "pure" seeing and "exact" description. But James is only bringing the scientific enterprise within his phenomenology of human action, according to which all purposeful activities, whether scientific, philosophical, artistic, or practical, are ways of ordering the flux of experience to answer to our needs. But once having acknowledged the "world" as a human context that sets up and makes possible and explicable particular acts, it does not necessarily follow that within these constraints the "real" world may not be disclosed as it really is. Since the disclosure is tied to our subjective interests, some additional moves are still required to determine whether what anyone takes to be the case is actually the case. James could never, to his own satisfaction, provide such a "bridge" from the phenomenal world of experience to the "real" world. He did not seem to realize that his philosophy of radical empiricism had already demonstrated that the phenomenal/realist distinction is reflectively generated to answer particular problems and does not refer to an original ontological difference. By understanding his natural history methodology as a radically empiricist phenomenological rather than empirical explanation, the difficulties inherent in the realist model simply do not arise.

# Notes

1. William James, *The Will to Believe, The Works of William James* (Cambridge, Mass.: Harvard University Press, 1979; orig. 1897), p. 93.
2. Ibid., p. 112.
3. William James, *The Principles of Psychology,* 3 vols., *The Works of William James* (Cambridge, Mass.: Harvard University Press, 1981; orig. 1890), vol. 2, pp. 939ff.
4. William James, *The Varieties of Religious Experience, The Works of William James* (Cambridge, Mass.: Harvard University Press, 1985; orig. 1902), pp. 359–60.
5. William James, *Some Problems of Philosophy, The Works of William James* (1911; Cambridge, Mass.: Harvard University Press, 1979), p. 22.
6. William James, *Essays in Psychology, The Works of William James* (Cambridge, Mass.: Harvard University Press, 1983), p. 273.
7. Ibid., p. 216.
8. Ibid., p. 217.
9. William R. Woodward says that the "fruitful tension" between James's emphasizing the physiological foundation of the problem of freedom and determinism and also insisting on the need for existential choice "was lost when behaviorists developed one side of James's theory of action and existentialists pursued the other." See introduction to James, *Essays in Psychology,* p. xxxvii.
10. James, *Principles of Psychology,* vol. 2, pp. 920ff.
11. James, *Essays in Psychology,* pp. 217ff.
12. Ibid., p. 224.
13. Ibid., pp. 59–61.
14. See James, *The Will to Believe,* pp. 58ff.
15. James, *Essays in Psychology,* p. 117.
16. William James, *The Letters of William James,* ed. Henry James, 2 vols. (Boston: Atlantic Monthly Press, 1920), vol. 1, p. 266.
17. William James, "Louis Agassiz," in *Memories and Studies* (Westport, Conn.: Greenwood Press, 1971), pp. 3–16.
18. Ibid., p. 12. This recalls T. H. Huxley's admonition to Charles Kingsley: "Sit down before the facts as a little child, be prepared to give up every preconceived notion, follow humbly wherever and to whatever abyss nature leads, or you will learn nothing." Huxley is quoted by Stephen J. Gould in "Between You and Your Genes," *New York Review of Books* 31 (Aug. 16, 1984), p. 38.
19. James, *Essays in Psychology,* pp. 2ff.
20. James, "Louis Agassiz," pp. 14–15.
21. His main objection to the "Kantian machine-shop" explanation of space, for instance, is that he has "no introspective experience of mentally producing or

creating space." He mistakenly takes as assertions of temporal succession a transcendental explanation of the conditions necessary to explain the fact of the synthetic unity of perceptions that James also agrees is what we do experience. He concurs with Kant that "the higher parts of mind . . . interweave the space-sensations with intellectual relations," but he takes the Kantian explanation to be an assertion that "one moment of passive inextensive sensation" is "succeeded by another of active extensive perception," rather than being grasped immediately as a synthesis. See James, *Principles of Psychology,* vol. 2, p. 905.

22. William James, *Collected Essays and Reviews* (New York: Russell and Russell, 1969), p. 138.

23. James, *Principles of Psychology,* vol. 1, p. 518.

24. See Daniel J. Wilson, "Science and the Crisis of Confidence in American Philosophy, 1870–1930," *Transactions of the Charles S. Peirce Society* 23 (Spring, 1987): 235–62.

25. H. S. Thayer, for instance, interprets James as being anti-intellectual and distrusting of science. He says that James cannot see the significance of scientific method. See H. S. Thayer, *Meaning and Action: A Critical History of Pragmatism* (Indianapolis: Hackett, 1981), p. 422.

26. James, *Principles of Psychology,* vol. 2, p. 1260.

27. Ibid., pp. 1260–61.

# GEORGE HERBERT MEAD

# George Herbert Mead on Social Fusion and the Social Critic

## JAMES CAMPBELL

I will explore here a roughly defined area of social life as it can be understood through the work of one of America's neglected thinkers. The area I have in mind is that of the nature of individuality, especially the individual's ability to disappear in the flow of social processes and his or her possible contribution to society's redirection. The thinker is George Herbert Mead. As befits any account of a frontier, I would not suggest that the account that follows is in any way complete or final. I do believe, however, that the area I am examining is one that merits all of our consideration.

Contemporary American life demonstrates how powerful is the human tendency to surrender our individuality, and how necessary it is for us to resist this tendency. We willingly give up our selves in pep rallies and race riots, in religious celebrations and patriotic warfare. In such cases we find ourselves "swept away" by the current, "lost" in the crowd, "fused" to our fellows. Although these fusion cases are related to a much broader social phenomenon — the fact that we can live much of our lives safe in thoughtless orthodoxy — my focus will be on the fusion cases and on our efforts as members of society to offer effective social criticism.

## Thoreau's Private Self

Surely the most frequently consulted guide for the attempt to overcome social fusion in the American tradition is Henry David Thoreau, who appeals to us from the shores of Walden Pond to awaken from the comfort of unquestioned custom and to deliberately seek spiritual well-being. "Moral reform," he writes, "is the effort to throw off sleep."[1] Once we are no longer asleep we will recognize that we "stand on the meeting of two eternities, the past and the future, which is precisely the present moment";[2] and we will be able to change our future lives. The prescription that Thoreau offers us is a harsh one: We must become more critical, and we must simplify. We must "reduce [life] to its lowest terms"[3] and "front only the essential facts of life."[4] Following Thoreau's presciption for spiritual well-being would probably cost us our microwaves and our dishwashers, our answering machines and our computers.

I am not going to dispute here Thoreau's call to us to simplify; I suspect he is largely right about our need to return to an uncomplicated life before we can attain and maintain a fuller level of self-consciousness. What I do want to challenge Thoreau on, however, is the psychology behind his call to reform, his understanding of the human self. He summons people to be themselves and to seek freedom, goals which for him seem to be equivalent. His method for staying out of "the ruts of tradition and conformity"[5] is to journey off by oneself. For Thoreau, the attempt to discover oneself is "private business."[6] And, for individuals to flourish, it is this privacy that we must defend. "If a man does not keep pace with his companions," Thoreau's familiar formulation goes, "perhaps it is because he hears a different drummer. Let him step to the music which he hears, however measured or far away."[7]

In his role as social critic, Thoreau calls upon people to rise above social conformity. Those who are "commonly esteemed good citizens," he writes, serve the state "not as men mainly, but as machines, with their bodies." He continues that "in most cases there is no free exercise whatever of the judgment or of the moral sense."[8] To be truly free individuals, we must clearly recognize that "it is not desirable to cultivate a respect for the law, so much as for the right" since each of us is bound only "to do at any time what I think right."[9] In his discussion of the role of the social critic, I am not troubled by Thoreau's claims that there is no complete correspondence between what is legal and what is right, or that evils must not be accepted, or even that on occasion violence is a necessary means to social reform. What I find troubling is Thoreau's description of the social critic as someone who rises, by a kind of self-insight, to a level of moral clarity not available to the others who are still asleep. "Any man knows when he is justified," he writes, "and all the wits in the world cannot enlighten him on that point."[10] The obvious problem with Thoreau's formulation is that he provides the critic with no social test of his or her insights; and consequently Thoreau's discussion of the critic's response to social fusion, however attractive it may initially appear to be, cannot be seen as adequate.

## Mead's Social Self

One figure in the history of classical American philosophy who addresses the issue of social fusion and the role of the social critic with a clear focus upon the limits of such personal insight is George Herbert Mead. We find in his work two overriding intellectual themes. The first of these is a fundamental commitment to furthering attempts at understanding the human being as a problem-solving animal who has risen to self-consciousness through the long process of evolution. The second central theme in Mead's work is the attempt to understand the human being as a thoroughly social creature, a creature whose self-conscious human life would neither be possible nor make sense outside of society.[11]

Mead is most widely known for his discussion of the "I" and the "me"; and it is his discussion of these two "phases" of the self that I will make use of here.[12] The "me" is that phase of the self that "contains" one's society. "We are individuals born into a certain nationality, located at a certain spot geographically, with such and such family relations, and such and such political relations," Mead tells us. "All of these represent a certain situation which constitutes the 'me.'"[13] It is this "me" aspect of the self that enables us to take the attitudes of others; and, when organized into "the attitude of the whole community" as "the generalized other," the "me" accounts for the individual's "unity of self."[14] The "I" phase of the self is what Mead calls the reaction of the organism to the ideas, values, and habits contained in "the generalized other." "The 'I' is the response of the individual to the attitude of the community as this appears in his own experience."[15] To be an individual member of a community at any given time, it is necessary that the person's self contain both aspects existing in a creative balance: the "me" bringing forth the possible ways of the community, and the "I" evaluating and choosing among them.[16]

From the perspective of the social arena, we can view these themes in terms of individual citizens and the language, customs, laws, and other habits that embody "the generalized other." Without such institutions there would be chaos — "The institution represents a common response on the part of all members of the community to a particular situation"[17] — but without free-thinking individuals there could be only narrow conformity. Knowing humans as we do, it is surely the latter situation that is more likely to be problematic: "As a rule we assume that this general voice of the community is identical with the larger community of the past and the future; we assume that an organized custom represents what we call morality."[18] Recognizing that "the novelty comes in the action of the 'I'"[19] and that "the action of the 'I' . . . involves a reconstruction of the society, and so of the 'me' which belongs to that society,"[20] Mead emphasized that without the constant influence of the "I" aspect of the self, society would slip into mindless uniformity and the danger of social fusion would increase.

Mead's discussion of cases where the "I" and the "me" do fuse is full of detail and offers a richer and more accurate picture of the interrelationship of society and the social critic than Thoreau does. One overriding point of Mead's analysis is that, unlike in cases of cooperative teamwork — for example, to save a person from drowning — where the individual balances "the sense of directed control"[21] with a keen sense of "his part" in the process,[22] in fusion cases the independent self really does disappear. In social fusion we have "a process of breaking down the walls so that the individual is a brother of everyone."[23] We find individuals in "complete identification with each other in the whole community,"[24] "feeling at one with everybody and everything about us,"[28] the sense "of having an intimate relationship with an indefinite number of individuals who belong to the same group."[26]

A second aspect of Mead's discussion of social fusion is his recognition of the pleasurable nature of such experiences. Fusion situations, he notes, "are peculiarly precious";[27] they result in "intense emotional experiences."[28] We accept, and even seek, social fusion because it brings us to the "ultimate heights of human experience"[29] and grants us "moments of priceless emotional experience."[30] The sense of solidarity "arouses like a burning flame" and "consumes the differences of individual interests."[31] Part of the reason for our delight in fusion is that as long as we can sustain the attitude that "everyone is at one with each other," we are freed from "that sense of control which hangs over us all because of the responsibilities we have to meet in difficult and trying social conditions."[32] In particular, in social fusion we are able to relax our ongoing evaluation of self and society, and identify our current situation with our highest possibilities.

A third emphasis of Mead's analysis is that the likelihood of social fusion in any community is enhanced by the existence (or at least the perception) of an external enemy. Such warfare can make "the good of the community the supreme good of the individual."[33] "There is no ground upon which men get together so readily as that of a common enemy," Mead writes; in self-defense against such an enemy, "we reach the ultimate form of self-assertion."[34] In social fusion brought about by hostility toward the common enemy "individual differences are obliterated":[35] "Those who fight together against common enemies instinctively tend to ignore the other social activities within which oppositions between the individuals engaged normally arise."[36] Moreover, Mead continues that the enemy need not be national. Domestic political struggles and religious factionalism work just as well: "It seems to be perfectly legitimate to assert the superiority of the nation to which one belongs over other nations. . . . It is just as true in politics and religion in the putting of one sect over against the others."[37] Loyalty as a social trait is something for which we seldom feel the need to apologize; and "devotion," he writes, "passes quite naturally into hatred of the enemy."[38]

A fourth aspect of Mead's analysis of social fusion is that it currently plays a fundamental yet harmful role in our social life. It is widely recognized that "we are not able to work out our own political institutions without introducing the hostilities of parties," he notes. "Without parties we could not get a fraction of the voters to come to the polls to express themselves on issues of great public importance, but we can enrol a considerable part of the community in a political party that is fighting some other party." Mead's explanation is that at present "it is the element of the fight that keeps up the interest."[39] Needless to say, such a method of political organization has serious costs. While "the attitude of hostility, either against the transgressor of the laws or against the external enemy, gives to the group a sense of solidarity," Mead writes, "the price paid for this solidarity of feeling is great and at times disastrous."[40] Especially in our use of external enemies to unify the populace must changes occur: "We can no longer depend upon war for the fusion of disparate and opposing elements in the nation. We are compelled to reach a sense of being a nation by means of rational self-consciousness." Rather than becoming one through feeling and emotion, "we must *think* ourselves in terms of the great community to which we belong."[41] In these patriotic cases, and in the other cases as well, the major result is the same: "Just in proportion as we organize by hostility do we suppress individuality."[42] And, to the extent that we suppress individuality, we make successful attempts at social criticism more difficult.

As these passages suggest, Mead believes that it is possible to overcome our reliance on social fusion if we develop the more rational approach to social organization that is already partly in use. "Over against the emotional solidarity of the group opposing the enemy," Mead writes, "we find the interests which spring up around the effort to meet and solve a social problem."[43] In these cases, "the interest shifts from the enemy to the reconstruction of social conditions."[44] Thus, although the appeal to emotion and personality may be essential at the founding of human associations,[45] and contribute heavily to the growth of larger communities,[46] it is possible to move beyond it to "a rational basis"[47] for social organization.

If we can develop a sense of "the larger social whole," hostile attitudes can "pass over into self-assertions that are functional instead of destructive,"[48] "rational" instead of "personal."[49] The sense of superiority that the individual then would have "is not a superiority over the other, but is grounded in that which he can do in relation to the functions and capacity of others."[50] Although his status does not offer the purely emotional satisfaction of social fusion, we recognize that it has other virtues: "The sense of the self obtained through the realization of a function in the community is a more effective and for various reasons a higher form of the sense of the self than that which is dependent upon the immediate personal relations in which a relation of superiority and inferiority is involved."[51]

Mead has in mind here a community in which there is a social life of cooperative inquiry and some level of participatory social democracy. He envisions a community in which individuals do not support or reject policies because of their sponsorship by party or union or religious group, and one in which public discourse contributes heavily to social education and social choices. This kind of "rational" politics would entail the acceptance by society of a high level of ongoing creative tension in the place of the emotional pleasure of homogenizing fusion. "A highly developed and organized human society is one," Mead tells us, "in which the individual members are interrelated in a multiplicity of different intricate and complicated ways whereby they all share a number of common social interests." At the same time as we have this intellectual focus on the common good, we recognize as well that these individuals "are more or less in conflict relative to numerous other interests which they possess only individually, or else share with one another only in small and limited groups."[52] But, through the development of a society that integrates "functional differentiation and social participation,"[53] we could come to benefit from the advantages that only this pluralistic type of society can yield.

In this creative tension of shared and conflicting interests we have an ongoing intellectual role for the social critic. Unlike Thoreau's social critic, who may live a private life aloof from social concerns until disaster looms, Mead's social critic is the citizen who continually contributes his or her evaluations with regard to social policies. When troubles do arise, it is this critical citizen who must attempt to keep "the prejudices of the community" under control while at the same time expressing "the principles of the community."[54] And, when serious troubles arise, it is this critical citizen who "appears as the representative of a different social order"[55] and who consequently can call on the community to reject its own values and adopt those of "a higher and better society than that which exists."[56]

It is important to stress, with Mead and against Thoreau, that the social critic is most effective in a society that has deliberately cultivated and integrated, not just tolerated, diversity. "The multiple social stimulation of an indefinite number of varied contacts of a vast number of individuals with each other is the fertile field out of which spring [cooperative] social organizations," Mead writes, because these diverse contacts "make possible the larger social life that can absorb the hostilities of different groups."[57] Such life is not the result of a smaller "me," as might be implied in the approach of Thoreau. Rather it requires a "me" that contains the greater "scope" that is necessary "for original, unique, or creative thinking and behavior."[58]

## Conclusion

As I suggested at the beginning, this paper is an initial attempt to address an important social issue using the work of a neglected thinker. I hope I have managed to convey some sense of the power of Mead's analysis of social fusion and social criticism. In this brief concluding section, I would like to discuss two specific points to be drawn from Mead's work here: first, a point about our social life; second, a point about Thoreau's self-understanding.

One of the important implications of Mead's approach to the problem of social fusion is that it is a difficult and ongoing task to maintain the duality of the self. To prevent the reduction of moral agents to social automata, to keep our critical moral "distance," we must strive to prevent social fusion.[59] In terms of Mead's analysis, this means first of all the continued development of the critical "I." "The novelty comes in the action of the 'I,'"[60] Mead notes, a claim that can also be rendered as "that which is novel must appear in the experience of an individual as an individual."[61] Consequently, if we are to minimize the dangers of social fusion, we must develop the agency of novelty. A second aspect of the struggle to avoid social fusion is the recognition that individuals must accept ultimate responsibility for the "me" that they select. We have available to us in our diverse society a large set of potential value frameworks to choose among. In our analysis of our situations, it is possible for us to move our focus "from a narrow and restricted community to a larger one,"[62] to use as our moral frame of reference societies other than our own whose values on occasion seem better than ours. And, if we are able to do this, it becomes our responsibility to do it. We cannot be satisfied merely with loyalty to our present selves. Concomitant with this responsibility of choosing a "me" is, of course, our social responsibility for education. If we reject Thoreau's insight approach, we must work to make these various options better known throughout society and to help all of us become better able to use them.

A second important implication of Mead's understanding of the problem of social fusion is that it offers us a far better explanation of the fundamentally social nature of the work that Thoreau was doing than appears in Thoreau's own familiar, highly individualistic account. In contrast to Thoreau's claim that "man thinking or working is always alone,"[63] Mead contends that an individual never is. "Selves," he notes, "can only exist in definite relationships to other selves."[64] For Mead, the individual's self arises "through its ability to take the attitude of the group to which he belongs."[65] One can be "a conscious and individual personality" only "in so far as he is a member of society, involved in the social process of experience and activity."[66] Thus, for Mead, social control is "actually constitutive of and inextricably associated with" human individuality rather than something "tending to crush out the human individual or to obliterate his self-conscious individuality."[67] Consequently, even "an absolutely solitary self" or "a person in solitary confinement for the rest of his life . . . still has himself" — and therefore his "me," his "generalized other" — "as a companion."[68]

In a comment that may have been directed at Thoreau, Mead writes, "even the man who haughtily withdraws himself from the crowd, thinks of himself in terms of an ideal community which is but a refinement of the world in which he lives."[69] Certainly this account offers a more accurate description of what Thoreau was actually doing than his own account does. Mead also suggests a better approach to the problem of social fusion and the role of the critic than Thoreau.

# Notes

1. Henry David Thoreau, *Walden,* ed. J. Lyndon Shanley (1854; Princeton, N.J.: Princeton University Press, 1971), p. 90.
2. Ibid., p. 17.
3. Ibid., p. 91.
4. Ibid., p. 90.
5. Ibid., p. 323.
6. Ibid., p. 19.
7. Ibid., p. 326.
8. Henry David Thoreau, *Reform Papers,* ed. Wendell Glick (Princeton, N.J.: Princeton University Press, 1973), p. 66.
9. Ibid., p. 65.
10. Ibid., p. 136.
11. For further explorations of these and other aspects of the thought of Mead, see James Campbell, "George Herbert Mead on Intelligent Social Reconstruction," *Symbolic Interaction* 4 (2) (Fall 1981), pp. 191–205; Campbell, "George Herbert Mead: Philosophy and the Pragmatic Self," in *American Philosophy,* ed. Marcus G. Singer (Cambridge: Cambridge University Press, 1985), pp. 91–114; David L. Miller,

*George Herbert Mead: Self, Language, and the World* (Austin: University of Texas Press, 1973).

12. George Herbert Mead, *Mind, Self, and Society from the Standpoint of a Social Behaviorist,* ed. Charles W. Morris (Chicago: University of Chicago Press, 1934), p. 192.

13. Ibid., p. 182.

14. Ibid., p. 154; see also p. 162.

15. Ibid., p. 196.

16. See ibid., p. 178.

17. Ibid., p. 261.

18. Ibid., p. 168.

19. Ibid., p. 209.

20. Ibid., p. 214.

21. Ibid., p. 273.

22. Ibid., p. 276.

23. Ibid., p. 219.

24. Quoted from *George Herbert Mead: Essays on His Social Philosophy,* ed. John W. Petras (New York: Teachers College Press, 1968), p. 151.

25. Mead, *Mind, Self, and Society,* p. 275.

26. Ibid., p. 219; see also ibid., pp. 274–76; see also Mead, *Selected Writings,* ed. Andrew J. Reck (Indianapolis: Bobbs-Merrill, 1964), pp. 234–35.

27. Mead, *Mind, Self, and Society,* p. 275.

28. Ibid., p. 274.

29. Quoted from Petras, ed., *George Herbert Mead: Essays on His Social Philosophy,* p. 151.

30. Ibid., p. 158.

31. Quoted from Mead, *Selected Writings,* p. 229.

32. Mead, *Mind, Self, and Society,* p. 274; also Mead, *Selected Writings,* pp. 356–57.

33. Mead, *Selected Writings,* p. 355.

34. Ibid., p. 236; cf. p. 292; Mead, *Mind, Self, and Society,* p. 219; and Petras, ed., *George Herbert Mead: Essays on His Social Philosophy,* pp. 153–54.

35. Mead, *Selected Writings,* p. 216.

36. Ibid., pp. 236–37; cf. Mead, *Mind, Self, and Society,* p. 219.

37. Mead, *Mind, Self, and Society,* p. 207; cf. p. 273.

38. Petras, ed., *George Herbert Mead: Essays on His Social Philosophy,* p. 152.

39. Mead, *Mind, Self, and Society,* p. 220; cf. p. 314.

40. Mead, *Selected Writings,* p. 229.

41. Ibid., p. 363; cf. p. 359; Petras, ed., *George Herbert Mead: Essays on His Social Philosophy,* p. 154.

42. Mead, *Selected Writings,* p. 228.

43. Ibid., p. 233.

44. Ibid., p. 239.

45. Cf. Mead, *Mind, Self, and Society,* p. 229.

46. Cf. ibid., p. 316.

47. Ibid., p. 313.

48. Mead, *Selected Writings,* p. 217.

49. Mead, *Mind, Self, and Society,* pp. 313–14.

50. Ibid., p. 285; cf. pp. 313–17; Mead, *Selected Writings,* pp. 230, 362.

51. Mead, *Mind, Self, and Society,* p. 316.

52. Ibid., p. 307.

53. Ibid., p. 326.

54. Ibid., p. 217.

55. Ibid., p. 386.

56. Ibid., p. 389; cf. pp. 167–68, 199, 265.

57. Mead, *Selected Writings,* p. 230.

58. Mead, *Mind, Self, and Society,* p. 221.

59. Just how easy it is to lose this "distance," especially in times of social crisis, can be seen by examining Mead's own ten-page World War I pamphlet, "The Conscientious Objector," Patriotism through Education Series 33 (New York: National Security League, 1918), unpaginated. In this brief essay, he writes that although there is a serious moral problem with punishing a person "for acting in accordance with the dictates of one's own moral judgment" (second page), we are handicapped because we have no way to certify the "sincerity of his attitude" (sixth page). In times of social crisis, he continues, we cannot allow "disobedience to laws" on the part of the minority, nor "organized effort to keep others from obeying the laws" (ninth page). Moreover, in time of war, even social criticism itself may be too dangerous to be tolerated: "Questions of policy which are debatable and must be debated under a democracy, if they involve the war itself and its successful conduct, cannot be debated while it is going on" (ninth page).

60. Mead, *Mind, Self, and Society,* p. 209; cf. pp. 177, 162.

61. George Herbert Mead, *Movements of Thought in the Nineteenth Century,* ed. Merritt H. Moore (Chicago: University of Chicago Press, 1936), p. 405.

62. Mead, *Mind, Self, and Society,* p. 199.

63. Thoreau, *Walden,* p. 135.

64. Mead, *Mind, Self, and Society,* p. 164.

65. Mead, *Movements of Thought in the Nineteenth Century,* p. 375.

66. Mead, *Mind, Self, and Society,* p. 255.

67. Ibid.

68. Ibid., p. 140; cf. Mead, *Movements of Thought in the Nineteenth Century,* p. 381.

69. Mead, *Selected Writings,* p. 357.

# Marx and Mead on the Social Nature of Rationality and Freedom

WILLIAM M. O'MEARA

A significant comparison can be made between Karl Marx and George Herbert Mead in order to examine Marx's theory of the social nature of rationality and freedom by discussing how language gives rise to consciousness and how consciousness gives rise to freedom.

Marx affirms that consciousness develops through the rise of language:

> Language is as old as consciousness, language *is* practical consciousness that exists also for other men, and for that reason alone it really exists for me personally as well; language, like consciousness, only arises from the need, the necessity, of intercourse with other men. Where there exists a relationship, it exists for me: the animal does not enter into "*relations*" with anything, it does not enter into any relation at all. For the animal, its relation to others does not exist as a relation. Consciousness is therefore from the very beginning a social product, and remains so as long as men exist at all.[1]

Marx himself did not explain how language and consciousness developed, but two Marxist philosophers, Tran Duc Thao and Mihailo Markovic, have offered explanations in agreement with Marx's intuitive hunches and compatible with George Herbert Mead's theory of the origin of consciousness. Markovic points out that the basis of human communication can be found in the conditioned and unconditioned reflexes of animals. Obviously commenting on the experiments of the Russian psychologist Pavlov with conditioned reflexes in dogs, Markovic notes that when a dog is conditioned to expect food only after a time period has passed after the ringing of a bell, the sound of the bell has become a signal for the food even though the animal will not be conscious of it as a significant symbol.[2] We have then some of the essential elements of meaning:

1. The designated object (food);
2. The dog's disposition to experience the representation of food (at least in the more highly developed animals, there is no reason to doubt

that the habit of reacting to a sign is formed by connecting the perception of the sign with the representation of the designated object);

3. The practical actions the dog undertakes upon the manifestation of the sign in order to satisfy its need (the sign manifests itself as a stimulus for a particular behavior).[3]

The isolated animal, however, cannot develop language. It is necessary that the previous elements of meaning begin to occur in a social context with other animals. In a group of animals that have a common practical goal, for example, of defense, these animals will need to coordinate their action, to transmit information, and to give mutual assistance. A specific warning cry might be an unconditioned reflex, genetically structured into the animals for common response, or might become a conditioned reflex evoking a shared response to a danger. What is further necessary for the development of conscious meaning is that an animal begin to grasp the similarity between its evoked response to its own gesture or cry and the response of another animal to the gesture or cry of the first. It is only in the similarity of their common practical response, for example, to the cry signaling a common danger, that the animals can become consciously aware of the cry as a meaningful gesture. Agreeing with Mead's theory of the origin of conscious meaning, Markovic notes that when the verbal gesture of one animal affects its hearing and evokes the same response in itself that it evokes in another animal who has heard the cry, then it is possible for consciousness of the meaning of the gesture to arise.[4] Markovic quotes Mead as follows: "We must identify for ourselves not only the object but also a readiness to respond to it in a particular way, and this identification must be done in the position or in the role of another individual to whom the object has been shown or may be shown. . . . A symbol becomes significant thanks to our capacity to be others at the same time that we are ourselves."[5]

Tran Duc Thao offers excellent insight into this human capacity to be others at the same time that we are ourselves as essential to the original form of human consciousness. Before consciousness of the meaning of a gesture develops, there must exist a sharing of the gesture in a social group. Mammals, such as chimpanzees, living together will repeat cries of warning to a common danger as they respond in a collective attack against the perceived threat. But in this situation, consciousness of meaning has not developed since an individual animal is not making the sign to itself in order to evoke the same response it evokes in the other animals. But Thao imagines how consciousness of meaning could have developed in a hunting situation engaged in by prehominids. When one hunter falls behind and the others call him by a gesture of the hand to join them, the hunter may repeat the gesture. But he cannot be calling the others to come to him; he is the one lagging behind.[6] "At the very moment when the subject begins to return the gesture to the others, he finds himself in contradiction with his own position as a lagger. The result of this is that . . . it is *for himself* that the subject repeats this call, which amounts to saying that *he calls himself* to rejoin the others."[7] By calling himself to rejoin the others, the individual becomes conscious of himself by looking upon himself from the viewpoint of the others. "Thus he is now in one and same gesture *both the giver and the receiver.*"[8] Furthermore, by calling himself to rejoin the others, the individual is conscious of the meaning of his gesture, namely, to catch up to the group, by becoming conscious of himself as the one who both gives and receives this gesture meaningful within the group's interaction. Whether we are talking about the origin of human consciousness in the prehominids or in a present-day infant, Marx's view is that "a man first sees and recognizes himself in another man. Peter only relates to himself as a man through his relation to another man, Paul, in whom he recognizes his likeness."[9]

Both Markovic and Thao have helped us to understand Marx's assertion, noted above, that language is practical consciousness as it exists for others and that consciousness is from the very beginning a social product. Consciousness arises within the social relationships of prehominids who are acting for practical goals such as defending themselves against predators or cooperating in a hunt. Only by interpreting one's physical and verbal gestures from the viewpoint of the others in a group can a prehominid become conscious of the meaning of his or her gestures. This ability to look upon the self from the viewpoint of the other is inherent in the very nature of self-awareness. The capacity of being simultaneously both self and others is essential to the nature of consciousness.

It would be a mistake to see human consciousness in the early stages of human evolution or of a child's development as identical with our contemporary, adult consciousness. Markovic points out that all investigators of early languages "have noted the presence of a number of concrete words that designate the various types of an object which is of practical significance, in the absence of an abstract word that would encompass all the varieties of the same type and that would hold conceptual significance."[10] For example, in many early languages there are various words to identify gray ducks, gray horses, and other gray objects, but there is no word which identifies the color gray itself. In the early speech of children we find a similar usage of names. They identify specific things in the immediate perceptual environment and use their words to get practical results, for example, by requesting adults to assist them. Words for the early humans and for children are useful means for interacting with others and for acting upon the environment.[11] For the child words are primarily a means of action having almost a magical effect. Merely saying the words is sufficient to make the desired people and objects materialize. Words are used as practical powers for achieving goals in the natural and social environment. [12]

Marx does affirm that consciousness is quite limited at the dawn of human awareness. Consciousness is focused primarily on the immediate sensory environment insofar as it acts upon people and insofar as people act upon it with their limited tools. Consequently, at this early stage, existing human relations and nature appear to be unable to be affected very much by human initiative. So there is little or no sense of creative freedom in early humans, ability to act upon society and nature. Human beings are like animals governed by instincts and dominated by the herd. Little or no deviation seems possible for human action. [13]

This early, tribal form of consciousness, which is so strongly determined by one's social relationships, undergoes historical enrichment as the human capability of working upon the environment develops over hundreds of thousands of years. Markovic writes: "Participation in the work process stimulated the further development of the capacity for generalization, abstraction and analysis. In work man constantly encountered instances of identity in diversity: he utilized the same tools in various ways, broke down objects into their component parts, got to know their various capacities, and utilized them for various purposes. And, conversely, he noted that various tools could have an identical practical function, and that various tools have similar characteristics and may satisfy the same use." [14]

Many mistakes were made, of course, in attempting to identify relevant similarities and differences useful for human work and for the satisfaction of human needs. But continuing practical involvement with people and objects helped to correct misunderstandings. Trial and error gradually enabled people to correct their practical ideas of how they could act upon the world with other people and be acted upon by the world and other people. [15]

The division of labor between mental and material labor, for example, between the master and the slave in Ancient Greece, was a crucial factor in humans becoming aware of the potential freedom inherent in consciousness. For the mind of the master can now be aware of himself as not enslaved, as freed from material labor, and as capable of directing the slave's labor towards the goals of the master. So the master develops a sense of the creative power of his mind in directing the labor of the slave. [16] Of course, the master is not aware of how his own culture and language set limits to the ways in which he thinks about and acts in the world with other people. Even Aristotle held that some people were fit to be slaves, not capable of giving rational directives to themselves but only capable of obeying them, either because they were born without adequate rational ability or because they had been degraded through prior enslavement.[17] But the positive point to be found in the distinction between mental and physical labor even in the master-slave relationship is that at least the master develops a sense of being freed from certain determinisms and of being freed for directing action towards self-chosen goals. Consequently, our awareness of conscious freedom in contemporary life, whether it be in democratic capitalism or democratic socialism, should not be recognized as truths obvious from the beginning of human awareness but as historical developments which may continue to change in the evolution of our concepts of human freedom.

Marx holds that human nature consists of active and passive powers enabling us to act and be acted upon by other natural realities.[18] As the prehominids developed labor, speech, and consciousness, and as labor became more complex in acting upon the world and divided into mental and physical labor, humans have developed their own human nature as consciousness and freedom. Human beings themselves have been the primary creative force in differentiating humans from animals.[19]

Marx essentially conceives of human labor as a manifestation of human freedom both in his early and later works. The connection between the social nature of consciousness and freedom is brought out quite clearly in his early writings in his use of the term "species-being," which he adapted from Feuerbach. In holding that human beings are species-beings, Feuerbach means that it is the presence of the species within the individual that makes possible human consciousness.[20] "The inner life of man is the life which has relation to his species, to his general, as distinguished from his individual, nature. Man thinks — that is, he converses with himself. . . . Man is himself at once I and Thou; he can put himself in the place of another, for this reason, that to him his species, his essential nature, and not merely his individuality is an object of thought."[21] We have seen that Marx's concept of consciousness involves the ability to be both self and other at the same time and that this ability evolved through the social interaction of prehominids. Thought is the incorporation of this social interaction into the self in that the conscious individual speaks to oneself as one speaks to another. This ability to be both self and other can free the individual by enabling one to look upon oneself and one's action from the viewpoint of the other or of a social group.

Marx explains how consciousness makes freedom possible: "The animal is one with its life activity. It does not distinguish the activity from itself. It is *its activity.* But man makes his life activity itself an object of his will and consciousness. He has a conscious life activity. It is not a determination with which he is completely identified. Conscious life activity distinguishes man from the life activity of animals. Only for this reason is he a species-being. Or rather, he is only a self-conscious being, i.e., his own life is an object for him, because he is a species-being. Only for this reason is his activity free activity."[22]

The mere animal is a member of a species but is not conscious. The mere animal does not become aware of itself from the viewpoint of another in its species and hence cannot free itself from its life activity. For the animal cannot criticize its activity or its point of view by using the point of view of another animal in the group. But human beings are species-beings since consciousness involves the ability to be both self and other. Consequently, human beings can be free. They are not determined to be self or other; they are not things but unfinished processes of becoming. They can evaluate their actions from the viewpoint of another, and they can evaluate another's actions from their own viewpoint. The conscious self need not be locked into one viewpoint. By using a future, imagined awareness, the self can be free from its present activity and can modify its activity in the light of that future point of view. Consequently, the human being as the species-being, that is, as the conscious being who is both self and other, is free.

The famous sixth thesis on Feuerbach sums up Marx's insight into the social origin of human consciousness and freedom: "But the human essence is no abstraction inherent in each single individual. In its reality it is the ensemble of the social relations."[23] Parsons's commentary on the ensemble of the social relations is quite significant:

> The French *ensemble* (Latin *insimul*) means at the same time, together; and the Latin *simulacrum* means image, representation, form. An *ensemble* is a group whose members are imaged or represented in each other and are hence together—after the manner of . . . Mead's role-taking self via the significant social symbol. "Since he comes into the world neither with a looking glass in his hand, nor as a Fichtian philosopher, to whom 'I am I' is sufficient, man first sees and recognizes himself in other men. Peter only establishes his own identity as a man by first comparing himself with Paul as being of like kind. And thereby Paul, just as he stands in his Pauline personality, becomes to Peter the type of the genus homo."[24]

Human consciousness and freedom have arisen through human social relationships via the development of labor and language, enabling people to be both self and other at the same time, that is, enabling them to be ensembles. Peter, by seeing himself in Paul, can evaluate himself from Paul's point of view, but Paul can do the same. Both in the cultural evolution of the human species and in the education of the human child, the continuing practical and social relationships between self and others are essential factors in the development of human intelligence and freedom.

In this paper, I have examined the social nature of rationality and freedom in the thought of Karl Marx, emphasizing the similarity between Marx and Mead on the nature of human consciousness. In accord with his dialectical concept of humankind as a historically developing essence, Marx affirms that language and thought have evolved primarily through people's practical relationships with nature and other humans. The social interaction of gesture and response between prehominids gives rise to the development of language and consciousness when individuals are able to be both givers and receivers of a meaningful gesture, thereby constituting the human essence as radically social. For language and consciousness enable the conscious individual to be both self and other at the same time. The ability to interpret one's actions and language gestures from the viewpoint of the other enables the individual to become free. Of course, one individual's understanding of another is not an intuitive certainty, rather it is a projected hypothesis which needs to be tested in the ongoing interaction between the individuals. Just as rational understanding of oneself and others undergoes historical development through the development of more complex labor upon nature and with other humans, so also does freedom undergo development. Marx clearly affirms that human freedom is present in labor both in his early and later writings because through consciousness of a goal people control their interactions with nature and use the laws of nature to achieve their intended purpose. At first, human consciousness and freedom in labor were dominated by the social group and by nature such that consciousness was a herd consciousness, an instinctive consciousness. However, the historical division of labor between mental and physical work was crucial in the development of human freedom, enabling people to become conscious of their own potential for self-directed action. At first, only the masters were thought capable of economic and political freedom, but with the historical development of the Industrial Revolution and the elimination of slavery and serfdom, all humans are capable, in Marx's view, of economic and political freedom. A key term that sums up the potential in humankind for the full development of rationality and freedom is species-being. As species-beings, human beings are capable of understanding the actions of any species in nature and of any human culture or individual and therefore are capable of creating freely from the viewpoint of any species or human culture or individual. As species-beings, humans are universal beings, capable of understanding and creating from the viewpoint of any being.


# Appendix

The following material is included to show that Engels and Marx agreed in their later writings that human conscious freedom is a development that differentiates humans from other animals. Engels sees humankind as developing from a prehominid state and gradually distinguishing human nature from its animal origins the more that humans through their labor learn to change physical nature through their conscious, goal-directed activity.[25] Mammal behavior is less controlled by instinct than the behavior of insects. As mammals became more capable of learning from their experience, the potential for a breakthrough to human self-control was developing. However, mere mammal behavior differs from true human behavior. A mammal such as a beaver will actively attack its environment in order to maintain its life cycle, but it is not aware of all the changes that it causes in its environment, nor is it capable of adapting to all those changes. The difference is that the human species, although it may not know all the consequences its behavior is causing in the environment, is capable of becoming aware of and of adapting to those consequences. This ability to labor actively upon nature with the capability of becoming aware of and adapting to all the consequences of human purposeful action in labor endows human beings with the ability to master nature. So Engels affirms that the essential difference between human nature and animal nature is found in the human ability to master nature, the ability to be free to adapt behavior in the light of knowledge, through conscious, goal-directed action.[26]

Just as Engels affirms that human labor reveals conscious freedom, so also does Marx. In *Capital,* human freedom is present in labor since "man of his own accord starts, regulates, and controls the material reactions between himself and Nature" for a consciously intended goal.[27] Furthermore, freedom is present in human labor because of a consciously intended goal. As Marx writes:

> We presuppose labour in a form that stamps it as *exclusively human.* A spider conducts operations that resemble those of a weaver, and a bee puts to shame many an architect in the construction of her cells. But what distinguishes the worst of architects from the best of bees is this: that the architect *raises his structure in imagination before he erects it in reality.* At the end of every labour process, we get a result that already existed in the imagination of the

labourer at its commencement. He not only effects a change of form on the material on which he works, but he also realizes a purpose of his own that gives the law to his modus operandi, and to which he must subordinate his will.[28]

Labor presupposes, of course, both humans as corporeal beings with organic needs and nature, the object labored upon, as a variety of living things and processes that can be used to satisfy human needs. However, nature is not directly usable for human beings as it is for other species. Humans must labor upon nature to make it suitable to satisfy their needs.[29] This labor begins with "imagining the goal, that is, the form of the object which the labouring subject wants to obtain, since it is only in terms of this form that definite matter can be a means of satisfaction of a definite need."[30] After consciousness determines the goal, it must then choose the means to attain that goal, and finally the human beings must act with an appropriate means to shape nature so that it will satisfy their goal. Both the determination of the goal and the selection of the means reveal a spiritual quality to human consciousness in that consciousness of the goal and the means are not determined by material nature but that consciousness makes nature serve human purposes.[31] "In setting goals which he wants to accomplish, man is not determined by nature, is a sovereign being with respect to it; he himself, his biological-spiritual nature is the primary source of these goals. . . . Thus, nature does not set goals for him, but only limits the possibilities of their attainment, compels realism in mapping out these goals. Nature is an order from which teleology is absent; only determinism is present in it."[32] The laws of nature are only an external limit upon the laborer's choice of the goal of labor and of the means to be used. Humans use the determinism inherent in physical nature to serve their purposes. Hence, although labor is limited externally by the laws of nature, labor reveals human conscious freedom, the spiritual side of human nature.

McMurtry emphasizes this combination of consciousness and freedom and calls "this special property of human nature, which for Marx enables man uniquely to 'raise a structure in his imagination' and 'erect it in reality,' the capacity of *projective consciousness.*"[33] This projective consciousness is a creative freedom which enables people to go beyond the limits of their present perception of the world and to see it from the point of view of a future that can be realized through human action. This capacity of projective consciousness has arisen and should find its fulfilment in human labor, especially in the labor or activity of creative art. For example, in the work of the creative writer there is the raising of a structure in the writer's imagination and then the actualization of that structure in the words of the story. Here, the materials of the writer offer practically no limitation to his or her imagination, unlike the limitations that primitive tools and the forces of nature impose on the primitive laborer. All labor should become like the labor of the creative artist, a manifestation of human projective consciousness, of creative freedom.[34]

# Notes

1. Karl Marx and Friedrich Engels, *The German Ideology* (New York: International Publishers, 1970), p. 51.

2. Mihailo Markovic, *Dialectical Theory of Meaning* (Dordrecht: D. Reidel Publishing Co., 1984), p. 333.

3. Ibid.

4. Ibid., pp. 335–38.

5. Ibid., p. 338.

6. Tran Duc Thao, *Investigations in to the Origin of Language and Consciousness,* trans. Daniel J. Herman and Robert L. Armstrong (Dordrecht: D. Reidel Publishing Co., 1984), pp. 8–10.

7. Ibid., p. 10.

8. Ibid., p. 11.

9. Karl Marx, *Capital, book I,* ed. Friedrich Engels, trans. Samuel Moore and Edward Aveling (Moscow: Progress Publishers, 1965); quoted in Thao, *Investigations into the Origin of Language and Consciousness,* p. 8.

10. Markovic, *Dialectical Theory of Meaning,* p. 346.

11. Ibid., pp. 346–48.

12. Ibid., p. 348.

13. Marx and Engels, *The German Ideology,* p. 51.

14. Markovic, *Dialectical Theory of Meaning,* p. 348.

15. Ibid., pp. 349–50.

16. Marx and Engels, *The German Ideology,* p. 51.

17. Aristotle, *Politics,* in *Introduction to Aristotle,* ed. Richard McKeon (Chicago: University of Chicago Press, 1973), pp. 601–605.

18. Karl Marx, *Economic and Philosophical Manuscripts,* trans. T. B. Bottomore, in Erich Fromm, *Marx's Concept of Man* (New York: Fredrick Ungar Publishing Co., 1961), p. 181.

19. Marx and Engels, *The German Ideology,* p. 42.

20. Michel Henry, *Marx: A Philosophy of Human Reality,* trans. Kathleen McLaughlin (Bloomington: Indiana University Press, 1983), p. 55.

21. Ludwig Feuerbach, *The Essence of Christianity,* trans. George Elliot (New York: Harper and Row, 1957), p. 2; quoted in Henry, *Marx,* p. 55.

22. Marx, *Economic and Philosophical Manuscripts,* p. 101.

23. Marx and Engels, *The German Ideology,* p. 122.

24. Howard L. Parsons, "The Concept of Creativity in Marx," *Revolutionary World* 49/50 (1982): 212.

25. Friedrich Engels, *Dialectics of Nature,* trans. Clemens Dutt, in *Reflections on Man,* ed. Jesse Mann and Gerald F. Freyche (New York: Harcourt, Brace and World, 1966), p. 287.

26. Ibid., p. 388.

27. Karl Marx, *Capital, book I,* in *The Thought of Karl Marx,* ed. David Mc-Lellan (New York: Harper and Row, 1974), p. 148.

28. Marx, *Capital, book I,* ed. Friedrich Engels, trans. Moore and Aveling, p. 179.

29. Ryszard Panasiuk, "Marx: Anthropology and Praxis," *Dialectics and Humanism* 3 (1983): 147.

30. Ibid.

31. Ibid., pp. 147–48.

32. Ibid., p. 148.

33. John McMurtry, *The Structure of Marx's World-View* (Princeton: Princeton University Press, 1978), p. 23.

34. Ibid., pp. 25–26; see also Karl Marx, *Pre-Capitalist Economic Formations,* ed. E. J. Hobsbaum, trans. Jack Cohen (London: Lawrence and Wishart, 1964), pp. 84–85.

# Mead, Gadamer, and Hermeneutics

JON S. MORAN

Although initially there seem to be essential differences between the hermeneutical philosophy of Hans-Georg Gadamer and the pragmatism of George Herbert Mead, an investigation of basic themes in each philosophy points to areas of fruitful dialogue. In the pages that follow I will uncover several of these general themes in order to indicate avenues of further research. First I will outline aspects of Gadamer's treatment of historical understanding. I then will link these aspects with methodological considerations from Mead's pragmatism. Finally I will suggest several points for further investigation.

Following Heidegger, Gadamer highlights the historical situation of human understanding.[1] He rejects the idea of human being as consisting of an eternal essence and instead views human existence as a function of temporal perspectives. For this reason he rejects the idea of a regulative, objective, atemporal scientific knowledge, especially when dealing with the understanding of past texts.

For Gadamer the understanding of a text involves, not a grasp of the intentions of the author, but rather an interpretation of the text within the perspective of the reader. The use of the intentions of the author as a standard is rejected for at least two reasons. First, it is doubtful that one can ever reconstruct this intention. Temporal passage has created a new context for the present interpreter for whom the intention of the author can be dimly perceived, if at all. This inability to recapture intentions is a function of the second and more crucial difficulty of using intentions as standards: the fact that the present meaning of a text must be grasped within the context of the interpreter.[2] Even if the interpreter could theoretically recapture the intention of the author, it is likely that the resulting meaning would be stillborn. This is because the meaning of the text within the experiential world of the interpreter must differ from the meaning within the perspective of the past author. This is not because the text says nothing specific. Rather the specific content of the text yields a meaning only within the experienced possibilities of the interpreter.

Thus for Gadamer all understanding involves interpretation from within the horizon of the present. A document then should not be viewed as an object detached from an interpreter who is capable of assuming a disinterested position which reveals an eternally objective meaning. Instead the document must be made present by seeing its application to present difficulties and concerns. The resultant is the meaning for the present interpreter.

In order to elicit the meaning of a document the interpreter should enter into an I-thou dialogue with the author.[3] But the interpreter does not come to the dialogue as a *tabula rasa*. The interpreter's anticipations of meaning form a horizon within which this dialogue occurs, raising questions about the authenticity of the resultant.

The prejudices and fore-meanings in the mind of the interpreter are not at his free disposal. He is not able to separate in advance the productive prejudices that make understanding possible from the prejudices that hinder understanding and lead to misunderstandings.[4]

The inherent difficulties encountered in distinguishing productive from unproductive prejudices incline Gadamer against the project of developing a clearly delineated method for unraveling the meaning of texts. Nevertheless he suggests that the work of correction and discrimination can be accomplished through *horizontverschmelzung* or the fusion of horizons.

The fusion of horizons involves the combination of past and present horizons to form a new horizon.[5] Despite the implications of the English word "fusion" this blending does not cancel out differences between horizons. The past horizon is still perceived as past. Although it is not the past as it was in itself as a then present reality, this "pastness" of the past must be retained in the present experience. Therefore the fusion involves a combined awareness of the past from a present perspective. Using the notion of an I-thou dialogue, one places oneself in the perspective of a past authorial Thou in order to grasp the relation of one's present perspective to that of the past. In the same process one also should be aware that one's present horizon is historically conditioned and open to future reinterpretation. Thus, "true historical thinking must take account of its own historicality."[6]

The adequacy of the present interpretation must be judged by its application to the present situation. It must be put into practice. In Aristotelian terms theory involves *phronesis* or practical wisdom.[7] The notion of phronesis and its relation to theory is not to be identified with the distinction between the development and articulation of a theory and its unmodified application to a particular area of concern. Phronesis is an integral part of the development of understanding itself. In Wittgensteinian terms the understanding of a language game involves participation in a form of life. The use of language is an integral part of the form of life and not a detachable formal structure that can be separated from action.

Gadamer's procedures have been criticized by both Jurgen Habermas and Karl-Otto Apel on the grounds that they lead to a subversive historical relativism.[8] Habermas maintains that the only way of arriving at the truth involves a reliance upon principles that transcend one's historical context. Apel suggests that interpretation must be guided by the regulative ideal of an ideal community of interpreters. Gadamer on the other hand claims that it is sufficient to employ a regulative principle representing, as one commentator describes, "what any rational being in that particular situation would think."[9]

The presence of such a conflict and Gadamer's attempt to use a form of contextualism to guide interpretation suggest a variety of areas in which a comparison with Mead can be made. Mead's conception of the generalized other has an analogue in Gadamer's idea of a contextually grounded conclusion of an ideal rational investigator. For Mead, in order to develop a self one must learn to place oneself in the context of other individuals within one's social group. This capacity is fostered by the acquisition of language and by participation in organized games. One begins by adopting the attitudes of specific individuals and learns to generalize the resulting dispositions. Eventually the generalized other can come to represent the ideal community of all those who share in rational discourse. Yet this ideal is not some future state of perfect interpretation. The generalized other remains contextually bound to the present to the extent that its specific content may be reconstructed as significant problems arise. This is the context-bound ideal that Gadamer uses.

The continual reconstruction of situations can be approached in terms of Mead's idea of the "I" and the "me" as functional components of the self. The "I" is the response of the organism to the attitudes of others; the "me" is the organized set of attitudes of others that one assumes.[10] This twofold division is necessary because the self contains two essential moments. First, as the "me" one's activity is structured in order that it may be grasped as a whole. And, second, as the "I" one responds to oneself as socially integrated in order to provide the unique activity of the organism.

The "me" represents the individual insofar as the generalized other is internalized in one's conduct. It is the habitual self, the more or less predictable self. It is the result of the fact that "we cannot realize ourselves except insofar as we can recognize the other in his relationship to us."[11]

The "I" is the self as a subject; it is the self considered as an actor in the present situation. Human behavior takes place within the context of a social situation in which the limitations and creative possibilities of action are present as the "me." The "I" then reacts to this self which arises through the taking of the attitudes of others. The truly individual contributions to society are thus created.

When a problem arises the habitual responses governed by the "me" are seen to be inadequate. Recourse must be made to reflective intelligence having a reference to the "I." This use of consciousness, Mead says, "has no necessary connection with the other."[12] The individual acting as an "I" selects data from the presented world which may not have been noticed before. These data serve as a bridge between the old habitual activity and the yet-to-be-created novel solution to the problem. Once the problem is solved new modes of behavior are created. Although the change may be instigated by a single individual, the solution to the problem transcends the realm of private behavior and can become a shared alternative within the community.

Two points of comparison with Gadamer's procedure can be made here. First, despite differences in terminology, for Mead the solution to present problems involves a reinterpretation of past traditions in the light of the present context. Although Gadamer may stress the role of the tradition more than does Mead, as I will note below, tradition must be consulted in Mead's account if a meaningful interpretation of a problem is to be made. Second, the reinterpretation is guided by public aspects of the present. Although Mead's stress on scientific method differs from Gadamer, both stress the public contribution of language and the necessity of an application to practice.

To refine this comparison and to show in Mead an analogue of Gadamer's "fusion of horizons," we must examine Mead's view of time and its influence on method. Mead held that there is "no aspect of the universe that is not a perspective."[13] Reality consists of a series of perspectives that are temporal in nature. A basic contention of Mead's theory of time is that only the present exists. If the past and future are to be investigated, they must be analyzed as part of ongoing present activity. In general the present is conceived as relating itself to a past and as providing preconditions for possible future developments.

In discussing the relationship between the past and the future Mead characterized the past in terms of two seemingly incompatible propositions. First, the past is definite and complete. Second, each new present reorganizes the past from which it develops. These propositions can be reconciled if one maintains, as Mead did, that the past is definite as a set of preconditions for present development, but then adds that there is an emergent element in the process of change which leads one to the implications of the past in relation to the present.

In the background of these comments is the notion that there is no knife-edged distinction between the moments of time. There is no exact place at which the present can be said to arise from a past. There is a temporal passage in which a present, characterized as emergent, gradually arises. The past presents certain preconditions or possibilities for development. The present organizes the elements in the process in a concrete, unique fashion. Thus, while one can predict the general outlines of a future state, one cannot specify all of the features of this state in their concrete detail.

Inherent in Mead's view of time is a justification of Gadamer's defense of interpretations of past texts from within the present horizon. To Mead past influences cannot be fully understood until one knows the outcome of these influences. Once the outcome is grasped the past can be understood as concretely influencing this outcome. Thus one cannot grasp the full import of the present until the present becomes a past in another present moment. Once this is accomplished one can outline and relate the structure of these two past moments. In Gadamer's terms such a procedure retains the historicity of historical thinking.

Mead and Gadamer also agree that the truth of a particular interpretation is contextually determined, rather than depending upon a set of contextually transcendent principles. Truth, Mead maintained, is "synonymous with the solution of the problem."[14] For Mead, "there is no such thing as truth at large. . . . [Truth is] always relative to the problematic situation. What is not involved in the problem is not true nor is it false; it is simply there, though there is no suggestion that a problem may not break out anywhere within it."[15] This nonproblematic situation of the problem is called "the world that is there."

Essentially questions concerning truth arise when our habitual conduct or interchange with the world is halted. We desire to continue but do not know how. This situation is problematic and constitutes the beginning of a series of acts that strive to readjust to the world.

In the constitution of a problematic situation the horizon constituted by the world that is there is crucial. It is only within the context of a world that is not placed in doubt that a problem or doubtful situation can be recognized. In Gadamer's language a problem arises within a tradition. The solution of the problem depends upon one's ability to bring the solution into harmony with the nonproblematic tradition. The establishment of this harmony consists in the reconstruction of the meanings involved in the problematic situation.

Similar to Gadamer's idea of the applicability of an interpretation is Mead's contention that the test of truth is "the ability to act where action was formally stopped."[16] We know the meaning of something when we know how to respond to it. When action is halted, we do not know how to respond. Thus in attaining the further ability to act, we must reconstruct the situation in order to clarify its meaning in regard to action.

For Mead interpretation is made possible by "sociality", defined as "the capacity of being several things at once."[17] Like the fusion of horizons, sociality necessitates that one place oneself in both the past and present perspectives in order to see the present interpretation as a solution to a problem that has arisen in the past. Sociality allows for both continuity and change. Continuity is found in some of the relations that exist between past and future. Yet the new interpretation or solution necessitates a change from the past. The same is true of the interpreter or problem solver. The creative activity of the "I" allows for both continuity and change to be found in the transition between an old and a new "me."

Given the considerations discussed in the paper, I suggest the following points upon which to base further investigation into relationships between the views of Mead and Gadamer. First, Mead's view of temporality complements Gadamer's contention that interpretation by present investigators involves no malicious distortion of the past. Second, the similarities between Mead's principle of sociality and Gadamer's fusion of horizons suggests ways of linking analyses of interpretation with conceptions of the contextual nature of reality. Third, Mead's views of the self and its relation to methods of inquiry relate to Gadamer's ideas about the implications of interpretations for the interpreter and the I-Thou stance taken toward texts. Finally, points of comparison such as these may suggest ways of linking pragmatic, scientific methods of historical investigation with the resources of the continental tradition from which Gadamer springs.

# Notes

1. Hans-Georg Gadamer, *Truth and Method,* ed. Garrett Barden and John Cumming (New York: Crossroad, 1985), pp. 225–34.

2. Ibid., pp. 263–64.

3. Ibid., pp. 321ff.

4. Ibid., p. 263.

5. Ibid., p. 273.

6. Ibid., p. 267.

7. Ibid., pp. 278–89.

8. David Couzens Hoy, *The Critical Circle: Literature, History, and Philosophical Hermeneutics* (Los Angeles: University of California Press, 1978), pp. 101–130.

9. Ibid., p. 110.

10. George Herbert Mead, *Self and Society from the Standpoint of a Social Behaviorist,* ed. and introd. Charles W. Morris (Chicago: University of Chicago Press, 1934), p. 175.

11. Ibid., p. 194.

12. Ibid., p. 167.

13. George Herbert Mead, *The Philosophy of the Act,* ed. and introd. Charles W. Morris, in collaboration with John M. Brewster, Albert M. Dunham, and David L. Miller (Chicago: University of Chicago Press, 1938), p. 495.

14. George Herbert Mead, *Selected Writings,* ed. and introd. Andrew J. Reck (New York: Bobbs-Merrill Co., 1964), p. 330.

15. Ibid., p. 324.

16. Ibid.

17. George Herbert Mead, *The Philosophy of the Present,* ed. and introd. Arthur E. Murphy, pref. John Dewey (Chicago: Open Court, 1932), p. 49.

# PEIRCE:
# UNEXPLORED ISSUES

# Pragmatism and the Normative Sciences

IRWIN C. LIEB

## I

The Lectures on Pragmatism, which Peirce gave in Cambridge in 1903 are supposed to be about what pragmatism is and whether it is true. Peirce begins them by saying that formidable objections had forced themselves upon him, and that he proposes to examine the *pros* and *cons* of pragmatism and to show "the result of allowing to both the *pros* and *cons* their full legitimate values."[1] In fact, however, Peirce never mentions the objections that either he or others had come to have; he hardly talks about pragmatism at all. The lectures are mainly about the categories and the normative sciences. Surprisingly, though, in the last lecture, Peirce says that "the substance of all sound argumentation about pragmatism has, as I conceive it, been already given in the previous lectures."[2] Peirce's audience would probably have been grateful for the arguments themselves. The "substance" of the "argumentation" is very difficult to follow. I don't know how much of his audience Peirce was able to keep, and James's remark about "brilliant light" and "Cimmerian darkness" is well known.

The lectures could have been very simply organized. Peirce might have said that, in the twenty-five years since he had formulated the pragmatic maxim, there had been some searching criticisms of it and that he himself had come to think that, at least to forestall certain kinds of misunderstanding, the maxim should be revised. He could have listed the criticisms, noted their insight, responded to remaining issues, and formulated a more acute and ample pragmatism. However, Peirce did nothing so direct. What he did instead is call for a "methodical, scientific and thorough examination of the whole question"[3] and — for some of us, unexpectedly — his plan for the study begins with "a preliminary glance at ethics."[4]

The reason for beginning with ethics, Peirce says, is that "if, as pragmatism teaches us, what we think is to be interpreted in terms of what we are to do, then surely *logic,* or the doctrine of what we ought to think, must be an application of the doctrine of what we deliberately choose to do, which is ethics."[5]

Important questions should have been raised over this first step. How exactly does pragmatism bear on what we might do? What does logic have to do with either how we think or how we ought to think? And if it has some bearing on our thought, what principles of ethics apply to it and how do they apply? Peirce raises none of these questions. He goes on, at once, to announce the second step, claiming that "we cannot get any clue to the secret of Ethics . . . until we have first made up our formula for what it is that we are prepared to admire."[6] Ethics depends on aesthetics: "It is evidently the basic normative science upon which as a foundation, the doctrine of ethics must be reared to be surmounted in its turn by the doctrine of logic."[7]

Where we might have thought, then, that we could simply ask what pragmatism is and whether it is true, Peirce tells us that our study will not be thorough unless we turn first to ethics and then to aesthetics. Peirce adds, however, that before we can turn to ethics and aesthetics, we have to make a more preliminary study: "Before we can attack any normative science, any science which proposes to separate the sheep from the goats, there must be a preliminary inquiry which shall justify the attempt to establish such dualism,"[8] an inquiry that "does not draw any distinction between good or bad in any sense whatever . . . [but that] just contemplates phenomena as they are and simply opens its eyes and describes what it sees . . . stating what it finds in all phenomena alike."[9]

This preliminary inquiry is phenomenology. It isolates the three elements that Peirce thinks are to be found in all phenomena. Phenomenology, in turn, depends on a precedent science, pure mathematics, and there is an inquiry that follows on the normative sciences, metaphysics. In the lectures, Peirce does not go into pure mathematics; nor does he provide an ordered discussion of metaphysics. His discussion of it is, unfortunately, mixed with phenomenology. Mainly, though, Peirce's order is phenomenology, then logic, then ethics, and then aesthetics. These, he thinks, will give us a thorough answer to the question of pragmatism, whatever that question is.

This is also the order in which the lectures proceed. After a genial introduction, Peirce repeats the original French formulation of the pragmatic maxim and illustrates its use in an overly long and too technical example about the meaning of probability. He goes on to the universal categories, then to a discussion of the reality of thirdness; he talks about three kinds of goodness next; then he discusses three types of reasoning, and his concluding lecture is on pragmatism and abduction. In the last lecture Peirce notes, though only very briefly, that pragmatism should be understood to be the logic of abduction.

What should we make of this indirection, of all this having to take up other subjects first? The indirection is part of what makes the lectures so difficult to follow, even when they are read. Why have so many difficult and controversial themes to be established before Peirce could come to say what pragmatism is? The answer is that they explain what pragmatism is. It seems to me, then, that we should regard the ordering of the lectures as brilliant. Though they are appalling as general lectures, the lectures are brilliantly conceived. The themes Peirce discusses are just the themes that have to be considered to amplify and to amend pragmatism. They show us what questions to ask; they show us the order to ask them in; they also show us where to look for the answers.

In the remainder of this paper, I will try to show that this is mainly so. I will also suggest that Peirce's way of working on philosophical questions is a very good way of working. We know that philosophy leads from one question to another; we also know that the answers to any of our questions are tentative until the notions they depend on are developed in a larger body of thought. What we understand less well is how such bodies of thought are themselves to be justified. It is on this point, perhaps, that we can learn most from Peirce. We can learn that thought can proceed systematically from appearances to realities and that it can be organized by principles which it itself will study. We can also learn, I think, that the final issue for us is not whether we can sustain by argument what we have come to think, but whether what we have thought sustains and enlarges us in all of our activity.

## II

I will be concerned with two issues: one calls for an explanation of a part of pragmatism, and the other calls for a modification of an important point in its first formulation.

The first formulation of the pragmatic maxim gives us what may be good advice about how to decide whether ideas have the same meaning or not. Compared with two other familiar ways of making ideas clear — Why did Peirce review only two other ways of making ideas clear? Why did he neglect the great empiricist notion of clarity? — Peirce thought that the pragmatic maxim introduced a third grade of clearness and, in a way, it does. But when we see what Peirce understood by a conception, we will see that the pragmatic maxim is really a definition. It is not a hitherto neglected way of making ideas clear. We will also see that we cannot have a complete conception of the meaning that the maxim asks us to consider. Peirce has, therefore, extensively, to modify his notion of *the* meaning of a term.

The pragmatic maxim tells us to consider the conceivable practical consequences of the object of our conception or, more accurately, it asks us to think of the consequences of acting in different ways on the objects of the kind that we have conceived. How, though, do we know what the consequences are or what they might be? How can we draw them out of the conception? The obvious answer — and Peirce gives it — is that our conception of the conceivable consequences of acting on an object is our conception of the object itself.

Peirce's notion of a conception is very close to Kant's; he said that he "was led to the maxim by reflection on Kant's *Critique*."[10] His third grade of clearness, then, does not depend on his going deeper into the meaning of an idea than, for example, Descartes or Leibniz did; it depends on his having a different idea of a conception. Given their own understandings of a conception, Descartes and Leibniz gave us the only doctrines of clearness they could have consistently devised. Since Peirce's notion is different from theirs, his idea of clearness is also different, and it is only because Peirce classifies their notions as being of a first and a second kind that he says, rhetorically and ambiguously, that the pragmatic maxim offers, not a third kind of clearness, which is what Peirce should have said, but a third grade, a relatively high grade, of clearness.

What does Peirce think a conception is? Like Kant, Peirce's view is that no sensations, none of the forceful and none of the qualitative characters we experience, are in themselves significant; impressions do not, of themselves, become ideas. Kant said that they are made to be significant when, in a construction, they are connected in certain ways with other actual or possible characters; they are made to be significant when they are connected into a conception. The forms of these connections are, for Kant, categorial. The categories are used — we know the difficulties of understanding and using them — to organize portions of actual and possible manifolds into conceptions and judgments. By contrast, Peirce thinks that the forms that make for significance are not categories; they are general features that fall under one of his own categories and are given to us in phenomena. Our experience, Peirce says, consists basically of perceptual judgments which we do not deliberately construct and which result from inferences we cannot criticize.

Peirce's views on these points are so important and interesting that I want to set them out again.

1. The general features that make for the meaning of what we perceive

are given to us in experience itself; they are not imported to further organize a manifold. Thirdness, Peirce says, "pours in on us." "Every general element of every hypothesis, however wild or sophisticated it may be, (is) given somewhere in perception . . . every general *form* of putting concepts together is, in its elements, given in perception."[11]

2. Our perception is, therefore, not a manifold of sense; it is judgmental, and it results from inference. Perceptual judgments are not Kantian "judgments of perception"; they are "judgments of experience," but they are not constructed. They are, or seem to be, the result of acritical inferences. There can, therefore, be no logical criticism of them. We may discard some of them. But that will not be because we think they are false; it will only be because they do not fit into the simplest view that we think we can have of the facts.

3. Our acritical inferences, our perceptual judgments, are abductive inferences. Peirce says that "abductive inference shades into perceptual judgment without any sharp line of demarcation between them . . . our first premises, the perceptual judgments, are to be regarded as an extreme case of abductive inferences, from which they differ in being absolutely beyond criticism."[12] The form of abductive inferences, the form of perceptual judgments, is owed to our having an insight into what would explain something that has surprised us. A conception, then, is introduced as a part of an inference, and when we think that it is or can be true of anything, we are thinking that its *object* is the cause of the surprising effect we had observed.

Peirce argued, again and again, that abduction is a genuine mode of inference. Some of his readers think it a matter of indifference whether we think of it as a mode of inference. The importance of Peirce's seeing it as a mode of inference, however, is that, if it is an inference, he can change Kant's view on important points about the categories and about the *introduction,* not the *construction,* of the conceptions in perceptual judgments.

This last note makes obvious the answer to the question of how, when we think of a conception, we are able to think of the conceivable practical results of acting on the object of the conception. The answer is that we come to have conceptions by a process of explaining the occurrence of just such effects. If we are reflective, then, if we can think of how one of our conceptions was introduced, we can collect our conception of the effects that the conception was introduced to explain. We can also see, now speaking very carefully, that, according to Peirce, our conception of a kind of object is the same as a conception of the effects that acting on the object of the conception could conceivably cause. What is unclear in Peirce's view — and part of it is probably irremovably unclear — is what is meant by "the object of a conception," by "acting on the object of a conception," and by "an action's or an object's causing observable effects." These are also Kantian difficulties and Peirce did not remove them.

Peirce's notion of a conception, then, is the same as the pragmatic maxim. The pragmatic maxim is a definition. Because it is, and because conceptions are introduced in judgments which are themselves the results of abductions, Peirce says in his last lecture that pragmatism is the logic of abduction. "Pragmatism," he says, and this is almost all he says about it, "proposes a certain maxim which, if sound, must render needless any further rule as to the admissibility of hypotheses to rank as hypotheses ... and, furthermore, this is *all* that the maxim of pragmatism really pretends to do."[13] All, that is, that pragmatism does or pretends to do is point out that an occurrence that surprised us is explained by understanding that it is a consequence of our having acted on the object of one of our conceptions. Two conceptions will, therefore, be the same if they explain the same occurrences; they will be different if they explain different ones. Abductions explain occurrences; occurrences are explained as consequences, and pragmatism is the maxim which tells us that our conception of objects is our conception of the consequences of acting on them. Is this, though, all that we should say?

If Peirce's notion of a conception is sound, then, of course, the pragmatic maxim enables us to distinguish conceptions; it has to distinguish them. But how does it fare when we use it to set out the meaning of one idea? The maxim can be used for doing this, and Peirce often uses it to bring out an important part of the meaning of an idea. There is, however, a difficulty in the idea of *the* meaning of a term. The difficulty is that, in detail, *the* meaning of a term cannot be complete. The pragmatic maxim is about the complete conception of an object. But on the pragmatic maxim our conception of an object is never a whole and single meaning. Words mean more, or can mean more, than we can ever say, and we also know that to be true. What we have to think, then, is how to understand *the* meaning of a term even while we know that we cannot set out what *the* meaning is.

Why can't we, using the pragmatic maxim, set out *the* meaning of a term? The answer is that the number of details in the meaning are indefinitely large. We cannot list all of them, or even make a rule for listing them. According to the maxim, the meaning of a conception is the conception of the conceivable practical effects of acting on the objects of the conception. But the number of the kinds of actions that might be taken toward such objects is indefinite, and the number of the conceivable practical consequences of different kinds is also indefinite. We, therefore, cannot give *the* complete meaning of a conception by citing conceivable practical results. We cannot even say all that we might mean. The original maxim is mistaken in saying that we can.

If we are to think of *the* meaning of a term, if we are to have an idea of *one* conception, then we have somehow to take account of all of the conceivable actions that might be taken toward the object of a conception and we also have to take account of all of the conceivable consequences of those actions. How are we to do this? How are we to sum them up in a general conception that explains the *all* in the *all* that a conception means? Peirce turns to ethics to answer these questions. He thinks there is an "ultimate meaning"[14] for a term, and he thinks of this meaning in connection with the idea that actions have an ultimate aim.

Here is Peirce's turn to ethics: "If the meaning of a symbol is in *how* it might cause us to act, it is plain that this 'how' cannot refer to the description of mechanical motions that it might cause, but must intend to refer to a description of the action as having this or that *aim*. In order to understand pragmatism, therefore, well enough to subject it to intelligent criticism, it is incumbent upon us to inquire what an ultimate aim, capable of being pursued in an indefinitely prolonged course of action, can be."[15]

This is an important but very condensed statement. It introduces the notion of "an ultimate aim" and it says that *the* meaning of a symbol has to do with actions' having such an aim. How are meanings and aims connected? Perhaps the easiest way to understand what Peirce means is, again, to compare his thought with Kant's. Peirce is nearly a Kantian about the meaning of conceptions; he is also nearly a Kantian in ethics, or he finds his way in ethics by criticizing and modifying Kant.

The major difference between them is that where Kant thinks that it is enough to acknowledge that a rational being is an end in itself, Peirce thinks that, setting, as he says, formalisms aside, we have to "ascertain what end is possible";[16] we have to think what aim is "immutable under all circumstances," what aim accords "with a free development of the agent's own esthetic quality" and what aim, at the same time, does "not ultimately tend to be disturbed by reactions upon the agent of that outward world which is supposed in the very idea of action."[17] The Kantian end in itself and Peirce's ultimate aim are very much alike—only they are *located* differently. We may be no more aware of having an ultimate aim than we are of being bound by the imperative, but perhaps no less. We may also be no more clear about what our aim is than we are about the rule of the imperative. But Peirce thinks that, in reasoning about actions, we can become clearer, not only about our aim, but about the meaning of our conceptions too. This greater clearness about conceptions has to do with the contribution that ideas can make to our thinking about what we should do.

In the matter of reasoning about what we should do, there is also a difference between Peirce and Kant. It derives from their different conceptions of our ends. In morals, for Kant, there is very little reasoning; for Peirce, we are to reason for as long as we can. According to Kant, to settle what we should do, we have to think whether the maxim on which we propose to act comports with the imperative. However, Kant gives us no account of the reasoning by which maxims are devised, or of the reasoning by which they should be devised. It is not even sure, for Kant, that there could be a course of reasoning that confidently concludes in a maxim that the imperative would have to endorse. What would one think of? What steps would one take? Once devised, and however devised, the imperative pronounces for or against our maxims. Then, it remains to decide whether, approved or not, we will act on a maxim that we have proposed for ourselves. For Kant, this too is not a matter for reasoning. There is no further reason for doing what we know that we should do, and there is no good reason for doing what we are not obliged to do. In either and any case, we cannot tell what maxim we have acted on. There is no sensible, no phenomenal, difference between acting morally and not. In morals, then, Kant's view seems to be that there is not much reasoning and that there is little effect or upshot from such reasoning as we may do.

Peirce does not think highly of "the logic of the ordinary attempts"[18] to refute the authority of the categorical imperative. "The whole question," he says, "is whether or not the categorical imperative be beyond control. If this voice of conscience is unsupported by ulterior reasons . . . *why should* we pay any more attention to it than to the bark of a cur . . . but if it can be disregarded, it is, in one sense, not beyond control. It leaves us free to control ourselves."[19] For Peirce, this means that we can reason about what we should do, and we can reason about our reasoning, and we can reason still further until we can no longer control our thought and are in sight of an end that commends itself just because of what it is. The categorical imperative is, perhaps the voice of reason but then we have no further reason to guide us as we contend with its demand and with the inclinations of our natures. For Peirce, it is only in an ultimate aim that our aspirations in both thought and feeling can be reconciled.

Peirce's notion of moral reasoning is that it is an inquiry in which, as in other inquiries, we think what we might do to secure the object of our desires, we have to think of an action that will conform to our ultimate aim. Nothing will seem to us an admissible maxim unless we think of it as possibly conforming to our aim; and to determine whether it will in fact advance our aim we have also to consider what the consequences of our actions will be. Our reasoning about what we should do is abductive. Just as we try to think what would render a surprising observation a matter of course, we think what action would settle our circumstance and also, as a matter of course, be in accord with our final aim. Pragmatism is the logic of abduction. Peirce also thinks that it yields a fourth grade of clearness as we think how our conceptions contribute to our thought about our possible action.

Peirce makes no statement in the lectures about the differences between the third and fourth grade of clearness. But there is one in the paragraphs that are printed as his preface. There, Peirce says that the maxim of pragmatism has "great utility in leading to a relatively high grade of clearness of thought . . . it should always be put into practice with conscientious thoroughness, but . . . when that has been done, and not before, a still higher grade of clearness of thought can be attained by remembering that the only ultimate good which the practical facts to which it directs attention can subserve is to further the development of concrete reasonableness; so that the meaning of a concept does not lie in any individual reactions at all but in the manner in which those reactions contribute to that development,"[20] in the manner in which the meaning of a conception contributes to the development of actions "becoming governed by law, becoming instinct with general ideas,"[21] conforming to our idea of an ultimate aim.

The ultimate meaning of a term, then, consists in our conception of the contribution that a term is capable of making to thinking what actions would conform to an ultimate aim. Why is this the ultimate meaning of a term? It is the complete meaing because it is the only conception we can have of *all* that we might do and of *all* that might follow on our doing it. It is the only conception we can have of all that a term might come to mean. It leads us toward greater clearness by having us consider what use, what good use, we can make for our ideas. The first formulation of pragmatism leaves us with an indefinite number of conceivable actions and an indefinite number of conceivable consequences. The meaning of a term is not some definite subset of either these actions or these consequences. We have therefore to think of a way of having *the* meaning embrace all of these, and also to include all that a word might come to mean in the future. Peirce's way of doing this is to think, generally, of all the conceivable actions involving an object that might contribute to an ultimate aim and of all of the consequences that might test the fittingness of the actions to the aim. All that a term means, then, and all that it can mean, has to do with an end that embraces every conceivable deliberate action involving the object of our conception. If there could be an action that does not have such an aim, it would not be deliberate and it should, perhaps, not even be thought of as an action, any more than an earthquake is.

An ultimate aim, then, embraces and tests all conceivable actions — its generality matches the *all* of the *all* that a word can mean. The pragmatic maxim should therefore be revised to read that all that a term means, all that it can ever mean, is our conception of the conceivable bearings of the conceivable consequences of its objects on what we might conceivably be deliberately prepared to do. This formula contains almost as many "conceivables" as Peirce's first formulation.

The original maxim of pragmatism, Peirce says, lends itself to being understood "in too individualistic a sense";[22] it directs attention to definite kinds of practical effects. When we amplify the maxim, we have also to understand that what we aim at is wider than the immediate aim of any one of our own actions. Peirce did not explicitly refer to Kant's Kingdom of Ends, but his idea of a community of inquirers, extended now to a community of those who act deliberately, is very much like Kant's. Our ultimate aim is not ours alone. It is no more possible that the world will finally allow a plurality of ultimate aims than that it will allow a plurality of final opinions. Just as we tend toward the same opinion, we tend toward having the same aim. Peirce says that "we cannot expect to attain a complete conception of it."[23] But he also says that "we can see that it is a gradual process, that it involves a realization of ideas in man's consciousness and in his works, and that it takes place by virtue of man's capacity for learning, and by experience continually pouring upon him ideas not yet acquired,"[24] ideas that, when acquired, are to be realized in new meanings and, perhaps, in more finely controlled and aimed activity.

# III

The question that concerned me at the start of this paper is what Peirce is doing in the Lectures on Pragmatism. He doesn't seem to be doing what he said what he was going to do. He said that he was going to consider the *pros* and *cons* of pragmatism and then consider how it might be vindicated or rectified. However, he did not deal with these topics directly. He seemed to deal instead with everything else he had ever thought, and at inordinate length and in dozens of too often long and vain asides.

The reading of the lectures I am recommending is that, in the lectures, Peirce did deal with all the *pros* of pragmatism that he could think of and that he also deals with, perhaps all, the *cons* he left us to imagine. He did this through an elaborate construction whose bearing on pragmatism he did not explain as plainly as he should have. I have tried to suggest, though for only two issues about pragmatism, how Peirce's construction shows us what pragmatism supposes and what its further or final good might be.

Pragmatism is the logic of abduction. Abduction supposes that, in addition to qualitative characters, there is always some token of exteriority in experience, and there is always some regularity, generality and significance. These are the features that phenomenology had distinguished, and pragmatism depends on them. It will, however, be firmly established only if one goes on to think whether what is real must coerce our judgments and our conception of our aims. In the lectures, Peirce leaves this last work undone. His only venture into it is in an absorbing discussion which has no bearing on ethics and is out of the order he proposed to follow. The largest portions of Peirce's lectures are about the categories and the normative sciences, and he is occupied with them because of the amendment they provide for the first formulation of the pragmatic maxim. The original maxim does not, as Peirce has said it did, provide for a complete conception of an object; there is no summary *all* for conceivable consequences. This is not a disadvantage in the project of distinguishing conceptions. But if we also take account of the normative sciences, we can enlarge pragmatism by asking what good there is in distinguishing conceptions. The answer is that the ultimate meaning of different terms does not consist in different specific practical consequences. It consists in a general conception of the different contributions that different objects might make to deciding what will advance an ultimate aim; it has to do with *whatever* we might do. This difference between a summary *all* and a *whatever* makes for an important improvement on the first formulation of pragmatism. Sometimes Peirce seems to regard it as a version of what he all along had in mind. This may simply be Peirce's vanity. Even so, it seems plain that, in his ordered rendition of the provinces of philosophy, in his moving from one to the other, in his drawing out of the support and dependency the provinces have for one another, Peirce located his pragmatism. He did not leave it isolated, as he had done earlier. He sees what comes before it and what comes after it; he sees what has to be said to explain it and he sees, as well, how comprehensive a careful review of it should be. I believe, of course, that there is much more that we can still learn from Peirce, and much that we can learn to do from the way in which he worked. This last is the last point I wish to emphasize. Perhaps, though, as in Peirce's lectures, in all that has been said, there has already been enough argumentation about the point.

# Notes

1. Charles Sanders Peirce, *Collected Papers of Charles Sanders Peirce,* ed. Charles Hartshorne, Paul Weiss, and Arthur Burks (Cambridge, Mass.: Harvard University Press, 1931–58), vol. 5, para. 15. Hereafter, this work will be cited as CSP, followed by a volume number and a paragraph number, in the standard fashion.

2. CSP 5.201.
3. CSP 5.34.
4. CSP 5.35.
5. Ibid.
6. CSP 5.36.
7. Ibid.
8. CSP 5.37.
9. Ibid.
10. CSP 5.3.
11. CSP 5.186.
12. CSP 5.181.
13. CSP 5.196.
14. CSP 5.179.
15. CSP 5.135.
16. CSP 5.134.
17. CSP 5.136.
18. CSP 5.133.
19. Ibid.
20. CSP 5.3.
21. CSP 5.4.
22. CSP 5.402n.
23. Ibid.
24. Ibid.

# Charles S. Peirce:
# American Backwoodsman

NATHAN HOUSER

Charles Peirce was city born and bred. He grew up in Cambridge, Massachusetts, where his grandparents had settled and where his father, Benjamin Peirce, taught mathematics and astronomy at Harvard University. Why, then, do I refer to him as a backwoodsman? For two reasons. First, he spent the final third of his life, his most philosophically productive years, in relative seclusion with his second wife at Arisbe, their home on the Delaware River, two and a half miles from Milford, Pennsylvania. Milford was a village of about a thousand persons located seventy miles from New York City, the nearest metropolitan center. For Peirce, a trip to New York would begin with a buggy ride of several miles to the nearest railroad station at Port Jervis (no railroad passed through Milford), then a train to New Jersey across the Hudson River from New York and, finally, a ferry to the city. Travel to other major eastern cities was by way of Manhattan. The inconvenience and expense of travel kept Peirce at Arisbe for most of his last thirty years. Because Peirce actually lived so far off the beaten track, he literally was, in that respect, a backwoodsman.

It is not primarily in that sense, however, that I refer to Peirce as a backwoodsman, even though his seclusion — a seclusion he never expected when he moved to Milford — was greatly detrimental to him, and may have cost him leadership in American thought in his own day — even, perhaps, world leadership in logic. As it turned out, Peirce's isolation in the backwoods of Pennsylvania was a portent of the fate of his deepest philosophical contributions. The kind of backwoodsman that I have in mind is the kind we find not at the frontiers of civilization, but rather at the frontiers of knowledge. Peirce was far more notably that kind of backwoodsman. He worked ceaselessly and painstakingly to push back boundaries and to cultivate uninhabited or sparsely inhabited intellectual wild lands. He was an intellectual backwoodsman.

In reflecting on the theme of frontiers in American philosophy, it occurred to me that the subject might be approached either historically or from the standpoint of current philosophical pursuits. Taking the historical approach, we could say that Peirce opened, or helped to open, a number of frontiers during his lifetime. His seminal work on the logic of relations might be cited, or his successful axiomatization of the natural numbers several years before the equivalent axiomatizations of Dedekind and Peano,[1] or his effective introduction of quantifiers,[2] or his discovery and introduction of truth-function analysis,[3] or his introduction of evolutionary conceptions into several areas of philosophy, or, perhaps, his behavioral account of belief.[4] But frontiers are not static; the unheard of in one age may be common knowledge in another. I decided that the frontiers I would consider as those of philosophy today. So I asked myself if any of Peirce's pioneering achievements now stand at the forefront of philosophy, whether in America or abroad, and promise to stimulate research for years to come.

It is to Peirce's great credit that a number of his contributions might be said to pass muster, but the contribution that stands out is Peirce's general theory of signs, his semiotic. This is an area in which he undertook the most remarkable and sustained labors and of which he is rightly regarded as a founder. Long before semiotic came to be regarded as a valuable discipline — some would say that time has not yet come — Peirce saw, as few before him had, its fundamental importance. Locke, whose work inspired Peirce, saw it to some extent. But when Locke introduced the term "semeiotica" into philosophy it was more or less an afterthought.[5] Peirce took up the study of signs with a clarity and purpose never before brought to it — unless by Poinsot, whose work on signs was virtually unknown until recently[6] — and he developed at least the outlines of an imposing science. To a large extent Peirce worked alone. Few understood then, and perhaps not many more understand now, what Peirce was up to. Peirce never faltered in his conviction that his work was of great value, although there is a certain pathos in some of his reflections: "I am," he said, "as far as I know, a pioneer, or rather a backwoodsman, in the work of clearing and opening up what I call *semiotic*, . . . and I find the field too vast, the labor too great, for a first-comer."[7] Peirce hoped that others would take up his vision and help construct an intellectual edifice which he supposed would dominate philosophy. Indeed, some have followed Peirce, but it is disappointing how many American philosophers dismiss semiotic as a study not to be taken seriously.

I can now safely say, however, that the writing is on the wall. Semiotic is a field of study whose time has come. It is a branch of philosophy that even the most reluctant will eventually have to accept. Many of those who resist welcoming semiotic into the fold of philosophy have little idea what it is. In the remainder of my paper I will attempt to locate semiotic within Peirce's system of thought, and to characterize it as a field of study. I will not attempt to characterize semiotic beyond Peirce's conception of it. I do not mean to imply that Peirce's general theory of signs is the only viable theory; certainly there are others. But Peirce has succeeded better than anyone else in developing a comprehensive theory that makes semiotic central to philosophy. I would not be surprised if some philosophers would just as soon see their departments offer courses in transcendental meditation as in semiotic. Those who feel this way doubtless know very little about Peirce's theory (or, you may say, about transcendental meditation). Others have a more tolerant, but hardly less uninterested, attitude toward Peirce's semiotic. The fact is, semiotic is simply not regarded by mainstream American philosophers as a mainstream subject. It is not thought to be central to the philosophic enterprise, and if someone takes it to be so, *that* is taken as a sign that *he* or *she* is off base. It is this disparagement of Peirce's semiotic that I hope to weaken by giving a more balanced, though very summary, account of his theory.

Peirce's philosophy, as is well known, is quite systematic. Some would say it is systematic to a fault. Central to Peirce's system is the idea that certain conceptions are fundamental to others, and those to still others, and so on; so that it is possible to analyze our various theoretical systems (our sciences) into a dependency hierarchy. At the very top of the hierarchy of conceptions we will find a set of universal categories, an idea Peirce shares with many of the greatest systematic thinkers, including Aristotle, Kant, and Hegel. Peirce's universal categories are three: firstness, secondness, and thirdness. Firstness is the conception of something that is what it is independently of what anything else is. Firstness does not go much, if at all, beyond the conception of a pure monad. Secondness is the conception of something that is what it is in relation to, or in reaction to, something else. It is, or is similar to, the conception of a pure dyad. And thirdness is the conception of a relation, or mediation, *between* two things —a conception of triadicity (or of a pure triad). In Peirce's opinion, all conceptions at the most fundamental level can be reduced to these three.

This theory of categories stands at the pinnacle of mathematics, which, in turn, is at the pinnacle of the sciences. Mathematics presupposes none of, but is presupposed by all of, the other sciences. Following mathematics, we come to philosophy, which has three main branches: phenomenology, the normative sciences, and metaphysics, which are dependent on each other in that order. Not surprisingly, Peirce's categories, fleshed out in different ways, make their appearances in each of these parts of philosophy (as, of course, they must if they are universal categories). There are three normative sciences at the center of philosophy: aesthetics, ethics, and logic, again dependent on each other in that order. Logic, in turn, has the following three branches: speculative grammar, critic, and methodeutic. The first branch studies the relation between representation and meaning, or what is requisite for meaningful representation. It corresponds in large measure to what we would call epistemology. The second branch of logic, critic, is sometimes called logic proper. It is the formal science of the truth conditions, or trustworthiness, of representations. The third branch of logic, methodeutic, sometimes called speculative rhetoric, studies how knowledge is attained and transmitted. It might be called the science of interpretation. These three branches correspond to some extent to Carnap's syntactics, semantics, pragmatics triad, which he learned from Charles Morris, who derived it from Peirce.

Following the three normative sciences, in Peirce's classification, comes metaphysics, the third and last branch of philosophy. Logic, the normative science immediately preceding metaphysics, sets the course for our metaphysical investigations. The special sciences — physics, psychology, and the like — follow philosophy.

You may be wondering, where does semiotic fit in Peirce's scheme? It may surprise you to learn that it is *equivalent* to logic. The normative science of logic *is* semiotic. The three branches of logic are the three branches of semiotic. Sometimes Peirce inclines toward limiting logic to what I have already called "logic proper," the science of the truth conditions, or trustworthiness, of representations. In that case logic would correspond roughly to semantics as one branch of semiotic, with the other branches corresponding roughly to syntactics and pragmatics. But Peirce's more usual practice was to equate logic and semiotic.

That is Peirce's conception of semiotic. It is, indeed, the general science of signs, as is commonly thought, but that is also what logic is. The science of signs is far broader than the formal study of the sign relation, even though the sign relation is a fundamental conception. Peirce's theory of signs in its most abbreviated form goes something like this. First there is speculative grammar, the study of the "general conditions to which thought or signs of any kind must conform in order to assert anything."[8] It is this part of semiotic that is most commonly dealt with, and is sometimes taken to be the whole of semiotic. For example, when Quine outlined Peirce's theory in his philosophical dictionary, *Quiddities,* he did not go much beyond Peirce's speculative grammar.[9] Often Peirce scholars impose this same limitation. Speculative grammar begins by inquiring into the general nature or structure of signs: those things which stand *for* something *to* something (or someone). What the sign stands for Peirce calls its object. What it stands to he calls its interpretant. The sign relation is *fundamen-*

*tally* triadic; eliminate the reference either to the object or to the interpretant and you annihilate the sign. This is the fundamental insight of Peirce's semiotic, and one that distinguishes it from theories of representation that attempt to make sense of signs that are related only to objects.

This is, of course, a most elementary part of Peirce's theory of signs. Peirce goes on to distinguish between different kinds of objects and interpretants. He explains that signs can be divided in three ways: according to what they are in themselves (either qualities, existent things or occurrences, or laws); according to how they are connected with their objects (they are either *like* their objects [icons]; are physically connected with their objects [indexes]; or are related by convention to their objects [symbols]); or according to how the object is represented by the sign (as a possibility, an actual existent, or as a law). Since every sign is something in itself, has a relation to its object, and represents its object in some way or other, the above divisions can be used to yield a classification of signs that makes more distinctions than any rival theory I know of, and therefore affords a richer analysis of representation of all sorts.

After speculative grammar comes critic, the study of the truth conditions of representations and "the kinds and degrees of trust that are appropriate to different ways of reasoning."[10] It is in this part of semiotic that we would study Peirce's famous triadic classification of arguments into retroduction (or abduction), induction, and deduction. Naturally, there is an important connection between the three classes of arguments and the analysis of signs, which results from speculative grammar and in turn rests on the universal categories.

Finally, we come to the last part of semiotic, speculative rhetoric or methodeutic. I have called this the study of interpretation or of how knowledge is attained and transmitted. I will admit that I have gone somewhat out on a limb with this characterization. But I believe it is clear enough that whereas the focus of critic is on the relation of signs to their objects (without ignoring altogether the role of interpretants), the focus of methodeutic is on the relation of signs to interpretants (without ignoring altogether the role of objects). In my opinion the chief doctrine to be elaborated in this part of semiotic is pragmatism.[11] Although pragmatism is often thought of as nothing more than a maxim for determining the meaning of words or abstract concepts, it is sometimes put forward by Peirce as a method of thinking[12] or of logic, and occasionally as the method of methods. In one place Peirce says that pragmatism is "a far-reaching theorem solidly grounded upon an elaborate study of the nature of signs."[13] In any case, the very essence of pragmatism seems to be its insistence on the fundamental role of interpretants in representation.

In brief, that is Peirce's semiotic — probably more encompassing than some philosophers have realized, and perhaps less esoteric than they supposed. Naturally there are many spin-offs and ramifications of Peirce's semiotic philosophy, some within epistemology, logic, and methodology, and others when Peirce addresses problems in metaphysics. I cannot even begin to catalogue Peirce's findings, let alone list all of the areas where we might fruitfully apply semiotic today, but I will conclude by stressing the importance of approaching Peirce's work with his semiotic theory in mind. Peirce's analysis of the sign relation as fundamentally triadic motivated much that is unique and significant in his philosophy. I will conclude with a few brief examples intended to illustrate how fundamental Peirce's semiotic is to his general philosophy.

Peirce's theory of cognition is a case in point. Arguing that all thoughts are signs, Peirce developed a sign theory of cognition which, according to Klaus Oehler, answers some of the more troublesome questions raised by Kant's transcendental idealism (while retaining the benefits). Oehler says that Peirce's sign theory enabled him to leave "the level of the controversy between idealism and realism behind him in a revolutionary way" and to lay "the foundation for a totally new way of considering the problem of cognition and reality."[14] One message is clear. To understand how Peirce deals with the idealism-realism question we must first understand his theory of signs.

Given Peirce's insistence that all thought is in signs, his inclusion of the interpretant as a correlate in the sign relation shows that all thought *is to some degree* a matter of interpretation. Of course interpretation is constrained, and to some extent directed, by facts beyond our control. But there is another side of interpretation, especially when we are dealing with symbols, the kind of signs involved in all advanced thought. Symbols are conventions. In other words, they are signs by agreement. That means they are part of a language, and they must be part of *our* language if we are to use them. Language is a communal affair. To accept a linguistic convention is tantamount to identifying with the linguistic community. Peirce stressed the significance and importance of *community* in his philosophy. He appealed to the conception of a community of inquirers for his theory of truth, but perhaps more important he regarded the *identification with community* as fundamental for the advancement of knowledge (the end of the highest semiosis) and the advancement of human relations as well. Concerning this latter point Peirce made the following provocative remark: "Here, then, is the issue. The gospel of Christ says that progress comes from every individual merging his individuality in sympathy with his neighbors. On the other side, the conviction of the nineteenth century is that progress takes place by virtue of every individual's striving for himself with all his might and trampling his neighbor under foot whenever he gets a chance to do so. This may accurately be called the Gospel of Greed."[15]

Presumably, on this point at least, Peirce was a Christian. A prominent German philosopher, Karl-Otto Apel, who among others finds something useful in Peirce's work for reflective Marxists, refers to Peirce's semiotic theory of inquiry as "logical socialism."[16]

Perhaps I am going rather too far afield, but it is worth noticing how Peirce's emphasis on the role of interpretants brings community to the forefront of his philosophy. This aspect of Peirce's work was much developed by Josiah Royce. Hilary Putnam has raised an interesting objection to Peirce's appeal to identification with community for explaining rational choice. He poses the problem (which he calls "Peirce's Puzzle") of explaining why it is rational to choose what is most probable in unrepeatable situations (where appeal cannot be made to success frequency). Peirce's answer, that one's identification with the ongoing community explains why it is rational to choose what is most probable in such cases, is dismissed by Putnam as unrealistic altruism. He opts instead for the Wittgensteinian nonanswer that we simply cannot explain why we choose to do what is probable in unrepeatable cases beyond saying that this is just what we do.[17] At present I cannot answer Putnam's objection, but I am confident that the Peircean reply will be a semiotic one. (I suspect that *convention*, a telltale mark of rationality for Peirce, has been mistaken for altruism by Putnam.)

I have remarked that interpretation is constrained and directed by facts beyond our control. This might lead a reader to ask, "What is a fact of the matter?" and "How does it relate to the truth of the matter?" By raising these questions we launch ourselves into an investigation of Peirce's pragmatic theory of truth, or so we should were we really intent on answering our questions—which the limit of space does not permit. Fortunately, Apel has recently made an excellent study of Peirce's theory of truth in his contribution to Eugene Freeman's *Monist* series on Peirce's relevance.[18] Apel situates Peirce's theory squarely within his semiotic. Peirce's theory of truth can be understood best (perhaps only) from within the framework of his theory of signs.

Perhaps the importance of a semiotic approach to Peirce's theory of truth can be brought out by a few suggestive remarks. Clearly, all representations are representations *of* this or that, but it is equally the case that every representation is a representation *to* or *for* someone; there is always an interpretant. Thus, truth is always knower-relative, we might say, but not entirely so. There is what we might call a correspondence side to Peirce's theory, for truth is relative to an object or a fact of the matter; but there is also what we might call a coherence side, that truth is relative to interpreters (or interpretants). This recognition of both factive and interpretive correlates in the sign relation is the key to Peirce's semiotic approach. We would not want to say, of course, that the truth concerning any given fact of the matter is in any way dependent on how that fact is represented to you or to me. Peirce agrees. Truth is not relative to the knower in *that* sense. The truth of a proposition is relative to an ideal community of inquirers, that is, to an ideal interpretant. This ideal interpretant is one that would result from intelligent and deliberate and exhaustive efforts to find out the truth, or, in other words, from a completed process of perfecting adjustments that result from a sustained and systematic program of verification (deliberate confrontation with the facts of the matter). To dismiss either of the so-called correspondence or coherence components of Peirce's pragmatic theory of truth involves a failure to appreciate the triadic character of all representation. The semiotic approach never loses sight of the triadic nature of signs.

I will make one final point about Peirce's pragmatism, in particular about the motivation for his pragmatic maxim, quoting a passage Peirce wrote in 1905 where he explains the purpose of his maxim: "It will serve to show that almost every proposition of ontological metaphysics is either meaningless gibberish — one word being defined by other words, and they by still others, without any real conception ever being reached — or else is downright absurd; so that all such rubbish being swept away, what will remain of philosophy will be a series of problems capable of investigation by the observational methods of the true sciences."[19] Peirce's pragmatic maxim, as here characterized, was intended as a test of whether our conceptions, and our theories, are indexed to experience, and whether they are tied to interpretants with performative and not only intellectual value, or whether they are part of a mere language game. I submit that this can be understood most clearly from within the context of Peirce's general theory of signs, and that within that context its message is one that semioticians, in particular, should heed. Semiosis that never escapes its web of symbolic interpretants (e.g., words) is condemned as meaningless gibberish.

These are only a few of many areas in which a study of Peirce's theory of signs appears to be necessary for a complete understanding of Peirce's contributions. The full import of his semiotic theory is yet to be worked out. Great strides have been made by dedicated individuals, but it is too much to expect that lone scholars will make the most of Peirce's work. It is a task for a great community of scholars. The great communal mind that for two hundred years has put so much of its immense power to the task of understanding Kant and developing his doctrines would do well to shift its collective attention to Peirce.

# Notes

1. Paul Shields, "Charles S. Peirce on the Logic of Number," Ph.D. diss., Fordham University, 1981.

2. Hilary Putnam, "Peirce the Logician," *Historia Mathematica* 9 (1982): pp. 290–301.

3. Atwell R. Turquette, "Peirce's Icons for Deductive Logic," in *Studies in the Philosophy of Charles Sanders Peirce,* ed. Edward C. Moore and Richard S. Robin (Amherst: University of Massachusetts Press, 1964), pp. 95–108.

4. Willard Van Orman Quine, "The Pragmatists' Place in Empiricism," in *Pragmatism: Its Sources and Prospects,* ed. Robert J. Mulvaney and Philip M. Zeltner (Columbia: University of South Carolina Press, 1981), pp. 21–39.

5. John Locke, *An Essay Concerning Human Understanding,* vol. 2, ed. Alexander C. Fraser (Oxford: Oxford University Press, 1844), chap. 21.

6. John Poinsot, *Tractatus de signis,* ed. John N. Deely (Berkeley: University of California Press, 1985).

7. Charles S. Peirce, *Collected Papers of Charles Sanders Peirce,* 8 vols., ed. Charles Hartshorne, Paul Weiss, and Arthur Burks (Cambridge, Mass.: Harvard University Press, 1931–58), vol. 5, para. 488. Hereafter, this work will be cited as CSP, followed by a volume number and a paragraph number, in the standard fashion.

8. CSP 2.206.

9. Willard Van Orman Quine, *Quiddities* (Cambridge, Mass.: Harvard University Press, 1987), pp. 210–11.

10. Beverley Kent, *Charles S. Peirce: Logic and the Classification of the Sciences* (Kingston: McGill-Queen's University Press, 1987), p. 134.

11. William Paul Haas, *The Conception of Law and the Unity of Peirce's Philosophy* (Fribourg: The University Press, 1964), pp. 83–85.

12. CSP 8.206.

13. CSP 8.191.

14. Klaus Oehler, "Peirce's Foundation of a Semiotic Theory of Cognition," *Peirce Studies* 1 (Lubbock: Texas Tech University Press, 1979), pp. 67–76.

15. CSP 6.294.

16. Karl-Otto Apel, *Charles S. Peirce: From Pragmatism to Pragmaticism* (Amherst: University of Massachusetts Press, 1981), p. 193.

17. Hilary Putnam, *The Many Faces of Realism* (LaSalle, Ill.: Open Court, 1987), pp. 80–86.

18. Karl-Otto Apel, "C. S. Peirce and Post-Tarskian Truth," in *The Relevance of Charles Peirce,* ed. Eugene Freeman (LaSalle, Ill.: Hageler Institute, 1983), pp. 187–223.

19. CSP 5.423.

# Peirce's Contribution to Ethics

VINCENT MICHAEL COLAPIETRO

In *The Development of Peirce's Philosophy,* Murray G. Murphey states that the "religious spirit was always present in Peirce's work, whether overtly expressed or not, and was an important factor in determining the nature of his philosophy."[1] One of the most important ways this spirit shaped Peirce's philosophy concerns how he conceived self-control. It was principally in the context of ethics and aesthetics that he explored self-control. The purpose of this paper is, accordingly, to investigate how Peirce's life-long commitment to a traditional form of religion or theism informed his mature conceptions of ethics and aesthetics.

## I

Peirce was disposed throughout his life to draw a sharp distinction between religion and theology.[2] He took religion to be a practical affair rooted in our instinctual nature[3] and theology to be a theoretical undertaking often far removed from religious practice and even more often animated by a polemical spirit.[4] For him, the central concern of the former is to bring individuals into communion with the ultimate ground and goal of their being;[5] the chief preoccupation of the latter is to separate the goats from the sheep, the heterodox from the orthodox.

Peirce was also inclined, especially before his mature investigation of the normative sciences, to draw an equally sharp distinction between morality and ethics. In his own words, "morality consists in the folklore of right conduct. A man is brought up to think he ought to behave in certain ways. If he behaves otherwise, he is uncomfortable. His conscience pricks him. That system of morals is the traditional wisdom of ages of experience. If a man cuts loose from it, he will become the victim of his passions.

It is not safe for him even to reason about it, except in a purely speculative way."[6] Just as theology is reason reflecting on religion, so ethics is reason reflecting on morality. In both cases, there is a strong tendency to overlook the dangers inherent in such reflection.

Peirce connected religion primarily with the disclosures of direct, personal experience and morality principally with the exigencies of our daily, interpersonal interactions. All attempts to give expression to the disclosures of the divine in our experience, including those forms of expression which have been inherited from tradition, more or less grossly distort the character of what has been directly encountered.[7] In contrast, most attempts to meet the exigencies arising from our interactions are, by and large, adequately illuminated by the maxims bequeathed to us by our elders. Despite these points of emphasis, Peirce by no means neglected the traditional and communal aspects of religion[8] or the experiential and personal facets of morality.[9] What religion and morality most deeply have in common is that they are not originally based on reason; both are first and foremost woven out of instinct, experience, tradition, and habit.

In contrast, Peirce saw theology and ethics as attempts on the part of reason to grasp more fully the substance of religion and morality, respectively. So conceived, religion and morality are primary, while theology and ethics are, at best, derivative and, at worst, destructive of the practices they are ordained to serve. Ideally, theology should provide an interpretation of what is revealed in experience, an interpretation set forth in the very spirit of the experience from which it sets out. There is no better name for this spirit than agape.[10] Historically, however, theology has been an arena in which "the inhumanity of a polemic spirit"[11] has dominated; moreover, it has not so much provided insights into direct experience as it has demanded assent to some speculative hypothesis regarding, say, the origin or nature of the cosmos.[12] In doing so, it has sinned twice — first, by blocking the road of inquiry[13] and, second, by misdirecting the instinctive impulse toward religious adoration. Ideally, ethics should provide an explanation of how persons in community must act in order to realize their individuality in and through participation in community. Historically, while ethics has occasionally performed a noble task, it has characteristically served an ignoble cause. In this context, reason has been used far more often to rationalize the unconscionable disregard of some morally sound folkway than to justify the conscientious refusal of some regenerate soul to engage in a traditionally sanctioned yet inherently immoral practice.[14]

In his critiques of theology and ethics, Peirce undoubtedly overstates — and, in certain respects, *wildly* overstates — the case against reason.[15] Yet, if we look beyond his explicit strictures to his actual practice, and if we take into account the ironic nature of Peirce's most disparaging remarks about the power of reason,[16] what we discover is, in effect, a threefold distinction in each case. In the one case, it is imperative to differentiate religion, theology as it has been historically undertaken, *and* theology as it ought to be reformed in light of a critical commonsensism. In the other, it is essential to differentiate morality, ethics as it has been historically practiced, *and* ethics as it ought to be reformed in the same light. The abuse of reason in the contexts of theology and ethics is not a justifiable warrant for prohibiting the use of reason in these contexts. It should, however, serve as a warning that any employment of our reason in these spheres is fraught with the possibility of our conclusions being simply rationalizations of the ego.[17] Thus, here as well as elsewhere, our only hope is to be guided by "a *contrite* fallibilism."[18]

## II

We are now in the position to turn directly to the way in which Peirce conceives the process of becoming an ethical agent. This process should not be seen as the pursuit of a fixed end by beings with preset capacities; rather it should be seen as an attempt to "further the realization of an ideal not definable in advance" of its pursuit[19] by beings who transform themselves into agents in the very pursuit of such an ideal.[20] While the ideal is "equally capable of inward and of outward realization,"[21] it can never be completely actualized in either dimension: "It must always be in a state of incipiency, of growth."[22] In a very general and formal way, we may characterize this ideal as the continuous growth of concrete reasonableness;[23] however, in order to give specificity and content to this ideal, it needs to be interpreted contextually and historically.[24] So, too, in any equally general and formal way, we may describe the task of becoming an ethical agent as participation in the growth of reasonableness; yet what this existentially means for any individual person can only be discovered by that person in the actual circumstances in which he is destined to live.

In the course of cosmic evolution, autonomous agents have emerged. These agents themselves are, in part, responsible for their own emergence; given the nature of autonomy, it could not be otherwise. The process by which such agents come into being is essentially a task to which they must voluntarily devote themselves. This task is summed by Peirce himself in this way: "It is by the indefinite replication of self-control upon self-control that the *vir* is begotten, and by action, through thought, he grows an esthetic ideal, not for the behoof of his own poor noodle merely, but as the share which God permits him to have in the work of creation."[25]

This passage brings into focus what Peirce takes to be the key factors in the process of becoming an ethical agent. Most prominent among these factors is the cultivation of ever higher grades of self-control.[26] What results from the self-controlled cultivation of self-controlled conduct is maturity — "the *vir* is begotten," the individual attains manhood.[27] However, the highest form of maturity demands assuming radical responsibility not only for how we act but also for what we love.[28] "In general, the good is the attractive — not to everybody, but to the sufficiently matured agent; and the evil is the repulsive to the same."[29] Accordingly, such maturity involves cultivating an ever more penetrating sense of that which is worthy of devotion; the moral agent conscientiously "grows an esthetic ideal." The cultivation of this ideal is, in its very essence, a *communal* undertaking: it can only be accomplished through a dialogue with others.[30]

But the conscientious cultivation of what Peirce understands by an aesthetic ideal drives toward a religious interpretation of this ideal, of the process through which this ideal discloses itself, and of the task to which it calls persons. First of all, the aesthetic ideal itself needs to be conceived in religious terms. Thus, we read in a letter from Peirce to James, dated July 23, 1905: "To Schiller's anthropomorphism I subscribe in the main. And in particular if it implies *theism,* I am an anthropomorphist. But the God of my theism is not finite. That won't do at all. For to begin with, existence is reaction, and therefore no existent can be *clear supreme.* On the contrary, a finite being, without much doubt, and at any rate *by presumption,* is one of a genus; so that it would, to my mind, involve polytheism. In the next place, anthropomorphism for me implies above all that the true Ideal is a living power. . . . That is, the aesthetic ideal, that which we *all* love and adore, the altogether admirable, has, *as admirable,* necessarily a mode of being to be called living."[31] Because our ideas of the infinite and thus of the divine are necessarily vague in the extreme, they become contradictory almost the moment we attempt to render them precise.[32] But, even so, they are "not utterly unmeaning, though they can only be interpreted in our religious adoration and the consequent effects upon conduct. This I think is good sound solid strong pragmatism. Now the Ideal is not a finite existent. Moreover, the human mind and the human heart have a filiation to God. That to me is the most comfortable [comforting?] doctrine. At least I find it most wonderfully so every day in contemplating my misdeeds and shortcomings."[33] If aesthetics concerns the *absolutely* admirable and adorable, and if this turns out to be not only infinite but also living and personal, then the principal conclusion of Peircean aesthetics merges with the central claim of traditional theism.[34]

Second, an indispensable phrase in the ongoing process by which this ideal is cultivated is either identical with, or at least analogous to, what traditionally has been called prayer.[35] The Ideal vaguely resembles a Person;[36] thus, it is a being with whom we can communicate in some fashion.[37] According to Peirce, "we, one and all, have an instinct to pray; and this fact constitutes an invitation from God to pray."[38] The purpose of prayer is simply to give expression to "the soul's consciousness of its relation to God."[39]

Finally, the task of becoming an ethical agent involves nothing less than assuming a unique role in the drama of divine creation.[40] "We must look to see what little and definite task our circumstances have set before our little strength to do. The performance of that task will require us to draw upon all our powers, reason included."[41] The creation of the universe "did not take place during a certain busy week, in the year 4004 B.C., but is going on today and never will be done."[42] Moreover, "such vague idea as we can have of the power of creation is best identified with the idea of theism (i.e., belief in a personal, infinite God). So then the ideal would be fulfilling our appropriate offices in the work of creation. Or to come down to the practical, every man sees some task cut out for him. Let him do it, and feel that he is doing what God made him in order that he should do."[43]

## III

While Murphey acknowledges (as we have seen) that the religious spirit influenced Peirce's philosophical reflections, he claims Peirce formulated very early and affirmed ever after a "prohibition against the mixing of matters religious and matters philosophic."[44] There is no question that Peirce endeavored to make philosophy "a strict science, passionless and severely fair."[45] There is equally no question that, for him, this meant being moved not by the desire to defend a truth allegedly in our possession but by the desire to discover a truth presently beyond our grasp.[46] However, he saw this very quest for truth as a form of worship.[47] Thus, while Peirce drew a sharp distinction between philosophy and religion (and an even sharper one between philosophy and theology), he did not advocate a complete "separation" of these distinct endeavors.[48]

In fact, Peirce's mature conception of the normative sciences (in particular, ethics and aesthetics) exhibits a *deliberate* attempt to interpret aspects of these sciences in religious terms. In the last decade or so of his life, he devoted considerable attention to what he called the normative sciences.[49] He came to identify these sciences as aesthetics, ethics, and logic. The overarching task of the normative sciences is finding out "how Feeling, Conduct, and Thought, ought to be controlled supposing them to be subject *in a measure,* and only in a measure, to self-control, exercised by means of self-criticism, and in the purposive formation of habit, as common sense tells us they are in a measure controllable."[50]

While Peirce regarded logic as "the Ethics of the Intellect," he regarded ethics in general as "the science of the method of bringing Self-Control to bear to gain our Satisfactions."[51] Ethics was understood as a theory of the intrinsically admirable. In one context, Peirce described this theory as follows: "If conduct is to be thoroughly deliberate, the ideal must be [on the side of the agent] a habit of feeling which has grown up under the influence of a course of self-criticisms and hetero-criticisms; and the theory of the deliberate formation of such habits is what ought to be meant by *aesthetics*."[52] In another context, he wrote: "Meantime, instead of a silly science of aesthetics, that tries to bring our enjoyment of sensuous beauty,—by which I mean all beauty that appeals to our five senses,—that which ought to be fostered is meditation, ponderings, day-dreams (under due control) concerning ideals—oh, no, no, no! 'ideals' is far too cold a word! I mean rather passionate admiring aspirations after an inward state. . . . Our contemporary religious doubt will prove a terrible calamity indeed, if the sort of meditations I mean is to be weakened, lying as they do at the very bottom, the very lowest hold of the ship that carries all the hopes of humanity."[53]

However, Peirce's name for this theory, "aesthetics," and his most characteristic ways of designating the *summum bonum* (the admirable, the fine, the beautiful) may induce the careless reader to overlook what, at bottom, motivated Peirce to ground ethics in aesthetics. What so moved Peirce becomes apparent only when we take seriously his not unusual characterization of the *summum bonum* as that which is in itself *adorable* in the original sense of this word (worthy of adoration). "The man of science has received a deep impression of the majesty of truth, as that to which, sooner or later, every knee must bow."[54] "It is not too much to say that he worships the divine majesty of the power of reasonableness behind the fact. From that sentiment springs the desire to further the discovery of truth."[55]

Deliberation, for Peirce (no less than for Dewey), is a dramatic rehearsal in the imagination of alternative courses of conduct.[56] However, to be thoroughly deliberate turns out—at least, for Peirce—to require one to be deeply prayerful. In an unpublished manuscript, we read: "All reasoning, even solitary meditation, is essentially of the nature of an appeal to a person held in high regard."[57] In the light of this, prayer would appear to be an appeal to that person held in the highest possible regard—in short, to the Most High.[58]

Peirce did "not see why prayer may not be efficacious, or if not the prayer exactly, the state of mind of which the prayer is expression."[59] This state of mind primarily consists in "putting oneself into an attitude of receptivity," of readiness to be grasped by the intrinsically admirable and to respond to this grasp.[60] Such an attitude provides what, in the final analysis, is the only adequate perspective from which we can effectively clarify our needs and purify our desires. "The fault of the vulgar utilitarian is not that he asks what would be the use of this or that, but that he never does ask. He simply rests in his present desires and never submits them to any criticism at all."[61] However, if we are to be thoroughly deliberate, an ongoing critique of our desires is necessary. We are obligated to ask, "What are our 'needs'? We know what we have an impulse to seek, and *if we have considered the matter deliberately* we are convinced that those things are far from being the same as our true needs."[62] The most advantageous perspective for the ongoing clarification of our true needs is one that results from dialogue with not only other human beings but also the Most High Other imaginable.[63] This perspective requires that the question of idolatry in the strict sense be raised in a formal and explicit manner.

It is only in light of purified desires that we can catch a more or less accurate glimpse of our moral destiny either in its most general character or its most personal form. In light of such desires, "the very first command that is laid upon you, your quite highest business and duty, becomes, as everybody knows, to recognize a higher business than your business, *not* merely an avocation after the daily task of your vocation is performed, but a generalized conception of duty which completes your personality by melting it into the neighboring parts of the universal cosmos."[64] What this individually means can only be decided by unique individuals themselves in their actual circumstances.

Given the traditional cast of his religious outlook, it should be no surprise that, for Peirce, the completion of one's personality, the realization of one's self, depends on the overcoming of egoism. This is accomplished only through a *series* of surrenders.[65] The text in which Peirce most carefully delineates the phases in this series is (of all places!) a review of Mach's *Science of Mechanics*. Here he asserts: "having once surrendered to the power of nature, and having allowed the futile ego in some measure to dissolve, man at once finds himself in synectic union with the circumambient non-ego, and partakes in its triumph. On the simple condition of obedience to the laws of nature, he can satisfy many of his selfish desires; a further surrender will bring him the higher delight of realizing to some extent his ideas; a still further surrender confers upon him the function of cooperating with nature and the course of things to grow new ideas and institutions.[66] Almost everybody will admit there is some truth in this: the question is how fundamental that truth may be."[67] For Peirce, it was difficult, if not impossible, to exaggerate the importance of this truth.[68] "Self-control seems to be the capacity for rising to an extended view of a practical subject instead of seeing only temporary urgency. This is the only freedom of which man has any reason to be proud; and it is because love of what is good for all on the whole, which is the widest possible consideration, is the essence of Christianity, that it is said that the service of Christ is perfect freedom."[69]

# Conclusion

Let me conclude by very briefly juxtaposing the views of Peirce with those of Dewey on three fundamental issues. In *The Quest for Certainty* as well as elsewhere, Dewey contrasts the arts of propitiating supernatural powers with those of controlling natural forces. However, what Peirce in his discussions of religion is driving at does not fall into either one of these categories. His concern here is to underscore the need for "arts" of surrendering egoistic control. In *A Common Faith,* Dewey himself calls attention to there being "changes in ourselves in relation to the world in which we live."[70] Such changes "relate not to this and that want in relation to this and that condition of our surroundings, but pertain to our being in its entirety."[71] While such changes involve "a note of submission," they are nonetheless voluntary. However, this does not mean that they depend on particular resolves or volitions.[72] Any such transformation of the self "is a change *of* will conceived as the organic plentitude of our being, rather than any special change *in* will."[73] While individuals themselves cannot effect such a transformation *of* will, they can open themselves to such a transformation by a type of reflection that is not directed toward controlling the course of events. It is in this connection that Peirce glimpses a dimension of deliberation that Dewey more or less overlooks, though not entirely.[74]

The second juxtaposition concerns the most appropriate way to describe the ultimate end of human action. According to Dewey, this "end is no longer a terminus or limit to be reached. It is the active process of transforming the existent situation. Not perfection as a final goal, but the ever-enduring process of perfecting, maturing, refining is the aim in living. . . . Growth itself is the only moral 'end.'"[75] As we have seen, Peirce's characterization of this end is more specific; it is the continuous growth of concrete reasonableness. For both, this end is evolutionary: It becomes defined in the very process of being pursued. However, at this point in the process, we can, according to Peirce, specify — albeit vaguely[76] — the direction in which it is desirable to grow.

Third, Dewey asserts: "There is nothing in which a person so completely reveals himself as in the things he judges enjoyable and desirable."[77] For Peirce, it would seem that there is nothing in which persons so completely reveal themselves as in what they deem admirable and adorable. Moreover, in the case of such persons as Buddha, Confucius, and Socrates, there is suggested the possibility of another sort of revelation.[78] The lives of these persons are themselves taken to be revelations of the divine. Is there any way of testing the authenticity of this type of revelation? For Peirce, its "ultimate test must lie in its value in the self-controlled growth of man's conduct of life."[79] Such a test renders the suggestion, at best, plausible; however, it can never eliminate the possibility that religion is the desperate illusion of a being terrorized by cosmic solitude and radical responsibility.

For Peirce, it is imperative not to misinterpret what the dramatic advances of the natural sciences in the last several centuries imply for the religious believer. These advances have rendered obsolete certain ways of articulating and defending this belief but they have not outmoded the most fundamental questions or answers concerning religious belief. Is there an intrinsic connection between autonomy and adoration? Do the highest forms of self-control demand the most complete form of self-surrender to what is intrinsically worthy of adoration? Or does the growth in human freedom point away from ingenuous participation in some more or less traditional form of religious worship? Is religion an illusion that, given the inevitable future advances in technology and science, has itself no future?

Or, precisely given these "advances," is not a conscientious refusal to absolutize the human will, in either its individual or collective form, needed in order to make *our* future a reality?[80]

# Notes

1. Murray G. Murphey, *The Development of Peirce's Philosophy* (Cambridge, Mass.: Harvard University Press, 1961), p. 16; also Robert J. Roth, *American Religious Philosophy* (New York: Harcourt, Brace and World, 1967), p. 65; and Donna Orange, *Peirce's Conception of God* (Lubbock, Texas: Institute for Studies in Pragmaticism, 1984).

2. Cf. John E. Smith, *Reason and God* (New Haven, Conn.: Yale University Press, 1961), p. 76.

3. Charles Sanders Peirce, *The Collected Papers,* ed. Charles Hartshorne, Paul Weiss, Arthur W. Burks (Cambridge, Mass.: Belknap Press of Harvard University Press, 1960), vol. 6, para. 216. Hereafter, this work will be cited as "CSP," followed by a volume number and a paragraph number, in the standard fashion. See also Richard L. Trammell, "Religion, Instinct, and Reason in the Thought of Charles S. Peirce," *Transactions of the Charles S. Peirce Society* 8 (1972), pp. 3-25.

4. CSP 6.3.

5. CSP 6.429; cf. John E. Smith, *Experience and God* (London: Oxford University Press, 1968), p. 17.

6. CSP 1.50; cf. CSP 1.600; CSP 1.666.

7. CSP 6.429.

8. See, for example, CSP 6.443; cf. Smith, *Reason and God,* p. 69.

9. At MS 675, pp. 13-14, Peirce writes: "God has created every man *free,* and not 'bound' to any kind of conduct but that which he freely selects. It is true that he finds he cannot be satisfied without a firm and stiff government over his impulses; but then it is a self-government, instituted by himself to suit himself; — copied, it is true, largely from the government his parents wielded when he was a child, but only continued because he finds its answers his own purposes; and not in the least because he is 'bound' in any proper sense whatever."

10. CSP 6.289; CSP 6.302; cf. Paul Tillich, *Morality and Beyond* (New York: Harper and Row, 1963), pp. 39-40; and Carl Hausman, "Eros and Agape in Creative Evolution: A Peircean Insight," *Process Studies* 4 (1975), pp. 11-25.

11. Charles Sanders Peirce, *Writings of Charles S. Peirce: A Chronological Edition,* vol. 1: *1857-66* (Bloomington: Indiana University Press, 1982), p. 5.

12. CSP 6.3.

13. CSP 1.136.

14. Cf., however, John Dewey, *Human Nature and Conduct,* in vol. 14 of *The Middle Works of John Dewey, 1899-1924* (Carbondale: Southern Illinois University Press, 1981), p. 177.

15. Cf. Smith, *Reason and God,* pp. 73-74, 90.

16. Trammell, "Religion, Instinct, and Reason in the Thought of Charles S. Peirce," pp. 12-14.

17. CSP 1.631.

18. CSP 1.14, emphasis added; cf. CSP 5.583.

19. CSP 1.589.

20. CSP 6.156.

21. CSP 1.589.

22. CSP 1.615.

23. See, for example, CSP 5.3 and CSP 5.433.

24. Cf. Tillich, *Morality and Beyond,* pp. 42-43.

25. CSP 5.402n.3; cf. CSP 1.607; see Walter P. Krolikowski, "The Peircean *Vir,*" in *Studies in the Philosophy of Charles Sanders Peirce (Second Series),* ed. Edward C. Moore and Richard S. Robin (Amherst: University of Massachusetts Press, 1964), pp. 257-70.

26. See, for example, CSP 5.533.

27. Krolikowski, "The Peircean *Vir,*" pp. 257-58.

28. Cf. Beverly Kent, *Charles S. Peirce: Logic and the Classification of the Sciences* (Kingston: McGill-Queen's University Press, 1987), p. 32.

29. CSP 5.552; however, cf. Kent, *Charles S. Peirce,* p. 155.

30. CSP 1.574.

31. CSP 8.262.

32. Ibid.

33. Ibid.

34. Cf. Murphey, *The Development of Peirce's Philosophy,* p. 364.

35. CSP 6.507; CSP 6.156.

36. CSP 6.516; cf. Vincent Potter, "'Vaguely Like a Man': The Theism of Charles S. Peirce," in *God Knowable and Unknowable,* ed. Robert J. Roth (New York: Fordham University Press, 1973), pp. 241–54.

37. Orange, *Peirce's Conception of God,* p. 15.

38. CSP 6.516; cf. CSP 1.906.

39. CSP 6.516.

40. CSP 7.572; CSP 8.138n.4.

41. CSP 1.647; cf. Kent, *Charles S. Peirce,* p. 27.

42. CSP 1.615.

43. CSP 8.138n.4.

44. Murphey, *The Development of Peirce's Philosophy,* p. 42.

45. CSP 5.537.

46. CSP 1.620.

47. See, for example, CSP 7.136; also Murphey, *The Development of Peirce's Philosophy,* p. 13; Mary Mahowald, "Peirce's Concepts of God and Religion," *Transactions of the Charles S. Peirce Society* 12 (1976), p. 368.

48. CSP 7.136.

49. Richard Robin, "Peirce's Doctrine of the Normative Sciences," in Moore and Robin, eds., *Studies in the Philosophy of Charles Sanders Peirce (Second Series),* pp. 271–88. See also Vincent Potter, *Charles S. Peirce on Norms and Ideals* (Amherst: University of Massachusetts Press, 1967); and Kent, *Charles S. Peirce.*

50. Peirce manuscript number 655, p. 24. The MS number refers to the manuscript number as given in Richard S. Robin, *Annotated Catalogue of the Papers of Charles S. Peirce* (Worcester, Mass.: University of Massachusetts Press, 1967). Hereinafter, such manuscript numbers will be cited as, for example, MS 655.

51. Charles S. Peirce, *Charles S. Peirce: Selected Writings* (New York: Dover Publications, 1958), p. 415.

52. CSP 1.574.

53. MS 675, pp. 15–16.

54. CSP 8.136.

55. CSP 8.136n.3.

56. MS 288, p. 29; Dewey, *Human Nature and Conduct,* p. 132.

57. MS 634, variant p. 1.

58. Cf. Orange, *Peirce's Conception of God,* p. 15.

59. CSP 6.516.

60. Orange, *Peirce's Conception of God,* p. 23.

61. MS 313, p. 12.

62. CSP 6.517, emphasis added; cf. MS 649, pp. 36–37.

63. See, for example, CSP 6.467.

64. CSP 1.673.

65. Cf. Mahowald, "Peirce's Concepts of God and Religion," p. 371.

66. Cf. Richard J. Bernstein, "Toward a More Rational Community," in *Proceedings of the Charles S. Peirce Sesquicentennial Congress,* ed. Kenneth L. Ketner et al. (Lubbock: Texas Tech University Press, forthcoming).

67. Charles Sanders Peirce, *Contributions to The Nation: Part One: 1869–1893,*

ed. Kenneth L. Ketner and James Edward Cook (Lubbock: Texas Tech University Press, 1983), p. 189.

68. Cf. CSP 5.402n.2.

69. CSP 5.339n.1.

70. John Dewey, *A Common Faith* (1934; New Haven, Conn.: Yale University Press, 1971), p. 16.

71. Ibid.

72. Ibid., p. 17.

73. Ibid.

74. Dewey, *Human Nature and Conduct,* pp. 179–81.

75. Ibid., p. 181.

76. Potter, "'Vaguely Like a Man': The Theism of Charles S. Peirce," pp. 247ff.

77. Dewey, *Human Nature and Conduct,* p. 262.

78. CSP 6.503.

79. CSP 6.480.

80. Cf. Smith, *Experience and God,* pp. 183–205; also Sergio Cotta, *Why Violence?* (Gainesville: University of Florida Press, 1985), pp. 113–36.

# ETHICAL THEORY

# Rights and Norms

BETH J. SINGER

In opposition to other theories, traditional and contemporary, which attribute rights to individual humans as such, and also to the conventional view that rights are held by individuals against society or against one another, I see rights to be norm-governed social relations; social institutions in which the members of a community jointly and mutually participate. Rights are therefore traits of communities, not of individuals. But the view of rights I shall present is not "communitarian." It is intended to transcend the opposition between individualism and communitarianism.

According to George Herbert Mead, on whose analysis of communicative interaction my theory of rights is largely based, individual selfhood and community are inextricably linked, and both evolve in the same process.[1] To become a self, as Mead explains it, is to learn to respond to oneself as others would: not merely to take the attitude of another individual or individuals toward oneself, but to view oneself as a member of a community of selves, all of whom are expected and required to behave in ways that community has determined to be appropriate or necessary. In Mead's own words, to become a self is to learn to take the attitude of the community, the "generalized other." It is "to be ready to act with reference to [one's] own conditions just as any individual in the community would act."[2] "One of the greatest advances in the development of the community arises when this reaction of the community on the individual takes on what we call an institutional form. What we mean by that is that the whole community acts toward the individual under certain circumstances in an identical way. . . . We call that the formation of the institution."[3] A social institution, then, may be defined as a way of behaving that is governed by a community, by the attitude of a generalized other; alternatively, we may identify the institution with the attitude itself. "An institution is, after all, nothing but an organization of attitudes which we all carry in us, the organized attitudes of the others that control and determine conduct."[4] Such an internalized and controlling attitude is commonly referred to by sociologists as a "social norm." All who share such an attitude, according to Mead, constitute a community, and to distinguish this sense of "community" from others, I call it a "normative community."

When a social norm is operative in a community, all the members have internalized the normative attitude, making it part of their individual perspectives. In the relevant circumstances, they are ready to take this attitude, not only toward one another but toward themselves. To have the attitude of a generalized other is to expect of the individual others that they, too, have governed and will govern themselves by this attitude and that they expect the same of us. (What "is expected of one" is not only what it can be predicted that one will do, but what it would be correct to do.) For rights to be operative is for such an attitude to be in place.

Rights are not anything (e.g., "powers" or "claims") we possess as individuals, but ways in which we behave toward one another. They are social relations, forms of social interaction, in which we jointly participate. As I have elsewhere shown, a rights-relation involves two reciprocally defined roles, that of being entitled ("having a right") to have, do, or say something, and that of being obligated to respect this entitlement. Where a right is operative, the entitlement and concomitant obligation are defined and established as normative by the attitude of the community. Thus the rights-relation is a triadic one, involving the community as such, as well as the role players, who have those roles in virtue of their membership in it.[5] To perform either role in this relation requires one to have the same normative attitude, the attitude establishing the entitlement and defining it as one it is obligatory to respect. One cannot treat something as being what one is entitled to by right without respecting that entitlement and holding all, including oneself, obligated to do so. Similarly, one cannot have the attitude that respect for anyone else's entitlement is obligatory without (supposing the same circumstances) taking that same attitude toward oneself, for if we could exempt ourselves from it, the respect would not be obligatory. Everyone in the community, therefore, everyone who shares the normative attitude that constitutes a right, has both roles. All have, and are equally obligated to respect, the same rights-entitlements.

But does this obligation outweigh other obligations? Do rights take precedence over other social institutions? The term "right" has a special force. When we talk of rights, we consider the entitlements they involve to take precedence over weaker entitlements or claims, such as desert. I do not base rights on any "greatest good" principle, or on the interests of "rights-bearers." Nevertheless, a criticism of "utilitarian" theories of rights could be taken to apply to the view to be developed here, namely, that if rights are institutions in the same sense as any other, their exercise must be weighed on the same benefit-scale as any other conduct or good. If this be the case, it has been said, then rights can be violated with impunity whenever enough people derive sufficient benefit from the violation. Moreover, proponents of "natural rights" raise another and, I think, more serious objection: If rights are social institutions, operative norms, then no one can claim to have a right that is not operative in the society of which he or she is a member. Are there, then, no universal rights? My treatment of both these issues will rest on an analysis, based on that of Mead, of the nature and function of social norms. The response to the first criticism will rest on the reply to the second.

In the language of the theory of operative rights, the question of universal rights becomes the question, "Are there rights-norms that ought to be operative in every normative community?" To answer this question, we must inquire more deeply into the nature and function of norms. Since normative behavior is expected of any member of the community in which the norm is operative, it must have the same meaning to all. For Mead this means that all respond to it in the same way or ways, the response being that of the generalized other. Any norm-governed act or gesture, that is, is a significant symbol. Part of its meaning is that it is (or is not) appropriate or allowable, whether at all or in specifiable circumstances. Regarding that which is allowed, appropriateness is only a minimal requirement. Behaviors may be defined by the norms as not only appropriate, but as *called for* in certain situations. They may be so in the strong sense of being mandatory or imperative; or in the weaker sense of being alternatives, one or another of which is expected; or in the still weaker sense of being invited, but optional. (This categorization is not exhaustive; there may be further shades of difference.) That we require laws to be obeyed and promises to be kept are norms of the first sort; the allowable responses to a move in a card game express a norm of the second sort; that one may or may not reply to a friendly letter exemplifies the third sort. The variety of ways in which members of our society may satisfy the expectations that they earn a living belongs to the second category. Rights-norms, imposing a mandatory obligation, belong to the first. That is, contrary to what is often held, not all norms are imperatives.[6] Furthermore, as I shall show, the nature of normativity is such that even those norms that are imperatives are not, *qua* norms, coercive or repressive. Acceptance of coercion may become a norm.[7] But it is the acceptance, whether tacit or overt, that makes even a coercive institution (such as the mandatory payment of income tax) normative.

When a norm is operative, the attitude it embodies is a constituent of the general perspective of a community, internalized by the members as a component of their individual perspectives and used by them in determining both their own behavior and their expectations regarding one another.[8] Both factors are essential. To have internalized a norm is to recognize when it is applicable, to know how to judge or behave in terms of it, and to feel or acknowledge its authority and legitimacy. However, to apply the norm, to govern oneself by it, is not necessarily to do what it calls for or defines as appropriate, even though one acknowledges its normativity. It is not even necessarily to refrain from doing what is prohibited. As Hans Joas points out in his book on Mead, "the understanding of morality as sociality does not come down to a morality of conformity."[9] To adopt and apply a normative perspective or attitude is to determine one's behavior or judgment in the light of what this perspective defines as relevant and irrelevant, permissible and impermissible, required or optional. Having internalized a particular norm, we must still, in any situation to which it is applicable, determine whether and how we will apply it; and factors other than the norm itself may enter into this determination.

We can explain this in terms of Mead's concepts of the 'I' and the 'me'. The attitude of the generalized other, embodied in the social norms, is incorporated into the 'me', which Mead speaks of as "the organized set of attitudes of others which the self assumes," and as representing "a definite organization of the community there in our own attitudes."[10] For Mead, that is, the 'me' is the self insofar as it is social, equipped with the responses — the knowledge, expectations, understandings, and other normative attitudes — shared by the members of the community (or communities) to which the individual belongs.[11] "Through taking those attitudes," Mead says, "we have introduced the 'me' and we react to it as an 'I'."[12] The 'I' is the self as dynamic and agential; it is the moving subject, aware of and reacting to the attitudes of the 'me' called out by the situations in which the individual becomes involved. Both 'I' and 'me' respond to the situation; both take positions, attitudes; but it is 'I' that decides and acts. And whereas the 'me' is cumulative, the product of past experience and social interaction, the 'I', continuously moving into the future, is not.[13]

As soon as I become aware of myself acting, I am no longer the actor; the actor I now remember is a 'me' that was an 'I' at an earlier time. "I cannot turn around quick enough to catch myself." The other side of this is that neither are we aware of what we will do; the as-yet-unrealized 'I' is not predictable. In addition to being active, that is, the 'I' is creative, originative, capable of introducing new factors into the dialogue with the 'me'. Reacting to the 'me', the 'I' stands outside the 'me's' perspective, which it judges in relation to the situation that has called it forth. The most important feature of the 'I' is this independence. While it must respond to the 'me', it is not bound by the latter's attitude. Not only does the 'I' determine how the perspective of the 'me' is to be applied, it can select and apply alternative perspectives from among those the self has acquired, and it can generate new perspectives which it may oppose to the 'me' and to the social norms. Thus the 'I' can criticize the 'me' and in decision and action can override it, though it need not do so. In social communication and interaction the 'I' can also criticize the community and so may exercise a determinative influence upon the community's perspective and, through it, upon the perspectives of other selves, other 'me's'. The interplay between the 'I' and 'me', while it plays a part in the reinforcement of social norms, is also an engine of social and cultural (i.e., normative) change. And, as Mead points out, the 'I' can appeal for support and justification of its own attitude, not only to other communities, present and past, but also to ideal, future communities which it projects.[14]

In its transiency, the 'I' is an object to itself only in memory, when it has become part of the 'me'. "The 'I' of this moment," Mead says, "is present in the 'me' of the next moment." The 'I' that acted a moment ago is now "the 'I' of the 'me'."[15] The 'me', then, must include the 'I' of the past; it is continuously incorporating the 'I' of the passing present, an 'I' that sometimes adopts the attitude of the community but does not always do so. Yet Mead repeatedly identifies the 'me' solely with the perspective of the community, leaving individuality to be the province of the 'I' alone. This not only fails to define adequately the status of past 'I's'; it denies the possibility of a cumulative and evolving personal or individual perspective which differs from that which is acquired from the community (i.e., the communities to which the self belongs). I shall therefore distinguish between a social 'me' and an individual 'me', to both of which the 'I may respond. The social 'me' comprises the internalized attitudes of the community or generalized other. The individual 'me' is the cumulative fund of individuated attitudes taken by the 'I', now available, with the attitudes of the community embodied in the social 'me', to be elicited in the future. In the moving present, attitudes of both the individual and the social 'me' may be called out. Responding to the situation as it unfolds, the 'I' evaluates those attitudes; but then it can also judge that response, which is its own essential past now encompassed by the 'me'.[16] The dialogue continues until the 'I' acts, decides, or comes to a conclusion. In this process, whether the 'I' is responding to the social or the individual 'me', the latter is being progressively shaped and reshaped. And just as it can project an ideal community, in criticizing the individual 'me' the 'I' may project an ideal individual 'me', an ideal self, to justify its critical stance.

As constituents of the social 'me', social norms have their field of operation in our governance of ourselves; but the social control that they exercise is mediated by self-control. Self-governance, even by means of the application of social norms, is self-determination. Rather than automatic or imposed conformity, normative behavior is self-determination with references to what is called for by those norms taken by the 'me' to be applicable. It is a process of reflexive communication between the social 'me' and the 'I'. Deliberation is the methodic elaboration of this same process. Taking the normative attitude in the person of the 'me', as 'I' one interprets and appraises the relevance of this attitude for the situation at hand, bringing to bear as well the attitude of the individual 'me' in determining whether and how to apply the norms. Decision and volition are acts of the 'I' reacting to the response called out in the 'me' by the situation, and the 'I' may endorse, reject, or adopt a modification of the social attitude.

Most often, in practice, we do follow the norms: we conform to the general mandates and taboos of the community or select from among the options with which its norms present us, whether we do so deliberatively or the 'I' simply permits us to act habitually. But we need not remain within the limits established by the community. Every situation is complex, and diverse perspectives may be relevant to different aspects of it. Many factors may come into play in shaping decision and correspondingly many perspectives be brought to bear by the 'I', including not only perspectives of the individual 'me' but also new perspectives of the 'I's' own devising. Even when the norms embodied in the attitude of the social 'me' define a particular mode of behavior to be mandatory, and even though in other circumstances the 'I' might decide to carry out that mandate, in a particular situation its response may be to give priority to some other perspective, social or individual, institutionalized or ideal. This response, in turn, is open to appraisal. But the independence of the 'I', its ability to transcend and appraise the attitudes of the 'me' and to accept or reject them or call for their revision, is intrinsic to the reflexive process of self-governance and cannot be denied without negating the self-determining character of normative behavior itself. We must conclude, therefore, that freedom to exercise this independence, that is, *personal autonomy,* is a necessary condition of those norms being efficacious, and hence a necessary condition of normative community.

Self-governance has additional prerequisites. The social 'me' embodies or personifies the normative attitude of the community. But the community is constituted by its interacting members, who together shape that attitude and give the norms their authority. It is of crucial importance that for social norms to be established is for them to be voluntarily adopted: Supposed or intended norms that are merely legislated or are imposed by some individuals or groups upon others are not operative, they do not have normative force, do not have the meaning of norms, unless and until they are *taken as* normative by those for whom they are to have this weight. This is true, not only for the individuals among whom a norm is first instituted, but also for those to whom it is subsequently taught. Transmission of the norms of a community is their reinstitution, their adoption by successive generations who thereby accept their normativity. Initially, those who are growing up in a community and come to internalize its attitude may take its norms for granted. But in every situation that elicits the normative attitude from the 'me', if the self is to act, the applicability and validity of that attitude are judged, whether explicitly or implicitly, by the 'I'. Even to act in accordance with habit or conform to a normative standard or prescription without question is to judge it, to evaluate it, albeit uncritically or unthinkingly. The action *is* a judgment of the 'I'. And each time a normative attitude is accepted as applicable and appropriate, even if for other reasons it is set aside, its authority is to that extent reinforced; each time it is either ignored or repudiated, its normative force is lessened. If they are to continue to be efficacious, therefore, the norms of a community must be recurrently ratified. But for them to be so is for them to be always open to criticism and subject to change.

Enforced conformity, autocratic control, is only a counterfeit of norm-governed behavior. What is accepted in such a case is not the authority of the norms but that of the enforcing power. To the extent that behavior is coerced it is not norm governed, and to the extent that it ceases to govern itself by its own norms, the integrity of a community is undermined. A common history and geographic proximity alone are not sufficient conditions of normative community. Where the norms cease to be efficacious, there is *anomie,* alienation, the antithesis of community. If there is to be genuine normative community, it must be instituted and perpetuated by its members, by whom the norms must be accepted and felt to be compelling. For this to be the case, not only must the members of the community decide how to use the norms in determining their judgment and behavior, they must participate in their institution, transmission, and revision. This means that each must be granted the authority to do so: authority to play a part in shaping the common perspective as well as autonomy in applying it. To put it another way, because the members of a normative community are by definition self-governing individuals who jointly adopt and autonomously apply the norms by which that community is defined and in terms of which it is organized and unified, both *personal authority* and *personal autonomy* are necessary conditions of normative community.

Normative community is a prerequisite of human life. Not only is all organized human social life governed by the norms embodied in culture; all symbolic communication, resting on shared understanding, involves the development and operation of norms.[17] Therefore, maintenance of the conditions of community ought to be ensured, as a matter of right. This is to say that the exercise of both personal authority and personal autonomy ought to be established at rights-entitlements in every community, to be uniformly respected. This is not all: Since without the exercise of both personal authority and personal autonomy no normative community could exist, that exercise is also a universal responsibility, for wherever they fail to be exercised, a fundamental requirement of human life is in jeopardy.

But doesn't the assertion that there are rights which ought to be universally operative mean that these rights are an exception to the principle that all norms are subject to criticism and to the autonomous judgment of the 'I'? Since rights-norms are norms in the same sense as any others, this cannot be the case. The authority of norms is not absolute, the independence of the 'I' entailing that they always remain open to criticism and subject to revision. In every situation in which they are called into play, norms are subject to the demand that they be justified. But so are the judgments of the 'I' in criticizing them. The special feature of the rights of personal authority and autonomy is that they are dictated by the very critique to which they are subject. But to exempt them from criticism is to deny them.

Much recent controversy over the nature and justification of rights has centered on the contention that rights cannot be based upon "utility," that is, on their being components of human good or human welfare. If they are so based, it is held, in the calculation of relative good or benefit, rights count no more than other goods and may be infringed in the interest of a greater social good. The rights to personal autonomy and authority are justified because of a particular benefit to both the community and its members. If the conditions of community did not obtain, individuals could not live in community with one another. But this means that the achievement of any goods within the ongoing process of social living presupposes what the fundamental rights are designed to protect. For this reason, those rights, together with any additional rights they necessitate, should be given priority over any other goods attainable within the social framework. In cases of conflict with other goods these rights, at least, take precedence. This is still not to say that they are absolute. It is conceivable that in a given situation compelling reasons might be given for abrogating them. There may be good reasons to imprison a convicted criminal, limiting the scope of that person's autonomy and authority. But to decide such cases (including the degree of limitation permissible) requires a principle of adjudication. In accordance with the fundamental rights, the (normative) principles in accordance with which such decisions are to be made should be established by the community, as indeed they must be, and as must the basic rights themselves, if they are to have normative authority.[18]

# Notes

1. In what follows I shall use several of Mead's concepts, but in my own way, and in some cases I shall modify or extend them, so that this paper should not be read as an essay on Mead.

2. George Herbert Mead, *Mind, Self, and Society: From the Standpoint of a Social Behaviorist,* ed. Charles W. Morris (Chicago: University of Chicago Press, 1934), p. 167.

3. Ibid.

4. Ibid., p. 211.

5. Beth J. Singer, "Having Rights," *Philosophy and Social Criticism* 11 (4) (Fall, 1986): 391–412.

6. Cf. Jürgen Habermas, *The Theory of Communicative Action,* vol. 1, trans. Thomas McCarthy (Boston: Beacon Press, 1987), pp. 33–39.

7. See, for example, David K. Shipler's newspaper report on the persistence of authoritarianism in Russia since the time of the czars: David K. Shipler, "In Soviet, Change Struggles to Emerge," *The New York Times,* Sunday, May 8, 1988.

8. I.e., in both their predictions of one another's behavior and what they take to be called for on the part of each.

9. Hans Joas, *George Herbert Mead: A Contemporary Re-examination of His Thought,* trans. Raymond Meyer (Cambridge, Mass.: MIT Press, 1985), p. 135.

10. Mead, *Mind, Self, and Society,* pp. 175, 178.

11. Mead is inconsistent, sometimes speaking of "I" or "me" as a response or responses and sometimes as that which responds, as if the responder were an entity. I believe the inconsistency is resolved by his term "phase." The self is "essentially a process with these two distinguishable phases." See ibid., p. 178.

12. Ibid., p. 174.

13. Ibid., p. 177.

14. Ibid., pp. 168, 174.

15. Ibid., p. 174.

16. The term "judgment" is used here in the sense, defined by Justus Buchler, in which it encompasses action and the shaping of materials as well as assertion and reasoning. See Justus Buchler, *Toward a General Theory of Human Judgment* (New York: Columbia University Press, 1951; New York: Dover Publications, 1979).

17. It is not impossible that some nonhuman animals may develop norms of communicative interaction, as is suggested by recent ethological studies. But this does not mean that they can participate in rights-relations. See Singer, "Having Rights."

18. An expanded and somewhat different version of this paper was read at the Conference on Praxeologies and the Philosophy of Economics in Warsaw, Poland, September 2–5, 1988.

# Pragmatism, Prudence, and Morality

### KONSTANTIN KOLENDA

One of the legacies of pragmatism, according to Richard Rorty, is its misgivings about the quest for a theory of truth.[1] These misgivings arise from the suspicion that any philosophical *theory* of truth is likely to restrict the commendatory function of "true." It so happens that this generous little word is applicable to any proposition which, in William James's phrase, is "good in the way of belief," and in John Dewey's rephrasing, expresses what is warrantedly assertible. And there are many different *kinds* of warrants for accepting a proposition as true. To suppose that truth has an *essence,* discoverable in a formal or informal definition, is to privilege *some* warrantedly assertible propositions at the expense of others. The history of the attempts to arrive at a universal theory of truth is a history of exclusionary moves that undermine the legitimacy of some parts of discourse, or even relegate it to the domain of nonsense, as was done in their heyday by logical positivists.

To reject the essentialist approach to truth is to abandon other essentialist claims. To say, for instance, that there is such a thing as an essential human nature is to eliminate certain attributions to human beings. If it is the case, as Rorty is prepared to claim, that descriptions of human beings are at the same time *evaluations,* then the search for some factual criteria of human nature will push aside as illegitimate or irrelevant any normative attributions.[2]

For similar reasons, the traditional distinction between prudence and morality loads the dice in favor of the latter. Prudence is seen as motivated by self-interest, and morality as commitment to the well-being of others. Thus Marcus Singer quotes a classical definition of prudence given by the nineteenth-century writer, Richard Whateley: "Whatever is done wholly and solely from motives of personal expediency — from calculations of individual loss or gain — is always accounted a matter of prudence, and not of virtue."[3] Singer agrees with this view of prudence as always involving reference to one's own interest, coupled with "the exercise of intelligence or rationality or forethought with respect to that interest."[4] Morality, on the other hand, has to do with acting on behalf of the interests of others. "In evaluating the prudence of an action, we must consider its effects on the agent. But its morality depends on its effect on others."[5]

Rorty credits Freud with having undermined the distinction between prudence and morality. Freud showed that moral deliberation is "just as finely-grained, just as detailed and as multiform, as prudential calculation has always been." Thus, he helped to "break down the distinction between moral guilt and practical inadvisability, blurring the prudence-morality distinction into invisibility."[6] The point is that when people deliberate what to do they are not getting all the help they need from clear criteria of what is either in their self-interest or good for the community. If it were enough to be guided by such criteria, practical deliberation — self-interested or other-directed — would be much easier than it is. Of course, one *begins* with scanning available criteria. There is much knowledge about the desirable objects of self-interest and of common good, and each person has an opportunity to draw on such truths about humanity individually and collectively. It is natural to start with propositions that are warranted by tradition and experience. But no collection of such propositions adds up to an account of a complete human nature to be realized, whether in private or in public life.

Therefore, any serious practical deliberation cannot be limited to scanning available criteria. Nor can it be assumed that the possession of certain character traits will guarantee wise decisions, when by specification of desirable character traits one means spelling out just what gives expression to essential human nature. The object of deliberation is not just to *discover* what our character is but also to *make* ourselves into beings we can respect. As in regard to truth, Rorty recommends that we switch from metaphors of finding to metaphors of making.[7]

One of the reasons why this shift is desirable is that preoccupation with human nature is likely to skew our view of ourselves. It tends to encourage the thought that what is essential about individuals, communities, nations, and humanity as such is already completed, done, finished. From this vantage point, all we can do is to be copycats — improve a bit here or there, add a flourish or two, or at most attempt variations on a theme. The theme itself, however, is deemed to be fully stated. Like Athena from the head of Zeus, humanity is seen as fully emerged.

But this view seems to suggest that humanity suffers from arrested development. It forgets that life is inherently forward looking. It is bent on creation, is hungry for novelty, fresh prescriptions, and new endeavors. This is true of individuals and of groups, geographically, politically, or professionally defined. Neither the individuals nor the collectivities are ever completed. As long as they exist, they are in the making.

Nothing else can be concluded from the study of history, especially as it is reflected in the arts and the humanities. The humanities become useful when they are not confined to describing what has been but are also perceived as pointing to what will or might be. At their best, they *challenge* our conception of what humanity is. They keep reminding us that human history is not something for which there is a preexistent pattern or model but rather something *worked on* by particular individuals and cultures. They encourage us to think of ourselves as contributors to the creation of a *better* humanity, as taking part in an ongoing process of adding something new rather than expressing something predetermined. Instead of regarding human nature as ready-made equipment with which we start, we can think of it as a product toward which we aim.

So when in his lecture on the "Contingency of Selfhood" Rorty takes sides with Freud against Kant, he follows up the implications of the view that humanity has no essential nature. By embracing this view he throws into doubt Kant's contention that only those decisions are moral which affirm something common to all human beings. To act in accordance with universalizable maxims is to regard that commonality as paramount. Kant's view is an elaboration on what he means by rationality: the capacity to act in accordance with the conception of a law.

Rorty questions this view. It assumes, he believes, that there is an essential human nature and that the central part of it is captured in the Categorical Imperative. He finds Freud's account of how human beings ought to shape themselves more convincing and more attractive than Kant's. A rough way of describing this distinction would be to say that while Kant favors dull, conventional people, Freud is alive to the creative, open-ended human possibilities. When Rorty credits Freud with discovering that there are no dull people because there is no dull unconscious,[8] his very description, like almost any description applied to human beings, is meant to be evaluative. Who would not prefer being creative to being dull?

But this is not just a matter of preference, or of mere aesthetics. Behind evaluative descriptions there is usually a recognition of the idiosyncratic dimension in the human search for selfhood. Rorty credits William James with being sensitive to this fact. James came to see the importance of paying attention to the contingencies and particularities of the setting within which moral judgments are made. He caught himself unjustly condemning the activity of a backwoods farmer when he observed him in the process of despoiling the virgin forest while preparing land for cultivation. To the farmer the sight of the uprooted trees was a sign of moral victory, a concomitant of a noble struggle for survival and subsistence, not a mindless destruction of nature. Conversely, the farmer would be unfair and insensitive to James's contingencies if he found the way of life of a Harvard professor curiously idle and useless.

Rorty finds that the vocabulary invented by Freud to describe human reactions and behavior is more sensitive to the multiplicity of factors at work in a human psyche than is Kant's language. Instead of offering uniform, monolithic prescriptions, Freud describes the multiple ways in which we try to come to terms with our contingencies. Kant encourages us to *flee* from the contingencies of human existence, to level them out, to deny that we are products of time and chance, historically conditioned. (One might add that Kantian language favors the acceptance of other people's descriptions of ourselves. Pushed hard, this view may lead us to conclude that other people are hell, as Garcin, in Sartre's *No Exit,* discovers.) Freud corrects Kant's mistaken belief that there must be one single context for all human lives and that morality consists in discovering a common mold for all important decisions. Over against this view, Freud the moralist encouraged us to try to break away from contemplating the universal in favor of recognizing the sheer contingency of individual existence.[9]

Does this mean that in doing so we deliver ourselves into the hands of irrationality? Such a conclusion would be premature. It would assume that all human thinking and coping occurs within the confines of universalizable criteria. Rorty, following Freud, denies that this is the case. Without denying that the rationality/irrationality distinction is useful, he points to its *limited* applicability.[10] It is quite proper to describe a move as irrational when it violates a relevant criterion. But if the situation with which we are dealing is not clearly covered by a set of relevant criteria, the challenge of irrationality is out of order. The question "What ought I to do?" may arise in contexts in which the applicability of familiar criteria is in doubt or uncertain. If so, the insistence that one should be rational in such contexts amounts to no more than urging that one *try* to find such criteria. But the invitation to look for them does not guarantee that one will find them.

This is where the switch from the metaphor of finding to that of making is appropriate. If we are respectful of the idiosyncratic components of the situation, we will not force them into the procrustean bed of already available criteria. This would amount to shortcircuiting the path of deliberation and self-exploration in favor of some preexistent picture of what is humanly possible and desirable. For a struggling psyche trying to come to terms with its own self-image in the light of its particular situation, the advice to look for a universalizable formula amounts to a monotonous and contentless incantation: Be rational! The problem, however, is that what is presented as a candidate for rationality comes from contexts that

are felt to be quite different from the one in which one actually finds oneself. It is, therefore, of no help at all to invoke here the Categorical Imperative, or any theory of rationality, because such an invocation would
ignore the special features of the individual case. A moral agent who feels
the "pinch of individual destiny" may find the voice of conventional morality intrusive or even impertinent; it is not sufficiently sensitive to the idiosyncratic components of the situation.

It would be of course irrational and immoral to hold at arm's length
considerations that legitimately clamor for recognition. A moral person
will not ignore moral rules when they *are* relevant. But the situations we
are now talking about are not of this sort. They are characterized by the
absence of a clear-cut applicability of moral rules dues to idiosyncratic
features of the situation. This is why Rorty says that in contexts in which
we are scanning the entire language in search of vocabulary that would
help us cope with their uniqueness, the rational/irrational distinction does
not do any work. Rationality is at home in the territory of consensus, where
the borderline cases do not fit. To step out of that territory is not to deliver
ourselves to irrationality but to acknowledge that the charge of irrationality would beg the question.

But can we in such situations appeal to the virtue of prudence? We can
if we do not insist that it be limited to the specification that it must aim
exclusively at satisfying the agent's self-interest. In situations of the sort
we have just described the agent is not clear whether what he ought to
do will *either* result in satisfying his self-interest *or* realize some common
good — both are on the line. This is why Rorty suggests that in such a situation the prudence/morality distinction shrinks into invisibility.

It is desirable to blur this distinction because the process of deliberation in idiosyncratic situations is also the process of self-definition. One
is motivated by the desire to shape a self that one can respect, a self that
seems acceptable to the one undergoing the process of deliberation. The
envisioned course of action may seem prudent in the sense that it promotes
the person's well-being — not in the sense of living up to some familiar
criteria but in a sense that moves beyond such criteria. It would be problematic to call such a judgment either premoral or postmoral, but a concern with value is at work here as well.[11] It expresses itself in the desire
to answer such questions as these: Who am I? What is my self-image? What
is possible for me under these unique circumstances? What resources does
my psyche offer me in order to cope with the situation? If I am contributing
to the shaping of morality, or rationality, or humanity, what would they
look like after my decision has become a precedent?

The blurring of the distinction goes both ways because the moral dimension is not wholly absent from such prudential, admittedly self-interested

deliberations, especially when one is concerned that the emerging self be something one can respect. Because "respect" and "self-respect" naturally belong to moral discourse, the prudential considerations are at the same time moral. Consequently, it is not to be expected that judgments made in such frontier situations will result in immediate consensus. Here we move outside the territory in which settled conventional or traditional wisdom prevails, and therefore, the projected new self-images are likely to look problematic. People who are invited to accept such newly forged self-images will be asked to revise accordingly their own possible self-conceptions. In periods of rapid cultural change, this may carry in its wake serious repercussions for the familiar forms of life.[13]

Where familiar distinctions can no longer serve as confident guides, it is natural to move away from the vocabulary of science and to favor the language of art. It is sometimes suggested that a human life is like a work of art because what we are is the result of crafting a response to our idiosyncratic contingencies and possibilities. The materials of our existence are shaped into particular forms by our choices, some of which in time crystallize into character traits. Our psyches are affected by the actions and personalities of others—parents, siblings, teachers, and actual and imaginary heroes, villains, and models. Many significant events in our lives flow from our reactions to accidental encounters with other people and to unpredictable situations. We define ourselves in the process of meeting or failing to meet challenges put in our path by human and nonhuman circumstances. Thus, the resulting personality is something *made,* a work of art.

But perhaps it is premature and not quite realistic to invoke here this honorific term. Art, after all, is not as common as the analogy would suggest. Not everything that is made deserves to be called "artistic." Perhaps the analogy can be rightly applied only to *some,* exceptional human beings—not to the common run of us.

Still, the assimilation of human personality to something made or created rather than found or discovered is not wrong and only calls for a more modest description. In looking for such a description, we may make use of two helpful words, one French, one German. By *bricolage,* the French mean something that is put together with a degree of ingenuity and success out of a medley of materials that do not lend themselves to a neat, elegant, organization or packaging. Up to a point, it is hodgepodge, contrived, improvised. The German word *basteln* similarly connotes the process of putting things together out of ordinary, easily available materials not covered by technological know-how. Yet, what emerges in this process, which in English could be called *tinkering,* is something that has a definite, particular character and can be valued for its own sake, without aspiring to the status of a work of art. Perhaps we can view a human self as such a *bricolage, etwas Gebasteltes,* arrived at by the modest means and talents at our disposal. This view may be more realistic precisely because the materials are so heterogeneous, unpredictable, and often surprising, even implausible, governed by nonlaws of contingency.

But this circumstance makes the challenge of living no less difficult and no less demanding. In responding to positive or negative factors affecting our lives, we must draw upon all the energies available to us — physical, psychological, emotional, and intellectual. If it is the case that human nature is still in the making, if it requires thinking in directions that do not insist on dichotomizing human action into either moral or prudential, then it is also important to create social and political conditions under which the creative process of humanity's self-making can proceed in optimal ways.

As a philosophical stance, pragmatism is willing to be the servant of the inexhaustible impulse of life to seek new forms for itself. It recognizes that if there were such a thing as essential human nature and predetermined common destiny, and if humanity were to convince itself what they are, the result would be a depressingly uniform behavior governed by universal criteria. But openness to novelty is an enemy of rigid rules and of the slavery to literal meanings. As Rorty puts it, the mark of an active human life is an effort to clothe itself in its own metaphors. While the poet's tools of self-making are words, human beings work with material provided by all of life: "their spouses and children, their fellow workers, the tools of their trade, the cash account of their businesses, the possessions they accumulate in their homes, the music they listen to, the sports they watch and play, and the trees they pass on their way to work."[14] Where prudence and morality merge there are no signposts, no clear guidelines, no proven recipes, no final blueprints. In such a no man's land, where one acts because one does not know what one *is* but has to go on living, solving problems, reacting to unforeseen circumstances, two cardinal virtues are in demand: courage and hope. Pragamtism is a champion of both.

# Notes

1. Richard Rorty, *Consequences of Pragmatism* (Minneapolis: University of Minnesota Press, 1982), p. 162.

2. Ibid., p. 195.

3. Marcus G. Singer, *Generalization in Ethics* (New York: Knopf, 1962), p. 302.

4. Ibid., p. 303.

5. Ibid.

6. Richard Rorty, "Contingency of Selfhood," *London Review of Books,* May 8, 1986, p. 11.

7. Richard Rorty, *Philosophy and the Mirror of Nature* (Princeton, N.J.: Princeton University Press, 1979).

8. Rorty, "Contingency of Selfhood," p. 14.

9. Ibid., p. 12.

10. Richard Rorty, "Contingency of Community," *London Review of Books,* July 24, 1986, p. 10.

11. George Santayana spoke of prerational morality as embodying actual interests and rooted habits and claimed that they "flare up of themselves in impassioned judgments." See George Santayana, *The Life of Reason* (New York: Charles Scribner's Sons, 1954), p. 442.

12. David L. Norton defends the view that each person contributes to the self-definition of humanity by actualizing his or her *daimon.* See David L. Norton, *Personal Destinies* (Princeton: N.J.: Princeton University Press, 1976), chap. 1.

13. Moral repercussions of such a change are dramatically illustrated in the decision faced by Captain Vere in Melville's *Billy Budd.* Unsurprisingly, an assessment of such repercussions is likely to be inconclusive. See Konstantin Kolenda, "Moral Conflicts and Universalizability," *Philosophy,* vol. 50 (1975), pp. 460–65.

14. Rorty, "Contingency of Selfhood," p. 12.

# William James and Our Moral Lives

RUTH ANNA PUTNAM

The title of William James's only systematic essay in what is now called ethical theory is "The Moral Philosopher and the Moral Life." I find James's use of the word "life" of great interest. One of the complaints that has been raised by contemporary ethical theorists against the dominant post-Enlightenment moral theories is that these theories are act centered rather than agent centered, that they take the notion of a right action, or of an obligatory action, as the central notion of morality. An agent-centered ethics, on the other hand, might ask "what is the best life to live?" or "what is a moral life?" It seems to me obvious that there is no reason to believe that a life consisting of a string of right actions, chosen as obligatory one by one, would be a coherent life. Such a life would have any kind of larger coherence, any pattern, any foreseeable development only by accident. That does not mean, however, that a life devoted to what James calls an ideal, or shaped by what Bernard Williams calls a project, might not then consist of a string of morally correct actions.[1] For (a) an action may well be morally correct without being obligatory—James insists both on the legitimacy of moral holidays and on the fact that when we have done our duty, we are done with it, we are not responsible for all the world's ills. And (b) what is for a particular agent morally correct depends often on what his projects or ideals are. I do not claim that what James calls an ideal is what Williams calls a project. What James means by an ideal is one of the questions I shall consider presently; here, I mean to suggest only that projects and ideals are the sorts of things that give shape to a life. In any case, James's title suggests that the moral life should be the center of attention rather than the moral actions which, to be sure, are an important part of it, and that is a suggestion that many contemporary ethical theorists welcome.

There is another way in which ethical theory may be agent centered rather than act centered. It can make the character of the agent, her virtues and vices, central. Virtues and vices are dispositions to act; but they are not only that. Virtues and vices are, importantly, dispositions to see the world in certain ways, to appreciate certain features and ignore others. The generous person does not only give freely of her money or her time, she also is more sensitive to the occasions when her money or her time are wanted. Once again, there is no reason to assume that a person who decides, action by action, what is the correct action and then does it, will develop a good character. She may well develop some virtues to excess and others only to the most rudimentary degree, if at all. That is the spectacle Susan Wolf paints for us in "Moral Saints."[2]

In James's language what I called dispositions are habits. Habits are formed by repeated actions; but the thought James impresses upon his readers is that in choosing the action, we are choosing the character we are going to have. He begins a very important paragraph in the *Principles*[3] by saying that "an act has no ethical quality whatsoever unless it be chosen out of several all equally possible," but continues after some examples, "in these critical ethical moments, what consciously *seems* to be in question is the complexion of the character itself. The problem with the man is less what act he shall now choose to do, than what being he shall now resolve to become."[4] Thus, though actions flow from character, actions also build and destroy character. This appears to lead to paradox. It is easy enough to understand that character limits the choices that are actually open to the agent, that are what James calls "live options"; but then it appears that the adult agent willy-nilly reinforces her virtues as well as her vices. Children on the other hand have their virtues reinforced and their vices discouraged by others. An ethical theory that makes character central seems then to be good only for the guidance of parents and others in charge of educating the young. James was aware of this problem. But he assures us that new habits can be formed as the result of new experiences. "Now life abounds in these, and sometimes they are such critical and revolutionary experiences that they change a man's whole scale of values and system of ideas. In such cases, the old order of his habits will be ruptured: and if the new motives are lasting, new habits will be formed, and build up in him a new or regenerate 'nature.'"[5] Moreover, it is quite clear that James believed that we can choose our character. Though there are examples of sudden conversions, the dynamics of character formation, or character change, in the adult must be understood for the most part as a slow process. Surely all of us know regretfully of virtues lost through neglect, and perhaps some of us know of virtues gained through determined vigilance. Finally, it is precisely because James believes that we can form our own character that he offers advice on how to form habits; I am suggesting that this advice is directed not merely at teachers attempting to aid their students in developing good habits but at anyone committed to leading a moral life. How else are we to understand the cautionary tale of Darwin, who lost the ability to enjoy poetry because he failed to read it regularly, or the maxim offered both in the *Principles* and in the *Talks* "Keep the faculty of effort alive in you by a little gratuitous exercise every day."?[6]

The task of the moral philosopher appears then to be to tell us what the moral life is, or at least to give us a method that will lead us to it. James tells us, indeed, that "the deepest difference, practically, in the moral life of man is the difference between the easy-going and the strenuous mood,"[7] and it is the latter which James advocates again and again. It is for the sake of the strenuous moral life that we are to believe in free will, that is, in real possibilities. For only if our actions can make a real difference to the world are they really good or bad, and only if we believe in real goodness and real badness will we be willing to act "no matter how we feel."[8] For the sake of the strenuous moral life James rejects any optimistic belief that the world is already perfect. It goes perhaps too far to say that James believes in God for the sake of the strenuous moral life, but it does not go too far to say that he defends our right to believe because "without a God the appeal to our moral energy falls short of its maximal stimulating power."[9] Even the moral philosopher questing for "the stable and systematic moral universe" is assured of success "only in a world where there is a divine thinker with all-enveloping demands."[10]

All this, however, fails to tell us anything about the content of the moral life. In the end we shall find that there is very little that the moral philosopher can tell us about that content; but to that little we must now turn. The moral life is a life that realizes as much as is humanly possible (and that may vary from one agent to another), the most inclusive coherent system of ideals. The moral philosopher's aim, accordingly, is to weave "the ideals he finds existing in the world" into "the unity of a stable system."[11] But what are "the ideals he finds existing in the world"?

They cannot be simply the ideals of the moral philosopher herself; insofar as she is a philosopher, she is to bring only a single idea of her own to the task, namely the ideal of producing a unified stable system of ideals out of the ideals she finds existing in the world. Otherwise she "would *pro tanto* cease to be a judicial investigator, and become an advocate for some limited element of the case."[12] And that idea fills James with the most lively apprehension: "Better chaos forever than an order based on any closet-philosopher's rule, even though he were the most enlightened possible member of his tribe."[13] Yet as individual moral agents who have to choose what lives to live, what characters to become, "we should incessantly seek, with fear and trembling, . . . to bring about the very largest total universe of good *which we can see.*[14] It is ultimately our character, "our personal aptitude or incapacity for moral life" that will be revealed in our choice, even if we "invoke any so-called philosophy."[15] Philosophy here can only guide; echoing Emerson, and anticipating contemporary American philosophers such as Martha Nussbaum,[16] he writes "that books upon ethics, therefore, so far as they truly touch the moral life, must more and more ally themselves with a literature which is confessedly tentative and suggestive rather than dogmatic,—I mean with novels and dramas of the deeper sort" but also, in a different sense of "tentative and suggestive," with "books on statecraft and philanthropy and social and economic reform."[17] The moral philosopher, it turns out, is a political philosopher as well. Her suggestions, one hopes, will enable us to see more clearly "the very largest total universe of good" both as private individuals and as citizens actively involved in the life of our community.

Still the moral philosopher, qua philosopher, is left with the task of finding the most comprehensive ideal based on the ideals she actually finds in her moral community, a community that consists, one is inclined to say, of all human beings whose ideals she can understand—not embrace, merely understand. But that is not enough. James was fully aware of the difficulty we have in understanding the ideals of others, of "the blindness with which we all are afflicted in regard to the feelings of creatures and people different from ourselves."[18] Having presented his audience with a long list of quotations illustrating a variety of ideals, he concludes that we are forbidden to regard as meaningless forms of life other than our own, and that we are commanded to "tolerate, respect and indulge those whom we see harmlessly interested in their own ways, however unintelligible these may seem to us."[19] This must not be mistaken for a quest for a Nagelian "view from nowhere,"[20] as he makes clear in the Preface to the *Talks to Teachers.* "There is no point of view absolutely public and universal." Rather, "the practical consequence of such a philosophy is the well-known democratic respect for the sacredness of individuality—is, at any rate the outward tolerance of whatever is not itself intolerant. . . . Religiously and philosophically, our ancient national doctrine of live and let live may prove to have a far deeper meaning than our people now seem to imagine."[21] The relevant community in today's shrunken world includes at least all human beings.

What, then, are ideals, and what makes one ideal more inclusive than another? I take it that an ideal is not any object of desire, rather it is the sort of conception, aim, or project that shapes a significant part of a life, either the life of an individual or that of a community. Thus James speaks of the philosopher's ideal of "a genuine universe from the ethical point of view,"[22] which sets her a lifelong task of the "punitive ideal," that is, the notion of retributive justice, which has shaped criminal law so far. Speaking of moral dilemmas, James says that the philosopher sees perhaps more clearly than the ordinary person that what is at stake is a choice of two universes, that the good to be chosen must be the one that fits into "a more inclusive whole."[23] This, it seems to me, is but another way of saying that in making a moral choice in difficult, momentous cases one chooses not so much an action as a way of life, one's character, and perhaps also the sort of society of which one will be a part. Given this life-shaping nature of ideals, their frustration will indeed give rise to persistent dissatisfactions. If, therefore, we dare to attempt to establish a new, a more comprehensive ideal—whether it be a nonracist society or, less ambitiously, to include new concerns in an already full life—we must take the attempt to be an experiment. That means both that we must be willing to take the risks ourselves, and that we must judge the experiments "by actually finding out, after the fact of their making, how much more outcry or how much appeasement comes about."[24]

I turn now to the question of inclusiveness. There are several possibilities. An ideal may be more inclusive than another because it is espoused by a greater number of persons or because it encompasses a greater number of lesser ideals, perhaps as the result of a process of compromise and accommodation. Thus we might say that the ideal of freedom of conscience is more inclusive than the ideal of toleration for Christian sects only; we might also say that the ideal of respect is more inclusive than the ideal of mere tolerance. In both cases the first ideal encompasses the second, in the first case it is also in this country at this time espoused by and benefits a greater number of people. However, the ideal of freedom of conscience, though its realization would have benefited the greater number of persons at all times, was espoused, for most of human history, only by a small number of persons. Should we then say that one ideal is more inclusive than another if it benefits a greater number of persons than that other? This too leads to difficulties; for we must recognize that the question of benefit depends, at least sometimes, on what people demand. Religious fundamentalists believe that freedom of conscience threatens the very values it leaves them free to pursue in our pluralist society. Were they the majority, they would attempt to impose their faith on everyone and consider themselves the beneficiaries. Nevertheless, religious freedom is the more inclusive ideal since it permits the realization of the greater part of the fundamentalists' ideals as well as the realization of the greater part of the ideals of those of other persuasions. I believe that for James moral progress occurs when more and more human beings—in their demands and in their actions—realize ideals that encompass greater and greater numbers of lesser ideals.

The task of finding more inclusive ideals is, therefore, truly formidable. One is tempted to fall back on the wisdom of humankind, which in practice means endorsing the scale of values of the society to which one happens to belong. This temptation is further encouraged by the fact that James believed, as we perhaps do not, that humankind had made, was making, and would continue to make moral progress. He was "confident that the line of least resistance will always be towards the richer and the more inclusive arrangement, and that by one tack after another some approach to the kingdom of heaven is incessantly made."[25] To the extent that present ideals clash with earlier ones, it would then appear that the earlier ones gave way to the later ones because they could not be accommodated in a coherent, comprehensive scheme. Nevertheless, may there not be ideals espoused by our predecessors which might offer solutions to some of our pressing contemporary ills? Should we not, in the interest of both objectivity and further moral progress, reconsider all past ideals? That would appear to be a waste of effort; surely, the result of humanity's experiments with slavery are sufficiently clear that we need no longer ask what is wrong with it. Nevertheless, as philosophers we must resist the temptation to be blind partisans of the present. On the one hand, any past ideal, such as the communitarian ideal, that has contemporary champions must be reconsidered, even if that serves only to remind us why we rejected it before. On the other hand, though the presumption both in science and in morality is in favor of the accepted opinion, progress in both is due to those courageous individuals who "may replace old 'laws of nature' by better ones [or] by breaking old moral rules in a certain place, bring in a total condition of things more ideal than would have followed had the rules been kept."[26] Since James mentions Tolstoy's ideal of nonviolent resistance, we may think of Martin Luther King as an American who broke the old rules to bring about more ideal conditions.

More ideal conditions according to whom? James insists that there would be no ideals in a world without sentient beings, that values and obligations are real if and only if there are minds who feel them and make demands. Nevertheless, he is not a subjectivist. For he asserts that there is, for moral judgments, a standard of truth outside the individual, just as there is such a standard for judgment in physics. That standard is provided by the existence of other people for whom we care and who care for us. Thinkers who are "indifferent to each other's thoughts and acts" would give us "only a multitude of 'subjective' opinions,"[27] but "one rock with two loving souls upon it . . . would have as thoroughly moral a constitution as any possible world . . . there would be real good things and real bad things . . . obligations, claims and expectations; obediences, refusals, and disappointments, . . . a moral life, whose active energy would have no limit but the intensity of interest in each other."[28] Objectivity in ethics depends, then, on the possibility of resolving conflicts, of arriving at shared values, of espousing jointly more inclusive ideals. That possibility rests on the fact that we have sympathetic as well as egoistic instincts, which "arise, so far as we can tell, on the same psychological level."[29] Mere intersubjectivity, however, is not enough. James's insistence on the imperfections of the world and on the possibility of moral progress suggests that there is a standard outside not only this or that thinker but outside any particular collection of them, just as scientific truth is not determined by the opinions of any particular collection of scientists. "There can be no final truth in ethics any more than in physics until the last man has had his experience and said his say."[30] Even if one has difficulty with the notion of a final truth, James's constantly reiterated faith in moral progress and in the importance of moral and social experiments suffices to show that he is neither a subjectivist nor a cultural relativist.

Both in science and in ethics the philosopher can do no more than to articulate a method, or methods, that will enable us to approach closer to truth. In the moral case, this appears to be the method:

> Since everything which is demanded is by that fact a good, must not the guiding principle for ethical philosophy (since all demands conjointly cannot be satisfied in this poor world) be simply to satisfy at all times *as many demands as we can?* That act must be the best, accordingly, which makes for the *best whole,* in the sense of awakening the least sum of dissatisfactions. In the casuistic scale, therefore, those ideals must be written highest which *prevail at the least cost* or by whose realization the least possible number of other ideals are destroyed.[31]

Unfortunately, this passage raises the suspicion that James is simply inconsistent. I shall argue that he is not. The suspicion arises as follows. If the *guiding principle* for ethical philosophy is

(1) that act is best which awakens the least sum of dissatisfactions,

then James appears to be after all an act-utilitarian, though not a hedonistic one since he denies that all demands are reducible to desires for physical pleasure and aversion to physical pain; "the elementary forces in ethics are probably as plural as those of physics are."[32] But this "guiding principle" is glossed by

(2) those ideals must be written highest by whose realization the least number of other ideals are destroyed.

Though (2) is vague — how would one count ideals? — it coheres far better than (1) with the account I have given of James's views. We should, therefore, let (2) guide us in our interpretation of (1). This results in the following reading of our troubling passage.

James does not intend us to take all existing desires as they happen to be and to seek what will satisfy the greatest number of them; rather we are to pursue those ideals that can be realized at the least cost in other ideals. If I am right that not every object of desire is an ideal, but only those which shape lives, or at any rate significant parts thereof, then large numbers of more or less temporary desires may well be sacrificed for the realization of an ideal. That, it seems to me, is an accurate description of how we actually manage to lead reasonably contented, reasonably coherent lives. We do, all the time, sacrifice small desires to long-range projects. Why should we not apply to the public domain what stands us in good stead in our private lives? If I am right, then "the best act" is that act which fits into the most comprehensive ideal and which, of all facts that so fit, awakens the least sum of dissatisfactions.

What James has to offer is richer and more complex than what I have been able to present in this limited space. I have merely begun to develop an interpretation of James's moral philosophy that stresses those aspects that speak to the concerns of contemporary virtue ethics. A juster appreciation of James's insights would, I believe, be a helpful contribution to the current problematic in ethical theory.

# Notes

1. Bernard Williams, *Moral Luck* (Cambridge: Cambridge University Press, 1981), passim. Also, Williams, *Ethics and the Limits of Philosophy* (Cambridge, Mass.: Harvard University Press, 1985), passim.

2. Susan Wolf, "Moral Saints," *Journal of Philosophy* 79 (1982): 419–39.

3. William James, *The Principles of Psychology,* 3 vols. (1890; New York: Dover Publications, 1950), vol. 1, pp. 287–88.

4. Ibid. (italics is original).

5. William James, *Talks to Teachers on Psychology and to Students on Some of Life's Ideals* (1899; Cambridge, Mass.: Harvard University Press, 1983), p. 53.

6. Ibid., p. 52; also James, *The Principles of Psychology,* vol. 1, p. 126.

7. William James, *The Will to Believe and Other Essays in Popular Philosophy* (New York: Dover Publications, 1956; first published 1897), p. 211. "The Dilemma of Determinism" is on pp. 145–83 and was first published in 1884; "The Moral Philosopher and the Moral Life" is on pp. 184–215 and was first published in 1891.

8. Ibid., p. 175.

9. Ibid., p. 212.

10. Ibid., pp. 213–14.

11. Ibid., pp. 184–85.

12. Ibid., p. 185.

13. Ibid., p. 204.

14. Ibid., p. 209; emphasis added.

15. Ibid., p. 214.

16. Martha Nussbuam, "Flawed Crystals: James's *The Golden Bowl* and Literature as Moral Philosophy," *New Literary History* 15 (1983): 25–50.

17. James, *The Will to Believe and Other Essays,* p. 210.

18. James, *Talks to Teachers,* p. 132.

19. Ibid., p. 149.

20. Thomas Nagel, *The View from Nowhere* (New York: Oxford University Press, 1986).

21. James, *Talks to Teachers,* pp. 3–4.

22. James, *The Will to Believe and Other Essays,* p. 185.

23. Ibid., p. 210.

24. Ibid., p. 207.

25. Ibid., p. 208.

26. Ibid.

27. Ibid., p. 192.

28. Ibid., p. 197.

29. James, *The Principles of Psychology,* vol. 1, p. 325.

30. James, *The Will to Believe and Other Essays,* p. 184.

31. Ibid., p. 205.

32. Ibid., p. 201.

# ROYCE:
# HERMENEUTICS, LOYALTY,
# AND RELIGION

# Loyalty to Loyalty:
# A Plan for America Today

JACQUELYN A. KEGLEY

In 1929, Paul Tillich provided us with an amazingly prophetic view of our world today when he wrote the following:

"Self-sufficient humanity's unrest is evident . . . in the constant speeding up of the tempo of all our activities, that is, in the concentration of a great variety of the experiences of life into a limited amount of time — with the consequent devaluation of every individual experience. . . . It is also revealed in the purely manipulative attitude towards nature and in the ceaseless mutual antagonism of all interests in society . . . humanity is forced into egocentric loneliness and surrounded by an infinite emptiness."[1]

Life in America is chopped up. People are lost, confused, conflicted. There is scandal on Wall Street, in the government, and even within our churches. There are calls for reform all about us — reforms in education, in government, in business. And we in philosophy have not escaped. Richard Rorty, in his *Mirror in Nature*, declared traditional philosophy bankrupt. Bernard Williams has concluded that "the resources of most modern philosophy are not well adjusted to the modern world."[2] Alasdair MacIntyre has argued that we have lost our comprehension, both theoretical and practical, of morality and that the powers of philosophical analysis and the dominant philosophies of the present will not help us.[3]

The situation is one of "boundary" or "frontier"; we are at the edge. The "Kairos," as Tillich would say, is here. We can begin to forge new roads, build new ground. We can begin, as Robert Bellah has urged, to build, in the United States and in the philosophical community, a sense of common problems, a new community of memory and of hope.[4] It is my contention that there is no better foundation for such building than our own roots, our American philosophy, and more particularly, the work of the frontier philosopher, Josiah Royce, who forged a philosophy of "community" and an ethic of "loyalty to loyalty" out of his own struggles with loneliness and experiences of rampant individualism on the frontier in California, a state always on the boundary.

In his *Philosophy of Loyalty* and *The Problem of Christianity,* Royce sought to develop a philosophical and ethical viewpoint that is person centered and yet at one and the same time community building. Today a stance is needed that allows respect for persons and for individual rights without developing a contentious situation in which rights are pitted against rights and the only remedy becomes litigation, judgment of right in courts of law or enforcement of rights through the police power of the state. To see that this is the case, one only needs to ponder on the tragic aspects of the "Baby M" case or those court cases determining for terminally ill patients the right to refuse treatment. Royce's work, I believe, can provide some fruitful ground for the ethical analysis in these kinds of complex cases. Drawing on the ethic of loyalty to loyalty, the doctrine of interpretation and Royce's analysis of community and the process of community building, it is my belief that we can pay better attention to the unique situational aspects of issues as well as to the motives, character and personhood of the agents involved. Royce also gives us a ground for an ethic of mutual self-empowerment in which our social interaction can allow us to develop as unique individuals with our own life plans and also as persons empowered with skills as well as the courage to make decisions in situations of great complexity and uncertainty.

In *The Philosophy of Loyalty* and his *Urbana Lectures,* Royce makes it quite clear that ethical analysis must be person centered and that ethical decision making must be highly personal. The student of values, says Royce, "has to begin and end his task with the study of personality."[5] What the study of personality reveals is a paradoxical situation, namely the paradox of moral autonomy and social dependency. Before I can become an autonomous moral agent I must first become a unified self. Indeed, for Royce it is a profound psychological fact that the quest for selfhood is a fundamental concern of all persons. What is desired is self-possession, a cohesive life plan. Yet what a person finds in himself is a chaos and conflict of wills. What one finds within is that passions, desires, wants all "speak too volubably [*sic*] with an incoherent babble of voices. I have no innate unity of life plan."[6] Thus, I discover and we know from experience that the only way one can become a unified self is in a social context and with the help of one's fellow human beings. "I myself, in so far as I have yet to learn my ideals, am dissatisfied with my inner situation. . . . It is I, then, who as a social being, continually require myself to look for guidance to my social world. My comrades, my teachers, my rivals, yes, even my enemies teach me what it is that I want. Through imitation I at length learn self-mastery. Through my social docility I come to attain my independence. My very freedom, in so far as I ever attain such freedom, will be due to the fact that I am able to learn through social contact with others, what it is I myself want to be."[7]

Through my social contact, my imitation of models, and my divergence from others, I begin to develop a life-plan, a cause or causes. It is my loyalty to my cause that unifies life, to give it a "center, finite, stability."[8] Becoming loyal to a cause, Royce argues, brings one's own will to self-consciousness, helps one become morally aware and autonomous. "My duty is simply my own will brought to self-consciousness . . . that which I can rightly view as good for me is simply the object of my deepest desire set plainly before my sight."[9]

The process of self-development and of coming to moral autonomy is, for Royce, a delicate balance of the individual and the social. Loyalty helps center and create a unique self but also helps self transcend private advantage. Loyalty is instrumentally valuable, it unifies the self, but it also is intrinsically valuable. It is something objective which is valued and loved for its own sake.

> For if you are loyal, your cause is viewed by you as something outside of you. Or if, like your country, your cause includes yourself, it is still much larger than your private self. It has its own value, so you as a loyal person believe. This essential value it would keep (so you believe) even if your private interest were left out of account. Your cause you take, then, to be something objective — something that is not your private self. It does not get its value merely from your being pleased with it. You believe, on the contrary, that you love it just because of its own value, which it has by itself, even if you die.[10]

Further, loyalty to loyalty is a supreme value, the supreme virtue, the ground for all other virtues. Royce declares as his thesis: "that all commonplace virtues insofar as they are indeed definable and effective are special forms of loyalty to loyalty."[11] I shall return to this later.

Royce, then, says moral autonomy develops within a social context, the social context is necessary to this self-development. But this does not mean that the self makes no contribution. Indeed, one takes a very active part in self-creation. Thus, declares Royce, "loyalty is perfectly consistent with originality."[12] Indeed, loyalty helps us develop "conscience," which Royce defines as "that ideal of life which constitutes your moral personality."[13] It is the "spirit of self" which informs all of one, true self, yet is nowhere expressed in any deed.[14]

We do develop a uniqueness of self — a plan different from that of all others. One grows to self-consciousness through role models, through imitation. But one doesn't just imitate, one begins to change the role, to develop a divergence from the model, to do things differently. Royce argues that individualism and collectivism, self will and social will grow together in an interactive process. Thus Royce concludes that "our social training thus teaches us to know ourselves through a process which arouses our self will; and this tendency grows with what it feeds upon. The higher the training and the more cultivated and elaborate is our socially trained conscience — the more highly conscious our estimate of our own value becomes, and, so, in general, the stronger grows our self-will."[15]

The social context, of course, can thus foster rebellion and continual contention and conflict of wills. This seems true of our social scene today, but this need not be the case. Royce offers us the possibility that mutual interaction can lead to support and self-improvement, to a sense of one's own worth. Commenting on the interaction between imitativeness and self-assertion, Royce writes, "The normal relation between the two is that we constantly use our imitativeness to give us opportunities for self-assertion. Having followed a given model, I can make use of the power thus acquired to display myself in the presence of other fellows — beings — to distinguish myself by my skill in a given act."[16]

We become unique selves; selves with worth and not necessarily rebellious selves. But we need "genuine community," a situation of interaction, some understanding, a mutual growth and empowerment.

Genuine community, for Royce, is one where some common memories and bonds exist, and this is built up by a process of interpretation and a will to harmonize. Individuals are separated in many ways. First, we are put asunder by the privacy of our immediate feelings, such as pain. I cannot know that you are experiencing pain unless you are publicly and truthfully displaying it in some manner. Second, my opinions, intentions, and plans are my secrets unless I reveal them in some way to you. Third, a common moral assumption of our behavior is respect of privacy, namely, your ideas and feelings are your inalienable possessions; they constitute your worth and you have a right to keep them private as well as to hold them. These facts speak strongly for a radical "social pluralism," a Liebnizian world of "windowless monads" and thus a contentious world of potentially conflicting wills. This is a world very much like our world today.

To this situation Royce brings three assertions: (1) Persons desire harmony in their lives, both within and without; (2) harmony is possible through the building of genuine community; and (3) genuine community requires the process of interpretation. Throughout his life Royce argued that harmonization of wills was a goal sought by persons and a necessary goal ultimately for self-fulfillment. In the *Urbana Lectures,* Royce argues for several procedural principles that he believes to constitute the "moral attitude." One of these is the principle of harmony, which is essentially a principle prescribing maximum reconciliation of all conflicting values at a minimum cost by compromise or redirection of each. In other words, other things being equal, the harmonization of conflicting interest results in more value being realized than is the case when conflict persists. Royce puts the matter as follows:

> If matters can be so arranged that A's will and B's will can cooperate with each other and help each other, instead of hindering each other, then the new and transformed situation possesses more objective value than the old situation. That is, a state of thing in which A's will cooperates with B's will is better, other things being equal, than the situation in which A's will conflicts with B's will. And this again is an objective truth about the world of values. For the conflict, if it occurs, can end at best in the success of only one of us. The peace and consequent cooperation of both of us would by hypothesis accomplish what we are both seeking and this would be an objectively valuable result, and would possess at least the value which both of us give to our own distinct purposes.[17]

Notice that the principle of harmony is a rule of attitude, but not one of substantial value or justification. It specifies a goal to seek in moral action; it does not yet give action guides to the rightness or wrongness of specific actions.

This ultimate principle, for Royce, is loyalty to loyalty, the broadening of bonds of loyalty and the building of genuine community. Loyalty to loyalty means to work for the harmonizing of conflicting loyalties, for community and common purpose. The loyal self works for community and the spirit of community. The communal context is necessary, says Royce, not only for self-development, but also for making clear what it is that love and true humanitarianism require. Royce's discussion of love in *The Problem of Christianity* is highly illuminating. He says that although we know we are to love God and our neighbor, the question is how we can be practically useful in meeting our neighbor's needs. "What is sure about love is that it indeed unites the lover, in spirit, to God's will. What constitutes, in this present world, the pathos, the tragedy of love, is that, because in our imperfect vision, we do not know how to make him (our neighbor) happy, to relieve his deepest distresses, to do him the highest good."[18]

Does my neighbor need a cup of water? This is why "Loyalty to loyalty" becomes associated, in *The Problem of Christianity,* with the "will to interpret." Interpretation is a triadic process that brings about unity and a community of understanding. For example, I am now interpreting Royce's thought to you and thus hope I am creating a community of common understanding. Loyalty to loyalty now is to engage in genuine community building. Interpretation, for example, is the process whereby I continually build a unified self. I interpret my present self, in terms of my past self, to my future self. The voluntary commitment to engage in an unlimited process of mutual interpretation is essential to a unified self, to genuine community, and to practicing "loyalty" and ethical action in the concrete.

In community we can come to know each other, to see what each others' needs are, to know what is trust, justice, true friendship. "Who is my neighbor?" My neighbor and I are members of one and the same community and I know what is my loyalty and my honor and my duty in this context.

Royce gives an excellent example of loyalty practiced in the concrete in the third lecture of the *Urbana Lectures*. In January of 1642, a conflict occurred between King Charles I and Parliament. Charles had resolved to arrest certain leaders of the opposition party in Parliament. He had sent his herald to the House to demand the surrender of these members into his custody. The speaker of the House in reply appealed to the ancient privilege of the House, which gave it jurisdiction over its own members and which forbade their arrest without its consent. The following day, the king, accompanied by his soldiers, went to confront the speaker directly, whereupon the speaker fell upon his knees before the king and said, "Your Majesty, I am the Speaker of the House, and being such, I have neither eyes to see, nor ears to hear, nor tongue to speak, save as this House shall command; and I humbly beg your pardon if this is the only answer that I can give to your Majesty."[19]

What does this example illustrate for us about both Royce's ethical theory and its application to our own present situation? First, ethical situations usually involve conflicts of will, either conflicting loyalties of one person or of several persons. This makes it imperative that the moral agent be clear about his or her loyalties and how they are to be upheld in situations. Second, as Royce makes clear in his discussion of the example, each ethical situation has not occurred before — it is a unique conflict of unique individuals, and thus they must all be clear about their goals and who they are but also be open to possibilities of harmonizing wills. It means that no mere application of abstract principles can resolve the situation. What principle is applicable in the situation of the speaker of the House? Further, says Royce, it is not a matter of self-sacrifice, heroism, or personal dignity. It is loyalty to the cause, namely loyalty to a community with a common history, traditions, and understanding. The speaker also calls himself and the king to a higher loyalty, that of the country. It is an attempt to build common bonds.

Third, there is the self-consciousness of the act. The speaker is unquestioning, decisive, clear, and independent of any merely external authority. Royce asserted often that the injunction "loyalty to loyalty" meant acting in the world with courage and conviction. It meant being a "committed self" and not the "emotivist, democratized self" described by Alasdair Mac-Intyre in his book *After Virtue*.[20] That is one type of self with no social context, a self entirely set over against the social world as well as a self that lacks any ultimate criteria. It is a self without care, concern, and commitment, and therefore without courage. Royce's loyal self is decisive, even in complex situations. Your conscience, says Royce, is fallible; it can be blind just like choice and loyalty. It can change and grow. Conscience does not dictate what one's effective cause or vocation is. All choices are open to error; they are expressions of my general ignorance of the world and of my limited powers. All one can do, finally, is act.

Royce's loyal self is precisely the self of commitment and courage. Two inseparable characteristics of loyal conduct are *decisiveness* on the part of the loyal individual and *fidelity* to loyal decisions once made.[21] In full agreement with James, Royce forbids us to play Hamlet's part and he provides this principle: "Decide knowingly, if you can, ignorantly if you must, but in any case decide and have no fear."[22]

This decisiveness partly comes from loyalty to a specific cause, as is the case of the speaker of the House. He speaks as the servant of the cause he has freely chosen. Loyalty is not loyalty to abstract entities. Rather, Royce addresses the question of "impractical humanitarism." He asks, in *The Philosophy of Loyalty:* "Is there a practical way of serving the universal cause of loyalty to loyalty, given the narrowness of our powers and the complexity of human nature which we try to improve?"[23] Royce's answer to this question is to limit undertakings to some decidedly definite personal range and one's own special personal cause. Loyalty to loyalty must be lived out in terms of specific loyalties to specific peoples, groups and causes. Royce worked on this idea in dealing in *War and Insurance*[24] with the analysis of dyadic, dangerous situations in which two parties, such as borrower and lender, or manager and worker, were in highly conflictual situations, with conflicting rights and interests. What was needed was a third party—a banker or judge to mediate, to interpret each to the other in order to build some common causes or bonds. This is interpretation, building community. This notion of specific loyalties to specific peoples, groups, and causes was also explored in Royce's call for a "wise provincialism." Indeed, the speaker's action is an example of a wise provincialism—standing for a specific community. However, the speaker also speaks for broadening the scope of loyalty, for he reminds the king of their common loyalty to the peace of the realm. And he speaks in a communal context that he interprets to the king, reminding him of a common understanding of the peace of the realm.

The important points here are as follows. First, we must develop skills of ethical analysis that are sensitive to the uniqueness of each ethical situation, to the life-plan, purposes, and goals of each agent involved. Royce is clear that universal moral law is practically speaking impossible, and the quest for it misguided. "The notion of a moral law which is in all respects absolutely and abstractly the same for all of us is a notion that is simply unjust to the very nature of our individuality. Your duty to be yourself differs in some respects from the duty of anyone else, and therefore involves some truths that are simply inaccesible to any individual besides yourself."[25]

Take again the command to love thy neighbor. How do we do so if we really do not know what he needs? He needs to be understood by us. This is why Royce saw justice and benevolence as dependent on loyalty — on community understanding. Justice, without loyalty, without the understanding community provides, is mere duty, a vicious formalism. It needs a proper attitude of love and concern and an understanding of what is just desert in *this* case, what is *this person's* due. Likewise, benevolence without communal commitment and understanding is a dangerous sentimentalism — giving a cup of water when it is not needed or forcing something on someone out of kindness.

This is why the will to interpret and to build common understanding is so important to resolution of ethical conflict. It may, indeed, take a third party — recall the pairs in *War and Insurance*. It required the court in the "Baby M" case. Perhaps we could seek patient advocates or ethical mediators, as in labor disputes. I am reminded of the whole informed consent issue in which the building of a community of mutual decision making is so important. One cannot hold that the doctor, with best intentions, truly speaks for the patient's "best interests," for how do we know the doctor really understands the patient's life plan? Nor does the patient necessarily understand the doctor's constraints or goals. Interpretation and community building need to take place. Self-empowerment needs to occur for the patient and doctor. Royce's views offer fruitful ground for exploration in this regard.

Royce does offer us the possibility of a new ethical stance — one beautifully described in the following analogy that Royce draws between science and ethics, the goal of both being the building of community among persons.

But beneath this contrast between the methods of the descriptive sciences and the methods of the doctrine of values lies, after all, a certain deep analogy between these methods. For the first rule in the scientific study of external things is: 'Be objective: consider the facts as they are.' And the first rule of the doctrine of values is: 'View every valuation from the point of view of the one who makes the valuation. Put yourself in his place.' And again the second rule of descriptive science is: 'Look for the laws that bind the facts together.' But the second rule of the doctrine of values is: 'See whether some lawful plan of action can be discovered whereby the valuations with which men begin can be harmonized.'[26]

# Notes

1. Paul Tillich, "The Class Struggle and Religious Socialism," trans. James Luther Adams, rev. Garrett E. Paul, in *Paul Tillich on Creativity,* ed. Jacquelyn Ann Kegley (Washington, D.C.: University Press of America, 1988), pp. 101–102.

2. Bernard Williams, *Ethics and the Limits of Philosophy* (Cambridge, Mass.: Harvard University Press, 1985).

3. Alasdair MacIntyre, *After Virtue* (London: Duckworth, 1981), p. 2.

4. Robert N. Bellah, Richard Madsen, William M. Sullivan, Ann Swidler, and Stephen M. Tipton, *Habits of the Heart: Individualism and Commitment in American Life* (New York: Harper and Row, 1987), p. 6.

5. Josiah Royce, "Urbana Lectures, I," *The Journal of the History of Philosophy* 5 (1967), pp. 63ff.

6. Josiah Royce, "Urbana Lectures, II," *The Journal of the History of Philosophy* 5 (1967), pp. 273ff.

7. Ibid., p. 273.

8. Josiah Royce, "Selections from *The Philosophy of Loyalty,*" in *The Philosophy of Josiah Royce,* ed. John Roth (New York: Thomas Y. Crowell Co., 1971), p. 290. All references to *The Philosophy of Loyalty* will be from this source.

9. Ibid., p. 281.

10. Ibid., p. 280.

11. Ibid., p. 257.

12. Ibid., p. 290.

13. Ibid., p. 306.

14. Ibid., p. 307.

15. Josiah Royce, *The Problem of Christianity,* 2 vols. (Chicago: Henry Regnery Co., 1968), vol. 2, p. 145.

16. Royce Papers, Harvard University Archives, folio 69, no. 3, pp. 4–5.

17. Ibid.

18. Royce, *The Problem of Christianity,* vol. 1, p. 88.

19. Josiah Royce, "Urbana Lectures," Harvard University Archives, folio 76, no. 3, pp. 2–3.

20. MacIntyre, *After Virtue,* p. 17.

21. Alasdair MacIntyre, "After Virtue", in Bellah et al., *Habits of the Heart: Individualism and Commitment in American Life,* pp. 224–25.

22. Royce, *The Philosophy of Loyalty,"* pp. 310–11.

23. Ibid., p. 296.

24. Josiah Royce, *War and Insurance* (New York: Macmillan, 1914).

25. Royce, "Urbana Lectures, II," p. 273.

26. Royce, "Urbana Lectures, I," p. 76.

# Major Developments in Royce's Ethics after the Problem

### FRANK M. OPPENHEIM

Sixty-year-old Josiah Royce reminisced about how as a boy he had wondered at the vistas stretching westward from his Avon Farm home near Grass Valley, California.[1] Climbing a hill on that gentle western slope of the Sierras, this lad could also gaze eastward to behold the mountains forming the Sierras' nearest range and then, far beyond them on the horizon, those colossal peaks of the Sierras' massive front wall.

This eastward vista of the boy Royce symbolizes in outline my view of the ethical peaks that arose in Royce's moral philosophy after he drafted *The Problem of Christianity* in 1912. I find some ethical developments during his final years that resemble four mountains on his nearest range of the Sierras.

Beyond them, however, I spy four other colossal peaks of his final ethical achievement. I invite you, as intellectual copioneers with Royce, to ascend to these peaks. If we wish to explore even cursorily the four major peaks of his final ethical growth, we have time merely to point out in passing those lesser insights on the nearer range.

Facilitating our uphill hike is the mature Royce's new 1912 mode of knowing: his method of interpretively musing upon signs. This Peirce-inspired way of thinking brings to light the new meta-ethical and methodological emphases in Royce's final ethics. Years earlier when William James had examined the question "Is life worth living?" Royce recognized that this profound meta-ethical question had to be answered positively before ethics could begin.[2] By 1915, however, Royce had reinterpreted this starting question into *three meta-ethical problems:* (1) In what sense can one direct one's life? (2) In what does the good of happiness lie? (3) Is the human self called to respond to a divine directive?[3] These problems needed positive interpretations that balanced each other for ethics to proceed at all.

The maturest Royce fashioned his fitting response with three methodological requirements: first, start ethics by considering these three problems;[4] second, insist on Peircean interpretation as the only mode of knowing that can answer them;[5] and last, show that such an interpretive method can *only* arise if one's fundamental orientation towards life is a loving loyalty towards the whole processing universe.[6] Such loving loyalty shows that others count as much as oneself and that real human life has its unavoidable "bumps and bruises." Hence, genuine ethics cannot arise from such individualisms as are primarily self-assertive or self-negating.

Our first brisk hike through these upgrades of meta-ethics and methodology brings us to the mountains — that is, to the content of Royce's maturest ethics. Focusing first on four significant yet lesser peaks in his late moral thought, we find that Royce then pointed to the *family* as both a starting point for, and a symbolic sign of, ethical life in community.[7] Moreover, he now more frequently employed the term "solidarity" to point up how concrete the thick life of community really is.[8] Third, focusing on business, Royce *tested* the moral soundness of various economic investments by asking whether investors through their choice intend to develop the *entire* human family (Royce's Great Community).[9] Fourth, he purified the idea of *mediator* to free us from regarding the divine as "the hostile One."[10]

Breathing more rapidly, perhaps, we are now confronted with the main range of Royce's most mature ethics. On it I discern four pinnacles that arose after Royce wrote *The Problem of Christianity:* (1) he synthesized ethics' "three principal ideas"; (2) he recognized three kinds of genuine loyalty within humankind's three basic interpersonal relationships; (3) he pioneered in creating a *cathekontic*[11] ethics, "an ethics of the fitting"; and (4) he explicated *genuine hope* as an indispensable dynamic within true loyalty.

Concerning his first major achievement, which principal ethical ideas did Royce synthesize in 1915 and how did he do so? He claimed "Loyalty, as you remember, is an effort to bring into union, into a sort of synthesis and cooperation the three leading ethical ideas, the idea of independence, the idea of the good, and the idea of duty."[12] Familiar with the history of ethical thought-systems, Royce chose to organize his 1915–16 Extension Course in Ethics around the following "three leading ideas": *independence* (or the autonomous free initiation of ethical choices primarily from one's own unique personhood), *the good* (or the generally successful quest for becoming humanly happier), and *duty* (or the acceptance of both equality and diversity within the human community along with the consequent bonds of mutuality, justice, and other variegated exigencies between members and communities that this acceptance of equality and diversity carries with it).[13] Royce's final ethical quest had become the endeavor to weave together these leading ideas of personal freedom, happiness, and duty by using the interpretive process. His synthesis of these leading and cooperating ideas allowed him to bring his art and philosophy of loyalty to greater balance and nuance in his final year. That he used interpretation to integrate these principal ideas (of autonomy, the good, and duty) constituted a new and major development in Royce's 1915–16 ethics. [14]

Moving to Royce's second major peak, we find that in 1915 Royce specified *three fundamental kinds of genuine loyalty*. [15] After the *Problem,* he kept interpreting loyalty and disloyalty ever more profoundly. His attention zeroed in on the three relationships that establish the family as humankind's most basic community, namely: the relationships between siblings, between friends or lovers, and between parent and child. He also realized that these relationships deeply affect other forms of communal life. He came to identify three forms of estrangement that endanger these three relations: "(1) the lovers' quarrel, (2) the fraternal strife, (3) the conflict of the successive generations." [16] When alienation soured any of these relations, Royce identified which of the three principal ideas needed most emphasis if the relation were to be healed properly. For unless a unique kind of loyalty transformed each of these three relations, each would slip back into that estrangement and conflict which only too frequently turned these seeming "pair relationships" into tragedies.

If the ethical idea most characteristic of that relationship were fittingly emphasized, however, then that distinctive type of fundamental loyalty proper to this particular relationship would arise. Hence, to deal remedially and insightfully with these three family relations, Royce needed to identify which leading ethical idea should be *most* emphasized in each case. Without violating his central synthesis of the three principal ethical ideas, this emphasis on one would let the other two play their indispensable, if less central, role. Thus each idea would in its turn seed a distinct kind of loyalty — one most suited for a particular basic family relation.

To be specific, with *siblings,* each is called to emphasize the other's *equal freedom and autonomy,* the first leading ethical idea. [17] If each sibling does so, increased union will arise — perhaps even reconciliation and a healing of past alienation. If a brother or sister principally respects the independence of the other, both will enjoy physical and psychological "free space." Both need this if each one's self-development is not to be interfered with or diminished by one's fellow-sibling. Sibling loyalty, then, respectfully creates "free space" for the other.

Second, Royce saw that the interpersonal bond between *friends or lovers* is based primarily on the second leading ethical idea, *goodness.* Friends and lovers fulfill their basic need when they share happiness continuously. Nevertheless, this kind of goodness can arise only if their love is constantly without estrangement. So Royce was led to hold that if they are to grow enduringly in this kind of love, it must, like joy, be "born a triplet." That is, since the *goodness* distinctive of friends and lovers tends to be fruitful, friends and lovers in some way must tend to be generative of their kind of loving loyalty if they are to attain lasting happiness.

Finally, in the *parent-child kind of loyalty,* Royce saw the need for a primary emphasis on *duty* if successive generations are to be bonded together fittingly. Parents must transmit, and children need to receive, life in all its forms — physical, sociocultural, affective, intellectual, moral, and religious — as well as the refined wisdom that previous generations have purified from received traditions. To transmit so much life and wisdom unharmed and even enhanced to the next generation requires a clear recognition and faithful observance of each one's duties in both the senders and receivers within each familial community of interpretation.

In brief, then, by 1916 Royce had worked out a significant development of his doctrine and art of loyalty. His doctrine of loyalty now explicitly integrated three leading ethical ideas. He had found that each of these was a more suitable principal interpreter than the other two in loyalty's three specific kinds: sibling loyalty, friendship loyalty, and parent-child loyalty.

The third major peak in Royce's maturest morality was his *cathekontic* ethics. That is, the heart of his interpretive process required the discovery of "the fitting." As we saw, Royce insisted that for genuine ethical life his three leading ethical ideas had to be appropriately integrated. This kind of apt integration occupied more of his ethical heartland than did the utilitarians' pragmatic fittingness, which also had its place. They thought ethical activity lay in securing, through the measuring of foreseeable consequences, a greater balance of pleasurable over painful results. Although Royce knew that sound moral decision making required a fitting calculation of good and bad results, he regarded as "*wholly inadequate*" for genuine loyalty the suggestion from Bentham that we calculate the sum of pleasures and pains to find the "good for us."[18] Besides calculating consequences, the genuine loyalist also had to be effectively committed to the common good, to keeping promises faithfully, and to treating all persons respectfully and without manipulation.

Beyond this fitting balancing of practical consequences, and beyond this apt synthesis of the three leading ethical ideas, Royce extended the norm of the fitting into other areas — to the moral agent's taking of a present decision that dovetails with both his chosen life-plan and his future hope,[19] to the thinker's search for that question which next suits her inquiry,[20] to the secular agent's fitting choice in any "agent community,"[21] and especially, to any human self (X) who tries to relate ethically to another human self(-ves) (Z) within the processing context of an interpretive community (Y).

   In this last-named paradigmatic ethical situation, a similar interpretive
finding of the fitting is needed to create and build a fundamental ethical
relationship. X lives with her partly unique and partly shared memories,
hopes, freedom, interests, and promises. So, too, do other selves (Z) live
with their partly unique and partly shared memories, hopes, freedom, interests, and promises. The problem becomes how to unite these two without violating either. Because the interpretive process operating in their community (Y) heads to a wise reasonableness that inserts self-correction, it
tries to discern a "fitting" way either to overcome alienation between X
and Z or to further unite them. Thus only through the influence of the
life and agency of this Community of Interpretation will X's individual
human self be led to *prefer what is better* for the whole community, for
herself, and for the other members who make up the community(-ies)
involved—local, national, or human. It is this interpretive process operating in the community (through its language, customs, religion, discoveries,
and hopes) that leads the individual self X to find or invent that "third
idea" which *fits in better* with the long-range consequences. While leaving
the personal decision making to X's own autonomy, the communal process calls her to *this* mode of action rather than any other.
   A fourth and final peak in Royce's maturest ethical growth is the *bold
hope*[22] that he experienced and expressed, especially in his *Hope of the
Great Community*. Here within genuine loyalty he identified foundational
hope as an affect indispensable for ethical life. Such hope is stifled by basic
pessimism. Such hope is overwhelmed by popular "ethical individualism,"
with its disregard of the universal common good. Royce's decades-long
struggle against these two "spoilers of mankind" reached fruition in his
*Hope of the Great Community* (1916). Here, as if sketching a tree, he identified the trunk of genuine hope. Onto this he grafted the psychic branches
needed to balance that trunk. Moreover, in the rich soils of human life
he found the roots that sustain this kind of hope.
   Like a tree trunk, the core of Royce's critically honed hope supports
that other hope which must operate in his "communities of expectation."[23]
Nevertheless, because attached to the Spirit's most fundamental and im-
mortal intent, Royce's central hope lies in human selves' commitment to
the ideal of the universal community. This ideal has "to do not merely with
the sentimental and romantic aspirations of humanity,"[24] but with the basic
intent of the Spirit of the universal community. Human selves' commitment to this ideal rests on an "unearthly confidence that, beyond all sor-
row, all shall be, for the dutiful, somehow good."[25] Thus Royce's central
hope uplifts the heart in a way that only genuine loyalty can. It relies
ultimately on the love, direction, and pedagogy of the Spirit-Interpreter
of the universal community.

Roycean commitment to this ideal opens up a *via media* whereby one escapes from radical pessimism and from the corrosive forms of ethical individualism. Lacking this commitment, some Americans caught today in consumerism and a merely functional existence reveal faces that exude such pessimism.[26] Or at the other extreme, ethical individualists seek their own personal or collective aggrandizement so impetuously or shrewdly that they kill genuine hope in others and even in themselves.[27] In contrast to these attitudes of will, Royce positively delineated his third attitude: the kind of hope that fits genuine loyalty.[28] It is found only in the genuinely loyal, for they alone have been ethico-religiously transformed by their commitment. Royce described them as persons who "walk not after the flesh, but after the spirit" of the universal community, and who live by genuine Pauline charity.[29] They form that consciously unified community which alone can offer salvation to distracted humanity and to detached individuals.

Royce balanced this kind of hope by integrating into it a critical wisdom, a sense of fallibility (that inserts both humility and humor into this hope), and a wholehearted practical commitment to further promote the coming of the universal community. Roycean hope clearly did *not* rest on any Pollyanna-ish daydream that humankind's Great Community would *inevitably* be realized or even that our human race would *surely* survive on this planet. He clearly foresaw, among other future possibilities, that unchecked destructive forces might extinguish the whole human race as completely as similar forces had rendered the saber-toothed tiger extinct.[30] He also foresaw that some fanatic's dream of worldwide conquest — military, economic, or other — would only lead to a "more or less universal community of hate."[31] Unlike many "pragmatists of the short range" who dodged talk of human death, ultimate tragedy, and nature's overwhelming calamities, but very much like William James's facing his own "going down in the wreck," Royce confronted head-on these dread issues that seem irredeemably hopeless.[32]

He located the roots of his central hope less in political structures and more in philosophy, humanities, science, art, economics, ethics, and religion. Philosophically, Kant's third basic question, "What may we hope for?" deeply impressed Royce. So, too, did Kant's postulate of immortality as a requisite for any rational ethics. Convinced by these insights, the mature Royce held as the vital nerve of philosophical ethics that *if* justice were permanently wrecked here on earth, then human life would be utterly worthless and therefore at bottom hopeless.[33]

Besides this philosophical taproot for hope, Royce found indispensable the vision of the Great Community proposed by our poets and prophets. Although political processes may supply some support for this hope,[34] stronger sustenance will come from the progress achieved during the nineteenth and twentieth centuries in art, industry, science, and social development.[35] Humankind's slowly growing *social arts* foster this hope and fashion interpretations that fit pluralistic communities and selves. When agents in insurance, banking, counseling, and other forms of nonforensic mediation exercise these social arts, they promote humankind's Great Community by generating that "ideal significance" to which prophets and poets first awaken us.[36] As an example of this secular stimulation of hope, Royce proposed, as wholly novel, the creation of an international board of trustees who would reinsure the nations' own insurance policies against war. The leaven-like effect of this board would gradually make all people aware of the Great Community of the future and thus increase their hope.[37]

Beyond philosophical, scientific, cultural, economic, and some political warrants for his hope, Royce emphasized above all the ethico-religious root of hope. As mentioned, the divine side of this root lay in the love, direction, and pedagogy of the Spirit of the Universe. This root's human side lay in "this salvation of a community through an human transformation that is universally significant."[38] Little wonder, then, that the mature Royce viewed such hope as supremely important. For the heart of this hope lies in that transformed life of loyalty within some genuine community that promotes the Great Community, or as Royce sometimes called it, "the church universal."[39] Ethico-religious transformation (or "salvation") radiates from the Great Community, which is missioned to hold the ideal of human community before the eyes of all people so that this vision keeps hope alive in human hearts that struggle amid tragedy.

Besides this sketch of the trunk, branches, and roots of hope, we find in some of his final deeds a concluding witness to what Roycean hope prompts a person to do.[40] This hope led Royce in his Tremont Temple and *Lusitania* addresses of 1914–15 to proclaim those prophet-like, biblically resonant, clarion calls to the consciences of his fellow Americans, still slumbering while German U-boats torpedoed innocents. Royce's hope in a concrete Community of Interpretation and in its embodiment in an "International Mutual Insurance Corporation," was strong enough to lead him, in the face of many objections but with the support of financial experts, to publish his plan for the reinsurance of the nations against war.[41] At his sixtieth birthday celebration in December of 1915, Royce confidently closed his autobiographical sketch with a quote from Swinburne's hope-filled "Watchman, What of the Night?"[42] Finally, Royce counterbalanced his frustration and grief over the war with his final collection of essays, appropriately entitled *The Hope of the Great Community*.

In summary, our frontier hiking has led us to a glimpse of the four pinnacles that mark Royce's final development in ethics: his integrated triad of three principal ethical ideas, his three kinds of genuine loyalty, his pioneer work in an ethics of the fitting, and his bold hope that is the inseparable companion of genuine loyalty. Nevertheless, in the Sierra Nevada of Royce's beloved California, the U. S. Geological Survey has, in paradoxical counterpoint to the claims of this essay, named one peak with four lakes on its eastern side as "Royce Peak with its four Royce Lakes."[43] I hope there can be further discussion to adjudicate between such rival claims.

## Appendix: Chronological List of Royce's Mature Writings

1913, *The Problem of Christianity,* 2 vols. (New York: Macmillan, 1913; 1 vol. Chicago: University of Chicago Press, 1968).

1914a, *War and Insurance* (New York: Macmillan, 1914).

1914b, "The Berkeley Conferences," Royce Papers, Harvard University Archives, vol. 84, three MSS.

1914c, "The Spirit of the Great Community," — an undelivered address to Berkeley's Philosophical Union, Royce Papers, Harvard University Archives, vol. 91, MS no. 3.

1915, "Extension Course in Ethics, First Semester, Fall 1915," Royce Papers, Harvard University Archives, vol. 94, MSS of four extant lectures.

1916a, *The Hope of the Great Community* (New York: Macmillan, 1916).

1916b, "Extension Course in Ethics, Second Semester, Spring 1916," Royce Papers, Harvard University Archives, vol. 95, MS, "Comments upon the Problem of the Mid-year Examination."

## Notes

1. Josiah Royce, *The Hope of the Great Community* (New York: Macmillan, 1916), p. 123. See the chronological arrangement of Royce's mature writings in the appendix.

2. William James, *The Will to Believe and Other Essays* (New York: Longmans, Green, and Co., 1899), pp. 32–62. In his 1911 eulogy of James, idealist Royce offered a positive answer to James's question: "What makes life worth living is not what you find in it, but what you are ready to put into it by your ideal interpretation of the meaning that, as you insist, it shall possess for you. This ideal meaning is always for you a matter of faith. . . . Your deeper ideals always depend upon viewing life in the light of larger unities than now appear, upon viewing yourself as a coworker with the universe for the attainment of what no present human game of action can now reveal." Josiah Royce, *The Basic Writings of Josiah Royce,* ed. and introd. John J. McDermott, 2 vols. (Chicago: University of Chicago Press, 1969), vol. 1, pp. 219–20; see also pp. 249–53.

3. Josiah Royce, "Extension Course in Ethics, First Semester, Fall 1915," Royce Papers, Harvard University Archives, vol. 94 (MSS of four extant lectures), Lecture 1, pp. 1–4, 10.

4. Ibid.

5. Josiah Royce, *The Problem of Christianity* (2 vols., New York: Macmillan, 1913; Chicago: University of Chicago Press, 1968), p. 318. Also, Royce, "The Berkeley Conferences," Royce Papers, Harvard University Archives, vol. 84 (MSS of three lectures), Lecture 1, pp. 31–33. Peircean interpretation fits these three problems because it is built, not upon a Hegelian dialectic of conflict, but upon a simple Peircean "will to promote union." See Royce, *The Problem of Christianity,* pp. 305, 317. See also Royce, "The Spirit of the Great Community," an undelivered address to Berkeley's Philosophical Union, Royce Papers, Harvard University Archives, vol. 91, MS no. 3, p. 11; Royce, "Extension Course in Ethics, Second Semester, Spring 1916," Royce Papers, Harvard University Archives, vol. 95, MS of "Comments upon the Problem of the Mid-year Examination," pp. 5, 15.

6. Royce, *The Problem of Christianity,* p. 349. Royce's three initial problems and his three methodological requirements are not to be confused with the three principles of his 1914 philosophy of loyalty, for which see Royce, "The Berkeley Conferences," Lecture 3, pp. 31–33.

7. Josiah Royce, *War and Insurance* (New York: Macmillan, 1914), pp. 36–37, 42–43, 49, 56, 71.

8. Ibid., pp. 7, 9, 39, 92.

9. Royce, "The Spirit of the Great Community," pp. 29–35; see also Royce, *The Hope of the Great Community,* p. 76.

10. Royce, "The Spirit of the Great Community," pp. 3, 7, 9. H. Richard Niebuhr, a close reader of Royce, skillfully elaborated this theme in his *Responsible Self* (New York: Harper and Row, 1963), pp. 136–45, 174–78.

11. Derived from Aristotle, the term is H. Richard Niebuhr's; see *The Responsible Self,* p. 87.

12. Royce, "Extension Course in Ethics, Second Semester," p. 20; see also Royce, "Extension Course in Ethics, First Semester," Lecture 1, p. 4.

13. Ibid., pp. 1–4

14. Already in 1908, in his significant address on the problem of truth, Royce had given signs of this trend to synthesize a triad of leading ideas. He then showed that a statement could not be true unless it integrated the three motives of unique self-fulfillment, pragmatic adaptation to changing environment, and genuine objectivity. See *The Basic Writings of Josiah Royce,* vol. 2, pp. 681–709.

15. Royce, "Extension Course in Ethics, Second Semester," pp. 18–32, 11–17.

16. Ibid., p. 19. Similarly, in 1912, Royce found that his trio of most essential "Christian ideas" — community, lost state, and atonement — if integrated by Grace as by a "gift from above," formed Christianity's most vital "doctrine of life." If these ideas are viewed as pointers toward his 1916 ethical synthesis, we find that the separated individual's lost state at least highlights how indispensable for ethics is *autonomous choice* — whether wisely or less wisely directed. Second, if the climactic idea of the *Problem* was atonement, Royce intensified this focus in the following years. For from 1912 to 1916 he embraced the tragic element in human life as inescapable but transformable. He thus revealed that our human quest for the *goodness* of authentic human happiness must enter into a "dying and a rising" to be successful. Finally, his leading Christian idea of "community" found its ethical counterpoint in his 1916 interpretation that life in community entails *duties*

for all its member-selves. The community both gifts them with a higher life and requires of them those "modes of action" that fit each one's membership in such a life.

17. Ibid., pp. 11–32. The three following paragraphs in the text are also based on this source.

18. "Extension Course in Ethics, First Semester," Lecture 4, p. 14.

19. "The Berkeley Conferences," Lecture 1, pp. 30–31.

20. Royce, *War and Insurance,* p. 26.

21. Royce, "The Spirit of the Great Community," pp. 12–35. Whether this agent be banker, insurer, counselor, judge, salesperson, or some other intermediary, his or her central role is to discover the fitting (*ta hekonta*). This includes listening discerningly enough to his or her principal to *concur with* the intent of the principal. It includes listening discerningly enough to the needy client to *adapt* to that person's mentality. It especially includes his or her discoveries both of that *suitable* "third idea" which first bonds those two selves by means of some common interest of theirs, and then of those subsequent "*fitting* thirds" which will keep creating and inspiring the life and unity of this agent-community for as long a time as is mutually "profitable" for all its members. See also Royce, *War and Insurance,* pp. 55–64, 86–93.

22. Unfortunately, Clendenning's statement that Royce "was still unconvinced that the universal community was more than a faint hope" is ambiguous. See John Clendenning, *The Life and Thought of Josiah Royce* (Madison: University of Wisconsin Press, 1985), p. 392. If his "faint" points to "dim" or "barely perceptible," he signals accurately; but if he means "faint" in its prior senses of "feeble" or "lacking conviction or courage," then he seems to be sending a misleading signal. Hence, I here place a greater counterbalancing emphasis on the vigor in the mature Royce's hope than does Clendenning.

23. Royce, *The Problem of Christianity,* p. 248.

24. Royce, *The Hope of the Great Community,* p. 37.

25. Royce, "Extension Course in Ethics, First Semester," Lecture, 1, p. 10.

26. For Royce, radical pessimism showed itself clearly in the southern Buddhists. Since they taught that any desire entraps a person in illusion, they urged all humans to eradicate from their hearts any desire for bliss.

27. The presence of such individualism in American life is amply documented by Robert Bellah, in Robert H. Bellah, et al., *Habits of the Heart: Individualism and Commitment in American Life* (Berkeley: University of California Press, 1985). For some positive philosophical and theological resources to build community and counter such individualism, see the volume tentatively entitled, *A Jesuit Response to Habits of the Heart,* ed. Donald Gelpi, (Georgetown University Press, forthcoming).

28. In this context of hope, Royce's three attitudes clearly expressed the three basic attitudes of will that he had sketched earlier in *The Problem of Christianity,* pp. 348–57.

29. Royce, *Hope of the Great Community,* pp. 48–49.

30. Ibid., p. 28.

31. Ibid., p. 53.

32. In my opinion, Royce philosophically confronted the depths of the problem of evil most starkly on November 22, 1896, when he read to Harvard's Philosophical Conference an essay entitled "Introduction to Paper on Problem of Job." The manuscript of this essay of eleven pages is in Royce Papers, Harvard University Archives, vol. 52, no. 1.

33. Royce, *War and Insurance,* p. 27. Here Royce reminded his audience, "We often do our best when we fix our mind on the thought which Kant expressed in the words: 'If justice meets utter wreck, then there is no worth whatever in the continued existence of human life in this world."

34. Royce, *Hope of the Great Community,* p. 57.

35. Ibid., pp. 38–39.

36. Ibid., p. 59.

37. Ibid., p. 69.

38. Ibid., p. 35.

39. Ibid., p. 33.

40. The Royce of 1912 experienced a hope that led him to direct the practical portions of the *Problem* "for the strenghtening of hearts"; see *The Problem of Christianity,* p. 40. It led him to close the work on p. 405 with the statement, "we can look forward to a time when the work and the insight of religion can become as progressive as is now the work of science."

41. Royce, *The Hope of the Great Community,* p. 66.

42. Ibid., pp. 132–36.

43. Royce Peak rises 13,282 feet in Fresno County, California, and lies seven tenths of a mile north by northwest of Marian Peak, at coordinates 37° 19′ 7″ and 118° 46′ 13″.

# Hermeneutics and Loyalty

ROBERT S. CORRINGTON

The current obsession with language and with written texts has blunted the generic drive of hermeneutics and its more legitimate quest for a categorial structure that is truly responsive to the various dimensions of meaning manifest in the ongoing human process. More important, this artificial constriction of the scope of interpretation theory has made it increasingly difficult to develop a proper social and political horizon within which acts of interpretation can find legitimation and transparency. The deeper emancipatory forces of nature and history remain bereft of a proper location for their appearance in nondestructive social orders. As a consequence of this, hermeneutics is all too frequently allied to those forces that would foreclose the evolution of shared values and meanings. As a corrective to this self-imposed alienation, hermeneutics needs to find an emancipatory stance that will allow it to go beyond linguistic and textual artifacts toward the horizonal structures and powers of nature and worldhood. The concept of loyalty, as the fundamental access structure of the human process, will provide the means by and through which hermeneutics can reclaim its legacy.

While it is clear that meanings, whether expressed in signs or not, are to some degree a product of human manipulation, it should be equally clear that meanings are found, assimilated, and encountered, before their transformation by constitutive acts. To ignore the assimilative dimension of the human process is to privilege the much narrower and less powerful manipulative dimension. Further, it ignores the sovereignty of nature and its infinite semiotic and interpretive wealth. The human process receives its direction and measure from a nature that cannot be reduced to the "sum" of all actual and possible categorial projections. Meanings evolve, as do organisms, and both must pay heed to antecedent conditions that govern and locate all products and their subsequent forms of legitimation. If the class of meaning events is larger than the class of truths, then it follows that validation emerges from the indefinitely ramified web of meanings made and meanings found. It does not follow that validation is a concept that functions outside of hermeneutics.

The individual interpreter thus lives within antecedent natural structures and forces that exert their own forms of compulsion. Gadamer's focus on the fusion of historical and temporal horizons, while not inappropriate, needs to be located within a more encompassing naturalism that provides access into the innumerable dimensions of the nature that makes it possible for history and temporality to prevail at all. By the same token, Heidegger's stress on the giving of language as the self-giving of Being needs to be gathered into the emancipatory forces of the worldhood that such language struggles to serve. These emancipatory forces drive toward hermeneutic and social transformation and cannot be inverted to serve rigid and self-justifying powers.

No interpreter can hope to fully prescind from the compulsive orders of nature and history. To interpret is to respond to felt lines of convergence within orders not of the self's own making. Cultural artifacts, whether linguistic or not, serve to present and preserve generic traits of prehuman and prehermeneutic orders. Of course, such artifacts also represent momentary or enduring expressions of personal and social manipulations of this natural material. Any isolated trait may participate in both human and prehuman configurations and thus convey greater interpretive value than a similar trait that is not so constituted. No meaningful act of interpretation can take place unless it fully participates in the orders of nature that empower it. The individual interpreter is always permeable to that which transcends meanings known or orders encountered. Analogous to the encompassing power of nature and history is the clearing provided to the individual by the structures of the community of interpretation. Such a community, no matter how fragmented its manifestation in time, lives as the origin and goal of all hermeneutic acts. The community is rooted in the vast evolutionary matrix of nature but is not restricted to the conditions of origin or empowerment. It lives between the antecedent realm of natural transaction and the hermeneutic kingdom in which all meanings will become known to finite interpreters. As such, the community of interpretation serves both origin and the deeper impulses of expectation that gather the traces of origin into the kingdom of hermeneutic transparency. The enabling condition for the finite interpreter is thus the community that lives as the sphere of transparency and eventual validation.

We have thus exhibited a generically incremental series moving from the least generic order of the individual interpreter to the more encompassing order of the community of interpretation, which in turn finds itself embedded in the innumerable orders of a nature that forever lies beyond the reach of all finite hermeneutic acts. The tensions between and among these orders are all integral to the evolution of shared meanings. Insofar as contemporary hermeneutic theory attempts to prescind from these tensions and flee to the illusory security of the alienated individual, it violates the very meaning structures that enable the self to have and endure meanings at all. Natural and communal orders govern and locate all personal transactions and, under the proper conditions, empower such transactions to overcome the forces of alienation that constrict personal meaning horizons.

The community of interpretation has traits that are distinct from those merely derived from the sum of all finite interpreters. These traits are deeply wedded to sign systems and meaning horizons that vastly eclipse the sum of all individual hermeneutic acts. Further, the community encompasses the horizonal plenitude of its members by providing the seed bed for all emergent horizons and their internal configurations. The power of origin, itself derived from the orders of nature, is gathered under the deeper power of social expectation that both supports and humbles all horizons. Origin without the governing power of expectation is demonic. Expectation without the antecedent gift of origin is willful and without embodiment.

The community is sustained by the loyal deeds of its interpreters who struggle against the opacity and reticence of natural and conventional sign systems. While any given sign system will have its own telos and movement toward totality, such a system will also contain innumerable traits that are recalcitrant to human analysis and articulation. The sheer hermeneutic and semiotic drift that characterizes the human process works against the counter movement of transparency and validation. Loyalty, as the constantly self-renewing attitude of radical openness, serves to rescue sign systems and meaning horizons from their own tendencies toward opacity. More important, loyalty is the fundamental social attitude that struggles toward the transformation of meanings into truths. In the words of Josiah Royce, "Truth seeking and loyalty are therefore essentially the same process of life merely viewed in different aspects."[1] Loyalty is social in that it seeks to reinforce and secure other genuine loyalties rather than to impose an alien and private cause onto the evolution of the community of interpreters. For Royce, loyalty to loyalty is more basic than mere loyalty to a cause. The principle of loyalty provides an existential grounding for the Kantian categorical imperative, which would ask us to transform private maxims into a truly universal law. Any given loyalty, insofar as it excludes other genuine loyalties, must surrender its idiosyncratic claims to the deeper social impulses of a transpersonal loyalty.

The community of interpreters provides a categorial clearing within which the individual interpreter can maximize the depth and scope of social communication. Hermeneutic acts are protected against premature closure by the loyal deeds that empower and guide each community toward the ideal of shared horizons and values. On a higher generic level, any given community of interpretation will be the locus of an indefinite number of other communities. The individual loyal interpreter has the social obligation to translate the horizonal values of each of these communities into some sort of reasonable and sharable perspective. No such higher order translation will be successful if it is not facilitated by democratic structures. Hermeneutics and radical democracy entail each other.

The relations between nature, communities, individuals, and sign systems are infinitely complex. Nature is the all-encompassing actuality within which history, social orders, and finite selves are included. The emancipatory power of loyal and democratic communities comes from a nature that is itself a hermeneutic process through and through. Nature exhibits emancipatory tendencies in the evolutionary processes that create room for greater organic complexity and a richer spectrum of response. Evolutionary success can be defined in terms of hermeneutic competence to derive leadings and meanings from situations fraught with tension and possible breakdown. Human interpretive communities intensify processes that are operative in other orders of nature. It does not follow from this that nature is constituted by mental acts or monads of proto-consciousness. The doctrine of panpsychism, defended by such thinkers as Peirce, Whitehead, and Hartshorne, privileges those traits constitutive of the human process and fails to understand how those precarious traits are embedded in vast and ofttimes hostile natural forces.

Loyalty has previously been defined as an access structure that enables the human process to become permeable to other horizons of value and meaning. A few further words are in order concerning the inner logic of this access structure. As noted, loyalty is not fulfilled if it is seen as loyalty to a specific cause. Beyond such limited loyalty lies the content-free loyalty that is directed to the furtherance of the cause of loyalty per se. In denying that loyalty to loyalty has a positive and pregiven content, we are asserting that it lives as a mobile region of intelligibility within which possible allegiances can appear. Any such appearance must satisfy the stringent criterion that it become emancipated from antecedent and finite embodiments. A commitment is allowed to function insofar as it points beyond itself toward the ultimate hermeneutic kingdom in which all loyalties will become transparent to the origins and goals that sustain them. In the words of Royce, "And so, a cause is good, not only for me, but for mankind, in so far as it is essentially a *loyalty to loyalty,* that is, is an aid and a furtherence of loyalty in my fellows. It is an evil cause in so far as, despite the loyalty that it arouses in me, it is destructive of loyalty in the world of my fellows."[2]

Evil causes reinforce the solipsistic tendencies of the isolated hermeneute who wishes to impose an insufficiently generic sign system onto the emergent horizonal structures of other selves. In the misplaced drive to become free from all origins, whether those of nature or of socially communicated perspectives, the solitary hermeneute removes himself or herself from those emancipatory structures that alone make transparency and democratic justice possible. it is not often noted that the quest for justice and true parity between and among selves is internally tied to the health and strength of those hermeneutic acts that refuse to privilege or condone the falsely autonomous self. Does this emphasis on communal justice impose its own form of control on the individual and thereby betray a dangerous paternalism? Put differently, is the principle of loyalty to loyalty simply a mask for the intolerance of difference? Can a genuine principle of radical alterity be combined with the emphasis on the evolution of shared perspectives and meanings? In what follows, I hope to show that genuine otherness is not threatened by the emancipatory structures of the community of interpreters.

Royce argued that the growth of individuality was only possible in the framework of social contrast in which the difference between the I and the not-I was clarified and deepened. The discovery of a personal center of will and action coincides with the awareness that other points of will limit the reach of the self. From this primal discovery unfolds the deeper hermeneutic understanding of the uniqueness and ultimate sovereignty of the other. The other, as a center of autonomous will and loyalty, helps in the very definition of the personal and social dimensions of my own finite self.

In allowing the other the freedom to live in and through specific loyalties, the realm of difference is preserved from the encroachment of an imperial transpersonal loyalty. At the core of the other self is a domain of mystery that cannot be penetrated by any hermeneutic act on my part. This hidden core cannot become fully transparent to the community of interpreters any more than it can become unhidden to the self that "contains" it. Within each self is its own otherness that points toward a more radical domain of alterity within which the richness of the human process is sustained.

In pointing toward the otherness within each self and between and among all social selves, it is important to note that such alterity does not negate or destroy the forms of presence that serve hermeneutics. The communication of shared meanings requires that signs and their referents, however ambiguous or attenuated, emerge before social inquiry to serve the needs of validation. A hermeneutics of suspicion that would overturn or unmask each presence cannot participate in the quest for social justice because of its denial of any meaningful transcendence. When meanings become filtered through loyal social selves, they abide as stable and reliable traces of that which transcends the sum total of all hermeneutic acts. Otherness and transcendence belong together in an eternal polarity. The evolution of shared values and meanings is one form of transcendence. As such, it does not negate or cancel that radical alterity that lives in the heart of the community of interpreters.

Loyalty to loyalty thus preserves both identity and difference but in alternative respects. Identity is preserved insofar as collectively generated meanings survive the relentless process of social query and point toward transcendence. Difference is preserved whenever the uniqueness and force of a given loyalty is protected from the destructive power of mere social conformity. The principle of loyalty honors both identity and difference in all their forms.

Thus far we have spoken of the incremental series composed of nature, communities, and individual interpreters. Loyalty to loyalty has emerged as the fundamental access structure that empowers finite interpreters to serve both the antecedent orders of nature and history and the emergent, and to a large extent consequent, orders of the community. What has remained veiled is the depth principle that moves between these three levels of reality. In rejecting panpsychism we have made it clear that the traits of human interpreters (such as self-consciousness, intersubjectivity, and temporality) are not to be projected onto nature as a whole. This temptation being rejected, we must look elsewhere for that empowerment that makes it possible for the community to receive the riches of nature without falling prey to the seductions of undifferentiated origin.

The movement from nature to meaning, and from meaning to truth, is made possible by the presence of what can best be called "Spirit." Spirit, itself without a positive semiotic content, is that dimension of nature that is captured in the phrase, "nature naturing." The Spirit is in one sense a product of nature and in another sense the animating principle within all natural transactions. In the words of Emerson, who was especially attuned to nature in its naturing: "that behind nature, throughout nature, spirit is present; one and not compound it does not act upon us from without, that is, in space and time, but spiritually, or through ourselves: therefore, that spirit, that is, the Supreme Being, does not build up nature around us but puts it forth through us, as the life of the tree puts forth new branches and leaves through the pores of the old."[3] Leaving aside the honorific rhetoric, it is clear that Spirit is the animating principle that lives between and through the great divisions of the world. The unity of Spirit is unique in that it refuses to become encompassed by any finite set of values or meanings. If Spirit is the source of unity within human communities, it follows that Spirit and the life of interpretation belong together. In what remains, we will examine the connections between Spirit, the nature of loyalty, and hermeneutics. Hopefully this will make it possible to find a deeper and more enduring measure for hermeneutics than that which has emerged from alternative paradigms.

The influence of Spirit is felt in the pressure to transcend antecedent horizons and their internal hermeneutic structures. This pressure is the most restless and creative aspect of the community of interpretation and drives each act of interpretation toward an ultimate expectation in which all origins are shriven of their hubris in the face of that which can never be an origin or finite horizon. The fissures opened within triumphalist and self-encapsulated horizons enable their semiotic plenitude to give way to an otherness that speaks from the future. This future is not that of calculated or projected consequences but stands as the total sublation of all present and past acts of meaning. The presence of Spirit manifests itself in the ever receding future that leaves traces of the hermeneutic kingdom. In the not-yet of the hermeneutic kingdom lies the true animating principle of social transformation. All acts of loyalty serve the not-yet that speaks beyond all attained horizons of meaning. To be loyal to loyalty is to experience the grace that comes from the Spirit. In a very real sense, the Spirit is the mediator between the powers of origin and the elusive presence/absence of the hermeneutic kingdom. Spirit, which stands behind and within all forms of empowerment, lives in the between that holds origin and expectation together. The identities emergent from antecedent orders stand under judgment by the alterity of expectation. This judgment forces each origin to acknowledge that which both supports and negates each finite potency. Since all empowerment comes from Spirit, it follows that the radical openness preserved by loyalty is itself made possible by the Spiritual Presence that quickens the life of interpretation.

The Spirit that guides and directs interpretation is the power that overturns merely finite meanings and their illusory self-validation. Spirit breaks through the concresced shells of given horizons and perspectives and thereby makes them permeable to each other in a way that would have been impossible outside of the presence of Spirit. Spirit, as the incarnation of meaning and truth, lives most dramatically in those communities that struggle toward the emancipation of all selves and their attendant horizons. On the deepest level, there is no contradiction between incarnation and otherness. In democratic communities of interpretation, otherness is preserved through the bindingness that is the gift of the incarnation. That is, the sheer imperative of the other is only felt when his or her meanings become incarnate in my own horizon of meaning. It is only a seeming paradox that the presence of Spirit, always advancing the scope of the incarnation, preserves the genuine otherness of the other. The forces of democracy are strengthened whenever the incarnation of Spirit gently undermines the misguided solipsism that refuses to acknowledge the radical equality of the other.

A democratic hermeneutic community is more than the sum of emancipated individuals. On the deepest level it is the enabling condition for all forms of personal and social liberation. The Spirit is unrelenting in its hostility to forms of domination and privilege. While finite powers frequently establish systems of priority, the Spirit demands absolute parity between and among selves. The structures of origin and the lure of expectation turn toward each other under the impress of Spirit. Origins give the community its hermeneutic wealth. The kingdom of expectation gives the community its concrete sense of justice. The Spirit creates that loyalty which enables all finite interpreters to find an equal place within the evolving community of interpretation.

# Notes

1. Josiah Royce, *The Philosophy of Loyalty* (New York: Macmillan Co., 1908), p. 314.

2. Ibid., pp. 118–19.

3. Ralph Waldo Emerson, *Nature, Addresses, and Lectures,* The Riverside Edition (New York: Houghton, Mifflin and Co., 1883); the essay "Nature" is reprinted from the 1836 edition, pp. 67–68.

# About the Contributors

Daniel Aaron
Harvard University

Mitchell Aboulafia
University of Houston, Clear Lake

Lynne M. Adrian
University of Alabama

Douglas Browning
University of Texas at Austin

Robert W. Burch
Texas A&M University

James Campbell
University of Toledo

Vincent Michael Colapietro
Saint Mary's College

Robert S. Corrington
Pennsylvania State University

Paul T. Durbin
University of Delaware

Webster F. Hood
Central Washington University

Nathan Houser
Indiana University-Purdue
University at Indianapolis

Jacquelyn A. Kegley
CSU Outstanding Professor

Konstantin Kolenda
Rice University

John Lachs
Vanderbilt University

Irwin C. Lieb
University of Southern California

Joseph Margolis
Temple University

John J. McDermott
Texas A&M University

Marjorie C. Miller
State University of New York
    at Purchase

Jon S. Moran
Southwest Missouri State University

Murray G. Murphey
University of Pennsylvania

William M. O'Meara
James Madison University

Frank M. Oppenheim
Xavier University

George S. Pappas
Ohio State University

Hilary Putnam
Harvard University

Ruth Anna Putnam
Wellesley College

Nicholas Rescher
University of Pittsburgh

John J. Ryder
State University College at Cortland

Herman J. Saatkamp, Jr.
Texas A&M University

Charlene Haddock Seigfried
Purdue University

Donald W. Sherburne
Vanderbilt University

Beth J. Singer
Brooklyn College, City University
    of New York

Ralph W. Sleeper
Queens College, City University
    of New York

Kenneth W. Stikkers
Seattle University

H. S. Thayer
City College, The City University
    of New York

Kathleen Wallace
Hofstra University